COLLECTED WHEEL PUBLICATIONS

VOLUME 3

NUMBERS 31 – 46

BPE

BPS Pariyatti Editions

BPS Pariyatti Editions
An imprint of Pariyatti Publishing
www.pariyatti.org

Although this is an American edition, we have left any British spelling of words unchanged.

First BPS Pariyatti Edition, 2019
ISBN: 978-1-68172-132-3 (Print)
ISBN: 978-1-68172-133-0 (PDF)
ISBN: 978-1-68172-134-7 (ePub)
ISBN: 978-1-68172-135-4 (Mobi)
LCCN: 2018940050

Contents

WH 31 & 32 The Manual of Insight
Ledi Sayādaw Mahāthera 1

WH 33 Advice to Rāhula: Four Discourses of the Buddha
Nyanaponika Thera 69

WH 34 & 35 Foundations of Buddhism: The Four Noble Truths
Francis Story 99

WH 36 & 37 Buddhism and the Age of Science
U Chan Htoon 153

WH 38 The Lamp of the Law
Soma Thera & Piyadassi Thera 203

WH 39 Purification of Character
Bhikkhu Vimalo (Germany) 227

WH 40 Purification of View
Dr. C. B. Dharmasena 247

WH 41 Buddhism and Peace
K. N. Jayatilleke 271

WH 42 & 43 Early Western Buddhists
Francis Story 299

WH 44 The Contribution of Buddhism to World Culture
Soma Thera 349

WH 45 & 46 Escape to Reality
Ānanda Pereira 369

Key to Abbreviations

A	Aṅguttara Nikāya	Paṭis	Paṭisambhidamagga
Ap	Apadāna	Peṭ	Peṭakopadesa
Bv	Buddhavaṃsa	S	Saṃyutta Nikāya
Cp	Cariyāpiṭaka	Sn	Suttanipāta
D	Dīgha Nikāya	Th	Theragātha
Dhp	Dhammapada	Thī	Therigātha
Dhs	Dhammasaṅgaṇī	Ud	Udāna
It	Itivuttaka	Vibh	Vibhaṅga
Ja	Jātaka verses and commentary	Vin	Vinaya-piṭaka
Khp	Khuddakapāṭha	Vism	Visuddhimagga
M	Majjhima Nikāya	Vism-mhṭ	Visuddhimagga Sub-commentary
Mil	Milindapañha	Vv	Vimānavatthu
Nett	Nettipakaraṇa	Nidd	Niddesa

The above is the abbreviation scheme of the Pali Text Society (PTS) as given in the *Dictionary of Pali* by Margaret Cone.

The commentaries, *aṭṭhakathā*, are abbreviated by using a hyphen and an "a" ("-a") following the abbreviation of the text, e.g., *Dīgha Nikāya Aṭṭhakathā* = D-a. Likewise the sub-commentaries are abbreviated by a "ṭ" ("-ṭ") following the abbreviation of the text.

The sutta reference abbreviation system for the four Nikāyas, as is used in Bhikkhu Bodhi's translations is:

AN	Aṅguttara Nikāya	DN	Dīgha Nikāya
MN	Majjhima Nikāya	Sn	Saṃyutta Nikāya
J	Jātaka story	Mv	Mahāvagga (Vinaya Piṭaka)
Cv	Cullavagga (Vinaya Piṭaka)	SVibh	Suttavibhaṅga (Vinaya Piṭaka)

The Manual of Insight

Vipassanā Dīpanī

by

Ledi Sayādaw Mahāthera

Translated by

U Ñāṇa Mahāthera

WHEEL PUBLICATION NO. 31/32

Publisher's Foreword to Second BPS Edition

The Venerable Ledi Sayādaw's *The Manual of Insight* was first published in book form by The Society for Promoting Buddhism in Foreign Countries, which was centred in Mandalay, Burma. It was later serialised in the journal "The Light of the Dhamma" (Rangoon), Vols. I and II. The full text appeared in a collection of Ledi Sayādaw's treatises, *The Manuals of Buddhism* (Rangoon: Union of Burma Buddha Sāsana Council. 1965).

The first BPS edition of *The Manual of Insight* introduced a few minor changes in style and terminology, and replaced a large number of the abundant Pali words by their English equivalents. This second edition carries through the same editorial policy which guided the work on the first edition. For the benefit of modern readers, the style has been simplified and streamlined, archaic and quaint expressions replaced by more contemporary ones, and the substitution of English for Pali executed more thoroughly. It is hoped that these revisions will make this valuable and illuminating treatise easier reading, and a useful and practical guide in achieving the purpose for which it was originally written: the development of meditative insight.

Vipassanā Dīpanī

The Exposition of Insight

The Three Hallucinations

Vipallāsa means hallucination, delusion, erroneous observation,[1] or taking that which is true as false and that which is false as true. There are three kinds of hallucination:

1. *Saññā-vipallāsa*: hallucination of perception
2. *Citta-vipallāsa*: hallucination of thought
3. *Diṭṭhi-vipallāsa*: hallucination of views

Of those three, hallucination of perception is fourfold. It erroneously perceives:

(i) Impermanence as permanence
(ii) Impurity as purity
(iii) Suffering as happiness
(iv) No-soul as soul

The same holds good with regard to the remaining two hallucinations, those of thinking and views.

All these classifications come under the category of "This is mine! This is my self or living soul!" and will be made clear later. The three hallucinations may be illustrated respectively by the similes of the wild deer, the magician, and a man who has lost his way.

The Simile of the Wild Deer

This is the simile of the wild deer to illustrate the hallucination of perception.

In the middle of a great forest a certain husbandman cultivated

---

1. Another rendering, "illusion" may be proposed, which fits better for all three varieties, while "hallucination" strictly refers only to erroneous sense perception.—Editor.

a piece of paddy land. While the cultivator was away, wild deer were in the habit of coming to the field and eating the young sprouts of growing grain. So the cultivator put some straw together into the shape of a man and set it up in the middle of the field in order to frighten the deer away. He tied the straw together with fibres into the semblance of a body, with head, hands, and legs; and with white lime painting on a pot the lineaments of a human face, he set it on the top of the body. He also covered the artificial man with some old clothes such as a coat, and so forth, and put a bow and arrow into his hands. Now the deer came as usual to eat the young paddy; but approaching it and catching sight of the artificial man, they took it for a real one, were frightened, and ran away.

In this illustration, the wild deer had seen men before and retained in their memory the perception of the shape and form of men. In accordance with their present perception, they took the straw man for a real man. Thus their perception was an erroneous perception. The hallucination of perception is as here shown in this allegory of the wild deer. It is very clear and easy to understand.

This particular hallucination is also illustrated by the case of a bewildered man who has lost his way and cannot make out the cardinal points, east and west, in the locality in which he is, although the rising and setting of the sun may be distinctly perceived by anyone with open eyes. If the error has once been made, it establishes itself very firmly, and can be removed only with great difficulty. There are many things within ourselves which we always apprehend erroneously and in a sense that is the reverse of the truth as regards impermanence and no-soul. Thus through the hallucination of perception we apprehend things erroneously in exactly the same way that the wild deer take the straw man to be a real man, even with their eyes wide open.

The Simile of the Magician

This is the simile of the magician to illustrate the hallucination of thought.

There is a sham art called magic by means of which, when lumps of earth are exhibited in the presence of a crowd, all who look at them think they are lumps of gold and silver. The power of the magical art takes from men their ordinary power of seeing and in its place puts an extraordinary kind of sight. It can thus for a time turn the mind upside down, so to speak. When persons are in command of themselves they see lumps of earth as they are. But under the influence of this magical art, they see the lumps of earth as lumps of gold and silver, with all their qualities of brightness, yellowness, whiteness, and so forth. Thus, their beliefs, observations, or ideas become erroneous. In the same way, our thoughts and ideas are in the habit of wrongly taking false things as true, and thus we delude ourselves. For instance, at night we are often deceived into thinking we see a man, when it is really the stump of a tree that we are looking at. Or, on seeing a bush, we imagine we are looking at a wild elephant; or, seeing a wild elephant, we take it to be a bush.

In this world all our mistaken ideas about things in our field of observation are due to the action of the hallucination of thought, which is deeper and more unfathomable than that of perception, since it deludes us by making false things seem true. However, as it is not so firmly rooted as the latter, it can easily be removed by investigation or by searching into the causes and conditions of things.

The Simile of the Man Who Has Lost His Way

This is the simile of the man who has lost his way to illustrate the hallucination of views.

There was a large forest haunted by demons, who lived there, building towns and villages. Some travellers who were not acquainted with the roads came through the forest. The demons created their towns and villages as splendidly as those of the *devas*, or celestial beings, and assumed the forms of male and female devas. They also made the roads as pleasant and delightful as those of the devas. When the travellers saw these, they believed that these pleasant roads would lead them to large towns and villages, and so, turning aside from the right roads, they went astray following the wrong and misleading ones, arriving at the towns of the demons and suffering accordingly.

In this allegory, the large forest stands for the three worlds—of sense existence, fine-material, and immaterial existence. The travellers are all those who inhabit these worlds. The right road is right views; and the misleading road is wrong views. The right views here spoken of are of two kinds, namely, those that pertain to the world, and those pertaining to enlightenment. Of these two, the former connotes this right view: "All beings are the owners of their deeds; and every deed, both moral and immoral, committed by oneself, is one's own property and follows one throughout the whole long course of life," while the latter connotes the knowledge of the doctrine of causal genesis, of the aggregates, of the sense bases, and no-soul. Of these two views, the former is the right road to the round of existences. The worlds of the fortunate—the abodes of human beings, devas, and Brahmas—are like the towns of good people. The erroneous views that deny moral and immoral deeds and their results or effects are like the wrong, misleading roads. The worlds of the unfortunate—the abodes of the tortured, of animals, *petas*, and *asuras*—are like the towns of the demons.

The right view of knowledge, which is one of the factors of enlightenment, is like the right road that leads out of the round of existence. Nibbāna is like the town of good people.

The views "my body" and "my soul" are also like the wrong and misleading roads. Viewed in this light, the world comprising the abodes of human beings, devas, and Brahmas, or the ceaseless renewing of existences, is like the towns of the demons.

The aforesaid erroneous views belong likewise to the hallucinations, and are deeper and more firmly established than the hallucination of thought.

The Three Fantasies (maññanā)

Maññanā means fantasy, egotistic estimation, high imagination, or feigning to oneself that one is what one is not. Through ignorance, hallucination arises, and through hallucination fantasy arises.

Fantasy is of three kinds:

1. *Taṇhā-maññanā*: fantasy caused by craving
2. *Māna-maññanā*: fantasy caused by conceit
3. *Diṭṭhi-maññanā*: fantasy caused by wrong views

Of these, "fantasy caused by craving" means the high imagination: "This is mine! This is my own!" in clinging to what in reality is not "mine" and "my own." In strict truth, there is no "I" and as there is no "I," there can be no "mine" or "my own." Both personal and impersonal (external) objects are highly imagined and discriminated as, "This is mine; that other thing is not mine"; and "This is my own; that other thing is not mine." Such a state of imagination and fanciful discrimination is called "fantasy caused by craving."

"Personal objects" means one's own body and organs. "Impersonal (external) objects" means one's own relations, such as father, mother, and so forth, and one's own possessions.

"Fantasy caused by conceit" means high imagination of personal objects expressed as "I" or "I am." When it is supported or encouraged, so to speak, by personal attributes and impersonal objects, it becomes aggressively haughty and fantastically conceited.

Here personal attributes means vigour of eyes, ears, hands, legs, virtue, intuition, knowledge, possession of power, and so forth. Impersonal objects means plenitude of family, relations, surroundings, dwellings, possessions, and so forth.

"Fantasy caused by wrong views" means overhestimation of personal objects as "my bodily frame; my principle; my soul; the core, substance or essence of my being." In the expressions "earthen pots" and "earthen bowls," it is understood that earth is the substance of which these pots and bowls are made, and the very earth so made, so shaped, is again called pots and bowls. In the expressions "iron pots" and "iron bowls," and so forth, it is also understood that iron is the substance from which iron pots and bowls are made, and the very iron so made, so shaped, is again called pots and bowls. In exactly the same way that in these instances earth or iron is the substance from which the vessels are made, so the element of extension, the earth-element which pertains to the personality, is assumed to be the substance of living beings; and of the "I" this fanciful estimation of the facts of the case arises: "The element of extension is the living being: the element of extension is the 'I'." What is here said in connection with the element of extension is in like manner to be understood in connection with the element of cohesion, the liquid element, and all other elements found in a corporeal existence. This overestimation or fantastic imagination will be expounded at greater length further on.

These three kinds of fantasy are also called the three *gāha*, or the three holds, to indicate their power of holding tightly and firmly. Since they also multiply erroneous, mistaken actions, which tend gradually but continuously to increase beyond all limits and never incline to cease, they are also called the three *papañcas* or the three multipliers.

The Two Dogmatic Beliefs (abhinivesa)

Abhinivesa means dogmatic belief, a strong belief set in the mind as firmly and immovably as doorposts, stone pillars, and monuments, so that it cannot be moved by any means or expenditure of effort. It is of two different kinds: (1) *taṇhābhinivesa*: dogmatic belief induced by craving; (2) *diṭṭhābhinivesa*: dogmatic belief induced by wrong views.

Of these, *taṇhābhinivesa* means the firm and unshakable belief in what is not "my own" body, head, hands, legs, eyes, nose, and so forth, as being "my own" body, head and so forth, throughout a long succession of existences, caused by attachment to the body.

Diṭṭhābhinivesa means the firm and unshakable belief in the existence of the soul or self or separate life in a person or creature, which is held, in accordance with this belief, to be an unchanging supreme thing that governs the body.

These two kinds of dogmatic belief are also called *taṇhā-nissaya* and *diṭṭhi-nissaya* respectively. They may also be called the two great reposers upon the five aggregates, and on body-and-mind; or the two great resting-places of *puthujjanas*, the ordinary men of the world.

The Two Stages (bhūmi)

Bhūmi (lit., soil, ground) means the stages where all creatures find their footing, generate, and grow. It is of two kinds: (1) *puthujjana-bhūmi*: the stage of the worldling; (2) *ariya-bhūmi*: the stage of the noble ones.

Puthujjana-bhūmi is the stage of the ordinary or normal being, the worldling (*puthujjana*); speaking in the sense of ultimate truth, it is nothing but the hallucination of views. All creatures of the ordinary worldly kind live in the world making this *diṭṭhi-vipallāsa*, or erroneous view, their resting place, their main support, their standing ground: "There is in me or in my body something that is permanent, pleasurable, and substantial."

The *diṭṭhi-maññanā* or fantasy through error, the *diṭṭhi-gāha* or erroneous hold, the *diṭṭhi-papañca* or multiplier of error, and the *diṭṭhi-abhinivesa* or strong belief induced by error, are also the landing stages, the supports, the resting places, and the standing grounds of all *puthujjanas*. Hence they will never be released from the state or existence of a puthujjana, so long as they take their firm stand on the ground of the aforesaid many-named error.

As to the *ariya-bhūmi*, it is the stage of an *ariya*, a noble and sanctified being, in whom hallucination is eradicated. It is, speaking in the ultimate sense, nothing but this right view, this right apprehension, the right understanding: "There is in me or in my body nothing permanent, pleasurable, and substantial." As an *h* lives making right view his main footing, this right view may be called the stage of the ariya. Upon the attainment of this right view, a being is said to have transcended the *puthujjana-bhūmi*, and to have set foot on the *ariya-bhūmi*.

Among the innumerable ordinary beings who have been treading the ground of the state of being puthujjana during countless existences of unknown beginning, if a certain person trying to eradicate the hallucination of error and to implant right view within himself, on a certain day succeeds in his attempts, he is said to have set foot that self-same day upon the ground of the ariya and to have become an ariya, that is, a sanctified being. Even if there should remain the hallucinations of thought and perception in some of the ariyas, they would not commit such evil deeds as would produce for them evil effects in the worlds of misfortune, for they have eradicated the weighty hallucination of error. The two remaining hallucinations would merely enable them to enjoy such worldly pleasures as they have lawfully earned.

The Two Destinations (gati)

Gati means literally "going," that is, going from life to life by way of rebirth; in other words, the change of existences, or the future destination of beings. It is of two kinds: (1) *puthujjana-gati*: the destination of worldlings; (2) *ariya-gati*: the destination of sanctified beings.

The former signifies the taking rebirth of the ordinary person, the worldling, which is dispersive (*vinipātana*). That is to say, he cannot be reborn into whatever kind of existence he might wish, but is liable to fall into any of the thirty-one kinds of existence, according as he is thrown by his past *kamma*. Just as, when a coconut, or any other fruit, falls from a tree, it cannot be ascertained beforehand where it will come to rest; so also when a worldling is reborn after his death, it cannot be known beforehand where he will be reborn. Every creature that comes into life inevitably has to face the evil of death; and after his death he is also sure to fall by dispersion into any type of existence. Thus the two great evils of death and dispersion are inseparably linked to every being born.

Of these two, the dispersion of life after death is worse than death; for the four realms of misery down to the Avīci hell stand wide open to a worldling who departs from the world of men; they are open to him like unobstructed space. As soon as his term of life ends, he may fall into any of the realms of woe. Whether far or near, there is no intervening period of time between two existences. In the wink of an eyelid, he may be reborn as an animal, as a wretched ghost (*peta*), as a titan or *asūra*, an enemy of Sakka, the king of gods. The same possibility holds if he dies in any of the six upper realms of the sphere of sense existence (*kāmāvacara-deva*). But when he expires from the fine-material (*rūpa-loka*), or immaterial worlds (*arūpa-loka*), there is no direct fall into the four realms of misery; there is a halt of one existence either in the abode of men or in those of devas, wherefrom he may fall into those four worlds of misery.

Why do we say that every being fears death? Because death is followed by dispersion to any sphere of existence. If there were no dispersion as regards existence after death, and one could take rebirth in any existence at one's choice, no one would fear death so much, although, to be sure, sometimes there may be thirst for death when a being, after living a considerable length of time in one existence, desires to move to a new one.

By way of showing how great is the dispersion of existence in the case of a worldling, the similes of the fingernail (Nakhasikha Sutta) and of the blind turtle (Kāṇakacchapa Sutta) may be cited from the discourses.

Nakhasikha Sutta (The Sutta on the Fingernail)

At one time the Buddha, showing them some dust which he had taken upon the tip of his fingernail, addressed the disciples thus:

> "If, O bhikkhus, these few grains of dust upon my fingernail and all the dust of the universe were compared in quantity, which would you say was less, and which more?" The disciples replied: "Lord, the dust on your fingernail is less, and that of the universe is more. Surely, Lord, the dust on your fingernail is not worthy of mention in comparison with the dust of the universe." Then the Buddha continued: "Even so, bhikkhus, those who are reborn in the abodes of men and devas when they have expired, are very few even as the few grains of dust on my fingernail; and those who are reborn in the four realms of misery are exceedingly many, even as the dust of the great universe. Again, those who have expired from the four miserable worlds and are reborn in the abodes of men and devas are few even as the grains of dust on my fingernail; and those who are repeatedly reborn in the four miserable worlds are innumerable, even as the grains of dust of the great universe."

What has just been said is the substance of the Nakhasikha Sutta. But, to say nothing of the beings of all the four realms of misery, the creatures that inhabit the four great oceans alone will suffice to make evident how great is the evil of dispersion (*vinipātana-gati*), the variety of possible kinds of existence after death.

Kāṇakacchapa Sutta (The Sutta on the Blind Turtle)

At one time the Buddha addressed the disciples thus:

> "There is, O bhikkhus, in the ocean a blind turtle. He plunges into the water of the unfathomable ocean and swims about incessantly in any direction wherever his head may lead. There is also in the ocean the yoke of a cart which is ceaselessly floating about on the surface of the water, and is carried away

> in all directions by tide, current, and wind. Thus these two go on throughout an incalculable space of time. Perchance it happens that in the course of time the yoke arrives at the precise place and time where and when the turtle puts up his head, and yokes on to it. Now, O bhikkhus, is it possible that such a time might come as is said?" "In ordinary truth, Lord," replied the bhikkhus, "it is impossible; but time being so vast, and an aeon lasting so long, it may be admitted that perhaps at some time or other it might be possible for the two to yoke together, as said: if the blind tortoise lives long enough, and the yoke does not rot and break up before such a coincidence comes to pass."

Then the Buddha said:

> "Bhikkhus, the occurrence of such a strange thing is not to be counted a difficult one; for there is a still greater, a harder, a hundred times, a thousand times more difficult thing than this lying hidden from your knowledge. And what is this? It is, bhikkhus, the obtaining of a human existence again by a man who has expired and been reborn once in any of the four realms of misery. The occurrence of the yoking of the blind tortoise is not worth thinking of as a difficult occurrence in comparison therewith. Because only those who perform good deeds and abstain from bad actions can obtain the existence of men and devas. The beings in the four miserable worlds cannot discern what is virtuous and what vicious, what good and what bad, what moral and what immoral, what meritorious and what demeritorious; consequently, they live a life of immorality and demerit, tormenting one another with all their power. Those creatures of the hells and the ghost world in particular live a very miserable life on account of punishments and torments which they experience with sorrow, pain and distress. Therefore, O bhikkhus, the opportunity of being reborn in the abode of men is a hundred times, a thousand times harder to obtain than the encountering of the blind turtle with the yoke."

According to this sutta, why those creatures who are born in the miserable planes are far from human existence is because they never look up but always look down. And what is meant by looking down? The ignorance in them by degrees becomes greater and stronger from one existence to another; and as the water of a river always flows down to the lower plains, so also they are always tending towards the lower existences; for the ways towards the higher existences are closed to them, while those towards the lower existences are freely open. This is the meaning of "looking down." Hence, from this story of the blind turtle, the wise apprehend how great, how fearful, how terribly perilous are the evils of the worldling's destination, i.e., the "dispersion of existence."

What has been said concerns the *puthujjana-gati.* Now, what is the *ariya-gati*, the destination of sanctified beings? It is deliverance from the dispersion of existence after death. It is also the potentiality of being reborn in higher existences or in existences according to one's choice. It is not like the fall of coconuts from trees, but is to be compared to birds which fly through the air to whatsoever place or tree they may wish to perch on. Those men, devas, and Brahmas who have attained the ariya state, can go to whatever better existence—as men, devas, Brahmas—they may wish to be reborn into, when they expire from the particular existence in which they have attained such ariya state. Though they expire unexpectedly without aiming to be reborn in a particular existence, they are destined to be reborn in a better or higher existence, and at the same time are entirely free from rebirth into lower and miserable existences. Moreover, if they are reborn again in the abode of men, they never become of the lower or poorer classes, nor are they fools or heretics, but become quite otherwise. It is the same in the abodes of devas and Brahmas. They are entirely set free from the *puthujjana-gati.*

What has been said concerns the destination of ariyas.

Explanation of the Two Destinations

Now we will explain the two destinations side by side.

When a man falls from a tree, he falls like a coconut because he has no wings with which to fly in the air. In precisely the same way, when men, devas, and Brahmas who are worldlings riveted to the hallucination of wrong views and not having the wings of the Noble Eightfold Path to make the sky their resting-place, are reborn after the dissolution of their present bodies into new ones. They fall tumbling into the bonds of the evils of dispersion. In this world ordinary men who climb up very high trees fall tumbling to the ground when the branches which they clutch, or try to make their resting-place, break. They suffer much pain from the fall, and sometimes death ensues because they have no other resting-places but the branches, neither have they wings to fly in the air. It is the same with men, devas, and Brahmas who have the hallucination of wrong views: when their resting-place of wrong views as regards self breaks down, they fall tumbling into the dispersion of existence. For their resting-places are only their bodies; and they have neither such a resting-place as Nibbāna nor strong wings like the Noble Eightfold Path to support them.

As for the birds, though the branches they rest on may break, they never fall, but easily fly through the air to any other tree. For the branches are not their permanent resting-places but only temporary ones. They entirely rely on their wings and the air. In the same way, men, devas, and Brahmas who have become ariyas and are freed from the hallucination of wrong views, neither regard their bodies as their self, nor rely upon them. They have in their possession permanent resting-places, such as Nibbāna, which is the entire cessation of all tumbling existences. They also possess the very mighty wings of the Noble Eightfold Path which are able to bear them to better existences.

The Two Truths (sacca)

Sacca or truth is the constant faithfulness or concordance of the term which names a thing, to or with that thing's intrinsic nature. It is of two kinds: 1. *sammuti-sacca*, conventional or relative truth; 2. *paramattha-sacca*, or ultimate truth.

Of the two, conventional truth is the truthfulness of the customary terms used by the great majority of people, such as "self exists," "men exist," "devas exist," "Sakkas exist," "elephants exist," "my head exists," and so on. This conventional truth is the opposite of untruth, and so one can overcome it. It is not a lie or lack of truthfulness when people say: "There probably exists an immutable, permanent, and continuing self or living soul which is neither momentarily rising nor passing away throughout one existence," for this is the customary manner of speech of the great majority of people who have no intention whatever of deceiving others. But according to ultimate truth, it is reckoned a *vipallāsa* or hallucination, which erroneously regards the impermanent as permanent and non-self as self. So long as this erroneous view remains undestroyed, one can never escape from the evils of *saṃsāra*, the wheel of life. All this holds good when people say "a person exists," and so on.

Ultimate truth is the absolute truthfulness of assertion or negation in full and complete accordance with what is actual: the elementary, fundamental qualities of phenomena. Here stating such truth in affirmative form, one may say: "The element of solidity exists," "the element of extension exists," "the element of cohesion exists," "the element of kinetic energy exists," "mind exists," "consciousness exists," "contact, feeling, and perception exist," "material aggregates exist," and so on. And expressing such truth in a negative form, it can be said: "No self exists," "no living soul exists," "no person exists," "no being exists," "nor do hands, nor any members of the body exist," "neither does a man exist nor a deva," and so on. In saying here: "No self exists," "no living soul exists," we mean that there is no such ultimate entity as a self or living soul which persists unchanged during the whole term of life, without momentarily coming to be and passing away. In the expressions "No being exists," and so forth, what is meant is that nothing actually exists but material and mental elements. These elements are neither persons nor beings, nor men, nor devas, etc. Therefore there is no separate being or person apart from the elements. This ultimate truth is the diametrical opposite of the hallucination, and so can confute it. One who is thus able to confute or reject the hallucination can escape from the evils of *saṃsāra*.

According to conventional truth, a person exists, a being exists; a person or a being continually transmigrates from one existence to another in the ocean of life. But according to ultimate truth, neither a person nor a being exists and there is no one who transmigrates from one existence to another. Here it may be asked: "Do not these two truths seem to be as poles asunder?" Of course they seem to be so. Nevertheless, we may bring them together. Have we not said: "according to conventional truth" and "according to ultimate truth"? Each kind of truth accordingly is truthful as regards its own mode of expression. Hence, if one man should say that there exists a person or a being according to conventional truth, the other to whom he speaks ought not to contradict him, for these conventional terms describe what apparently exists. And likewise, if the other says that there exists neither a person nor a being according to ultimate truth, the former ought not to deny this, for, in the ultimate sense, material and mental phenomena alone truly exist, and in strict reality they know no person or being.

For example: men dig up lumps of earth from certain places, pound them into dust, knead this dust with water into clay, and from this clay make various kinds of useful pots, jars, and cups. Thus there exist various kinds of pots, jars and cups in the world.

Now, when discussion takes place on this subject, if it were asked: "Are there earthen pots and cups in this world?" the answer according to the conventional truth should be given in the affirmative, and according to the ultimate truth in the negative, since this kind of truth admits only the positive existence of the earth out of which the pots and so forth were made. Of these two answers the former requires no explanation inasmuch as it is an answer according to the established usage, but as regards the latter, some explanation is needed. In the objects that we called "earthen pots," and "earthen cups," what really exists is only earth not pots or cups in the sense of ultimate truth, for the term "earth" applies properly not to pots and cups but to actual substantial earth. There are also pots and cups made of iron, brass, silver, and gold. These cannot be called earthen pots and cups, since they are not made of earth. The terms "pots" and "cups" also are not terms descriptive of earth but of ideas derived from the appearance of pots and cups, such as their circular or spherical shape and so on. This is obvious, because the terms "pots" and "cups" are not applied to the mere lumps of earth which have no shape or form of pots and cups. Hence it follows that the term "earth" is not a term descriptive of pots and cups, but of real earth; and also the terms "pots" and "cups" are not terms descriptive of earth but of pictorial ideas (*saṇṭhāna-paññatti*) which have no elementary substance other than the dust of clay, being mere conceptions presented to the mind by the particular appearance, form, and shape of the worked-up clay. Hence the negative statement according to the ultimate truth, namely, that "no earthen pots and cups exist," ought to be accepted without question.

Material Phenomena

Now we come to the analysis of things in the ultimate sense. Of the two kinds of ultimate phenomena, material and mental, as mentioned above, the former is of twenty-eight kinds:

(i) The four great essential elements:
1. Element of solidity (*paṭhavī*)
2. Element of cohesion, or binding, the fluid (*āpo*)
3. Element of heat, including warmth and cold (*tejo*)
4. Element of motion or vibration (*vāyo*)

(ii) The six bases:
5. Eye-base
6. Ear-base
7. Nose-base
8. Tongue-base
9. Body-base
10. Heart-base

(iii) The two sexes:
11. Male sex
12. Female sex

(iv) One species of physical life:
13. Vital force

(v) One species of material nutrition:
14. Edible food

(vi) The four sense fields:
15. Visible form
16. Sound
17. Odour
18. Savour

These last eighteen species are called genetic material qualities (*jāta-rūpāni*), as they possess the power of production.

(vii) One species of physical limitation:
 19. Element of space

(viii) The two communications:
 20. Intimation through the body
 21. Intimation through speech

(ix) The three plasticities:
 22. Lightness
 23. Pliancy
 24. Adaptability

(x) The four salient features:
 25. Integration
 26. Continuance
 27. Decay
 28. Impermanence or death

These last ten species are called non-genetic material qualities (*ajāta-rūpāni*) as they do not possess the power of production.

Four Great Essentials (mahābhūta)

Mahābhūta means to develop greatly.

1. The element of extension is the element of earth, that is, the fundamental principle or foundation of matter. It exists in gradations of many kinds, such as hardness, more hardness, stiffness, more stiffness, softness, more softness, pliability, more pliability, and so on.
2. The element of cohesion is the element of water, that is, the cohesive power of material qualities whereby they form into a mass or bulk or a lump. There are apparently many kinds of cohesion.
3. The element of heat is the element of fire, that is, the power to burn, to inflame, and to mature the material qualities. This maturative quality is of two kinds, namely, the maturative quality of heat and the maturative quality of cold.
4. The element of motion is the element of wind or air, that is, the power of supporting or resisting. It is of many kinds, such as supportive, resistive, conveying, vibratory, diffusive, and so on.

From these four great elements all other forms of matter are born. Or, expressed in another way: All matter is a combination, in one proportion or another, of these four elementary properties, together with a varying number of secondary material phenomena derived from the great elements.

Derived Materiality
(*upādā-rūpa*)

The Six Bases (vatthu)

A base, *vatthu*, is that where consciousness is generated, arises, develops, or that whereupon it depends.

5. The eye-base is the sensorium within the eyeball where consciousness of sight is generated: consciousness of sight connotes the power of seeing various kinds of colours, appearances, forms and shapes.
6. The ear-base is the sensorium within the organ of the ear where consciousness of sound is generated; and the consciousness of sound connotes the power of hearing various kinds of sound.
7. The nose-base is the sensorium within the nose organ where consciousness of smell is generated; and the consciousness of smell connotes the power of smelling different kinds of odours.
8. The tongue-base is the sensorium upon the surface of the tongue where consciousness of taste is generated; the consciousness of taste connotes the power of tasting many kinds of taste such as sweet, sour, and so forth.
9. The body-base is the sensorium locating itself by pervading the whole body within and without from head to foot, where consciousness of touch is generated; the consciousness of touch connotes the power of feeling or sensing physical contacts.
10. The heart-base (*hadaya-vatthu*) is a kind of very fine, bright, subtle matter within the organ of heart where mind consciousness, comprising sixty-nine classes of the same in number is generated.

From these six bases all classes of consciousness are generated and arise.

The Two Sexes (bhāva)

Bhāva means production or productive principle.

11. The *itthi-bhāva*, the female sex, is a certain productive principle of matter which produces several different kinds of female features or feminine characteristics.
12. The *puṃ-bhāva*, the male sex, is a certain productive principle of matter which produces several different kinds of male features or appearances and masculine characteristics.

The two sexes respectively locate themselves in the bodies of male and female; like the body-base they pervade the entire frame from the sole of the foot to the top of the head within and without. Owing to their predominant features the distinction between femininity and masculinity is readily discerned.

The Vital Force (jīvita-rūpa)

13. *Jīvita* means life, that is, the vital force which controls the material qualities produced by kamma, and keeps them fresh in the same way that the water of a pond preserves the lotus plants from decay. It so informs them as to prevent them from withering. The common expressions of ordinary speech, "a being lives" or "a being dies," are descriptive merely of the presence or absence of this material quality of life. When it ceases forever with reference to a particular form, we say "a being dies," and we say "a being lives" so long as it continues to act in any particular form. This also permeates the whole body.

Material Nutrition (āhāra-rūpa)

14. *Āhāra-rūpa* means the element of essential nutriment that nourishes or promotes the growth of material qualities. Just as the element of water that resides in earth or falls from the sky nourishes trees or plants, or mainly promotes their growth

and helps them to fecundate, develop and last long, so also this material quality of nutrition nourishes the four kinds of matter produced by the four causes kamma, mind, temperature, and food—and helps them to fecundate and grow. It is the main supporter of the material quality of life, so that undertaking various kinds of work in the world for the sake of getting one's daily food is called a man's living or livelihood.

The Four Sense Fields (gocara-rūpa)

Gocara means sense field or object of the five senses.

15. The object "visible form" is the quality of colour and shape of various objects.
16. The object "sound" is the quality of sound itself.
17. The object "odour" is the quality of scent or smell.
18. The object "savour" is the quality of savour or taste.

Mention is not made here of touch, the tangible object, as it consists of three of the great elements, namely, tangible extension, tangible temperature, and tangible movement. Counting the tangible also, we thus get five sense fields in all. Of these, visible form is the object of eye; sound, of ear; odour, of nose; savour, of tongue; and the tangible, of body.

The Element of Space (ākāsa-dhātu)

19. *Ākāsa-dhātu* means the element of space. In a heap of sand there is space between each particle of sand. Hence we may say that there are as many spaces as there are particles of sand in the heap; and we can also distinguish the particles of sand from one another. When the heap is destroyed, the particles of sand are scattered about, and the space enclosed between them disappears also. Similarly, in very hard lumps of stone, marble, iron, and other metals, there are innumerable atoms and particles of atoms, called *kalāpas* or groups. Even the finest, smallest particles of an atom contain at least the following eight qualities of matter: the four essentials and colour, odour, savour, and nutritive essence. And each group is separated by the element of space located between them. Therefore there is

at least as much space as there is matter in the lump. It is owing to the existence of this space that lumps of stone and iron can be broken up, or cut into pieces, or pounded into dust, or melted.

The Two Modes of Communications (viññatti-rūpa)

Viññatti-rūpa means mode of communication. It is a sign employed to communicate the willingness, intention, or purpose, of one person to the understanding of another.

20. *Kāya-viññatti* is that peculiar movement of body by which one's purpose is made known to others.
21. *Vacī-viññatti* is that peculiar movement of sounds in speech by which one's purpose is made known to others.

Those who cannot see the minds of others know the purpose, the intention, the willingness of others through the use of these two modes of communication. These two are employed not only in communicating one's purpose or intention to the understanding of another, but also in moving the parts of the body while walking, and so forth, according to one's will, as also in learning by heart, reading to oneself, and so forth.

The Three Plasticities (*vikāra-rūpa*)

Vikāra means the peculiar expression or distinctive condition of the genetic material qualities (*jāta-rūpa*).

22. *Lahutā* is the lightness of the material quality.
23. *Mudutā* is the pliancy of the material qualities.
24. *Kammaññatā* is the adaptability of the two media of communication.

When one of the Four Great Essentials falls out of order and becomes disproportionate to the rest in any parts of the body, these parts are not light as usual in applying themselves to some work, but tend to become heavy and awkward; they are not pliable as usual, but tend to become hard, coarse, and rigid; they are not as adaptable as usual in their movements in accord with one's will, but tend to become difficult and strained. Likewise, when the essentials are out of order, the tongue and the lips are not adaptable according to one's wish in speaking, but become firm and stiff. When the four great essentials are in good order and the parts of the body are in sound health, the matter of the body (*rūpa*) is said to be in possession of these qualities, lightness, pliancy, and adaptability, which are called the three plasticities (*vikāra-rūpa*).

The Four Salient Features (lakkhaṇa-rūpa)

Lakkhaṇa means the salient feature or mark by means of which it is decisively known that all material and mental qualities are subject to impermanence.

25. *Upacaya-rūpa* means both integration and continuance of integration; the former may be called *ācaya* (initial integration) and the latter *upacaya* (sequential integration).
26. *Santati-rūpa* means continuance. From the cessation of sequential integration to the commencement of decay the phenomenon continues without any increase or decrease. And such a continuous state of material phenomenon is called *santati* or *pavatti* (prolongation). The production (*jāti*) of the groups of material qualities alone is described by the three names, *ācaya*, *upacaya*, and *santati*.
27. *Jaratā* is the state of growing old, of decline, of maturity, ripeness (in the sense of being ready to fall), decay, caducity, rottenness, or corruption.
28. *Aniccatā* means impermanence, death, termination, cessation, brokenness or the state of disappearing.[2]

A plant has five periods, the *ācaya* period, the *upacaya* period, the *santati* period, the *jaratā* period, and the *aniccatā* period. It is first generated; then it grows up gradually or develops day-by-day; and after the cessation of growth it stands for sometime in the fully developed state. After that it begins to decay, and at last it dies and disappears.

---

2. It is our Ledi Sayādaw's style in writing to express an idea by means of as many synonymous terms as he can collect. A translator such as I, who has not fully attained the mastery of the English language, in which the treasures of Burmese literature are to be deposited, meets difficulty with furnishing the translation with a sufficient number of appropriate terms.—Translator

Here, the primary generation of the material qualities is called *ācaya* period; the gradual growth or development, the *upacaya* period; and their fully developed state, the *santati* period. However, during these three periods there are momentary decays (*khaṇika-jaratā*) and momentary deaths (*khaṇika-aniccatā*), but they are inconspicuous. The declining of the plant is called *jaratā* period. During the period of decline there are momentary births (*khaṇika-jāti*) and momentary deaths (*khaṇika-maraṇa*), but they are also inconspicuous.[3] The death of the plant and the final disappearance of all its constituents are called the *aniccatā* period. During what we call death there are also momentary births and decays but they are invisible. The five periods allotted to what is apparent to the view are shown here only in order to help one to grasp the idea of *lakkhaṇa-rūpas*.

In a similar manner we may divide, in the life of a fruit tree, the branches, the leaves, the buds, the flowers, and the fruits into five periods each. A fruit can be divided into five periods thus: the first period of appearance; the second period of growth or development; the third period of standing; the fourth period of ripening and decaying; and the fifth period of falling from the stem, total destruction, or final disappearance.

Just as we get five periods in the life of plants, so is it with all creatures, and also with all their bodily parts; with their movements or bodily actions such as going, coming, standing, and sitting; with their speech and with their thought. The beginning, the middle, and the end are all to be found in the existence of every material thing.

The Four Producers of Material Phenomena

There are four producers (*samuṭṭhāna*) which produce material phenomena: (1) *kamma*, (2) *citta*, (3) *utu*, (4) *āhāra*.

3. The commentator of the Dhammasaṅgaṇī, in his *Atthasālinī*, explains this by an illustration of a well dug out on the bank of a river. The first gushing out of water in the well, he says, is like the *ācaya* of the material phenomenon; the flushing up or the gradual increasing or the rising up of water to the full, is like the *upacaya*; and the flooding is like the *santati*.—Tr.

1. *Kamma* means moral and immoral actions committed in previous existences.
2. *Citta* means mind and mental concomitants existing in the present life.
3. *Utu* means the two states of *tejo-dhātu*, the fire-element: heat (*uṇha-tejo*) and cold (*sīta-tejo*).
4. *Āhara* means the two kinds of nutritive essence: internal nutriment that obtains from the time of conception, and external nutriment that exists in edible food.

Out of the twenty-eight species of material qualities, nine species—the six bases, two sexes, and life— are produced only by kamma. The two media of communications are produced only by *citta.*

Sound is produced by *citta* and *utu*. The three plasticities are produced by *citta, utu*, and *āhāra*. Of the remaining thirteen, excluding *jaratā* (decay) and *aniccatā* (impermanence), the eleven—comprising the four great essentials, nutriment, visible form, odour, savour, the element of space, integration, and continuance—are produced by the four causes. These eleven always appertain severally to the four classes of phenomena produced by the four causes. There are no phenomena that enter into composition without these. Material phenomena enter into composition with these, forming groups of eight, nine, and so forth, and each group is called *rūpa-kalāpa.*

Two salient features, decay and impermanence, are excluded from the material qualities born of the four causes as they disorganise what has been produced.

Mental Phenomena

There are fifty-four kinds of mental phenomena: *citta*, mind or consciousness; *cetasika*, mental properties or concomitants, fifty-two in number; and *nibbāna*, liberation from the circle of existences.[4]

Citta means the faculty of investigating an object (*ārammaṇa*); or of taking possession of an object; or of knowing an object; or of being conscious of an object. *Cetasikas* are factors of consciousness,

4. Nibbāna is here regarded as a mental phenomenon, not from the objective, but from the subjective point of view.—Tr.

or mental properties born of mind, or concomitants of mind. *Nibbāna* means freedom from all suffering.

Consciousness

Consciousness is divided into six classes:

1. Consciousness of sight
2. Consciousness of sound
3. Consciousness of smell
4. Consciousness of taste
5. Consciousness of touch
6. Consciousness of mind

Of these:

1. The consciousness arising at the eye-base is called consciousness of sight, and has the function of seeing.
2. The consciousness arising at the ear-base is called consciousness of sound, and has the function of hearing.
3. The consciousness arising at the nose-base is called consciousness of smell, and has the function of smelling.
4. The consciousness arising at the tongue-base is called consciousness of taste, and has the function of tasting.
5. The consciousness arising at the body-base is called consciousness of touch, and has the function of touching.
6. The consciousness arising at the heart-base is called consciousness of mind. In the immaterial world (*arūpa-loka*), however, mind-consciousness arises without any physical base.

Mind-consciousness is again subdivided into four kinds:

(a) *Kāma*-consciousness
(b) *Rūpa*-consciousness
(c) *Arūpa*-consciousness
(d) *Lokuttara*-consciousness

Of these:

(a) *Kāma*-consciousness is that which is under the dominance of desire prevailing in the world of sense desire (*kāma-loka*). It is fourfold, thus: moral (*kusala*), immoral (*akusala*), resultant (*vipāka*), and ineffective (i.e., kammically inoperative, *kriyā*).

(b) *Rūpa*-consciousness is the *jhānic* mind which has become free from sense-desire but still remains under the dominance of the desire prevailing in the fine-material world. It is threefold, thus: moral, resultant, and ineffective.

(c) *Arūpa*-consciousness is also the *jhānic* mind which has become free from desire for the fine-material, but still remains under the dominance prevailing in the immaterial world. It is also threefold, thus: moral, resultant, and ineffective.

(d) *Lokuttara*, or supramundane consciousness, is the noble mind (*ariya-citta*) which has become free from the threefold desire, and has transcended the three planes, *kāma*, *rūpa*, and *arūpa*. It is of two kinds, thus: noble consciousness in the path (of stream-entry, etc.) and noble consciousness in the fruition (of stream-entry, etc.).

Cetasikas or Mental Properties

Mental properties are of fifty-two kinds.
(a) The seven common properties (*sabba-citta-sādhāraṇa*), so called on account of being common to all classes of consciousness:

1. *Phassa*: contact
2. *Vedanā*: feeling
3. *Saññā*: perception
4. *Cetanā*: volition
5. *Ekaggatā*: concentration of mind
6. *Jīvita*: psychic life
7. *Manasikāra*: attention

(b) The six particulars (*pakiṇṇaka*), so called because they are features only of certain types of consciousness:

8. *Vitakka*: initial application
9. *Vicāra*: sustained application
10. *Viriya*: effort
11. *Pīti*: pleasurable interest
12. *Chanda*: desire-to-do
13. *Adhimokkha*: decision

The above thirteen mental properties are called "mixers"[5] (*vomissaka*), meaning that they can mix with both moral and immoral consciousness. Shwe Zan Aung calls them "un-moral properties."

(c) The fourteen immoral properties (*akusala*) are:

14. *Lobha*: greed
15. *Dosa*: hate
16. *Moha*: dullness
17. *Diṭṭhi*: error
18. *Māna*: conceit
19. *Issā*: envy
20. *Macchariya*: selfishness
21. *Kukkucca*: worry
22. *Ahirika*: shamelessness
23. *Anottappa*: recklessness
24. *Uddhacca*: distraction
25. *Thīna*: sloth
26. *Viddha*: torpor
27. *Vicikicchā*: perplexity

(d) The twenty-five moral properties (*sobhana*) are:

28. *Alobha*: disinterestedness; lit.: non-greed
29. *Adosa*: amity; lit.: non-hate
30. *Amoha*: reason; lit.: non-delusion
31. *Saddhā*: faith
32. *Sati*: mindfulness
33. *Hiri*: modesty
34. *Ottappa*: discretion
35. *Tatramajjhattatā*: balance of mind
36. *Kāyapassaddhi*: composure of mental properties
37. *Cittapassaddhi*: composure of mind
38. *Kāyalahutā*: buoyancy of mental properties
39. *Cittalahutā*: buoyancy of mind
40. *Kāyamudutā*: pliancy of mental properties
41. *Cittamudutā*: pliancy of mind
42. *Kāyakammaññatā*: adaptability of mental properties
43. *Cittakammaññatā*: adaptability of mind

5. *Vomissaka* literally means "mixed" or "miscellaneous".—Ed.

44. *Kāyapaguññatā*: proficiency of mental properties
45. *Cittapaguññatā*: proficiency of mind
46. *Kāyujukatā*: rectitude of mental properties
47. *Cittujukatā*: rectitude of mind
48. *Sammā-vācā*: right speech
49. *Sammā-kammantā*: right action
50. *Sammā-ājīva*: right livelihood
51. *karuṇā*: pity
52. *muditā*: appreciation.

The Common Properties

1. *Phassa* means contact, and contact means the faculty of pressing the object so as to cause the agreeable or disagreeable "sap" to come out. So contact is the main principle or prime mover of the mental properties in their uprising. If the sap cannot be squeezed out, then no object will be of any use.
2. *Vedanā* means feeling, the faculty of tasting the sapid flavour thus squeezed out by *phassa*. All creatures are sunk in feeling.
3. *Saññā* means perception, the act of perceiving. All creatures become wise through this perception, if they perceive things with sufficient clarity in accordance with their own ways, customs, creeds, and so forth.
4. *Cetanā* means volition, the faculty of determining the activities of the mental concomitants so as to bring them into harmony. In the common speech of the world we are accustomed to say of one who supervises a piece of work that he is the performer or author of the work. We usually say: "Oh, this work was done by So-and-so" or "This is such and such a person's great work." It is somewhat the same in connection with the ethical aspects of things. Volition is called action (*kamma*), as it determines the activities of the mental concomitants and supervises all the actions of body, speech, and mind. As all prosperity in this life is the outcome of the exertions put forth in work performed with body, speech, and mind, so also the conditions of a new existence are the results of the volitions[6]

6. "Asynchronous volition" is the name given to it in the Paṭṭhāna, and it is known by the name of *kamma* in the actions of body, speech and mind.

performed in previous existences. Earth, water, mountains, trees, grass, and so forth, are all born of the element of temperature and they may be quite properly be called the children or the issue of volition, or the element of kamma, as they are all born through kamma.

5. *Ekaggatā* means concentration of mind. It is also called concentration (*samādhi*). It becomes prominent in the *jhāna-samāpatti* the attainment of the supernormal modes of mind called *jhāna*.
6. *Jīvita* means the life of mental phenomena. It is preeminent in preserving the continuance of mental phenomena.
7. *Manasikāra* means attention. Its function is to bring the desired object into view of consciousness.

These seven factors are called common properties, as they always enter into the composition of all consciousness.

The Particular Properties

8. *Vitakka* means initial application of mind. Its function is to direct the mind towards the object of investigation. It is also called *saṅkappa* (aspiration), which is of two kinds: *sammā-saṅkappa* or right aspiration, *micchā-saṅkappa* or wrong aspiration.
9. *Vicāra* means sustained application of mind. Its function is to keep the mind engaged in the object (by considering, reflecting, etc.).
10. *Viriya* means energy, or effort of mind in actions. It is of two kinds, right effort and wrong effort.
11. *Pīti* means pleasurable interest of mind, or buoyancy, or rapture of mind.
12. *Chanda* means desire-to-do, such as desire-to-go, desire-to-speak, and so forth.
13. *Adhimokkha* means decision, or literally, apartness of mind from the object; it is intended to connote the freedom of mind from the wavering state between the two courses: "Is it?" or "Is it not?"

These last six mental properties are not common to all classes of consciousness, but severally enter into their composition in some cases. Hence they are called particulars. They make thirteen if they are added to the common properties; and both, taken together, are called mixers as they enter into composition both moral and immoral consciousness.

The Immoral Properties

14. *Lobha* ethically means greed, but psychologically it means agglutination of mind with objects. It is sometimes called *taṇhā* (craving), sometimes *abhijjhā* (covetousness), sometimes *kāma* (lust), and sometimes *rāga* (sensual passion).
15. *Dosa* in its ethical sense is hate, but psychologically it means the violent striking of mind at the object (i.e., conflict). It has two other names *paṭigha* (repugnance) and *vyāpāda* (ill-will).
16. *Moha* means dullness or lack of understanding. It is also called *avijjā* (nescience), *aññāṇa* (not knowing) and *adassana* (not seeing).

The above three are called the three immoral roots, as they are the main sources of all immorality.

17. *Diṭṭhi* means error or wrong view in matters of philosophy. It takes impermanence for permanence, non-soul for soul, and moral activities for immoral ones; or it denies that there are any results of action, and so forth.
18. *Māna* means conceit or wrong estimation. It wrongly imagines the name-and-form (*nāma-rūpa*) to be an "I," and estimates it as noble or ignoble according to the caste, creed, or family, and so on, to which the person belongs.
19. *Issā* means envy, lack of appreciation, or absence of inclination to congratulate others upon their success in life. It also means a disposition to find fault with others.
20. *Macchariya* means selfishness, meanness, or unwillingness to share with others.
21. *Kukkucca* means worry, anxiety, or undue remorse for what has been done wrongly, or for right actions that have been left undone. There are two wrongs in the world, namely, doing evil deeds and failing to do meritorious deeds. There are also two ways of repenting, thus "I have done evil acts," or "I have left undone meritorious acts, such as charity, virtue, and so forth." "A fool always invents plans after all is over," runs the saying.

So worry is of two kinds, with regard to forgetfulness and with regard to evil, "sins of omission" and "sins of commission."

22. *Ahirika* means shamelessness. When an evil act is about to be committed, no feeling of shame such as "I will be corrupted if I do this," or "Some people may know this of me," arises in him who is shameless.
23. *Anottappa* means utter recklessness as regarding such consequences as self-accusation ("I have been foolish; I have done wrong," and so forth), accusations by others, punishment in the present life inflicted by rulers, and punishment to be suffered in the realms of misery in the next life.
24. *Uddhacca* means restlessness or distraction of mind as regards an object.
25. *Thīna* means slothfulness of mind, that is, the dimness of the mind's consciousness of an object.
26. *Middha* means slothfulness of mental properties, that is, the dimness of the faculties of each of the mental properties, such as contact, feeling, and so forth.
27. *Vicikicchā* means perplexity or sceptical doubt, that is, not believing what ought to be believed.

The above fourteen kinds are called *akusala-dhamma* (immoral states); in fact, they are real immoralities.

The Moral Properties

28. *Alobha* means disinterestedness of mind as regards an object. It is also called *nekkhamma-dhātu* (the element of renunciation) and *anabhijjhā* (liberality).
29. *Adosa* or amity, in its ethical sense, means inclination of mind in the direction of its object, or purity of mind. It is also called *avyāpāda* (non-ill-will or peace of mind) and *mettā* (loving-kindness).
30. *Amoha* means knowing things as they are. It is also called *ñāṇa* (knowledge), *paññā* (wisdom), *vijjā* (true knowledge), *sammā-diṭṭhi* (right view).

These three are called the three moral roots as they are the main sources of all morality.

31. *Saddhā* means faith in what ought to be believed.
32. *Sati* means constant mindfulness in good things so as not to forget them.
33. *Hiri* means modesty, that is, hesitation in doing evil deeds through shame of being known to do them.
34. *Ottappa* means moral dread, that is, hesitation in doing evil deeds through fear of self-accusation, or accusation by others, or punishment in this world and in the realms of misery.
35. *Tatra-majjhattatā* is balance of mind, that is, the mode of mind which neither cleaves to an object nor repulses it. This is called *upekkhā-brahmavihāra*, equanimity of the sublime abodes, and *upekkhā-sambojjhaṅga*, equanimity that pertains to the factors of enlightenment.
36. *Kāya-passaddhi* means composure of mental properties.
37. *Citta-passaddhi* means composure of mind. Composure means that the mental properties are set at rest and have become cool, as they are free from the three immoral roots, which cause annoyance in doing good deeds.
38. *Kāya-lahutā* means buoyancy of mental properties.
39. *Citta-lahutā* means buoyancy of mind. Buoyancy means that the mental properties have become light, as they are free from the immoral properties, which weigh against them in the doing of good deeds. It should be explained in the same manner as the rest.
40. *Kāya-mudutā* means pliancy of mental properties.
41. *Citta-mudutā* means pliancy of mind.
42. *Kāya-kammaññatā* means fitness for work of the mental properties.
43. *Citta-kammaññatā* means the fitness for work of the mind.
44. *Kāya-pāguññatā* means proficiency of the mental properties.
45. *Citta-pāguññatā* means proficiency of the mind. Proficiency here means skilfulness.
46. *Kāyujukatā* means rectitude of mental properties.
47. *Cittujukatā* means rectitude of mind.
48. *Sammā-vācā* means right speech, that is, abstinence from the four wrong modes of speech: lying, slander, abusive language, and idle talk.
49. *Sammā-kammantā* means right action, that is, abstinence from the three wrong acts: killing, stealing, and sexual misconduct.

50. *Sammā-ājīva* means right livelihood.

The above three are called the three abstinences.

51. *Karuṇā* means pity, sympathy, compassion, or wishing to help those who are in distress.
52. *Muditā* means appreciation of and delight in the success of others.

These last two are called sublime abodes (*brahma-vihāra*) and are also called illimitables (*appamaññā*).

Nibbāna

Nibbāna may be classified into three kinds:

1. Freedom or deliverance from the plane of misery is the first Nibbāna.
2. Freedom or deliverance from the world of sense-desire is the second Nibbāna.
3. Freedom or deliverance from the fine-material and the immaterial worlds is the third Nibbāna.[7]

Consciousness, the fifty-two mental properties, and Nibbāna altogether make up fifty-four mental phenomena. Thus the twenty-eight material phenomena and fifty-four mental phenomena make up eighty-two ultimate things which are called ultimate facts. On the other hand, self, soul, creature, person, and so forth, are conventional facts.

7. The first refers to the first of the four stages of emancipation, stream-entry (*sotāpatti*), where rebirth in the lower worlds is excluded. Since, already at this stage, the final attainment of Nibbāna is assured after at most seven existences, the author calls it, in anticipation, the first Nibbāna. The second applies to the stage of the non-returner (*anāgāmi*) who has eliminated the fourth of the ten fetters, sensual lust (*kāma-rāga*). The third is the stage of Arahatship where all fetters are destroyed, among these the desire for fine-material and immaterial existence (*rūpa-* and *arūpa-rāga*).—Ed.

Causes I

Of these eighty-two ultimate things Nibbāna, inasmuch as it lies outside the scope of birth (*jāti*), does not need any cause for its maintenance since it also does not come within the range of decay and death (*jarā-maraṇa*). Hence Nibbāna is unconditioned and uncompounded. But with the exception of Nibbāna, the other eighty-one phenomena, both mental and material, being within the spheres of birth, decay, and death, are conditioned and compounded things.

Among the four causes already dealt with in connection with the material qualities, kamma is merely an originator and mind (*citta*) is simply a stimulus. The physical body develops, stands, and is maintained by the power of the heat element and by the power of the essence of nutriment. If the forces of the latter two come to an end, the forces of the former two also can no longer operate but cease simultaneously.

In the case of trees, for example, the seeds are only their origins. They grow, develop, and are maintained by the elements of earth and water. If these two principles fail them, the power of the seed also fails along with them. Here the physical body is like the tree; kamma is like the seed; the heat-element is like the earth; the nutritive essence is like the rainwater, which falls regularly at proper seasons; and mind is like the atmosphere and the heat of the sun, both of which give support from outside.

With regard to the causes of mind and mental properties, three things are needed for the arising of resultants: a past kamma, a base to depend upon, and an object. The first is like the seed of the tree, the base is like the earth, and the object is like the rain-water.

Two things are necessary for the arising of each of the mental phenomena of the moral properties, the immoral properties, and the ineffective properties: a base to depend upon and an object. However, to be more detailed, full rational exercise of attention (*yoniso manasikāra*, or rationally-directed attention) is needed for the moral properties, and irrational exercise of attention (*ayoniso-manasikāra*, or irrationally-directed attention) for the immoral properties. The ineffective properties which have apperceptional functions have the same causes as the moral properties. As for the two classes of consciousness called "turning towards (the object)," if they precede the moral properties they have the same causes as the moral properties; if they precede the immoral properties they have the same causes as the immoral properties. Here, *yoniso-manasikāra* means proper exercise of attention and *ayoniso-manasikāra* means improper exercise of attention. These are the functions of the two classes of consciousness called *āvajjana*, "turning towards." On seeing a man, if attention is rationally utilised, moral consciousness arises; and if attention is irrationally utilised, immoral consciousness arises. There is no particular object which purely of itself will cause to arise only a moral consciousness or only an immoral consciousness. The process of the mind may be compared to a boat of which the *āvajjana-citta* or "turning-towards-thought" is the helmsman. As the course of a boat lies entirely in the hands of the helmsman, so too the occurrence of moral and immoral consciousness lies entirely in the hands of the *āvajjana-citta*.

What the seed is to the tree, that the attention is to the moral properties and the immoral properties. What the earth is to a tree, that their base is to the moral properties and immoral properties. While what the rain-water is to a tree, that their object is to the moral properties and immoral properties.

Causes II

We will now set forth the causes in another way.

Each of the six classes of consciousness has four causes.

For the arising of consciousness of sight, there is needed the eye-base, a form-object, light, and attention. Unless there is light, the function of seeing will not take place, nor the process of cognition. Attention is a name for the *āvajjana-citta*, which turns the mind towards the cognition of the form-object.

For the arising of the consciousness of sound, there is needed the ear-base, a sound-object, space, and attention. Here, space is needed for the sound to be communicated to the ear. The function of hearing can take place only when it is present; the process of ear-door cognition also occurs only when hearing takes place.

For the arising of the consciousness of smell, there is needed the nose-base, a smell-object, air, and attention. Here, "air" means the air in the nose of the inhaled air. If this is not present, odours cannot come into contact with the nose-base, and consequently the function of smelling and the nose-base, and consequently the function of smelling and the nose-door cognition cannot take place.

For the arising of the consciousness of taste, there is needed the tongue-base, an object of taste, water, and attention. "Water" means wetness of the tongue. If the tongue is dry, the savour or sapidity cannot come into contact with the tongue-base and consequently the function of tasting and the tongue-door cognition cannot take place.

For the arising of the consciousness of touch, there is needed the body-base, an object of touch, a degree of coarseness (*thaddha*) in the object of touch, and attention. Only a somewhat coarse object of touch can make an impression upon the body-base. If the object of the touch is too subtle, it cannot impinge upon the body-base. And unless there is impingement, neither consciousness of touch nor the body-door cognition can arise.

For the arising of the consciousness of mind, there is needed the heart-base, an object of thought, the mind-door, and attention. "Object of thought" (*dhammārammaṇa*) comprises the following: all material qualities other than the five sense objects, all mental phenomena, all ideas, and Nibbāna. The five-sense objects also can become objects of mind-consciousness but in order to set forth what is not related to the five senses, only thought-objects are mentioned here. The mind-door means the continuum of sub-consciousness (*bhavaṅga*). Though the heart-base is the place where consciousness of mind arises, since it does not possess the appropriate kind of sensuous organs, the impressions of objects cannot appear in the mind-door only.

The Two *Abhiññanas* or Super-Knowledges

Abhiññā means super-knowledge, the faculty of knowing pre-eminently beyond the knowledge of ordinary mankind. It is of two kinds, *samatha-abhiññā* and *dhamma-abhiññā*.

Samatha-abhiññā means super-knowledge acquired by carrying out of the exercises in calm (*samatha*). It is of five different kinds:

1. *Iddhividha-abhiññā*
2. *Dibbasota-abhiññā*

3. *Cetopariya-abhiññā*
4. *Pubbenivāsa-abhiññā*
5. *Yathākammupagābhiññā*

The first is the supernormal powers of passing through the air, sinking into the earth, creating wonderful things, transforming oneself into different personalities.

The second is extreme sensitivity of hearing, as is possessed by celestial beings.

The third is the supernormal knowledge of others' thoughts.

The fourth is the supernormal knowledge of previous existences.

The fifth is the supernormal knowledge of the kamma in accordance with which living beings are thrown into the various spheres of existence; it resembles the supernormal vision possessed by celestial beings.

Dhamma-abhiññā means the insight by which are discerned all the things of ultimate truth (mentioned in the section on the truths) together with their respective characteristics, which are beyond the range of conventional truth. It is divided into three kinds:

1. *Sutamaya-ñāṇa*: knowledge acquired by learning
2. *Cintāmaya-ñāṇa*: knowledge acquired by reasoning
3. *Bhāvanāmaya-ñāṇa*: knowledge acquired by contemplation

The last of the three is again subdivided into two: (1) *anubodha-ñāṇa* and (2) *paṭivedha-ñāṇa*. Of these, the former is the triple insight into impermanence, suffering, and no-soul, or the insight into things with all their characteristics as they truly are. The latter is the supramundane knowledge of the four paths. By this knowledge, which can dispel the darkness of the defilements (*kilesa*) such as error, perplexity, and so forth, those who have attained the paths are brought into the light.

The Three *Pariññās* or Profound Knowledges

Pariññā means profound knowledge. It is of three kinds:

1. *Ñāta-pariññā*: autological knowledge (lit. "knowledge of what has been understood")
2. *Tīraṇa-pariññā:* analytical knowledge
3. *Pahāna-pariññā:* dispelling knowledge

Ñāta-pariññā or Autological Knowledge

Ñāta-pariññā means a profound and accurate discernment of mental and material phenomena with all their proximate causes, and also of Nibbāna, as shown in the previous sections on the truths and the causes. It discerns things deeply by means of *dhamma-abhiññāṇa* (philosophical knowledge) in their ultimate aspects, dispelling all merely pictorial ideas or representations (*santhāna-paññatti*), such as hair of the body, and so forth. Even if all of these are not discerned, if only the Four Great Essentials out of twenty-eight material phenomena are discerned in the aforesaid manner, it may be said that the function of *ñāta-pariññā* as regards *rūpa* (form) is accomplished. As regards *nāma*, the mental side, if only four of the mental things—mind, feeling, perception, and volition—are thoroughly discerned in the aforesaid manner, it may also be said that the function of *ñāta-pariññā* as regards *nāma* is fulfilled. If Nibbāna can also be discerned as shown above, the function of *ñāta-pariññā* would be fully realised.

Tīraṇa-pariññā: the Triple Knowledge of Impermanence, Ill, and No-Soul

Tīraṇa-pariññā means a profound and accurate discernment of momentary phenomena (both mental and material) with insight into rise and fall, by skilfully dissecting the continuity of mentality and materiality (*nāma and rūpa*) into momentary ultimates. It is of three kinds:

1. *Anicca-pariññā*: knowledge of impermanence
2. *Dukkha-pariññā*: knowledge of ill or suffering
3. *Anattā-pariññā*: knowledge of no-soul

Anicca-pariññā means either a perfect or a qualified knowledge of the law of death: conventional death and ultimate death. By "conventional death" we mean the kind of death concerning which we are accustomed to say, according to the conventional truth, that "to die some time is unavoidable for every living person or every living creature." By ultimate death we mean the momentary death of mental and material phenomena, which occurs innumerable times even in one day. The former neither possesses the real salient feature of impermanence, nor does it lie properly within the domain of *aniccā-pariññā*, but only of the recollection of death (*maraṇānussati*). In fact, it is only the latter, ultimate death, which exhibits the salient feature of impermanence, and lies within the domain of *anicca-pariññā*.

Dukkha-pariññā means either a perfect or a qualified knowledge of the intrinsic characteristic ill or suffering. Here ill is of two kinds:

1. *Vedayita-dukkha*: ill as painful feeling
2. *Bhayattha-dukkha*: fear-producing ill

Of these two, by *vedayita-dukkha*, bodily and mental pains are meant; and by bodily pain is meant the unbearable, unpleasant pain that comes to the various parts of the body; while mental pain means such pains as *soka* (sorrow), *parideva* (lamentation), *domanassa* (grief), and *upāyāsa* (despair), which are experienced by mind. *Bhayattha-dukkha* is that ill which falls within the sphere of *bhaya-ñāṇa* (knowledge of things as fearful) and of *ādīnava-ñāṇa* (knowledge of things as dangerous) to wit: *jāti-dukkha* (ill of birth), *jarā-dukkha* (ill of decay), *maraṇa-dukkha* (ill of death), *saṅkhāra-dukkha* (ill of conditionality), and *vipariṇāma-dukkha* (ill of changeability). The last two will be explained afterwards.

The Simile of the Dangerous Disease

Here is an illustration to show the difference between *vedayita-dukkha* and *bhayattha-dukkha*.

A man has a dangerous disease. He has to live on a simple diet, such as vegetables and fruit, so as to keep himself healthy and the disease in a subdued condition. If he takes rich food, such as poultry, fish, meat, and sweets, even though a sense of comfort and enjoyment may accompany such a dainty meal, after partaking of it he will suffer pain and indigestion for the whole day or maybe for many days, which will cause the disease to arise again in full force. The more dainty the meal is, the longer will he suffer. Now suppose that a friend of his, with a view to acquiring merit, brings him some nicely-cooked, buttered rice, fowl, fish, and meat. The man, fearing the agony of pain which he will have to undergo if he should eat the meal, has to thank his friend but decline it, telling him that the meal is too rich for him, and that should he eat it he would be sure to suffer. In this instance, the richly-prepared food is, of course, the pleasurable object, for it will probably furnish a nice savour to the palate while it is being eaten, which feeling of pleasure is called *vedayita-sukha*. But to him who foresees that it will cause him such pain as may break down his health, this same food is really an object devoid of pleasure. He shrinks from and fears it, for he knows that the better the savour the longer he must suffer; hence the pleasure his palate will derive from the food is to him a real fear-producing ill.

In the world, he who has not got rid of the error of ego and become safe against the danger of the dispersion of life (*vinipātana-bhaya*), and its passage to realms of misery, is like the aforesaid man who has the dangerous disease. The existences of men, devas, and Brahmas, and the pleasures experienced therein, are like the richly-prepared food and the feeling of pleasure derived from it. The state of being reborn in different existences after death is like the agony which the man has to suffer after the enjoyment of the food.

Here, *vedayita-dukkha* is synonymous with *dukkha-vedanā*, which is present in the *vedanā* triad of the "things conjoined with pleasant, unpleasant, and neutral feeling." *Bhayattha-dukkha* is synonymous with the truth of suffering (*dukkha-sacca*) and with *dukkha* as one of the intrinsic characteristics, i.e., impermanence, ill or suffering, and no-soul (*anicca, dukkha, anattā*).

Hence, the perfect as well as the qualified knowledge of the ill inherent in the existences of men, devas, and Brahmas, including also the pleasures experienced therein, is called *dukkha-pariññā*.

Anattā-pariññā means the perfect or the qualified knowledge of mental and material phenomena as possessing the characteristic of no-soul. By this knowledge of things as no-soul (*anatta-ñāṇa*), all the mental and material phenomena that belong to the ultimate truths are discerned as having no soul, self, or substance. By it also is discerned the personal nature of the "person" of conventional truth. Neither are persons and creatures discerned as the soul or personality of mental and material phenomena; nor is it assumed that there exists, apart from these, a soul or personality which never dies but transmigrates from one existence to another. If this knowledge attains to its highest degree, it is called *anatta-pariññā*. The triple knowledge of impermanence, ill, and no-soul is called *tīraṇa-pariññā*.

Pahāna-pariññā: Dispelling Knowledge

Pahāna-pariññā means the perfect or the qualified knowledge which dispels hallucinations. It dispels the three hallucinations of permanency (*nicca-vipallāsa*) by means of the insight acquired through the contemplation of impermanence; the three hallucinations of pleasure (*sukha-vipallāsa*) and the three hallucinations of purity (*subha-vipallāsa*) by means of the insight acquired through the contemplation of ill; and the three hallucinations of self (*attā-vipallāsa*) by means of the insight acquired through the contemplation of no-soul.[8]

Here *attā* or soul is the supposed underlying essence of a pictorial idea (*santhāna-paññatti*), and *jīva* or life is the supposed underlying essence of an aggregate-idea (*santati-paññatti*).

Of these two delusions, the former may be got rid of by a knowledge of the two kinds of truth, the ultimate and the conventional; but the latter can be got rid of only when the *anicca-pariññā*, the full knowledge of impermanence, reaches its summit.

Here, by *santati* is meant the continuum of aggregates of the same kind, and by *nānā-santati* is meant the continua of aggregates of different kinds.

This *santati* is of two kinds, mental and material. And the continuum of the material variety of aggregate is again subdivided into four classes, namely, into those produced by kamma,

8. The three hallucinations of permanency are erroneously perceiving, thinking and viewing the impermanent as permanent. Similarly, in the case of pleasure, purity, and soul, the three hallucinations each obtain by way of erroneous perception, thought and view.—Tr. & Ed.

by mind, by temperature, by food. Each of these four kinds of continua is liable to change if its respective causes change. When changes take place, the change of the continuum, of the kamma-produced class is not apparent but that of the mind-produced class is very apparent. In the one single act of sitting down many movements of the different parts of the body are to be observed. These movements and actions are nothing but the changes in the continua of aggregates.

The Growth, Decay, and Death of the Material Aggregates

In each aggregate there are three periods: birth, growth-and-decay, and death. In each step taken in the act of walking there are beginning, middle, and end. These are respectively birth, growth-and-decay, and death. Though we say "a step," this connotes the whole body; that is to say, the whole body undergoes change; the aggregates of the whole body undergo new births, new growth-and-decays, and new deaths. If a hundred steps or a thousand steps are taken in the course of a walk, then, a hundred or a thousand new births, new growth-and-decays, and new deaths take place in the whole body. A step may also be divided into two, the lifting-up aggregate and the laying-down aggregate of the foot. And in each single step, birth, growth-and-decay, and death must be noted. The same holds good with regard to all the postures of the body, such as standing, sitting, sleeping, stretching out, drawing in. Only what is to be understood here is that all tired, wearied, inflammatory, irritative, inflictive, painful states are changes in the continua of aggregates produced by temperature. Both in exhaling and inhaling, beginning, middle, and end are all discernible. The phase of continuance of stability in the existence of the aggregates is immediately followed by decay which, in connection with such matter, is called exhaustion or weariness. It is produced by inflammatory and irritative matter, and through it unbearably painful feelings arise. Then, through these painful feelings, people become aware that exhaustion is present; but they do not apprehend the perpetual growth-and-decay of the continua. Weariness is indeed the name applied to the growth-and-decay of the continua of aggregates which at first spring up strongly and cheerfully, while the end of each of these aggregates is the death of the continuum (*santati-maraṇa*). In the same manner it is to be understood that there are beginning, middle, and end in every aggregate produced by laughter, smiling, gladness, joy, grief, sorrow, lamentation, groans, sobs, greed, hate, faith, love, and so forth. Also, in speaking it is obvious that every word has its beginning, its middle, and its end, which are respectively the momentary birth, growth-and-decay, and death of speech.

With regard to matter produced by temperature, aggregates arise and cease at every stroke of our fan when, in hot weather, we fan ourselves. In exactly the same way, while we are bathing there arise and cease cool aggregates each time we pour water over ourselves. Tired, fatigued, ailing aggregates, generally speaking, are changes in the temperature-produced continua. Through hot and cold foods we observe different changes in the body that are sometimes due to temperature (*utu*). The arising, aggravation, and curing of diseases by unsuitable or suitable food and medicines are also due to temperature. Even in the mind-produced aggregates, there may also be many changes which are due to temperature.

With regard to the aggregates produced by nutritive essence, poverty or abundance of flesh, vigour or defect of vital force must be taken into account. By vigour of vital force, we mean that as soon as the food taken has entered the stomach, the vital force which pervades the whole body becomes vigorous and is strengthened. Therefore, the most necessary thing for all creatures is to prevent the vital force from failing, and to promote it. What we call "getting a living in the world" is nothing else but getting regular supplies of food for the maintenance of the vital forces. If people hold that it is of great importance to remain alive, it will be obvious to them that a sufficient supply of suitable food is also a matter of great importance. It is more necessary to supply food than to increase the blood; for if the supply of food to the stomach is reduced, all blood and flesh in the body will gradually decrease. The life of the kamma-produced material qualities, such as the eye, the ear, and so forth, is the *jīvita-rūpa*, or the vital force which depends upon the supply of food. If the supply of food fails, the whole body, together with the vital force, fails. If the supply of fresh food is suspended for six or seven days, the vital force and all the kamma-produced material qualities come to an end. Then it is said that a being dies. Now, it is not necessary to indicate the changes (i.e., the birth, the growth-and-decay, and death) of the aggregates of the food-produced material qualities, for they are apparent to everyone.

The Growth, Decay, and Death of the Mental Phenomena

What has been shown is the growth-and-decay and the death of the continua of material aggregates.

Now come the continua of mental phenomena. They are also very numerous. Everyone knows his own mind. There are continua of various kinds of greed, of various kinds of hate, of various kinds of dullness, of various kinds of love. In the single act of sitting, the arising of countless thoughts is recognised by everyone. Each process of thought has its birth, decay, and death. Everyone knows of himself: "Greed is rising in me now," or "Hate is rising in me now," or "Greed has ceased in me," or "Hate has ceased in me." But it cannot be said that it has ceased forever or that it has come to its final end, for this is only the temporary cessation or death of the process or continuum of thoughts. If circumstances are favourable, they will rise again instantly. What has just been said is in exposition of the mental continuum.

Ñāta-pariññā is relevant to *tīrana-pariññā*, which in turn is relevant to *pahāna-pariññā* which is the sole necessary thing.

The Exposition of *Tīraṇa-pariññā*

The Mark of Impermanence in Matter

The three salient marks or features are:

1. *Anicca-lakkhaṇa*: the mark of impermanence
2. *Dukkha-lakkhaṇa*: the mark of ill or suffering
3. *Anatta-lakkhaṇa*: the mark of no-soul

Anicca-lakkhaṇa, or the mark of impermanence, is the characteristic of the sphere of *vipariṇāma* and of *aññathābhāva*. *Vipariṇāma* means metastasis, that is, a radical change in nature: a change from the present state into that which is not the present state. *Aññathābhāva* means subsequent change of mode. If the spheres of *vipariṇāma* and *aññathābhāva* are exposed to the mind's eye, it will be distinctly discerned that the mental and material phenomena which are within the spheres of these two, vipariṇāma and aññathābhāva, are really impermanent things. Therefore we have said: "*Anicca-lakkhaṇa* or the mark of impermanence, is the characteristic of the sphere of vipariṇāma and of aññathābhāva." When we closely observe and analyse the flame of a lamp burning at night, we take note of the flame together with its five salient features: birth, growth, continuance, decay, and death. We note that the fire is momentarily arising. This is the birth of a material phenomenon; but it is not fire. We observe that the flame, after arising, is constantly developing. This is the growth of the material phenomenon; but it is not fire. We observe that the flame is uninterruptedly continuing in its normal state. This is the continuance of the material phenomenon; but it is not fire. We observe that the flame is dying down. This is the decay of the material phenomenon; but it is not fire. We observe that the flame is dying away. This is the death of the material phenomenon; but it is not fire. The property of hotness is, of course, fire. The flame quivers merely on account of the presence of these five salient features. Sometimes it may quiver when the lamp is removed, and in that case it may be said that the quivering is due to wind. These five salient features are therefore the subsequent changes (*aññathābhāva*) of the flame, called the marks of impermanence. By observing and taking note of these five salient features, it can be understood that the flame is an impermanent thing. Similarly, it should be understood that all moving things are impermanent things.

The mobile appearances of the most delicate atoms of matter, which are not discernible by the human eye, are discovered by the help of that clever revealer of nature's secrets, the microscope. Through the discovery of these moving appearances, it is believed by certain Western people—Leibnitz and Fechner, for example—that these material phenomena are living creatures. But in truth they are not living creatures, and the moving appearances are due only to the reproduction of the material phenomena through the function of the physical change (*utu*). By reproduction we here mean the *ācaya-rūpa*. In some bodies, of course, there may be living creatures in existence.

When we look at the flowing water of a river or a stream, or at the boiling water in the kettle, we discern moving appearances. These are the reproductions of material phenomena produced by physical change. And in water which seems still or quiet to the naked eye, moving appearances will also be seen with the help of a microscope. These two are reproductions of material phenomena produced by physical change. Here, "reproductions" means the constant integrations of new phenomena, which are called *ācaya-rūpas*. By discerning the integrations of new phenomena, the subsequent death or disappearances of the old phenomena, which are called the *aniccatā-rūpa*, is also discernible. When the integration of new matter and the death of the old matter take place side-by-side, the *santati-rūpa* is discernible. When the reproduction is excessive, the *apacaya-rūpa* is discernible. When the death of old matter is excessive, the *jaratā-rūpa* is discernible. We have shown above that in every tree, root, branch, leaf, sprout, flower, and fruit there are these five salient marks. So, when we look at them with the aid of a microscope, we see that they are full of very infinitesimal bodies moving about as if they were living creatures, but in fact these are mere reproductions of matter produced by physical change.

As regards the bodies of creatures or persons, these five salient marks are also discernible in every member of the body, such as hair, hair of the body, fingernails, toenails, teeth, the inner skin, the outer skin, muscles, nerves, veins, big bones, small bones, marrow, kidney, heart, liver, membrane, lungs, intestines, entrails, undigested food, digested food, and the brain. So, when we look at them with the help of a microscope, moving organisms like very small creatures are seen. These are the reproductions of matter produced by kamma, mind, food, and physical change. There may, of course, be microbes in some cases. Thus, if we look with the mind's eye, the mark of impermanence in all the matter of the whole body will clearly be discerned.

What has just been expounded is the mark of impermanence in matter.

The Mark of Impermanence in Mental Phenomena

In mental phenomena, i.e., mind and its concomitants, the mark of impermanence which has two distinct features, radical change (*vipariṇāma*) and the subsequent change (*aññathābhāva*), is no less clearly to be seen. In the world, we all know that there are many different terms and expressions applied to the different modes and manners of the elements of mind and body, which are incessantly rising and ceasing. For instance, there are two expressions, "seeing" and "not-seeing," which are used in describing the function of the eye. Seeing is the term assigned to the element of sight-consciousness; or, when we say "one sees," this is the term applied in describing the arising of sight-consciousness from the conjuncture of four causes, namely, eye-base, visual form, light, and attention. And when we say, "one does not see," this is the phrase we use in describing the nonexistence of sight-consciousness. When, at night in the dark, no source of light is present, sight-consciousness does not arise upon the eye-base; it is temporarily suspended. But it will arise when the light from a fire, for instance, is introduced. And when the light is put out, sight-consciousness also will again cease. As these are five salient marks present in the flame, if the light comes to be, seeing also comes to be, sight also arises. If the light develops, seeing also develops. If the light continues, seeing also continues. If the light decays, seeing also decays. And if the light ceases, then seeing also ceases. In the daytime also, these two terms "seeing" and "not-seeing" may be used. If there is no obstruction, one sees; and if there is obstruction, one does not see. As regards eyelids, if they are opened, one sees; and if they are shut, one does not see. What has just been expounded is the vipariṇāma and aññathābhāva of sight-consciousness through the occasioning cause, light. In cases where the destruction of the eye-base occurs after conception, sight-consciousness also is lost. If the visual form is taken away out of view, sight-consciousness also ceases. While sleeping, as there is no attention, sight-consciousness subsides for some time. The genesis of all classes of consciousness that take part in the process of eye-door perception is to be understood by the term "seeing"; and the subsidence of the same is to be understood by the term "not-seeing."

Similarly, in each function of hearing, smelling, tasting, and touching, a pair of expressions (existing or otherwise) is obtainable, and these must be dealt with as to their impermanency, i.e., vipariṇāma and aññathābhāva, in the same way as sight-consciousness. With regard to mind-cognition, it has many different modes, and each is apparent in its nature of vipariṇāma and aññathābhāva through the changes of the different kinds of thought. Among the mental concomitants, taking feeling for example, the changes of pleasure, pain, joy, grief, and hedonic indifference, are very evident. So also, the changes of perception, initial application, sustained application, from good to bad and vice versa, are very obvious. It may be easily noticed by anyone that in the single posture of sitting, greed, disinterestedness, hate, and amity, each arise by turns.

What has just been expounded is the impermanence of mental phenomena. So much for the mark of impermanence.

The Mark of Ill

Briefly speaking, the marks of impermanence in vipariṇāma and aññathābhāva may also be called the mark of ill, for they are to be feared by the wise in *saṃsāra*, the wheel of life. Why are they to be feared by the wise? Because, in the world, the dangers of decay and death are the dangers most to be feared. Vipariṇāma is nothing but momentary decay and death; it is the road to death, and to the dispersion of life into different spheres. All creatures remain alive without moving to another existence only because they are sustained by various methods of preservation. Vipariṇāma is also to be feared on account of the disadvantages which may fall on ourselves. *Ācaya*, *upacaya* and *santati*, the features of aññathābhāva, may also bring many disadvantages. They may establish in the physical body many kinds of disease and ailments. They may establish in the mental continuum many kinds of afflictions (*kilesa*), many kinds of hallucination, and many other disadvantages. Every material phenomenon possesses these two marks of impermanence; and also every mental phenomenon pertaining to the three realms of being has the same two marks of impermanence. Therefore the mental and material phenomena of men, devas, and Brahmas are all subject to ill. The two marks of impermanence being always present, there are approximately three different marks of ill, *dukkha-dukkhatā*, *saṅkhāra-dukkhatā*, and *vipariṇāma-dukkhatā*.

Dukkha-dukkhatā means both bodily (*kāyika*) and mental (*cetasika*) pain. *Saṅkhāra-dukkhatā* is the state of material and mental phenomena which exists only if they are always determined, conditioned, and maintained with a great deal of exertion in every existence. The existences of Brahmas have a great amount of *saṅkhāra-dukkha*. Hardly one out of a hundred, who has abandoned all sensual pleasures, renounced the world, and practised the sublime states (*brahma-vihārā*) without regard to his own life, hereafter attains the existence of a Brahmā. Though people know that such existence is a very good thing, they do not venture to practise them, for they take them to be very hard, difficult and pain-giving. When *jhānas* and supernormal intellections are attained, they must be maintained with great care and trouble, for if not, they are liable to be lost in a moment upon the most trifling lapse.

Vipariṇāma-dukkhatā is the state of destruction or death occurring at any time, day or hour, whenever circumstances are favourable to it. The existences of men, devas, and Brahmas are the real ills, since they are severally subject to the said three marks of ill.

The Eleven Marks of Ill

Speaking broadly, there are eleven marks of ill :

1. *Jāti-dukkha*: ill of birth
2. *Jarā-dukkha*: ill of decay
3. *Maraṇa-dukkha*: ill of death
4. *Soka-dukkha*: ill of sorrow
5. *Parideva-dukkha*: ill of lamentation
6. *Kāyika-dukkha*: bodily ill
7. *Cetasika-dukkha*: mental ill
8. *Upāyāsa-dukkha*: ill of despair
9. *Appiya-sampayoga-dukkha*: ill due to association with enemies
10. *Piyavippayoga-dukkha*: ill due to separation from loved ones
11. *Icchā-vighāta-dukkha*: ill due to non-fulfilment of wishes

Of these, *jāti* means birth or production. It is of three kinds: *kilesajāti*, birth of defilements; *kammajāti*, birth of actions; and *vipākajāti*, birth of effects.

Of these three, *kilesajāti* is the birth or the production of defilements such as greed, hate, dullness, error, conceit, and so forth.

Vipākajāti is the birth or production of different kinds of diseases, different kinds of ailments, and different kinds of painful feelings in the body, or the production of mean and low existence such as those of birds and animals, and so forth. Among the *kilesajātis*, greed is very fierce and violent. It will rise at any time it finds favourable circumstances, like fire fed with gunpowder. When it rises, it is very difficult to suppress it by any means whatever; it will grow in volume in an instant. Hence, it is a real "ill," since it is very much to be feared by all noble beings. The like should be understood in connection with hate, dullness, and so forth, which ethically are one thousand and five hundred in number. Just as a hill which is the abode of very poisonous serpents is feared and no one dares to approach it, so also the existences of men, devas, and Brahmās are feared; and no noble beings dare approach them with the views "my self" and "my body," for they are the birthplaces of the said defilements. Therefore they are real "ills" that are to be feared.

Of the *kammajāti*, immoral actions of body, speech, and thought are the development of the defilements. Therefore they are equally as fierce as the defilements. Hence this *kammajāti* is also a real "ill" to be feared by all noble ones. Just as the villages where thieves and robbers take up their quarters are feared, and good people do not venture to approach them, so also the existences of men, devas, and Brahmās are feared, and none bent on deliverance dare approach them with such views as "my self" and "my body," for they are the birthplaces of the said *kammajāti*.

As to *vipākajāti*, owing to the dreadfulness of *kilesajāti* and *kammajāti*, *vipākajāti*, rebirth into the planes of misery, is likewise always a terrible thing in the revolution of existences.

Therefore, the existences of men, and so forth, to which the *vipākajāti* together with the *kilesajāti* and the *kammajāti* are joined, are real "ill." The moral actions and the fortunate realms furnish food for the defilements, fuel for the flames of the defilements, so that the birth of moral actions and the birth of results therefrom, are all obtainable in the *kilesajāti*. So much for *jātidukkha*, the ill of birth.

Concerning the *jarādukkha* and *maraṇadukkha*: these are the momentary decays and deaths which follow a being from the moment of conception, and are at all times ready to cause him to fall in decay, death, or unfortunate realms whenever opportunities occur. They also obtain in connection with *vipariṇāma-dukkha*: and since they dog the steps of all living beings in every existence from the moment of conception, the existences of men, devas, and Brahmas are real "ill". So much for the ills of decay and death.

The ills of sorrow, lamentation, bodily pain, mental pain, and despair always follow the existences of men and devas, ready to arise whenever an opportunity occurs. The realms of the hells and the *peta* worlds are the realms of sorrow, lamentation, pain, grief, and despair. So much for the five kinds of dukkha.

To come into contact with persons, creatures, things, or objects with which one does not wish to unite or which one does not wish even to see is the ill due to association with enemies.

Separation from persons, creatures, things, and objects which one always wishes to meet or be united with, from which one never wishes to be parted in life or by death—this is the ill due to separation from loved ones.

To strive hard, but all in vain, to obtain anything is the ill due to non-fulfillment of wishes.

These "ills" or dukkhas arc very numerous and very evident, and are also frequently met with in the world. Hence the existences, of men, devas, and Brahmas are real "ills." Of these eleven varieties of dukkhas, birth, decay, and death are the most important.

So much for the mark of ill.

The Mark of No-Soul

The mark by which mental and material phenomena are to be understood as no-soul is called the *anatta-lakkhaṇa*, the mark of no-soul. In considering the word *anattā*, the meaning of *attā* ought first to be understood. *Attā* in ordinary sense means essence, or substantiality. By essence or substantiality is meant, as we already explained in connection with ultimate truth, for instance the earth which is the essence or the substantiality of a pot. The word "pot" is merely the name by which is indicated a certain pictorial idea (*santhāna-paññatti*); it is not a name for earth. And a pictorial idea possesses no essence or substantiality as an ultimate thing; here earth alone is an ultimate thing which possesses essence or substantiality. If the question is asked: "Does such a thing as pot exist in the world?" those who are unable to differentiate between the two kinds of truth, ultimate and conventional, would answer that the pot exists. These should then be asked to point out the pot. They will now point to an earthen pot near at hand, saying: "Is not that a pot?" But it is not correct of them to assert that earth is pot; it is a false assertion. Why is it a false assertion? Simply because earth is an ultimate thing and has essence or substantiality, while pot is a mere conception having no essence or substantiality, and thus, like space, is void. To assert of earth that it is pot is in effect to try to make out that essential earth constitutes the essence or substantiality of the pot, which is actual fact, seeing that pot as a mere representation of the mind possesses no substantial essence whatever. Here, what actually is non-existent pot becomes existent pot, and earth also becomes *attā* of the pot, so that earth and pot become one and the same thing; the identity of the one is confused with the identity of the other. It is for this reason that we call this a false assertion. In this illustration, earth corresponds to the five aggregates or their constituents, material and mental phenomena, while pot corresponds to persons and living creatures. Just as earth becomes the essence of pot in the statement that the earth is the pot, so also the five aggregates or their constituents become the attā or the essence of persons and creatures, when it is said that the aggregates are persons and creatures. This is the meaning of attā.

Now for *anattā*. In the expression "earthen pot," if one is able to discern that earth is one thing and pot another, and that earth is an ultimate thing and pot a mere conception of the mind; and again, that earth is not pot and pot is not earth, and also that it is false to call earth a pot, and to call pot earth; then the earth becomes not the essence or attā of the pot, but becomes anattā, void of essence; at the same time, the pot is seen to be void like space, since it is a mere conception of form. A like result is obtained if one is able to discern the five aggregates and the material and mental phenomena thus: The five aggregates are ultimate things; persons and creatures are ideas derived from their forms and continua; hence the phenomena are not persons and creatures; and persons and creatures are not the phenomena. If the phenomena are called persons and creatures, this is a false naming of them; and if persons and creatures are called the phenomena, this is false too. Accordingly, the phenomena become not the essence of persons and creatures, but become anattā, or the reverse of substantial essence. Also, persons and creatures become quite evidently void and empty, inasmuch as they are mere ideas derived from the forms and continua of the phenomena. What has just been said is in exposition of the meaning of anattā.

How the Marks of Impermanence and Ill Become Marks of No-Soul

The marks of impermanence and ill expounded in the foregoing pages are also the marks of no-soul. How? It is supposed that the ideas (*paññatti*) of persons and creatures are eternal and immortal[9] both in this existence and in those that follow, and it has been explained that the phenomena are not eternal since they are subject to momentary decay and death which are the marks of

---

9. In Buddhist philosophy there are three things which are "eternal and immortal," in the sense in which that phrase is used here in the text. These three things are, in Pāli, *paññatti, ākāsa,* and *nibbāna*; that is, concepts (or ideas), space, and that which supervenes when craving, hate and delusion are completely wiped out. It is held that the existence of these three has nothing whatever to do with time, never enters time, is never limited by time. The law of rise-and-fall, of arising and ceasing, which applies to all other things, does not apply to them. They exist independent of whether any particular being thinks them or not. In other words, they are eternal and immortal and independent of time, not in any sense of being unbrokenly continuous in time. Nibbāna is distinguished from the two other "eternal and immortal" things in that it has *santilakkhaṇa* or it is *santibhāva*, a word which may be rendered quite adequately in English as "the great peace" and all that this implies.—Translator.

The statement of the Translator, the Venerable U Ñāṇa, ascribing the teaching on the "eternal nature" of concepts and space to Buddhist philosophy in general, requires qualification. This teaching is obviously of late origin, being found neither in the Abhidhamma Piṭaka nor in the old Abhidhamma commentaries. The earliest reference might be in the Parivāra, a late summary of the Vinaya, appended as the last book to the Vinaya Piṭaka. There, in a stanza, it is said that "all formations (*saṅkhārā*) are impermanent, painful, not-self and conditioned (*saṅkhata*); Nibbāna and space are not-self"—which, by implication, may mean that the latter two (which do not include concept) are unconditioned (*asaṅkhata*). It was characteristic of the later schools (also the Śrāvakayāna school of the Vaibhāṣikas) to have enlarged the list of the *asaṅkhata-dhammā*, while the Dhammasaṅgaṇi (and so also the Sutta Piṭaka) speaks only of Nibbāna as unconditioned (*asaṅkhata*). It is also significant that the two Abhidhamma manuals, *Abhidhammatthasaṅgaha* and *Abhidhammāvatāra*, both have chapters on concept (*paññatti*), but make no mention of its eternal and unconditioned nature—Nyanaponika Thera

impermanence; and also because they are constantly ceasing and being reproduced innumerable times even in one day, the mark of that kind of impermanence is known as aññathābhāva.

But in the ideas of persons and creatures no marks of radical change (*viparināma*) and subsequent change (*aññathābhāva*) are to be seen. If such marks were to be found in the ideas of persons and creatures, then, of course, these ideas would also be subject to birth, decay, and death, and would be reborn and decay and die many times even in one day. But these marks are not to be found in the ideas; we discern these marks only in the mental and material phenomena. Therefore it comes to this, that the mental and material phenomena (*nāma-rūpa-dhammā*) are not to be regarded as the essence or substantiality of persons and creatures. It is in this way that the mark of impermanence becomes the mark of no-soul, in accordance with the text: *asārakatthena anattā*, "On account of being without a core, the word anattā is used."

How does the mark of ill become the mark of no-soul? The marks of ill are very evil, very disadvantageous, and very unsatisfactory; and all creatures desire to be in good states, to be prosperous, and to be satisfied. If mental and material phenomena are the true essence of persons and creatures, the phenomena and the person must be one and the same. And if this be so, their desires must also be one and the same; that is, the person's desire must also be that of the phenomena, and vice-versa. But if this is not so, then each must be a thing separate from the other.

Here, by a "person's desire" we mean greed (*lobha*) and desire-to-do (*chanda*); and by "the desire of phenomena," the happening of things in accordance with their causes. A main characteristic of persons and creatures is the craving for happiness of mind and body; and an outstanding feature of phenomena is their uniformity with their causes or conditions, that is, the arising and the ceasing of phenomena are subject to causes, and never occur entirely in accordance with the desires of persons in defiance of causes. For example: if warmth is wanted, the cause that produces warmth must be sought out; or if coldness is wanted, the cause that produces coldness must be sought out. If long life is wanted, the causes of long life, for instance, a daily supply of suitable food, must be sought out; for no man can live long merely by wishing to live long. And if rebirth in the worlds of the fortunate is wanted, then the cause of this, moral or virtuous deeds, must be sought out; for no one can get to the worlds of the fortunate merely by wishing to be reborn there.

It is sometimes erroneously believed that one can be whatever one wishes to be, because upon occasions something one has wished for is later on fulfilled. But in actual fact it has come about only in accordance with a cause that was previously sought out and brought into play. It is falsely believed by many people that one can maintain oneself according to one's wish when in sound health or at ease in any of the four bodily postures, ignoring the fact that the cause, the partaking of food on previous days, was sought by them and brought into play. They also mistakenly think that their wishes are always fulfilled, when they find themselves living happily in buildings previously in existence. But in truth, if one looks around in this world and sees how great and numerous are the businesses, affairs, occupations and so forth, of men in all their extent and variety, he will soon discern with the mind's eye that the *saṅkhāra-dukkha*, the suffering associated with conditioned phenomena, is great and manifold in precisely the same measure as men's activities. And this dukkha is due to the establishing of the causes necessary for acquiring of the desired effects; for the phenomena can never become exactly as beings wish them to be or order them to be. Thus, simply in beholding the marks of *saṅkhāra-dukkhatā* all about us, it becomes evident that phenomena do not spontaneously conform to the desires of persons and creatures, and hence they are not their essence or substance. In addition to this, it also should be well noted how conspicuous is non-substantiality with regard to the other types of ill aforementioned, as *dukkha-dukkhatā, vipariṇāma-dukkhatā, jāti-dukkha, jarā-dukkha, maraṇa-dukkha,* and so forth.

So much for the mark of no-soul from the standpoint of ill or suffering.

The Three Knowledges Pertaining to Insight of the Three Marks

The three knowledges pertaining to the insight that fully grasps the meaning of the three marks are called *tīraṇa-pariññā*.
These three knowledges pertaining to the insight are:

1. *Anicca-vipassanā-ñāṇa*: insight-knowledge in contemplating impermanence
2. *Dukkha-vipassanā-ñāṇa*: insight-knowledge in contemplating ill
3. *Anattā-vipassanā-ñāṇa*: insight-knowledge in contemplating no-soul

Of these three knowledges, the last-mentioned must be acquired primarily and fully in order to dispel the error of the soul doctrine. And in order to obtain fully this last-mentioned knowledge, the first must be introduced; for, if the first is well discerned, the last is easily acquired. As for the second, it does not culminate through the acquisition of the first. It is owing to imperfection in obtaining the second knowledge that the transcendental path has four grades, and that lust and conceit are left undispelled. Hence the most important thing for Buddhists to do is to free themselves entirely from the ills of the realms of misery (*apāyadukkha*), i.e., the suffering experienced through rebirth in subhuman worlds. There is no way of escaping from them open to men when the teachings of the Buddha vanish from the world. To escape from the ills of unhappy rebirths means to put away all immoral actions and erroneous views, and to put away all erroneous views means to put away utterly the view of soul. Therefore, in this life in which we are so fortunate to encounter the teaching of the Buddha, we should strive to contemplate or meditate upon the impermanence of things, and thus to bring to fullness the insight-knowledge of no-soul. In confirmation of this, here is a quotation from the texts:

> To him, O Meghiya, who comprehends impermanence, the comprehension of no-soul manifests itself. And to him who comprehends no-soul, the fantasy of an 'I' presiding over the five aggregates is brought to destruction; and even in this present life he attains Nibbāna.

There is no need for us to expatiate upon the truth of this text, for we have already shown how the mark of impermanence can become the mark also of no-soul.

The insight exercises can be practised not only in solitude, as is necessary in the case of the exercise of calm or *samatha*, but they can be practised everywhere. Maturity of knowledge is the main thing required. For if knowledge is ripe, the insight of impermanence may easily be accomplished while listening to a discourse or while living a householder's ordinary life. To one whose knowledge is developed, everything within and without oneself, within and without one's house, within and without one's village or town, is an object at the sight of which the insight of impermanence may spring up and develop. But those whose knowledge is, so to speak, still in its infancy, can accomplish this only if they practise assiduously the exercises in calm.

Consideration of the momentary deaths which occur innumerable times even during the wink of an eye is only required in discussion on Abhidhamma. But in meditating or practising the exercises in insight, all that is needed is consideration of the *santati-vipariṇāma* and the *santati-aññathābhāva*, that is, of the radical change and sequent change of the continua, things which are evident to and personally experienced by every man alive.

The exercises in insight that ought to be taken up are, first, the four great elements from among the material qualities, and the six classes of cognition from among the mental qualities. If one can discern the arising and ceasing of the four elements innumerable times in one day alone, the changes, arisings, and ceasings of the derivative material qualities are also discerned. Of the mental qualities also, if the changes of consciousness are discerned, those of the mental concomitants are simultaneously discerned. In particular, the conspicuous feelings, perceptions, volitions, and so forth, from among the mental qualities, and the conspicuous forms, odours, and so forth from among the material qualities may be taken as objects for the exercise, as they will quickly enable a meditator to acquire with ease the insight of impermanence.

However, from the philosophical point of view, the insight is acquired in order to dispel such notions as "creatures," "persons," "soul," "life," "permanence," "pleasures," and to get rid of the hallucinations. The acquisition of insight also mainly depends on a sound grasp of the three marks, which have been sufficiently dealt with already.

So much for the exposition of *tīraṇapariññā*.

The Exposition of *Pahāna-pariññā*

The Five Kinds of Dispelling

In Buddhist teachings there are five kinds of *pahāna*, i.e., the dispelling, putting away or giving up of mental defilements:

1. *Tadaṅga-pahāna*: the temporary dispelling of the defilements by substitution of the opposite
2. *Vikkhambhana-pahāna*: the temporary dispelling by suppression in the jhānas
3. *Samuccheda-pahāna*: the eradication of defilements effected at the moment of attaining the paths (*magga*) of emancipation (*sotāpatti-magga*, etc.)
4. *Paṭippassaddhi-pahāna*: the tranquillisation of defilements at the fruition-stage (*phala*) of emancipation (*sotāpatti-phala*, etc.)
5. *Nissaraṇa-pahāna*: the final escape or deliverance from the defilements on attaining Nibbāna

In order to make clear these five kinds of *pahāna*, the three periods or stages (*bhūmi*) must be mentioned here. They are:

1. *Anusaya-bhūmi*: the stage of latency, the inherent tendency for defilements
2. *Pariyuṭṭhāna-bhūmi*: the stage of mental involvement or obsession through the occurrence of defiled thought processes
3. *Vītikkama-bhūmi*: the stage of actual transgression in words or deeds.

Of these three, *anusaya-bhūmi* is the period during which the defilements lie latent surrounding the life-continuum (*bhavaṅga*), but have not come into existence as thought processes within the three phases of time.

Pariyuṭṭhāna-bhūmi is the period during which the defilements rise from the latent state and manifest themselves as thought processes at the mind-doors when any object that has the power to arouse them produces a perturbation at any of the six doors of perception.

Vītikkama-bhūmi is the period at which the defilements become so fierce and ungovernable that they produce evil actions in deed and word. Thus, during repeated existences without known beginning, every occurrence of greed that goes along with a being's life-continuum has these three periods. Similarly, all other defilements, like hate, ignorance, conceit, etc., have three periods each.

There are three kinds of training (*sikkhā*) in Buddhism, namely: the training of morality (*sīla*), in concentration (*samādhi*), and in wisdom (*paññā*). The training in morality is able to dispel only the third stage of the defilements, that of actual transgression. As there remain two stages undispelled, the defilements temporarily put away by morality can arise again and soon fill up until they reach the stage of transgression.

The second training, in concentration, through attaining the first jhāna, the second jhāna, and so forth, is able to dispel only the second stage of the defilements left undispelled by morality, that is, the mental involvement by evil thought process. As the stage of latency is still undispelled, if obstacles to jhāna were encountered, the defilements temporarily put away by jhāna would soon arise and grow until they reach the stage of transgression. Therefore the dispelling by concentration is called *vikkhambhana-pahāna*, which means the putting away to a distance by suppression. Here jhāna can dispose of the defilements for a considerable time so that they do not arise soon again, for meditation is more powerful in combating the defilements than morality.

The third training, the training in wisdom—the knowledge that belongs to insight and the knowledge that pertains to the supramundane path—is able to dispel the first, latent stage of the defilements left undispelled by morality and concentration. The defilements that are entirely got rid of through wisdom, leaving nothing behind, will never rise again. Therefore the putting away by wisdom that has reached the supramundane paths of stream-entry, etc., is called dispelling by eradication (*samuccheda-pahāna*).

The knowledge that pertains to supramundane fruition puts the defilements away by tranquillising the same defilements that have been put away by the knowledge that pertains to the supramundane path; this putting away is called the *paṭippassaddhi-pahāna*. The putting away by entering Nibbāna is called the *nissaraṇa-pahāna*, the utter escape from the ties of existence forever.

Now, we have seen that knowledge is of three kinds: knowledge of insight, knowledge pertaining to the supramundane path, and knowledge pertaining to supramundane fruition. Of these, though the knowledge of insight is able to put away the first, latent stage of the defilements (*anusaya-bhūmi*), it is not able to put it away completely. Only the knowledges pertaining to the paths are able to put away all the defilements that respectively belong to each path. The knowledge pertaining to *sotāpatti-magga*, the first path, utterly dispels and eradicates all erroneous views and perplexities. It also finally dispels all immoral actions that could result in rebirth in the realms of misery. The knowledge pertaining to *sakadāgāmi-magga*, the second path, dispels all coarse lust and hate. The knowledge pertaining to *anāgāmi-magga*, the third path, dispels all subtle lust and ill-will, left undispelled by the second path. To the *anāgāmi* or never-returner, the link of kinship with this world is broken, and the Brahmā world is the only sphere where he may take rebirth. The knowledge pertaining to *arahatta-magga*, the fourth path, dispels the defilements which were left undispelled by the lower paths. One who kills all defilements becomes an Arahat and escapes from the three worlds. In our Buddhist religion, the dispelling by eradication is the chief thing to be accomplished.

So much for the *pahāna-pariññā*.

The Practice of Insight Meditation

I will now indicate the main points necessary to those who practise the exercises of insight. Of the three knowledges of insight, the knowledge of impermanence must first and foremost be acquired. How? If we carefully watch the cinematograph show, we will see how quick are the changes of the numerous series of photographs representing the wonderful scene, all in a moment of time. We will also see that a hundred or more photographs are required to represent the scene of a moving body. These are, in fact, the functions of *viparināma* and *aññathābhāva*, or the representation of impermanence or death, or cessation of movements. If we carefully examine the movements in a scene, such as the walking, standing, sitting, sleeping, bending, stretching, and so forth, of the parts of the body during a moment of time, we will see that these are full of changes, or full of impermanence. Even in a moment of walking, in a single step, there are numerous changes of pictures which may be called impermanence or death. It is also the same with the rest of the movements. Now, we must apply this to ourselves. The impermanence and the death of mental and material phenomena are to be found to the full in our bodies, our heads, and in every part of the body. If we are able to discern clearly those functions of impermanence and death which are always operating in our bodies, we shall acquire the insight of the destruction (*bhaṅga-ñāṇa*), into the breaking-up, falling-off, cessation, and changes of the various parts of the body in each second, in each fraction of a second. That is, we shall discern the changes of every part of the body, small and great, of head, of legs, of hands, and so forth. If this be thus discerned, then it may be said that the exercise on the contemplation of impermanence is well accomplished. And if the exercise on the contemplation of impermanence is well accomplished, then that of the contemplation of non-soul is also accomplished. If this is thus discerned, then it may be said that the exercise on the contemplation of impermanence is well accomplished. By the word "accomplished," it is meant that the exercise has been properly worked out so as to remain a permanent possession, during the whole term of life; but it is not meant that the knowledge of the path and of fruition has been attained. The attainment of the knowledge of the path and fruition, however, is quick or slow, according to opportunity or lack of opportunity in the practice of higher virtues.

It is also very difficult to become correctly aware of the attainment of the paths and of the fruits. In fact, even the *ariya* who has attained the first path hardly knows that he has become an attainer of the stream-of-the-path. Why? Because of the unfathomableness of the latent stage of the defilements. Those yogis or meditators who do not know the unfathomableness of the latent stage of the defilements, sometimes think themselves to be attainers of the stream-of-the-path while as yet their erroneous views and perplexity are only partially, but not completely, put away. If error and perplexity, with all their latent states, are eradicated by the *samuccheda-pahāna*, they would become the real attainers of the stream-of-the-path. The meditators or practisers of insight, however, for the whole term of life, must gladly continue in the exercise on the contemplation of impermanence until the exercise is systematically worked out. Even the Arahants do not give up these exercises for the securing of tranquillity of mind. If meditators practise these exercises for the whole term of life, their knowledge will be developed till they pass beyond the *puthujjana-bhūmi*, the stage of the worldling, and arrive at the *ariya-bhūmi*, the stage of the noble ones, either before death or at the time of death, either in this life or in the life following, in which latter case they will be reborn as devas.

Conclusion

Here the concise *Vipassanā Dīpanī*, *The Manual of Insight*, written for the Buddhists of Europe, comes to a close. It was written in Mandalay, while I was sojourning in the Ratanasiri Monastery, where the annual meeting of the Society for Propagating Buddhism in Foreign Countries took place; and it was finished on the 14th waxing of Taboung in the year 2458 B.E., corresponding to the 26th February, 1915 C. E.

A Life Sketch of the Venerable Ledi Sayādaw

The author of this manual, the Venerable Ledi Sayādaw of Burma, was one of the outstanding Buddhist scholars and writers of this age. His numerous writings show not only his vast store of learning, of which he had a ready command, but also a deep penetration of the respective subjects derived from his meditative experience. During a long period of his later life he used to spend six months of the year teaching, preaching, and writing, and the other six months meditating.

He was born in 1846 at a village in the Shwebo District of Burma. Early in life he was ordained a novice (*sāmaṇera*) and at the age of twenty he received the higher ordination with the name Bhikkhu Ñāṇa. He received his monastic education under various teachers and later studied Buddhist literature under the Venerable San-kyaung Sayādaw in one of the large monastic colleges at Mandalay. He was a very bright student. His first book, *Pāramī Dīpanī* (*Manual of the Perfections*) was published fourteen years after his higher ordination while he was still at San-kyaung Monastery. It was based on twenty questions set by his teacher, which he alone among the numerous pupils had been able to answer fully and satisfactorily.

During the reign of King Theebaw he became a Pali lecturer at Mahā Jotikārāma Monastery in Mandalay. One year after the capture of King Theebaw, in 1887, he moved to a place to the north of Monywa town where he established a monastery under the name of Ledi-tawya Monastery, from which he derived the name Ledi Sayādaw under which he became widely known. In later years, he regularly toured many parts of Burma, teaching and preaching, and establishing Abhidhamma classes and meditation centres. He composed Abhidhamma rhymes (*abhidhamma-saṅkhitta*) and taught them to his Abhidhamma classes. Some of the Ledi meditation centres still exist and are still famous in the country.

He was awarded the title Agga-Mahāpaṇḍita by the Government of India in 1911. Later the University of Rangoon conferred on him the title D. Litt. (*honoris causa*). In later years he lived at Pyinma where he died in 1923, aged 77.

The Venerable Ledi Sayādaw wrote many essays, letters, poems and manuals, in Burmese and in Pali, and also some sub-commentaries (*ṭīkā*). A list of his writings has been published in the Buddhist quarterly, "Light of the Dhamma" (Vol. VIII, No. 1),[10] together with a biography on which this brief life sketch is based. Most of his expositions are called *dīpanī* ("manuals" or lit. "illuminators"), and became very popular in Burma. Some of these are short treatises; others are larger works, as for instance the *Paramattha Dīpanī*, *The Manual of Ultimate Truth,* written in 1897, which is a commentary on the *Abhidhammattha Saṅgaha*, a compendium of the Abhidhamma Philosophy.

Several of these manuals seven have been rendered into English and published or reprinted in the magazine "Light of the Dhamma": (1) *Vipassanā Dīpanī—Manual of Insight,* (2) *Paṭṭhānuddesa Dīpanī—Manual of the Philosophy of Relations*, (3) *Niyāma Dīpanī—Manual of Cosmic Order*, (4) *Sammā-diṭṭhi Dīpanī—Manual of Right Understanding*, (5) *Catusacca Dīpanī—Manual of the Four Truths*, (6) *Bodhipakkhiya Dīpanī—Manual of the Requisites of Enlightenment*, (7) *Maggaṅga Dīpanī—Manual of the Constituents of the Noble Path.*

The "Light of the Dhamma" has ceased publication, however, the manuals have been reprinted in a single volume under the title *Manuals of Buddhism* published by the aforementioned Council in Rangoon and by the Vipassaná Research Institute in Igatpuri, India.

The BPS has published a few other translations. A revised edition of the *Manual of the Requisites of Enlightenment* has appeared in the Wheel Series as Wheel no. 171/174 (now BP 412), likewise, the *Paṭṭhānuddesa Dīpanī* as Wh. 331/333 titled *Buddhist Philosophy of Relations*, the *Maggaṅga Dīpanī* as Wh. 245/247 titled *Noble Eightfold Path and its Factors Explained*, the *Uttamapurisa Dīpanī* as BP 420 titled *Manual of the Excellent Man*, the *Ānāpāna Dīpanī* as Wh. 431/432 titled *A Manual of Mindfulness of Breathing*, and

10. Published by the Union of Burma Buddha Sāsana Council, Kaba Aye P.O., Rangoon, Burma. An extensive list is also given in the B.P.S. translation of the *Vijjāmagga Dīpanī.*

the *Manual of Light (Alinkyan)* and the *Manual of the Path of Higher Knowledge (Vijjāmagga Dīpanī)* as BP 620.

A few more translations of Ledi Sayādaw manuals on vegetarianism, abstinence from liquor, and monks' etiquette can be found on http://www.aimwell.org.

Advice to Rāhula: Four Discourses of the Buddha

Translated from the Pali
With an Introduction

Edited by

Nyanaponika Thera

WHEEL PUBLICATION NO. 33

Introduction

"A son has been born to thee, O prince!" this was the message that reached Prince Siddhattha when returning from a drive through the city of Kapilavatthu and a day spent at a park nearby.

"A fetter (Rāhula) has been born, a bondage has been born!" said the prince upon hearing the news. And Rāhula was the name given later to the babe by Siddhattha's father, the Rāja Suddhodana.

These were indeed unusual words with which to welcome a first-born; but we shall understand them better when we set them against the background of another experience encountered by Siddhattha on that memorable day. We are told that it was on this very day that Siddhattha met on his way, the serene figure of an ascetic—or, as some would have it, saw a vision of it. This encounter showed him a way of life that could help him to find, for himself and mankind, the deliverance from the inflictions of old age, sickness and death which had made such a strong impact on him when he had grasped their full significance not long before during earlier outings.

Now, the sight of a monk was to him as if a door had opened in the golden cage, for a bird that longed for freedom. But the birth of his child threatened to close that door for him again, and Siddhattha knew that he had to come to a decision this very day. At the end of those fateful hours which Siddhattha spent in the palace after his return, his mind was firmly set on his quest for the Deathless. The time of the Great Renunciation had come; it was towards midnight that he went to the chambers of his wife, the Princess Yasodharā, to have a last silent glance at her and his son. But the mother's arm and hand enclosed protectively Rāhula's little head, and without having seen his child's face, Siddhattha went into the night and started on a road that, after six years, led him to his goal, to full enlightenment—Buddhahood.

It was not yet a full year after his enlightenment that the Buddha visited his paternal home, Kapilavatthu. During his stay there, while one day he was seated in the palace, Princess Yasodharā spoke to Rāhula: "This is thy father, Rāhula! Go and ask him for thy heritage!" Little Rāhula went and stood before the Enlightened One who was still seated, and exclaimed: "How pleasant is thy shadow, O ascetic!" The Master rose from his seat and when he had left the palace, Rāhula followed and, as told by his mother, spoke to him: "Give me my heritage, O ascetic!" Thereupon the Master turned to his disciple Sāriputta and said: "Ordain him, Sāriputta." Thus little Rāhula became a novice monk (*sāmaṇera*) at the age of seven. But henceforth, at the request of Rāja Suddhodana, no further *sāmaṇera* ordinations were given without the parents' consent.

The Master took constant interest in Rāhula's development and wisely guided him throughout the years, until Rāhula, in his twenty-first year, had attained to Sainthood (*arahatta*) and needed guidance no longer. The exhortations collected in these pages, are the greater and the most important part of those handed-down to us in the Sutta Piṭaka of the Pali Canon. About those not included here, some information will be given in the following:

The *first* of the texts translated here, the Exhortation to Rāhula given at Ambalaṭṭhikā (Ambalaṭṭhikā-Rāhulovāda Sutta), was spoken by the Buddha when Rāhula was seven years old. The discourse has two main subjects, truthfulness and mindfulness, which are indeed the cornerstones for building a character and for developing the faculties of mind. An education based on the fostering of these two qualities, will indeed have secure foundations. It is a counsel, however, which, in general, adults are as much in need of, as a young child. For impressing these teachings deeply on Rāhula's mind, the Buddha made ample use of similes in that discourse.

According to the commentators, in the same early period of Rāhula's novitiate the Master taught and explained to him the ten "Boy's Questions" (*kumāra-pañhā*) which begin with "What is One? All beings, subsist by nutriment." They are also called the "Novice's Questions" (*sāmaṇera-pañhā*) and were originally devised for the seven-year-old Arahant, Sopaka *sāmaṇera*. The text of these Questions can be found in the Khuddakapāṭha ("Minor Readings") of the Sutta-Piṭaka.

Our *second* text, the Great Discourse of Exhortation to Rāhula (*Mahā-Rāhulovāda-Sutta*), spoken to him when he was eighteen years, chiefly contains instructions on meditation. Those given by the Buddha himself pertain foremost to Insight-meditation (*vipassanā-bhāvanā*), namely to the not-self nature (*anattatā*) of the five categories of clinging (*pañcupadānakkhandhā*), and of the four material elements. Later the Buddha elaborated on the Venerable Sāriputta's suggestion to Rāhula, to practise Mindfulness of Breathing. The master also stressed here the importance of equanimity by giving five similes of which the first four refer again to the four material elements, thus linking up with the earlier instruction. In this same discourse, the Master also hands to Rāhula a little armoury of meditational weapons against various unwholesome states of mind.

In his twenty-first year, before he had completed a full year after his Higher Ordination, the Venerable Rāhula attained to the highest goal of a recluse's life, to Sainthood (*arahatta*). This occurred after the enunciation of the *third* text in our collection, the Shorter Discourse of exhortation (Cūḷa-Rāhulovada-Sutta). This discourse applies the three characteristics of all conditioned existence (impermanency, suffering, and not-self) to the entire realm of six-fold sense perception and all mental processes relating to it.

It was at this moment of Sainthood attained, that the Enlightened One, the incomparable teacher of men, the master of the skilful means of guiding them, gave to his son the full paternal heritage for which Rāhula had asked. The most precious legacy, indeed, that a father can bestow! When the Buddha preached the Discourse on the Heirs of the Dhamma (Dhammadāyāda Sutta, MN 3), in which he distinguished between the heirs to worldliness and the heirs to truth, this may well have evoked in him the memories of little Rāhula's request for his heritage.

Our *fourth* text, the verses from the Sutta-Nipāta, called "Rāhula-Sutta," circumscribes in brief the life of a monk, and the thoughts and the ideals that should be foremost in a monk's mind. These verses are, as it were, the monk's version of the Mahā-Maṅgala-Sutta ("Blessings"). The concluding sentence expressly states that these were frequently repeated by the Master for Rāhula's benefit. Since they contain terse references to meditation they may have originated in the period when our second text, the Mahā-Rāhulovada-Sutta, was spoken, that is at Rāhula's eighteenth year or after.

The same may hold good for the texts in the Rāhula-Saṃyutta of the Saṃyutta-Nikāya. Those twenty-two short discourses are all instructions for Insight-meditation, and are more or less variants of our third text. They are, as the commentary says, meant to promote those "qualities that bring deliverance to maturity" (*vimuttipācanīyadhammā*) spoken of at the beginning of the Cūḷa-Rāhulovada-Sutta (MN 147). To the same category belongs the Rāhula-Sutta of the Aṅguttara-Nikāya (AN 4:117) which deals with the four material elements in a similar way as our second text (MN 62).

In the Theragātha, the Verses of the Elders, there are stanzas spoken by the Venerable Rāhula himself (vv. 295-298); and in the "Questions of Milinda," there are ascribed to him some more verses which are not found elsewhere. These verses are the only utterances recorded of the Venerable Rāhula. There is also no other account in Pali literature indicating that he was active as a teacher or preacher or in any other way. It is possible that this reticence on the part of the Venerable Rāhula was intentional because, being the Master's son, he did not wish to come into any prominence.

The Venerable Rāhula passed away before the Master and also before the Venerable Sāriputta; but we have no information as to the time and circumstances of his death.

Though the Venerable Rāhula himself always kept modestly in the background, the Master placed him among those disciples who had gained excellence in specific ways of conduct or knowledge (*etadagga-sāvakā*; Aṅguttara-Nikāya I), praising him as one who was "foremost among those who are keen to learn, eager in following the Training" (*sikkha-kāma*). The Venerable Rāhula was always amenable to advice, and to this virtue of his, practised also in former lives, refer two Jātakas (Birth Stories): No. 16: Tipa-attha-miga-Jātaka, and No. 319: Tittira-Jātaka.

As one of the early Chinese pilgrims to India, Hiuen Tsiang, relates (Beal, *Records*, p. 180), King Asoka erected Stupas in memory of many of the great Disciples, and one of these Stupas was dedicated to the Venerable Rāhula, as the particular object of pilgrimage and veneration for novices, so that they may remember and emulate his devotion to the Training.

Since our age lacks an Asoka, may the texts presented here serve as a Stupa, an object of recollection, homage and inspiration, for all those who are "keen to learn and eager in following the

Training"—because "it is they who shall reach the topmost height"—as the Master gave assurance in the last period of his life.

"Tamatagge me te Ānanda bhikkhu bhavissanti ye keci sikkhakāmā'ti.

Mahā-Parinibbāna-Sutta

Nyanaponika Thera
Forest Hermitage,
Kandy, Sri Lanka
June 1961

Acknowledgements

The first two texts in this collection, translated in 1925 by the Venerable Bhikkhus Nārada and Mahinda, appeared first in the periodical *The Blessing* (Vol. I. No. 6), published by the "Servants of the Buddha," Colombo. We are obliged to that Society for kind permission to reproduce these translations. The introductions to each of these two discourses were written by the then President of that society, Dr. Cassius A. Pereira (now Venerable Kassapa Thera of Vajirārāma, Colombo). The original Notes appended to these two texts, in *The Blessing*, have been slightly abridged and a few new ones (marked "Ed.") added.

The third text, the Shorter Exhortation (MN 147), has been translated by Nyanaponika Thera.

The fourth text, the verses from the Sutta-Nipāta, is reproduced from *Woven Cadences of the Early Buddhists* (Sutta-Nipāta), translated by E. M. Hare, *Sacred Books of the Buddhists*, Vol. XV, London 1925, Pali Text Society. The explanatory notes have been supplied by the editor.

Buddhist Publication Society

Introduction to the Ambalaṭṭhikā-Rāhulovada Suttanta

It is the supreme characteristic of the great World Teachers—and, indeed, of all profound thinkers—that they invariably express themselves in the most natural, simple, and direct way; similarly, hairsplitting and quibbling over words is the mark of puny minds.

The greater the genius of the teacher, the more we become conscious of his desire to be understood by humanity, and of his effort to make his teaching comprehensible even to the dullest intellect. Thus it is that we perceive the genius of the Buddha strikingly revealed in the lucidity of his language, and in the homely incidents and everyday occurrences with which he illustrates and emphasizes his teaching.

At all times, he adapts his exposition to the capacity of his audience. To children, his words and illustrations are such as to appeal to and impress a child's mind; to an audience more mature, we find a mode of expression again calculated to appeal to its comprehension. To the wise, he elaborates his teaching in such a way that they become conscious of its profound and sublime nature, and dimly perceive, as it deeper grows, that finally it leads to those unfathomed depths to be attained only by personal realization—never by mere reasoning.

In the following Suttanta the Buddha is exhorting his son Rāhula, a *sāmaṇera* aged seven. The Blessed One delivers a short, but nevertheless profound, homily on the necessity of that elementary principle of moral conduct—truthfulness.

Continuing, he establishes the moral criterion by which to determine a good (*kusala*, lit. skilful) action, and a bad (*akusala*, unskilful) one. It is from the beneficial or harmful effects of an action upon both the doer and others, that we are to distinguish between good and bad. In other words, Buddhism judges by results; therefore its moral words may be said to be utilitarian.

Throughout the Suttanta, the supreme importance of reflection is the constant theme of the Buddha. The three stages he emphasizes being prior to action, during action and subsequent to action. Students of philosophy should find this Suttanta of particular interest, as it deals with one of the basic questions of Ethics: the criterion of good and evil.

Ambalaṭṭhikā-Rāhulovada Suttanta
The Ambalaṭṭhikā Exhortation to Rāhula.[1]

Thus have I heard:

On one occasion the Blessed One was staying at the Bamboo Grove, in the Squirrels' Sanctuary, near Rājagaha. Now at that time the Venerable Rāhula was residing at Ambalaṭṭhikā[2] and in the evening the Blessed One, having risen from meditation, proceeded thither to the Venerable Rāhula who—seeing him coming from afar—got ready a seat, and water for washing the feet. And the Blessed One sat on the seat prepared and, being seated, washed his feet. Then the Venerable Rāhula, having saluted the Blessed One, respectfully sat at one side.

Thereupon the Blessed One, having left a small quantity of water in the vessel, addressed[3] the Venerable Rāhula:

"Do you see, Rāhula, this small quantity of water left in the vessel?"

"Yes, Lord."

---

1. This Suttanta is referred to in the *Bhābrā Edict* of King Asoka.
2. Ambalalaṭṭhikā, "The mango sapling." The so-called 'palace' was a retreat for meditation, and for those desiring solitude, erected in the Bamboo Grove.—Comy.

In the Brahmajāla Suttanta, it is said that the Blessed One took shelter for one night in the royal rest-house at Ambalaṭṭhikā, together with the company of Bhikkhus. Commenting on this Buddhaghosa says: "Here *Ambalaṭṭhikā* is the king's park. At the entrance stood a young mango tree called *Ambalaṭṭhikā* by the people. Consequently, the park itself came to be known as *Ambalaṭṭhikā*. It was well watered, shady, surrounded by a rampart, securely fastened with gates, and protected like a casket. Within the park was a house ornamented with magnificent paintings, for the king's relaxation. This was known as the royal rest-house."

It would appear from the above that there were two buildings in this park; one, for the king's own use; the other for the use of the religious orders.

3. The Commentator states that the Buddha delivered this discourse to Rāhula, whose age was only seven, knowing that boys of tender years, thoughtlessly, often speak falsely.

"Similarly, Rāhula, insignificant indeed is the Samaṇaship[4] of those who are not ashamed of uttering deliberate lies."

Whereupon the Blessed One threw away that small quantity of water, and addressed the Venerable Rāhula: "Do you observe, Rāhula, that small quantity of water, thrown away?"

"Yes, Lord."

"Similarly, Rāhula, discarded[5] indeed is the Samaṇaship of those who fare not ashamed of deliberate lying."

Then the Blessed One turned the water-vessel upside down, and addressed the Venerable Rāhula:

"Do you notice, Rāhula, this water-vessel turned upside down?"

"Yes, Lord."

"Similarly, Rāhula, overturned[6] indeed is the Samaṇaship of those who are not ashamed of uttering deliberate lies."

Finally, the Blessed One set the water-vessel upright and addressed the Venerable Rāhula:

"Do you see, Rāhula, this water-vessel, empty and void"?

"Yes, Lord."

"Similarly, Rāhula, empty and void indeed is the Samaṇaship of those who are not ashamed of deliberate lies."

"Suppose, Rāhula, the king's elephant—with tusks like plough-poles, mature, well-bred, whose place is the battlefield—having gone into the strife, performs doughty deeds[7] with his fore-legs, with his hind-legs, with the fore-part of his body, with the hind-part of his body, and also with his head, ears, tusks and tail, protecting only his trunk; and the mahout thinks that—despite this elephant's prowess and the various feats he has performed—as he has protected his trunk, the life of the royal elephant has not really been risked. But, Rāhula, from such time as the king's elephant, having gone into battle and performed feats with various parts

4. *Sāmaññaṃ*, the state of a *samaṇa*. Generally rendered "asceticism" or "monasticism," but neither word is a suitable designation for the status of Bhikkhus.

5. In both places the same word is used—*chaddita* thrown away: abandoned, left, etc.

6. *Nikkujjita*, overturned, upset.

7. That is, he destroys everything that comes in his way. Comy.

of his body, also performs feats with his trunk: then the mahout thinks that the life of the king's elephant has really been risked. For now there is nothing that the royal elephant has not risked.[8]

"Similarly, Rāhula, I say, of anyone who is not ashamed of uttering deliberate lies, that there is no evil that could not be done by him. Accordingly, Rāhula, thus, indeed, should you train yourself: 'Not even in play will I tell a lie.'

"What do you think, Rāhula; for what purpose is a mirror?"

"For the purpose of reflecting,[9] Lord."

"Similarly, Rāhula, having reflected should bodily action be done; having reflected,[10] should verbal action be done; having reflected, should mental action be done.

"Whatever action you desire to do with the body, Rāhula, of that particular bodily action you should reflect: 'Now, this action that I desire to do with the body—would this, my bodily action, be conducive to my own harm, or to the harm of others, or to that of both (myself and others)?—Then, unskilful is this bodily action, entailing suffering and productive of pain.

"If, Rāhula, when reflecting you should realize: 'Now, this bodily action of mine, that I am desirous of doing, would be conducive to my own harm, or to the harm of others, or to that of both (myself and others)—hence, unskilful is this bodily action, entailing suffering and productive of pain'—such an action with the body, Rāhula, you must on no account perform.

"If, on the other hand, Rāhula, when reflecting you realize: 'Now, this bodily action that I am desirous of doing, would conduce neither to the harm of myself, nor to that of others, nor to that of both (myself and others)—hence, skilful is this bodily action, entailing pleasure and productive of happiness'—such bodily action, Rāhula, you should perform.

"Whilst you are doing an action with the body, Rāhula, of that

8. That is, he has fearlessly exposed every part of his body to the risks of battle, not protecting even his trunk.

9. *Paccavekkhaṇatthaṃ*; Comy: for the purpose of looking at, for seeing any blemishes in the face. (Ed.)

10. *Paccavekkhitvā paccavekkhitvā*. This expresses in simple language what is implied in the doctrinal terms *sati*, 'mindfulness', and *yoniso manasikāra*, wise consideration or thorough attention. (Ed.)

particular bodily action should you reflect: 'Now, is this action that I am doing with my body, conducive to my own harm, or to the harm of others, or to that of both?—Then, unskilful is this bodily action, entailing suffering and productive of pain.'

"If, Rāhula, when reflecting you realise: 'Now, this action that I am doing with my body is conducive to my own harm, to the harm of others, and to that of both, hence, unskilful is this bodily action, entailing suffering and productive of pain'—from such a bodily action, Rāhula you must desist.

"If, on the other hand, Rāhula, when reflecting should you realize: 'Now, this action of mine that I am doing with the body is neither conducive to my own harm, nor to the harm of others, nor to that of both—hence, skilful is this bodily action, entailing pleasure and productive of happiness'—such a bodily action, Rāhula, you should do again and again.

"Having done an action with your body, Rāhula, of that particular bodily action you should reflect: 'Now, is this action that I have done with my body conducive to my own harm, or to the harm of others, or to that of both?—Then, unskilful is this bodily action, entailing suffering and productive of pain.'

"If, Rāhula, when reflecting you should realize: 'Now, this action that I have done with my body is conducive to my own harm, to the harm of others, and that of both—hence, unskilful is this bodily action, entailing suffering and productive of pain'—such a bodily action of yours, Rāhula, should be confessed, revealed, and made manifest to the Teacher, or to the learned, or to your brethren of the Holy Life. Having confessed, revealed, and made it manifest, you should acquire restraint in the future.

"If, on the other hand, Rāhula, when through reflection you realize: 'Now, this action that I have done with my body is neither conducive to my own harm, nor to the harm of others, nor to that of both—hence, skilful is this bodily action, entailing pleasure and productive of happiness'—for that very reason, Rāhula, should you abide in joy and happiness, training yourself, day and night, in meritorious states.

"Whatever action you desire to do by word, Rāhula, of that particular verbal action you should reflect: 'Now, this action that I desire to do by word—would this, my verbal action, be conducive to my own harm or to the harm of others, or to that of both?—Then, unskilful is this verbal action, entailing suffering and productive of pain.'

And he should reflect similarly before, during and after, verbal action.[11]

"If, on the other hand, Rāhula, when reflecting you realize: 'Now, this action that I have done by words is neither conducive to my own harm, nor to the harm of others, nor to, that of both, hence, skilful is this verbal action, entailing pleasure and productive of happiness'—for that very reason, Rāhula, should you abide in joy and happiness, training yourself, day and night, in meritorious states.

"Whatever action you desire to do by mind, Rāhula, of that particular mental action you should reflect: 'Now, this action that I desire to do by mind—would this, my mental action, be conducive to my own harm or to the harm of others, or to that of both?—Then, unskilful is this mental action, entailing suffering and productive of pain.'

And he should reflect, similarly before, during, and after, mental action.[12]

"If, Rāhula, when reflecting you realize: 'Now this action that I have done by mind is conducive to my own harm, to the harm of others, and to that of both, hence unskilful is this mental action entailing suffering and productive of pain'—such mental actions of yours, Rāhula, should be loathed, abhorred and despised.[13] Thus loathing, abhorring and despising, you should acquire restraint in the future.

"If, on the other hand, Rāhula, when reflecting you should realize: 'Now, this action that I have done by mind is neither conducive to my own harm, nor to the harm of others, nor to that of both`h—hence skilful is this mental action, entailing pleasure and productive of happiness'—for this very reason, Rāhula, should

---

11. The detailed exposition of "verbal action" is identical with that of bodily action.

12. The detailed exposition of "mental action" is likewise identical with that of bodily action, with the exception of the penultimate paragraph. The last two paragraphs are accordingly given in full.

13. Being a mental offence, Rāhula is not exhorted (as in the case of bodily, and verbal, action) to confess it to anyone.

you abide in joy and happiness, training[14] yourself, day and night, in the meritorious states.

"For whosoever, Rāhula, in the distant past, Samaṇas or Brāhmaṇas, purified their bodily, verbal and mental actions, they all did so in exactly the same way—by constantly reflecting. Further, whosoever, Rāhula, in the distant future, Samaṇas or Brāhmaṇas, shall purify their bodily, verbal and mental actions, they too will all do so in exactly the same way—by constantly reflecting. And further, whosoever, Rāhula, at the present time, Samaṇas or Brāhmaṇas, purify their bodily, verbal and mental actions, they all do so in exactly the same way—by constantly reflecting.

"Accordingly, Rāhula, thus must you train yourselves: 'By constantly reflecting shall we purify our bodily actions; by constantly reflecting shall we purify our verbal actions; by constantly reflecting shall we purify our mental actions.'

Thus spoke the Blessed One. Delighted, the Venerable Rāhula rejoiced at his words.

Introduction to the Mahā-Rāhulovada Suttanta

In the following Suttanta the Buddha deals with a profound subject—meditation, or culture of the mind. Not by servile supplication to any Heavenly Father is the craving and hatred by which the world is rent and torn to be assuaged; but only by the cultivation of that sublime equanimity which, having comprehended the true nature of life, amidst delight or misery: "... like to a rock, unmoved stands, and shakes not."

According to the commentaries, this exhortation was delivered when the Venerable Rāhula was in his eighteenth year—an early age, surely, at which to appreciate the ultimate possibilities of mind-culture.

---

14. This refers to self-examination. The Commentator says that one should reflect whether any evil has been done through word or deed. If so, it should be confessed; if not, one should abide rejoicing in that knowledge. If, whilst reflecting, one finds that an evil thought has been harboured, then it should be loathed and a firm resolution made not to entertain it again. If no such thought has arisen, one should abide rejoicing in the fact.

The four great essentials to which the Buddha first directs the attention of Rāhula are: *paṭhavī, āpo, tejo,* and *vāyo*, known as "*dhātus*" in Pali. "*Dhātu*" is defined as "that which bears its own intrinsic nature"; it's most appropriate English equivalent being "element." But it must not be hastily assumed from this that we are here dealing with the four "elements" of the ancient Greek philosophers, namely: earth, water, fire, and air; since, in the Abhidhamma sense, the four *dhātus* imply extension or solidity (*paṭhavi*), cohesion (*āpo*), heat (*tejo*), and motion or vibration (*vāyo*).

In the Sutta-Piṭaka, however, we find compounds designated by the generic name of the '*dhātu*' which predominates in their composition. *Kesa* hair, for instance, although a compound consisting of the four essentials and the four derived material qualities, is classified under '*paṭhavī-dhātu*,' owing to the predominance in its composition of the element of solidity.

Having explained to Rāhula the nature of the 'dhātus' (including, space), the Buddha further exhorts him to be constantly mindful of them, and to cultivate that perfect equanimity of mind which remains undisturbed by likes and dislikes—comparable to the absolute passivity of earth, water, fire, air, and space.

In conclusion, the Buddha—after briefly enumerating certain subjects of meditation with the specific qualities inhibited by each—gives a profound statement as to how the meditation on breathing is to be practised. And practising, according to these instructions, it is said that, in no long time, Rāhula becoming Arahant, achieved Emancipation.

Mahā Rāhulovada Suttanta
The Great Exhortation to Rāhula

Thus have I heard: 'Once the Blessed One was staying at the monastery of Anāthapiṇḍika, in the Jeta Grove, near Sāvatthī. Then the Blessed One, having robed himself in the forenoon, took bowl and robe, and entered Sāvatthī for alms; and the Venerable Rāhula also, having robed in the forenoon, took bowl and robe, and followed close behind[15] the Blessed One. Thereupon the Blessed One looked back and addressed the Venerable Rāhula:

"Whatsoever form[16] there be, O Rāhula, whether past, future

---

15. The Commentator states that the Venerable Rāhula, whilst following the Blessed One, noted with admiration, the physical perfection of the Buddha, and reflected with satisfaction that he himself was of similar appearance. Rāhula was very handsome. The books say that as the Buddha went along, followed by Rāhula, the pair was comparable to an auspicious royal elephant and his noble offspring, a royal swan with its beauteous cygnet, a regal lion with its stately cub, etc. Both were golden in complexion, almost equal in beauty, both were of the warrior caste, both had renounced a throne. So Rāhula, admiring the teacher, thought, "I too am handsome, like my parent the Blessed One. Beautiful is the Buddha's form, and mine is similar." "What is the lad, Rāhula, considering," thought the Buddha, "as he follows me?" And the Master read Rāhula's train of thought. Thereupon the Buddha decided to reprove Rāhula at once. A small leak may sink a ship, if neglected by the captain. Rāhula's foolish, vain thoughts could lead the lad to states of ill, and such leaks brook no delay.

16. *Rūpaṃ*: According to Abhidhamma *rūpa* is that which changes owing to physical conditions, such as heat, moisture, etc. Twenty-eight of these material qualities, or *rūpas*, are enumerated in the *Abhidhammatthasaṅgaha.* (See *Compendium of Philosophy*, p. 154). *Rūpa* in its generic sense, means 'matter,' and in its specific sense, 'quality.' But, in popular language, it means 'form.' (Shwe Zan Aung) We believe that Abhidhamma scholars would unanimously agree that 'matter' is the best possible rendering for *rūpa.* 'Body' would likewise be a suitable equivalent for *rūpa*, denoting, as in this Suttanta, the physical form of an individual. We have, however, retained the general term 'form,' despite one great objection to the use of the word 'form' for *rūpa*—namely, the contrast in Western philosophy between the impermanency of 'form' and the permanency of 'matter.'

or present, personal[17] or external,[18] coarse or fine, mean or noble, far or near—all form, in accordance with fact and with perfect knowledge[19] should be regarded thus: 'This is not mine; this am I not; this is soulless'."

"Verily, form alone, Blessed One; form alone: Exalted One?"

"Form, Rāhula, and sensation, Rāhula, and perception, Rāhula, and the mental concomitants, Rāhula, and consciousness,[20] Rāhula."

Then the Venerable Rāhula (reflected): 'What individual, having been edified today with an exhortation from the Blessed One himself, would enter the village for alms?[21]

Thereupon he turned back and sat down at the foot of a certain tree, with legs crossed, the body held erect, intent on mindfulness.

Now, the Venerable Sāriputta[22] saw him seated thus, and addressed him:

"Cultivate, Rāhula, the meditation of mindfulness on inhaling and exhaling![23] Inhaling and exhaling with mindfulness, Rāhula,

---

17. *Ajjhattaṃ*: belonging to one's own life-flux; relating to the individual.

18. *Bahiddhā*: outside, without.

19. *Sammapaññā* is *vipassanā paññā*: intuitive knowledge.—Comy.

20. These are the five component parts (*khandha*) that together constitute an individual. As matter or *rūpa* comprises twenty-eight material qualities, so mind or consciousness comprises fifty-two mental properties. (*Compendium*, pp. 94, ff). Of these, two—*vedanā*, sensation and *saññā*, perception—are usually treated as separate groups. The remaining fifty are collectively designated "*saṅkhāras*, because, as concomitants, they perform their respective functions in combination as one whole, of act, speech, or thought." See note on *saṅkhāra, Compendium of Philosophy*, p. 273.

21. Rāhula is said to have felt like a thief who has been caught with the stolen goods. He was very wise and understood, in detail, anything concisely stated (a fact that handicaps one who reads this exhortation to him, without the elucidation of the Commentaries). The Master, having reproved Rāhula, proceeded on his begging-round, but the latter decided to forego food that day.

22. If the two chief disciples happen to be residing in the same monastery as the Buddha, not until he has departed on the alms round do they set forth.—Comy.

23. The Venerable Sāriputta, noting the cross-legged posture of his youthful pupil—which was the one always adopted for the Meditation on Breathing—

cultivated, and frequently practised, is productive of much fruit and manifold advantages."

And, at eventide the Venerable Rāhula rose from solitary meditation and proceeded to the presence of the Blessed One. Saluting him respectfully, he sat on one side. Seated thus, the Venerable Rāhula said to the Blessed One:

"How, Lord, is mindfulness on inhaling and exhaling cultivated; how frequently practised, to produce much fruit and manifold advantages?"[24]

"Whatever,[25] Rāhula, pertains to oneself as an individual, is hard, of a solid nature, and a product of grasping—as for example: hair of the head, hair of the body, nails, teeth, skin, flesh, sinews, bones, marrow, kidneys, heart, liver, diaphragm, spleen, lungs, stomach, intestines, mesentery, excrement; or anything else whatsoever pertaining to oneself as an individual, that is hard, of a solid nature, and a product of grasping— this, Rāhula, is called the personal 'element of earth.'[26] But even this personal earthy element, as well as the external earthy element, is merely the element of solidity. This, in accordance with fact and with perfect knowledge, should be regarded thus: 'This is not mine; this am

---

advised this practice, not being aware that Rāhula was practising another, on the Buddha's own instruction.

24. Rāhula's meditation bore no fruit. He was perplexed. The Buddha had instructed him to meditate on "Form," whereas the Venerable Sāriputta, his teacher, advised "Breathing." The Buddha had inculcated the importance of obedience to one's immediate teacher. So Rāhula decided to meditate on "Breathing," and to obtain the Buddha's instruction on the subject. But the Blessed One did not immediately satisfy this wish. Before the ship can be steered safely to the haven, its dangerous leaks must be stopped. The Master proceeded to do this by expanding on his first brief instruction of meditation on "Form," and its constituents. Thus does a wise physician dispense the needed medicine, ignoring the patient's desires. This done, the Buddha gave Rāhula instruction on "Breathing."

25. Instead of giving a direct answer to the question, the Buddha explains to Rāhula the nature of the four essentials (*mahābhūtā*) to which all bodies may be reduced, in order to dissipate his illusion regarding self.

26. According to Buddhism there are four essentials or primaries which are interrelated, viz: *paṭhavī*, solidity; *āpo*, cohesion; *tejo*, temperature; and *vāyo*, motion.

I not; this is soulless'; Having seen with perfect knowledge that such is the case, one becomes disgusted with he element of earth, and one's mind is detached from the element of solidity.

"What now, Rāhula, is the element of water? The element of water may be internal, may be external.

"And what, Rāhula, is the internal watery element? Whatever pertains to oneself as an individual, is liquid, of a fluid nature, and a product of grasping—as for example: bile, phlegm, pus, blood, sweat, lymph, tears, serum, saliva, nasal mucus, synovial fluid, urine, or anything else whatsoever pertaining to oneself as an individual, that is liquid, of a fluid nature, and a product of grasping— this, Rāhula, is called 'the internal element of water.' But even this internal watery element, as well as the external watery element, is merely the element of fluidity. This, in accordance with fact and with perfect knowledge, should be regarded thus: 'This is not mine; this am I not; this is soulless.' Having seen with perfect knowledge that such is the case, one becomes disgusted with the element of water, and one's mind is detached from the element of fluidity.

"What now, Rāhula, is the element of fire? The element of fire may be internal, may be external.

"And what, Rāhula, is the internal fiery element? Whatever pertains to oneself as an individual, is hot, of a fiery nature, and a product of grasping—as for example: that whereby there is deterioration,[27] whereby there is intense burning,[28] whereby what is eaten, drunk, chewed and tasted, is well-digested, or anything else whatsoever pertaining to oneself as an individual, that is hot, of a fiery nature, and a product of grasping— this, Rāhula, is called 'the internal element of fire.' But even this internal fiery element, as well as the external fiery element, is merely the element of heat. This, in accordance with fact and with perfect knowledge, should be regarded thus: 'This is not mine; this am I not; this is soulless.' Having seen with perfect knowledge that such is the case, one becomes disgusted with the element of fire, and one's mind is detached from the element of heat.

---

27. *Jīriyati*: to be old, worn out, decrepit. Also "oxidation."

28. *Paridayhati*: to be scorched. As, for instance, if a person were to say, 'I am burning! I am burning!' and were to long for something cool. Cf. *Sammohavinodanī*, p. 69.

"What now, Rāhula, is the element of air? The element of air may be internal, may be external.

"And what, Rāhula, is the internal gaseous element? Whatever pertains to oneself as an individual, is gaseous, of an airy nature, and a product of grasping—as for example: ascending and descending flatus, the vapours in the abdomen and bowels, the air passing through the various parts of the body, such as inhalation and exhalation, or anything else whatsoever pertaining to oneself as an individual, that is gaseous, of an airy nature, and a product of grasping— this, Rāhula, is called 'the internal element of air.' But even this internal gaseous element, as well as the external gaseous element, is merely the element of air. This, in accordance with fact and with perfect knowledge, should be regarded thus: 'This is not mine; this am I not; this is soulless.' Having seen with perfect knowledge that such is the case one becomes disgusted with the gaseous element, and one's mind is detached from the element of air.

"What now, Rāhula, is the element of space? The element of space may be internal, may be external.

"And what, Rāhula, is the internal element of space? Whatever pertains to oneself as an individual, is void, of an empty nature, and a product of grasping as for example: the cavities of the ear and nose, the mouth aperture, that whereby one swallows what is eaten, drunk, chewed and tasted; where such nourishment accumulates, that whereby such nourishment passes from the lower part (of the body), or anything else whatsoever pertaining to oneself as an individual, that is void, of an empty nature, and a product of grasping— this, Rāhula, is called 'the internal element of space.' But even this internal void element, as well as the external void element, is merely the element of space. This, in accordance with fact and with perfect knowledge, should be regarded thus: 'This is not mine; this am I not; this is soulless.' Having seen with perfect knowledge that such is the case, one becomes disgusted with the void element, and one's mind is detached from the element of space.

"Like unto earth,[29] Rāhula, practise meditation. For, O Rāhula, by practising meditation like the earth, the contacts

29. Why did he commence thus? In order to show the reasons for acquiring balance of mind (*tādi-bhāva*, imperturbability).—Comy.

that have arisen—agreeable and disagreeable—will not continue to obsess your mind. Just as pure and impure things, Rāhula—excrement, urine, saliva, pus and blood—are cast upon the earth, and yet the earth neither abhors, nor loathes, nor dislikes such things; even so yourself, Rāhula, earth-wise, practise meditation. For, Rāhula, by practising meditation like the earth, the contacts that have arisen—agreeable and disagreeable—will not continue to obsess your mind.

"Like unto water, Rāhula, practise meditation. For, O Rāhula, by practising meditation water-wise, the contacts that have arisen—agreeable and disagreeable—will not continue to obsess your mind. Just as pure and impure things, Rāhula—excrement, urine, saliva, pus and blood—are washed (away) in water, and yet water neither abhors, nor loathes, nor dislikes such things; even so yourself, Rāhula, like water, practise meditation, and the contacts that have arisen will not continue to obsess your mind.

"Like unto fire, Rāhula, practise meditation. For, O Rāhula, by practising meditation fire-wise, the contacts that have arisen—agreeable and disagreeable—will not continue to obsess your mind. Just as fire, Rāhula, burns pure and impure things—excrement, urine, saliva, pus and blood—and yet fire neither abhors, nor loathes, nor dislikes such things; even so yourself, Rāhula, like fire, practise meditation, and the contacts that have arisen will not continue to obsess your mind.

"Like unto air, Rāhula, practise meditation. For, O Rāhula, by practising meditation air-wise, the contacts that have arisen—agreeable and disagreeable—will not continue to obsess your mind. Just as air, Rāhula, blows upon pure and impure things—excrement, urine, saliva, pus and blood—and yet air neither abhors, nor loathes, nor dislikes such things; even so yourself, Rāhula, like air, practise meditation, and the contacts that have arisen will not continue to obsess your mind.

"Like unto space, Rāhula, practise meditation. For, O Rāhula, by practising meditation space-wise, the contacts that have arisen—agreeable and disagreeable—will not continue to obsess your mind. Just as the vault of heaven, Rāhula, is not attached to any place; even so yourself, Rāhula, like the vault of heaven, practise meditation. For, Rāhula, by practising meditation like space, the contacts that have arisen—agreeable and disagreeable—will not continue to obsess your mind.

"Develop the meditation on loving-kindness (*mettā*),[30] Rāhula. For, Rāhula, by developing loving-kindness, ill-will is abandoned.

"Develop the meditation on compassion, Rāhula. For, Rāhula, by developing compassion, cruelty is abandoned.

"Develop the meditation on sympathetic joy, Rāhula. For, Rāhula, by developing sympathetic joy, aversion is abandoned.

"Develop the meditation on equanimity, Rāhula. For, Rāhula, by developing equanimity, hatred is abandoned.

"Develop the meditation on impurity,[31] Rāhula. For, Rāhula, by meditating on impurity, lust is abandoned.

"Develop the meditation on the concept of transience, Rāhula. For, Rāhula, by meditating on the concept of transience, pride of self is abandoned.

"Cultivate the concentration of mindfulness on inhaling and exhaling, Rāhula. Inhaling and exhaling with mindfulness, Rāhula, cultivated and frequently practised, is productive of much fruit and manifold advantages. And how, Rāhula, is inhaling and exhaling with mindfulness cultivated; how frequently practised, to produce much fruit and manifold advantages?

"Here, Rāhula, a Bhikkhu having retired to the forest, or to the foot of a tree, or to a lonely place, sits with legs crossed, the body held erect, intent on mindfulness. Consciously he inhales; consciously he exhales. When taking a long inspiration, he knows 'I am taking a long inspiration'; when making a long expiration,

30. The Buddhist technical term *mettā* (Sanskr: *maitriya*) is here rendered "Benevolence"—(*bene*: well and *volens*, wishing or willing) which is exactly what *mettā* signifies. The only drawback is that 'benevolence' is, as generally understood today, too flaccid a word to convey the rapture of Buddhist *mettā*. We ourselves were driven to the use of 'Loving-kindness' for *mettā*. 'Love,' alone, is corrupted with the idea of the sexual; 'kindness,' alone, is too tame. In the combination 'loving-kindness,' 'loving' intensifies 'kindness,' modifies the possible taint of 'loving.' The reader will now appreciate something of the import of the Pali word *mettā*, which we intend to retain in future, in view of its deep significance, and the difficulty of offering a graceful English equivalent.

31. *Asubha*. The ten *'asubhas'* are the ten stages of increasing putrefaction of corpses, viz.: 1. bloated. 2. discoloured. 3. festering. 4. fissured. 6. dismembered. 7. cut and dismembered. 8. bloody. 9. wormy. 10. bony. (See *Expositor*, Part I, p. 264).

he knows 'I am making a long expiration.' When taking a short inspiration, he knows 'I am taking a short inspiration'; when making a short expiration, he knows 'I am making a short expiration.'

'Conscious of the entire body (-process)[32] I will inhale,' thus he trains himself; 'Conscious of the entire body (-process) will I exhale', thus he trains himself. 'Calming the bodily process I will inhale', thus he trains himself; 'Calming the bodily process will I exhale,' thus he trains himself. 'Experiencing pleasure I will inhale,' thus he trains himself; 'Experiencing pleasure will I exhale,' thus he trains himself. 'Experiencing happiness I will inhale,' thus he trains himself; 'Experiencing happiness will I exhale', thus he trains himself. 'Conscious of the mental process[33] I will inhale,' thus he trains himself; 'Conscious of the mental process will I exhale,' thus he trains himself. 'Calming the mental process I will inhale,' thus he trains himself; 'Calming the mental process will I exhale,' thus he trains himself. 'Perfectly conscious I will inhale,' thus he trains himself; 'Perfectly conscious will I exhale,' thus he trains himself. 'With enraptured mind I will inhale,' thus he trains himself; 'With enraptured mind will I exhale,' thus he trains himself. 'Thoroughly composing the mind I will inhale,' thus he trains himself; 'Thoroughly composing the mind will I exhale,' thus he trains himself. 'Emancipating the mind I will inhale,' thus he trains himself; 'Emancipating the mind will I exhale,' thus he trains himself. 'Reflecting on transience I will inhale', thus he trains himself; 'Reflecting on transience will I exhale', thus he trains himself. 'Reflecting on freedom from lust I will inhale,' thus

32. *Sabba-kāya.* Literally "the whole body." According to the *Visuddhimagga* (Vism VIII. 171–172.), *kāya* used in this connection, does not mean the physical body, but the whole mass of inhalation and exhalation.

33. *Kāya-saṅkhāra*, literally "body-process." This Prof. Rhys Davids renders this as "bodily organism" (*Dialogues*, Pt. II, p. 328). According to the *Visuddhimagga* it means "inhalation and exhalation." We find this word used in a similar sense in the Cūḷa-Vedalla Suttanta (MN 44, MI 301).

"*Assāsa-passāsā kho āvuso Visākha kāyikā ete dhammā kāyapaṭibaddhā, tasmā assāsapassāsā kāya-saṅkhārā.*"—Inhalation and exhalation, friend Visākhā, are indeed physical. These conditions are dependent on the body; therefore inhalation and exhalation are (called) *kāya-saṅkhārā*. (Vism VIII. 175ff.)

he trains himself; 'Reflecting on freedom from lust will I exhale,' thus he trains himself. 'Reflecting on Cessation I will inhale,' thus he trains himself; 'Reflecting on Cessation will I cxhale,' thus he trains himself. 'Reflecting on complete emancipation I will inhale,' thus he trains himself; 'Reflecting on complete emancipation will I exhale,' thus he trains himself.[34]

"Mindfulness on inhaling and exhaling, Rāhula, thus cultivated and frequently practised, is productive of much fruit and manifold advantage. When, Rāhula, inhaling and exhaling with mindfulness is thus cultivated and frequently-practised, even the last inspiration and expiration ceases consciously, not unconsciously."

This was spoken by the Blessed One. The Venerable Rāhula, delighted, rejoiced at his words.

Cūḷa-Rāhulovada Suttanta
The Shorter Exhortation to Rāhula

Thus have I heard. On one occasion the Blessed One was staying in the monastery of Anāthapiṇḍika, in the Jeta Grove, near Sāvatthī. There the following thought arose in the mind of the Blessed One whilst meditating in solitude:

"Mature are in Rāhula those qualities that bring deliverance to maturity.[35] Should I not now give further guidance to Rāhula, for the extinction of the corruptions?"[36]

---

34. This description of the meditation on Breathing is, we fear, too condensed for the general reader, to whom we are unable to offer a detailed exposition here. But it must be stated that each injunction of the Blessed One, in this connection, has a specific meaning and the practice proceeds, up and up, starting with merely noting the breaths, through the jhānas, and ending with Nibbāna attainment. The student is referred to the *Visuddhimagga*, Vism VIII. 145ff., 245ff., for further particulars.

35. *Vimutti-paripācanīyā dhammā*. The Commentary mentions two sets of fifteen 'things conducive to the ripening of deliverance' (i.e., of Arahatta or Saintship).

36. I. Three purifying factors for each of the five controlling faculties (*indriya*), faith, energy, mindfulness, concentration and wisdom. Briefly stated, these three purifying factors are: avoiding the company of those

Having robed himself in the forenoon, the Blessed One took bowl and robe, and entered Sāvatthī for alms. Having gone his round for alms in Sāvatthī, he returned; and after the meal he addressed the Venerable Rāhula thus: "Take your mat, Rāhula. We shall go to the Andha Grove, and spend the day there."—"Yes, Lord," replied the Venerable Rāhula, took his mat and followed close behind the Blessed One.

On that occasion, many thousands of deities followed the Blessed One, thinking: "Today the Blessed One will give further guidance to the Venerable Rāhula, for the extinction of the corruptions."

And the Blessed One, having entered the Andha Grove, sat down at the foot of a certain tree on a seat prepared for him. Then also the Venerable Rāhula, having saluted the Blessed One respectfully, sat at one side. Thereupon the Blessed One addressed him as follows:

"What do you think, Rāhula, is the eye permanent or impermanent?"

"Impermanent, Lord."

"Is that which is impermanent, painful or pleasant"?

"It is painful Lord."

"Is it justifiable, then, to think, of that which is impermanent,

---

possessing qualities opposed to the respective faculty; associating with those who possess these faculties to a high degree; reflection on those parts of the Teaching that are helpful to a development of the respective faculty.

II. The five controlling faculties; five contemplations: of impermanence, of the suffering in the impermanent, of not-self in suffering, of giving up, of dispassion; noble friendship, moral restraint, talk on the austere life, application of energy and penetrative wisdom. *Āsavanaṃ khaye. Āsava*, 'corruption,' elsewhere rendered by 'taints' or 'cankers,' means literally 'flux' or 'outflow.' There are three kinds of 'corruptions": by sense-desire (*kāmāsavā*), by (desire for continued) existence (*bhavāsavā*) and by ignorance (*avijjāsavā*); often a fourth kind is added: the corruption by wrong views (*diṭṭhāsavā*). The Arahant, or Saint, is often called 'one in whom the corruptions have become exhausted' or 'the extirpator of corruptions' (*khīṇāsavo*). *Arahatta*, Saintship, is the extinction, or exhaustion, of the corruptions (*āsavakkhaya*).

pain-laden and subject to change—'This is mine;[37] this I am;[38] this is my self?'"[39]

"Certainly not, Lord."

"What do you think, Rāhula, are forms (visual objects) permanent or impermanent?"

"Impermanent, Lord."

"Is that which is impermanent, painful or pleasant?"

"It is painful, Lord."

"Is it justifiable, then, to think of that which is impermanent, pain-laden and subject to change—'This is mine; this I am; this is my self?'"

"Certainly not, Lord."

"What do you think, Rāhula, are eye-consciousness[40] ... visual contact permanent or impermanent?"

"Impermanent, Lord."

"Is that which is impermanent, painful or pleasant"?

"It is painful Lord."

"Is it justifiable, then, to think of that which is impermanent, pain-laden and subject to change—'This is mine; this I am; this is my self?'"

"Certainly not, Lord."

"What do you think, Rāhula: that which arises conditioned by visual contact, namely all that belongs to feeling, perception, mental formations and consciousness, is that permanent or impermanent?"

"Impermanent, Lord."

"Is that which is impermanent, painful or pleasant?"

"It is painful, Lord."

"Is it justifiable, then, to think of that which is impermanent, pain-laden and subject to change—'This is mine; this I am; this is my self?'"

"Certainly not, Lord."

"What do you think, Rāhula, ear and sounds, nose and smells, tongue and tastes, body and tangibles, mind and ideas;

---

37. "This is mine"—as motivated by craving (*taṇhā*) or possessiveness.
38. "This I am"—as motivated by pride (*māna*).
39. "This my self (or soul)"—as motivated by wrong views (*diṭṭhi*).
40. *Cakkhu-viññāṇa*.

the (corresponding types of) consciousness and contact; and the feelings, perceptions, mental formations and consciousness which arise conditioned by that contact—are all these permanent or impermanent?"

"Impermanent, Lord."

"Is that which is impermanent, painful or pleasant?"

"It is painful, Lord."

"Is it justifiable, then, to think of that which is impermanent, pain-laden and subject to change—'This is mine; this I am; this is my self?'"

"Certainly not, Lord."

"The learned noble disciple, Rāhula, who sees thus, gets a disgust for the eye, gets a disgust for forms, for visual consciousness, visual contact,[41] and for that which arises conditioned by visual contact, namely all feelings, perceptions, mental formations and consciousness.

"He gets disgust for ear and sounds, nose and smells, tongue and tastes, body and tangibles, mind and ideas, gets a disgust for the (corresponding types of) consciousness and contact, and for that which arises conditioned by that contact, namely all that belongs to feeling, perception, mental formations and consciousness."[42]

"In him who gets disgusted,[43] passion fades out.[44] With the fading out of passion[45] he is liberated. Thus liberated, the knowledge arises in him: 'Liberated am I, birth is exhausted, fulfilled is the Holy Life, done what should be done, and nothing further remains after this': Thus he knows."

Thus spoke the Blessed One. Glad at heart, the Venerable Rāhula rejoiced in the words of the Blessed One.

---

41. *Cakkhu-samphasso.*

42. *Vedanāgataṃ saññāgataṃ saṅkhāragataṃ viññāṇagataṃ.* This refers to the last four of the five aggregates (*khandha*), comprising the mental part (*nāma*) of the individual.

43. "Gets a disgust for": *nibbindati* ("disgust": *nibbidā*).—Here where a high stage of penetrative Insight (*vipassanā*) is reached, 'disgust' should not be understood to mean a strong emotional revulsion, or loathing (which generally is linked with feelings of resentment or antagonism); it is rather an estrangement, a spontaneous recoiling or turning away.

44. *Virajjati.*

45. *Virāga*, 'through dispassion.'

Now, during that utterance the mind of the venerable Rāhula was freed from the corruptions through clinging no more. And also in those many thousand deities, there arose the stainless, immaculate Eye of Truth[46] : "Whatever is subject to origination is subject to cessation."

The Rāhula Sutta

(Sutta-Nipāta, Verses 335-342)

The Prologue

The Master:

From living constant, say,
Dost thou the wise man scorn?
The torch-bearer to men?
Is he revered by thee?

Rāhula:

From living constant, nay,
The wise man scorn I not;
The torch-bearer to men
Is aye revered by me.

The Teaching

The Master:

Loosed from the pleasure-strands,
Dear forms that charm the mind,
In faith renounce thy home,
Ender of ill become!

Seek thou for lovely friends!
Seek bed and seat remote,
Lone and of little noise.
Frugal in fare become!

46. *Dhamma-cakkhu*, the Vision of Dhamma, refers here (according to Comy.) to the attainment of Arahatta, Saintship; while elsewhere it applies only to Stream-entry (*sotāpatti*).

Robes, alms and requisites,
Thy bed and seat: for these
Beget no craving, nor
Turn to the world again!

Curbed by observance-rule,
Curbed in the senses five,
Mark thou thy body's ways[47]
And be wearied of it!

Shun thou the things of sign,[48]
Attractive and passion-fraught:
On foul things[49] quicken mind,
One-pointed and intent!

Quicken what has no sign,[50]
Be rid of warping pride.[51]
Then mastering the pride,[52]
You shall fare in calm.[53]

In this way the Master constantly instructs the Venerable Rāhula.

47. Literally: Have 'mindfulness directed to the body' (*sati kāyagatā-ty-atthu*).

48. "Sign" (*nimittaṃ*), that is, the sign or notion of greed. But *nimittaṃ* is here better to be linked with *subhaṃ* in the next line, and rendered by "attractive object" or "the idea of attractiveness."

49. "On foul things" (*asubhāya*), i.e., the unattractive or repulsive aspect of the inanimate body as considered in the cemetery meditations; and of the animate body, in the meditation of the 32 parts of the body.

50. "No sign" (*animittaṃ*), i.e., without a sign of greed, hatred or delusion, nor any notion of permanency. Comy.: 'Cultivate insight" (*vipassanā*).

51. Literally: "of any proclivity to pride" (*mānānusayaṃ*).

52. *Māna*, 'pride' has here also the wider meaning of self-conceit (*asmi-māna*) or ego-illusion.

53. This refers to the highest tranquillity of Sainthood.

Foundations of Buddhism
The Four Noble Truths

Francis Story
The Anagārika Sugatānanda

WHEEL PUBLICATION NO. 34/35

By walking thou canst not the world's end gain;
Nor, if ye win it not, be freed from pain.
But truly, he whose wisdom is profound,
Who rightly sees the world—by him 'tis found.
He that has lived in holiness shall know
With mind serene the ending of life's round,
Nor to this world nor other long to go.

Rohitassa Sutta SN 2:26
Verse translation by the author

Foundations of Buddhism

The Four Noble Truths

Mankind, pondering and disputing, has been engaged for so long in trying to find an answer to the enigma of existence, and so many first-class minds have been devoted to the task, that had the problem been open to solution by the intellect alone we should certainly have been furnished with the definitive blueprint of our being, beyond all doubt or conjecture, many centuries ago. From the time when prehistoric myth became merged into an attempt to give a rational account of the universe the questions, 'What is life? How did it originate? Has it a purpose, and if so, what is it?' have haunted the imagination; yet still for most people they remain unanswered. Reason has offered a wide range of ingenious possibilities from the speculations of the Eleatics down to the more sophisticated theories of the modern epiphenomenalists, but so far it has failed to provide any reasonable explanation that is not open to equally reasonable objections. And whilst reason has failed, its alternative, supernatural revelation, has shown itself equally contradictory and inconclusive, and has suffered an even worse defeat. Its historical record has weighed heavily against it because of the disastrous influence it has often exerted in human affairs. The private revelations of mystics, by their exclusively subjective nature, can never offer more than an insecure foothold for faith in those who have not directly shared them, and a doubtful faith is the father of fanaticism.

The record of man's speculative thought down the centuries has come to resemble a maze of tracks in a boundless desert. The tracks can be identified by their characteristics; they are the tracks of religion, of philosophy, and obliterating many of these, the more recent tracks of science. For the most part the tracks of religion go round in circles. Beginning as myth they continue as myth hardened into dogma, and so go over the same ground in endless repetition. Other tracks wander along aimlessly, drawn in this direction and that by new theories, new discoveries and new contacts, their path variable as the wind. These are the tracks of philosophy, the imprints of man's restless, inquiring mind—a mind which, despite its courage and adventurousness, has only the old material to work over and so is reduced to combining ideas in endless permutations, seeking to reconcile the irreconcilable and always failing to reach an end. Then, superimposed upon these there are the imprints of scientific thought, which has invaded philosophy to an ever-increasing extent, but which at the same time discourages any concern with ultimate issues, or with questions of value and purpose. Time and again the older tracks of philosophy and religion are seen to have crossed one another, and where they met there are signs of a scuffle. Too often, there is blood on the sands of history.

So it has been ever since man emerged as an animal capable of abstract thinking. Now we have entered a phase in which supernaturalism has given way almost entirely to scientific knowledge, and the approach to the problem is somewhat different. Yet science has not brought us any nearer to the answers. The tracks of thought still remain indecisive, their beginning a mystery, their end a mark of interrogation. Present day knowledge with its unprecedented accumulation of facts concerning the physical universe and the constitution of living organisms, has provided philosophers with a vast stock of new material to take into account, but so far the result has only been to give the mind more than it can handle. Far from clarifying the general picture, the effect has been to overcrowd the canvas. To correlate the various specialized branches of knowledge is a stupendous task, and one that is further complicated by the areas of uncertainty in each of them. The non-specialist is seldom in a position to be able to separate theory from established fact in the scientific disciplines, and this is particularly so in the case of those which relate to the life-processes, such as genetics and biochemistry, and are therefore the most relevant to the inquiry.

Besides this, the facts that science presents often seem to point to opposite conclusions. Despite the great advances that have been made in physics, technology is still working to a great extent with factors that are not completely understood, or even satisfactorily defined. There are, for example, certain radiations forming the basic structure of the universe which appear both as waves and as particles, although logically they cannot be both at the same time.

It is not even certain whether the expression 'at the same time' has any meaning in a universe where events can hardly be said to be simultaneous at all, and where the image of a star seen from a distance of many thousands of light years may be nothing more than the ghost of something that ceased to exist in space before man appeared on the earth. Expanding knowledge tends to cut us adrift from the apparent security of empirical facts, and in many ways the nature of thought itself has been brought into question.

There are people who entertain the hope that at some time in the not-too-distant future we may be able to get final answers to questions that have tormented men for generations by feeding all the relevant data into an electronic brain. But that hope is founded on two very large assumptions: first, that all the necessary data will eventually become available, and secondly that man can devise a machine more capable than its creator. So far, the most advanced electronic computer has not been able to do more in the field of mathematics than a human mind can do. It only does it more quickly. Even there it adds nothing new; there have been abnormal human brains that could extract cube roots with the same speed and accuracy. If a new and basically different mode of thinking is needed it must be sought for elsewhere than in electronic machines.

Does this mean that we shall never know any more about the ultimate things than we do now? The conclusions to which science moves at present are, in regard to the older beliefs, chiefly negative. They tell us what is no longer believable, but do not suggest alternatives or encourage any positive inferences. Yet in the quest for truth science contributes something of greater value than the facts it provides. It offers a method of inquiry, a disciplined use of the facts at hand, which is more productive than the pursuit of random theories. It indicates a method by which the data of experience, no matter how limited they may be, can be taken as starting points for a journey into unknown territory, and how from a few observed facts a general principle can be deduced. Furthermore, it includes as an important part of its method the readiness to discard whatever theory is found to be in disagreement with the observed phenomena, and this iconoclastic function of science points to a truth of the highest significance, namely, that in the search for reality what is most essential is not the gathering and tabulating of facts, but the understanding of those facts in their true relation to one another, and the preliminary stripping away of hitherto accepted ideas until we are left with nothing more than the bare bones of experience, but that experience of the most fundamental and universal kind. Science works on theories, certainly, but is prepared to abandon them when they fall flat; it does not build model cosmologies from selected materials.

This method, which has been responsible for everything we can claim to have derived from our knowledge of the physical universe, is the only profitable one to follow when we seek to enlarge our understanding beyond the world of immediate sensory perception. And it is towards the possibility of such an extension that the psychological sciences are now turning. There is an increasing recognition of the truth that the world of external phenomena is only a part—and by no means the most important part—of man's total experience. What goes on within ourselves, in our psychological responses and motivations, and also on the intuitive levels of the mind, is being given the same analytical scrutiny as that which is turned on the objective features of the universe. For the first time, scientists are making a serious study of the mental processes, conscious and unconscious. They are giving equal attention to the paranormal aspects of the mind, such as the phenomena of telepathy, clairvoyance and the recollection of previous lives. From this may develop an entirely new approach to the problem of being.

A new one, that is, so far as the West is concerned. But nothing in mental science, or in philosophy, is really new. More than six hundred years before the Christian era, the tracks of speculative thought had reached a stage of the utmost complexity, in India. There we find the familiar arguments of mysticism versus rationalism, of empiricism, pragmatism, logical positivism, the opposing views of 'eternalism' and 'annihilationism', and of so many intermediate doctrines that it can be safely said that later philosophers have been able to produce nothing that was not a duplication or variant of one or the other of them. When we examine the sixty-two *diṭṭhis* or theories regarding the nature of life and the universe, which were current in the time of Gotama Buddha and described by him in the Brahmajāla Sutta of the Dīgha Nikāya, we find there the seeds of all later thought, the archetype of every idea that has appeared in philosophy between Plotinus and Kierkegaard. That some of them were the doctrines of established schools which had been in existence long before the birth of the Buddha is evident from the accounts of the Buddha's own search for illumination, for on renouncing the world the prince-ascetic Siddhattha first placed himself under two teachers from among the many sects that were already laying claim to ultimate knowledge. Those teachers, Ālāra Kālāma and Uddaka Rāmaputta, were not logicians but exponents of yoga. As such they had their philosophy, but its final vindication was to be sought in the subjective realm, in an intensified perception outside the scope of formal reasoning. By the practice of *jhāna*, or mental absorption, they had in fact succeeded in raising consciousness to a higher power.

But great as were the achievements of these two eminent yogis, the ascetic Gotama did not find the full enlightenment he sought in their systems. Neither did he reach it by way of the extreme asceticism to which he turned later. He found, on the contrary, that an entirely new mode of approach was needed if he were to break through the tangle of conceptual thinking on the one hand, and sublimated consciousness on the other. By the traditional yogic methods, he had gone beyond the world of forms, but not beyond that of ideas or the mere suspension of ideas. He found that the degree of illumination these methods gave was far from that of absolute knowledge and liberation. Thrown back on his own resources, with no longer any guiding principle except what he might find within himself, he returned in thought to the original impulse of his quest. Its beginning, significantly enough, lay in a very early experience he had known, of an intuitive kind. He had been sitting watching his father, the king, carrying out the ritual of the spring ploughing. His attention had been caught and held by the flocks of birds that followed in the wake of the plough; they were eagerly scratching in the newly-turned furrows for worms and insects. Driven by hunger, the all-demanding hunger that is ever present in nature, and excited by the sight of their living prey, birds of all kinds were quarrelling and fighting one another, a noisy, turbulent mass of feathered bodies, striking and tearing with beak and claw, unmercifully.

A common enough sight, and one that carries no special meaning for most people. But to the young Siddhattha, it had been a troubling experience. So indeed it should be to anyone who believes in an overruling power, a Creator, whose chief attribute is love. Birds—among the most delicate and beautiful of nature's offspring, creatures so light and ethereal that when man thinks of spiritual beings it is with the wings of birds and something of their morning ecstasy that he pictures them—those same birds that have been the poet's inspiration and the nature lover's joy, at close quarters are seen to be fully as rapacious and as cruel towards smaller creatures and to their owns species as the most ferocious of the larger animals. By such a slight transformation the winged angel becomes the winged tiger.

Yet, as the young Siddhattha saw even then, it could not be otherwise. Birds had to satisfy the urge to live, and for their food they had to prey on others and compete with others. So it was throughout nature, and from whatever particular the generalization was drawn it expanded into the same universal truth. Not only is nature indifferent to cruelty and pain, but it actually imposes them upon all living creatures as the condition and price of their existence. To inflict or to suffer; or both to inflict and to suffer—that is the law of life.

The peculiar insights of childhood, which often have an extraordinary clarity and depth, are too commonly lost when we become submerged in the world's incessant and implacable demands. As we accumulate knowledge we lose percipience; we know the fact, but its true inner meaning is estranged from us. So, regardless of the moral indifference of nature, men build and try to maintain systems of ethics, in the comfortable belief that in some way they harmonize with natural law and an underlying principle of goodness, call it God or what you will. But while doing so they are walking a tightrope stretched across a mocking abyss of negation. Woe to him who looks into that dark gulf and tries to find there the features of an omnipotent, all-merciful ruler of the universe! If he sees anything of the sort it will be only in his imagination, the reflection of an idea instilled into him by tradition. If he sees nothing, he risks losing his balance. Unless he is strong enough to face this void, it is better for the tightrope walker to keep his gaze fixed elsewhere, on some defined point in the sphere of action, and trust solely to the labyrinth organs, his own interior instruments of balance. His innate sense of right and wrong must be his support. It is not always a trustworthy sense, but for most intelligent people today it is all that is left. As for the theologian, in order to remain on good terms with the birds, he has to forget their private lives and admit only the idealized convention; let the angels have their wings, but not the beak or claws.

To most thinking people now, there is no longer any question of reconciling theology with reality. Not many, however, have the courage to face the facts and say, with the Existentialists, that "the universe is absurd, because there is no reason for it to exist—no God has created it to declare his glory or serve as a dwelling-place for his creatures—and because nothing in it has any specific function to fulfil. Man has no destiny or privileged position, and not even the consciousness, which he has of himself, can save him from the universal absurdity of all created beings."[1] That disquieting knowledge lies like a cancerous growth in the background of man's mind, driven inwards yet injecting its poison into all that he says and does and believes in. Rationalism, humanitarianism and all the other substitutes that have been devised in place of the spiritual life lost to mankind are all essentially meaningless in face of the futility man feels, his sense of utter helplessness in an alien world. The Egyptians found no difficulty in worshipping a dead god, but modern man can only worship life.

When Siddhattha arrived at the most critical point of his quest, when all the traditional paths had been followed to their uttermost limits and still the truth beyond all truths had not been found, he recollected his early experience and what it had revealed to him. He remembered too that it had led him to another experience, on a different level of consciousness. At that time he had delved for the answer to the problem into the deepest layers of his being, for he knew instinctively that what he was seeing in nature was a true reflection of his own condition as a living, sentient organism doomed, like all others, to unceasing conflict. Each of us stands alone with each one's destiny, yet in another sense each is deeply involved with all others. If the solution to the world mystery was to be found anywhere it must be in the fullest, most intimate understanding of one's own nature.

1. Jean-Paul Sartre: *A Literary and Political Study* by Philip Thody, 1960

So he turned his mind back to that incident in early life which had shown him his true path, to the glimpse he had had of a knowledge he possessed before creed and tradition claimed him. After his Enlightenment, the Buddha described it in these words:

> I recalled how once I was seated under the shade of a jambu tree while my father, Suddhodana, was ploughing the royal furrow, and having put aside desires and impure states of mind, yet cognizing and reflecting in the bliss born of detachment, I attained the first mental absorption. Could it be that this was the way to realization? With that thought the clear consciousness came to me: Yes, indeed, this is the way to realization.

Now, the first mental absorption (*jhāna*) is reached by purifying and tranquillizing the mind, which can be done by the practice of *ānāpāna-sati*, contemplation of the breathing. The state of tranquillity is accompanied by joy and rapture, and in this jhāna refined and calmed thought-conception and sustained thought are still present though no longer engaged with a multitude of objects, but exclusively in the subject of meditation. Having risen from that absorption, the mind will be calm and concentrated, and being no longer disturbed by desires of the more active kind, it becomes able to examine the factors of experience with detachment, and so enjoys a new clarity of perception. It is as though the rippled surface of a pool were to become smooth and still. When that happens two things follow: the surface reflects external things more accurately, and at the same time it becomes possible to see through the surface to the depths below.

This is only the initial stage of the jhānic consciousness, which is progressive; but it opens the way to the succeeding levels. In these, the second, third and fourth absorptions, consciousness becomes more and more refined as the sensations of joy, the bodily perceptions, the reflex-perceptions and the remaining elements of self-awareness are discarded step by step. When the ascetic, Siddhattha, seated under the Bodhi Tree, remembered his first jhānic experience, he at once applied himself to inducing it once more, starting from the point of the first jhāna that he had reached spontaneously on that occasion. Then, having attained tranquillity, he went on to apply mental concentration to the analytical examination of his own interior world—the body, the mind and the mental objects. The technique of making the mind tranquil, known as *samatha-bhāvanā*, is the prelude to the cultivation of direct insight, or *vipassanā-bhāvanā*. It is in the latter form of meditation that the mind finally penetrates the Four Noble Truths and so comes to distinguish reality from illusion. The ultimate truth is then seen 'face to face'. From being descriptive truths, that are merely grasped intellectually, the Four Noble Truths become known and understood and felt as certainties, on a new level of realization. In a quite indescribable way they become *experienced*, just as we experience the sensations within our own bodies, our thoughts and emotions—indeed, with an even greater force and reality than these.

Thus it was by intuitive penetration that Siddhattha attained Buddhahood after all other means had failed. He stood outside the limitations of the consciousness centred in an illusory self and was able to see through and beyond the cosmic processes, past the boundaries of space and time. At last, after those six years of arduous, agonizing and fruitless austerities, he was able to say, "I discovered that profound truth, so difficult to perceive, difficult to comprehend, tranquilizing and sublime; *which is not to be grasped by mere reasoning*, and is visible only to the wise" (Majjhima Nikāya 26).

The truth he had penetrated was the fourfold division of knowledge, the basis of all that is comprehended in the term *ñāṇadassana*, insight-wisdom. Expressed as the Four Noble Truths, it comes first in the Buddha's teaching and summarizes everything that follows. Concerning the first declaration of these truths, the Buddha said:

> The Perfect One, O Bhikkhus, the Fully Enlightened One, has established at Isipatana the supreme Kingdom of Truth, which none can overthrow—neither ascetic nor Brahman nor heavenly being nor fiend, nor god nor anyone whomsoever in the universe—by proclaiming, pointing out, revealing, setting up, explaining and making clear the Four Noble Truths.
>
> And what are these Four Noble Truths? They are the Truth of Suffering, the Truth of the Cause of Suffering, the Truth of the Cessation of Suffering, and the Truth of the Noble Path that leads to the Cessation of Suffering.

Now, these truths, as we shall see, are something quite different from the usual bases of religious belief; so different, in fact, that it has been questioned whether Buddhism is a religion at all. It has been disputed whether it is a philosophy, a code of ethics, a religion or a science. The fact is that it contains all of these and transcends them. Superlatively, it is the science of the mind. The Focur Noble Truths crystallize the uniqueness of Buddhism and of the Buddha, for as the Teacher said:

> So long, O Bhikkhus, as the absolutely true knowledge and insight as regards these Four Noble Truths were not quite clear to me, so long I was not sure whether I had attained that Supreme Enlightenment which is unsurpassed in all the world ... But as soon as the absolutely true knowledge and insight as regards these Four Noble Truths had become perfectly clear to me, there arose in me the assurance that I had attained to that supreme, unsurpassed Enlightenment.

Dukkha Ariya Sacca

The Noble Truth of Suffering

The Buddha formulated the first truth in the following words, which run like a recurring theme through the Buddhist scriptures:

> What, Bhikkhus, is the Noble Truth of Suffering? Birth is suffering; decay is suffering; death is suffering; sorrow, lamentation, pain, grief and despair are suffering. To be separated from the pleasant is suffering; to be in contact with the unpleasant is also suffering. In short, the five aggregates of Existence connected with attachment are all suffering.

This is often interpreted as a fundamental attitude of pessimism, even of despair, in the Buddhist outlook. It does so appear, for instance, in the use Schopenhauer made of oriental ideas in his philosophy. There is a tendency to see it as being in opposition to the vigorous, life-affirming attitudes of the West.

If the first Noble Truth were the whole of the Buddha's message, there would be ground for the objection. And if it is insisted that Buddhism should fit into one or other of the pessimistic or optimistic, life-denying or life-asserting categories of thought, there would, on this truth alone, be little choice as to which it should be. But in the Buddhist view there is no justification for preferring one pole of thought to another; what is required is that the view of life should be objective, unbiased and realistic.

The first Truth is drawn from a critical examination, not only of the human predicament but of all aspects of the life of sentient beings. Its acceptance involves a correction and readjustment of the usual perspectives. It then appears as the recognition of a universal symptom, one that is normally disregarded only because it is a chronic condition. The Buddhist emphasis on it is the essential preliminary to diagnosis and treatment; it is the stage at which the physician tells the patient that he is ailing.

But it is not to be supposed that the first truth as formulated denies the existence of joy and laughter. It stresses the evils of life to counteract man's natural inclination to dwell on the pleasant and ignore and forget everything disagreeable—that psychological device by which the will to live is maintained despite the most discouraging experiences. At the same time it is a reminder that whilst at any given moment we may personally be enjoying what we call happiness there are incalculable numbers of sentient beings that are in misery, a reminder of which most people are continually in need. And in speaking of happiness it is useful to remember that while many people feel reluctant to admit the overwhelming preponderance of suffering in life, comparatively few are capable of true happiness on their own account. Their only refuge from reality is in pleasure.

The Buddha said that he himself had known both pleasure and pain in their most extreme forms. If life were unrelieved misery, no one would feel desire to continue with it, while if it were unalloyed happiness, there would be no need for the remedy which religion seeks to provide. It may be added that in a world of ideal happiness and security, one of the hypothetical Utopias that men have dreamed of and which, incidentally, each dreamer constructs according to his own peculiar ideas of perfection, so that scarcely any two of them have features in common, there would be no incentive for effort of any kind. It is only where the adverse conditions of the world, as we know it, prevail, where good and evil, virtue and vice are in perpetual conflict, that man's noblest endeavours could be born. It is only in such a world, in fact, that these opposites could exist at all. And so far as the Utopias are concerned, human beings exhibit such a diversity of tastes, inclinations and desires that it is rather childish to suppose that any ideal society, which must necessarily be uniform, could ever confer happiness on all its members.

We hear much today about anxiety-neuroses as a part of modern, urban civilization, and they are real enough, but there is another side of the picture as well. Man's nature, balanced between the primitive and the civilized, needs the alternation of states of consciousness. Even too much freedom from anxiety is alien to human nature, as the so-called affluent societies are beginning to show. The increase in crime, and particularly juvenile delinquency, the outbreaks of racial persecution and revolt against the established order are due as much as anything to the fact that the affluent society gives too much leisure to those who do not know how to use it, too much security to those whose natures demand risk and excitement, and too much orderliness to those who can express themselves only in violence. All these conditions are unnatural to perhaps the majority of men; the teenage boy, who joins in mass hooliganism, converts the highways into racing tracks or plays chicken with automobiles and trains, is only giving outlet to the primordial urge to face danger and assert himself against it. His self-esteem cries out for the thrill of conflict and the hazards that a too protective society denies him.

For the most part, man is still a primitive fighting animal; if it were not so, war would automatically have been abolished long ago. Augustine of Hippo said that all men desire peace, but all desire it in their own way. He was only partly right; all men want peace, but they also want it to be a kind of war. That is the unrecognized, 'unadmitted' fact behind all the talk of world peace at international conferences and in intellectual humanist circles: in the realm of his unconscious, man craves for the triumphs and pains of conflict.

The unrelieved boredom of eternal heavenly bliss would not suit man as he is now constituted. If suffering did not exist he would be obliged to invent it. Recognizing this fundamental fact of human personality, Buddhism attaches no importance to heavenly states, for it acknowledges that while the elements of personality with all their necessary imperfections continue to exist, an eternity of happiness would be insupportable. Without its opposite, happiness would have no meaning.

It is a worthy aim to strive for the improvement of worldly conditions and the perfection of the welfare state; yet there is a point beyond which it cannot be carried without leading either to internal disruption or some form of totalitarianism. The notion that a perfect human society can be evolved has taken the place of the hope of heaven which formerly prompted men to labour for their own perfection; and it has already given birth to more persecution and suppression of liberty than ever came out of the Inquisition. A perfect society cannot be fashioned by man who is imperfect; and if such a society were possible, man as he is would not fit into it. The historian and the anthropologist know that this is so, but unfortunately the demagogues are stronger. In a world ruled by the most vociferous elements, political and commercial, the individual is given little opportunity to seek one's own salvation. The only self-development he knows is the process of acquiring information which today goes by the name of education.

The implications of the Buddhist truth of suffering are considerably more than appear in the bare words of the formula. That birth (or as Buddhism defines it, the perpetual process of arising) is painful, and that mental and physical decay, with their culmination in death, are unavoidable evils, is a self-evident fact. But their evil is not only in their actual occurrence; it extends beyond it, for at every stage of life, man is overshadowed by the thought of them, as he is by the threat of sickness, accidents, bereavements and other misfortunes of greater or lesser likelihood. Whatever attitude of disregard he may adopt towards these threats to his peace of mind, it can never be anything more than a very fragile shield against possibilities that are too disturbing to contemplate. These vicissitudes are inseparable from life, and one who tries to ignore them is the true escapist. To be positively life-affirming it is these facts above all others that we must be prepared to assimilate into our Weltanschauung.

The realistic philosopher of today has good reasons for his pessimism. His mechanistic universe has no place for human values, for hopes of individual fulfilment. He takes the same direct and disillusioned view of life as that presented in the Buddhist truth of suffering, but he knows nothing of the remedy. For him there is no assurance of any higher truth, no relief from the oppressive actualities that surround him in a cosmos apparently hostile, or at best indifferent, to man and his aspirations. A certain pride in his heroic despair may sustain him, and yet in his heart he may envy those who can still make the choice of faith against reason, and like Kierkegaard, believe in a religion that is impossible because it is impossible.

Buddhism accepts the scientist's comfortless picture of the universe, but with a difference. In the Dhamma, both a. higher truth and the means of realizing it are present as vital and knowable facts, and it is this which lifts the realistic outlook into the realm of hope. The dialogue between Buddhism and scientific thought is only just beginning, and as it develops it may result in a number of new and significant interpretations.

So far as the ordinary man is concerned, the loss of faith in traditional religious systems has left a spiritual vacuum which can be filled only by preoccupation with material improvements, or else by the never-ending struggle for some cause or other—the kind of struggle in which so often what is right and just becomes imperceptibly twisted into injustice, and the means become unworthy of the goal. For those who have seen the pitfalls there is nothing left but a resigned submission to whatever the world may impose. Yet man cannot endure a life that is entirely without values; if they are not to be found in nature he is under a compulsion to create them artificially. This is seen even in science where, as Conant has pointed out,[2] value judgments intrude themselves at every turn. When we are forced to apply these value judgments to life itself, it as disconcerting to find that while the general scheme is apparently as devoid of ultimate purpose as it is of moral imperatives, the pain and misery with which it is fraught having no discernible end to serve, it is just those unpleasant features that predominate in man's total experience. An optimistic philosophy on late nineteenth century lines is hardly conceivable today. Even the possibility of one that is pragmatically constructive becomes more remote as humanity drifts helplessly from triumph to triumph in the conquest of nature. In the grip of nuclear politics and on the verge of gaining possession of the moon, most people find it best not to ask themselves what the word progress really means.

Literature and the arts tend to reflect the same bleak mood as contemporary philosophy. It is true that after *The Waste Land*, T. S. Eliot came to terms with religion, and Aldous Huxley's brittle and erudite wit turned to syncretic mysticism, but the note that had been struck continued to echo in their work and that of others. A later school of writers tried to find a substitute for the lost religious spirit in political attitudinizing, producing a certain effervescence but scarcely anything of real depth or enduring value. For the most part, literature at present has little to offer to mitigate the unpleasant aspects of life that it presents.

Formerly, the stock lament of the poet that joy quickly turns to grief, and the Elizabethan dramatist's concern with the night side

2. *Modern Science and Modern Man* by James B. Conant

of the soul were bearable, because they contained no foreboding of a final oblivion. For the effectiveness of his soliloquy it was necessary for Hamlet to picture death as the bourn from which no traveller returns—but he had in fact just seen his father return from it. Thus there was sadness, and a great deal of sheer horror in classic tragedy, but not the chill at the heart, the twentieth-century shudder at the stark futility of life, which the nihilism of today has given us. When man felt that suffering had meaning he could endure it; his suffering then provided the great underlying fact of all the finest art and literature, the truth that gave it depth and meaning. It is in the tragic that we recognize man's being, his commitment to the total human situation and his identification with all involved in it.

"There are three kinds of suffering," the Buddha said. "They are intrinsic suffering of mind and body (*dukkha-dukkhatā*), the suffering of the aggregates (*saṅkhāra-dukkhatā*) and the suffering of transience (*viparināma-dukkhatā*)" (Dīgha Nikāya 33). The statement is comprehensive, for it goes beyond the experiential modes of suffering into suffering as a cosmic necessity. Mental and physical suffering is the pain that is known in its most obvious form, but the 'suffering of the aggregates' lies in the state of disease, unrest and instability which is inherent in the arising and passing away of the momentary phases of existence, of which we are normally unaware, but which is present all the time. The suffering of transience comes from the impermanent nature of happiness; in the inevitability of its end, happiness, contains both the potentiality and realization of pain.

Of these three aspects of suffering it is the second alone that calls for a special understanding of the Buddhist world view. The aggregates here spoken of are the five *khandhas*, or groups, which constitute a living, sentient being. They are: *rūpakkhandha*, the visible, tangible body of form, the physical aggregate; *vedanākkhandha*, the aggregate of sensations derived from the six sensory organs—eye, ear, nose, tongue, tactile organs and mind; *saññākkhandha*, the perceptions arising from these organs in contact with their objects; *saṅkhārakkhandha*, the mental properties including intellection, imagination, memory and volition; and lastly *viññāṇakkhandha*, which is the sum content of consciousness at any given moment. All of these aggregates are compounded, conditioned and impermanent;

they are in a constant state of change—that is to say, of arising and passing away—so that there is nothing in the nature of a stable, persisting entity to be found in them.

Since they are no more than a flux of conditionality they cannot contain any self-existing, immutable core of personality; the conscious being is in reality a cause-effect continuum flowing through space and time, his existence in the moment of conscious awareness a cross-section of an eternal process. The suffering of the aggregates is inherent in their mutability; the process of coming to be which never attains the fulfillment of perfect being.

The problem of identity-in-change can be understood only by viewing identity as a relationship of cause and effect. So we find in the series of transformations undergone by the protozoa, which present no clear distinction between plant and animal life, a highly complicated pattern of individuality. It can hardly be said that a protozoon at one stage of its career is the 'same' protozoon as that which existed before or that which will exist subsequently. Yet the protozoa do not arise independently; each transformation is the consequence of those that preceded it, and each is dependent also on external conditions. The closer we get to the basic structures of life the more evident this principle becomes.

In the case of human personality we find, on analysis, no mental or physical constituents beyond these five aggregates; for this reason personality is devoid of anything that can be called a self-entity. The ego is a conditioned subjective phenomenon, the psychic life a series of mental events. All that goes to make up a human being is comprehended in the 'three signs' (*ti-lakkhaṇa*) of all phenomena: impermanence (*anicca*), suffering (*dukkha*), and soullessness (*anattā*). By *anattā* (Skt: *anātman*, void of soul) is meant the absence of any permanent, unchanging essence of being.

At the same time it is these aggregates of personality, which arise by way of antecedent and co-incidental conditions, both mental and physical, that are the cause of clinging to life. In their function of sustaining and perpetually renewing the life-urge they are called grasping aggregates (*upādānakkhandha*). They are the grappling hooks with which beings fasten themselves, willingly, to suffering.

Like all other organisms, man is conditioned to respond to irritation, for the principle of irritability plays a leading role in organic evolution. It is not surprising, therefore, to find that there are forms of suffering which he enjoys, and that pleasure and pain, as forms of stimulation, overlap one another and at times become indistinguishable. Bodily excitement moves from pleasure to pain by excess; aesthetic stimulation likewise crosses the border between joy and sadness. The beauty of a sunset can disturb and trouble the mind, yet no one avoids it on that account. Masochism is regarded as abnormal, yet perfectly 'normal' people go to the theatre to have their hearts moved to pity and terror by a great tragedy. Apart from this, pleasure in its very essence is a source of pain. While it lasts it is a disturbance and an agitation; when it ceases it leaves us dissatisfied and filled with longing for its continuation or repetition. The individual's personal reactions towards the experiences he finds pleasurable also involve some degree of suffering, as do the hazards he encounters in seeking them. Those who have a strong inclination towards luxury and sensual pleasures suffer when they are denied them, and find it difficult to practice restraint in their enjoyment of them. Yet the consequences of unbridled self-indulgence are likely to be even more painful, and of longer duration, than the pains of self-restraint. And this does not apply only to the grosser physical pleasures, even the most refined intellectual or aesthetic pleasures can become an obsession, and immoderate surrender to them may take the form of a spiritual orgy, destructive in its psychological effects. From whatever point it is viewed, pleasure either involves suffering as part of its function as an irritant, or brings suffering about as its result. Considered in the ultimate sense, as an irritation, all sensation is suffering; its desirability or otherwise depends upon a purely subjective distinction.

Buddhism makes a further fourfold classification of dukkha into unmanifested, manifested, indirect and direct suffering. 'Unmanifested' suffering is that in which the suffering and its cause do not appear, as in the tribulation of mind accompanying anger, passion and lust; or where they are not visible externally, but take the form of inward physical pain. 'Manifested' suffering is that in which both the pain and its cause are visible, as in suffering under torture. 'Indirect' suffering is that which contains in itself, as do the sensual pleasures, seeds of subsequent pain, while direct suffering is the pain as immediately experienced.

In its cosmological aspect suffering has an existence independent of man's awareness, for, as we have seen, it is one of the three signs of being, the characteristics of all phenomena. Since everything in the universe is subject to arising and passing away, the three characteristics, Impermanence, Suffering and 'Essencelessness' are found in all compounded things, material and immaterial.

Matter is made up of four Great Primaries (*mahā bhūtā*), representing the categories in which it manifests. For convenience they are defined as the 'elements' of solidity, cohesion, temperature and motion. Space is sometimes added as a fifth. For philosophic purposes this is an adequate description, denoting as it does the varied transformations as well as the functions of the atomic units (*kalāpa*) of matter. These atoms and their components are in a continuous state of movement and change, a process in which energy assumes the sensible aspect of solid physical substance. That this is nothing more than an appearance is fully confirmed by modern physics, for as Bertrand Russell has pointed out, "In pursuit of something that could be treated as substantial, physicists analyzed ordinary matter into molecules, molecules into atoms, atoms into electrons and protons. But now electrons and protons themselves are dissolved into systems of radiations by Heisenberg and into systems of waves by Schroedinger. The two theories amount mathematically to much the same thing. And these are not wild metaphysical speculation; they are sober mathematical calculations accepted by the great majority of experts."

Since matter has resolved itself into energy, whether it be as radiations or waves, all phenomena are seen as a succession of events in the space-time continuum, not as static entities. To be properly understood they must be observed as processes bearing the unitary characteristic of all forms of energy, that is to say, perpetual movement and transmutation. Here again the problem of individuality obtrudes itself, for like the protozoon the atom has no real identity from one moment to another in the phases of its hectic existence. The basic structure of the universe itself is energy, something which can only be described as an unceasing restlessness and agitation.

In analyzing the five aggregates of personality the Buddha began with the gross components of the physical body and of all other matter as being made up of the four Great Primaries, enumerating and classifying them according to whether they are internal or external, existing in one's own body or in the objective world. Thus, solidity (*paṭhavī*), whether it be of one's own body or of external objects, is all of one order; it belongs to the same category of phenomena and is subject to the same laws of arising and dissolution wherever it is found. The same is true of the factors of cohesion, temperature and motion, all of which are found internally and externally. Each classification ends with the assertion: "Now, whether it be the internal element, or whether it be the external element, both are one in their nature. This, one should understand according to reality and true knowledge—that this element does not belong to me, this is not 'I', this is not my 'Self'."

Wherever it may be found, physical substance is in fact of one kind in its fundamental structure. Instead of dividing matter into three classes, solid, liquid and gaseous, Buddhist cosmic analysis defines it by group characteristics, as *lahutā* (lightness, buoyancy), *muditā* (softness, plasticity) and *kammaññatā* (activity). Since in physics there is nothing that can be called absolutely solid, gaseous or liquid, but each partakes in some degree of the nature of the others, the Buddhist classification serves its philosophic purpose by referring all to the four Great Primaries. The purpose of applying the knowledge specifically to the body, and of establishing a universal principle embracing all matter, is to disabuse the mind of any belief that the human body is a supernatural organism distinct from other material objects, and to counteract the tendency to regard the body as the 'Self' or as integral to the self.

In like manner the Buddha deals with the four immaterial or mental aggregates. Sensation, perception, volitional activities and consciousness are all causally conditioned factors. Their 'life' consists of thought-moments (*cittakkhaṇa*) which arise and pass away with inconceivable rapidity. The real term of a being's conscious existence is no longer than the duration of one of these point-moments of consciousness which are strung, as it were, on the thread of cause and effect to give the illusory sense of self-identity.

So, in the Buddha's summary, "All aggregates are transient; all aggregates are subject to suffering, all things are devoid of self-entity. Body is transient; sensation is transient; perception is transient; mental aggregates are transient and consciousness is transient. And that which is transient is (necessarily) involved in suffering; and of that which is involved in suffering and change one cannot rightly say, 'This belongs to me, this is I, this is my Self.' Therefore, whatever constitutes bodily form, or sensation, or perception, or mental aggregates or consciousness, whether it be gross or subtle, exalted or low, far or near, one should understand according to reality and true knowledge, 'This does not belong to me, this is not I, this is not my Self.'"

In its fullest sense the word *dukkha* is to be understood as including all degrees of mental and physical uneasiness, from wild dissatisfaction to despair, mild discomfort to acute agony. The living organism, being impermanent in all its parts, is subject to that form of suffering which is inherent in its restless, ever-changing nature, the suffering that is inseparable from the process of coming-to-be which never reaches the state of true being. In the mental aggregates the characteristic of restlessness takes diverse forms, such as irritability, frustration, anger, worry, conflicting desires and emotions, all distressful states which are rightly to be understood as dukkha. Seen in this light, even what we know as happiness is not free from the dukkha of agitation. 'Happiness' exists only in contrast to its opposite mode of restlessness which we call 'sorrow.' Since pleasure and pain are merely relative states, neither of which can be experienced without its opposite, Buddhism denies the possibility of a perfect, unchanging and unalloyed happiness where the conditions of conscious life prevail. The reasons for this will become more apparent when we examine the second Noble Truth, which deals with the source and origin of suffering.

Dukkha Samudaya Ariya Sacca

The Noble Truth of the Cause of Suffering

If this life were the only one through which we have to pass, if death were the end of joy and grief, alike, the existence of pain would have no special significance. The problem would be restricted to the practical means of alleviating it, so far as that might be possible. At the same time there would be no place for moral values in a life which originated fortuitously and pursued its course through a series of meaningless events to an equally meaningless end. The abstract concepts of good and evil, right and wrong could be discarded in favour of whatever artificial and arbitrary standards happen to suit the needs of the moment. In such circumstances it is conceivable that compassion itself would not rank very high in the scale of human values; for, logically the highest achievement would be personified by the individual who was most successful in avoiding suffering himself, even though he did so by inflicting it on others.

But mankind on the whole has never accepted this view. Although the conditions of nature are of a kind that outwardly at least give very little reason for assuming a moral order in the universe, man in principle has always behaved as though there were in fact some absolute values to be taken into account. He has an innate conviction of the reality of right and wrong, and even in violating the law he has acknowledged it. It is this instinctive belief in moral order that prompts us to seek a cause, conformable to our notions of justice, for the ills that afflict the world of sentient beings.

Buddhism takes for granted a system of moral law which requires a continuation of the life-process. It is a continuation by way of cause and effect, the cause being *kamma*, or volitional actions, and the effect *vipāka*, the pleasant, unpleasant or hedonically neutral experiences that follow from them. The moral equilibrium is maintained by the operation of an impersonal law which produces good results from morally wholesome thoughts, words and deeds, and bad results from those that are morally unwholesome. The succession of lives which the term 'rebirth' signifies is not the reincarnation of a soul-entity. It is an individual current of relationships in a cause-effect continuum, expressed as 'That having been, this comes to be.' Identity from one birth to another derives solely from this causal relationship, as it does in a single life-course when the child becomes the adult, the adult the octogenarian; its analogy is that of milk turning to curd, and curd to cheese. It is the purely conventional 'identity' that is found in the different phases of the protozoon and the atom.

In teaching that there is continuity after death in the form of a succession of rebirths Buddhism does not stand alone, but in agreement with many of the oldest religious traditions of East and West. The difference—an ontologically important one—lies in its treatment of the phenomenal personality, in which no single element of the five aggregates survives, but all are incessantly renewed in accordance with the universal rule that where a cause has existed a result must follow from it. The doctrine of rebirth in Buddhism is frequently criticized on two grounds: that it is inconsistent with the principle of *anattā* (soullessness), and that it is a dogma at the root of a system which claims to be undogmatic. In regard to the first objection, a proper understanding of identity by way of causal connection as it appears in biological, psychological and even purely physical processes shows that the Buddhist dynamic concept of personality is the true one, and that it does not preclude the kind of identity which we commonly accept when we speak of the 'self'.[3]

The second criticism on closer scrutiny is found to be quite unjustified. Leaving aside man's intuitive feeling that some part of his subjective awareness, of his individualized cognitive experience, if not his total personality, will survive death, and also the more important consideration that if there is indeed any principle of justice and moral order in the cosmos it can be found only in a

3. "To deny plumply that 'consciousness' exists seems so absurd on the face of it—for undeniably 'thoughts' do exist – that I fear some readers will follow me no further. Let me then immediately explain that I mean only to deny that the word stands for an entity, but to insist most emphatically that it does stand for a function." William James, *Does Consciousness Exist?*, 1904. The reader is invited to contrast this with the static concept of Descartes' "*Cogito ergo sum*."

law of moral retribution extending beyond the present life, there is a great and increasing mass of evidence to show that rebirth is a reality, and that it is possible in certain circumstances (for instance in hypnotic trance) to remember previous lives. The doctrine of rebirth is far from being an unsupported assumption. It is a truth which is accessible to us in two ways: by reason of its necessity on teleological grounds, and directly through personal knowledge or the evidence provided by others. The sole 'common sense' objection to it—that one cannot personally remember a previous existence—falls to the ground when we consider the limitations of memory and the various circumstances which may impede and inhibit it. So far as heredity and other genetic considerations affect the question, they are not at all inconsistent with rebirth as it is understood in Buddhism. On the contrary, they provide a necessary part of the process by which mental energy produces organic life out of inorganic matter, and at the same time preserves the identity of species. Much that is still obscure in biological processes, such as the actual means by which hereditary characters are transmitted through substance that has only chemical properties, requires an additional factor to make it explicable. So too does an allied group of phenomena, the type of behaviour in animals, and to some extent in human beings, which is called instinctual. The persistence of such characters, for which biology provides no adequate explanation, becomes more intelligible when it is related to the Buddhist concept of a rebirth-continuum. Life is the outcome of two orders of causality the physical and the mental, and in the Buddhist view the genetic patterns through which hereditary characters are transmitted are the physical media of the mental energy conditioned by past kamma.[4]

It was in the light of this knowledge of the continuity of existence that the Buddha looked for the origin of suffering not only in the current life but in former states of being. He discovered it in a primordial urge, the thirst (*taṇhā*) for sentient existence:

> What now is the Noble Truth of the Cause of Suffering? Truly it is that Craving which gives rise to fresh rebirth,

4. For a fuller treatment of this subject the reader is referred to *The Case for Rebirth*, Wheel Publication 12/13

and conjoined with pleasure and lust, finds gratification now here, now there. It is of three kinds: sensual craving (*kāmataṇhā*), craving for existence (*bhavataṇhā*) and craving for self-annihilation (*vibhavataṇhā*).

Sensual craving, which is generated by contact of the organs of sense with their objects, is sixfold: craving for pleasurable sights, sounds, odours, tastes, tactile sensations, and mental impressions. These are known as the fields (*āyatana*) of sense-perception. The craving for existence takes three forms, corresponding to the spheres in which life manifests; that is, craving for existence in the sensual spheres (*kāma-loka*), in the fine-material spheres (*rūpā-loka*) and in the formless spheres (*arūpā-loka*) or mental planes. The craving for self-annihilation is the group of desires that accompany the erroneous view that the aggregates of phenomenal personality constitute a soul, which is annihilated at death.[5]

In another classification craving is considered under two heads: *vaṭṭa-mūla-bhūta-purima-taṇhā*, the primordial craving which is at the root of rebirth, and *samudācārataṇhā*, craving manifested in conduct. The first is the craving which promotes and sustains the round of existences, as it appears in the formula of Dependent Origination. There, "Conditioned by ignorance (of the true nature of existence) arise the kamma-formations (*saṅkhāra*);[6] conditioned by the kamma-formations arises consciousness (in the special sense of rebirth-linking consciousness, the mental impulse which like an electric spark bridges one life-continuum to another); conditioned by consciousness arises mind and body (of the new life-sequence); conditioned by mind and body arise

5. T. W. Rhys Davids, following Spence Hardy, takes *vibhava-taṇhā* to be "the love of the present life, under the notion that existence will cease therewith, and that there is no future state," therefore, "craving for success (in this present life)."—*Buddhist Suttas*, Sacred Books of the East Vol. XI, n. In the Commentaries, however, the emphasis is laid on the desire for self-extinction which accompanies the belief that there is a self-entity which is annihilated at death.

6. *Saṅkhāra:* In the context of Dependent Origination this term is adequately rendered as 'kamma-formations', on the analogy of 'habit-formations' as denoting a pattern of mental activity. Here the emphasis is on those volitional activities (*kamma*) which produce rebirth.

the six fields of sense-perception; conditioned by the six fields of sense-perception arises contact (between organ of sense and sense object); conditioned by contact arises sensation (*vedanā*); conditioned by sensation arises craving; conditioned by craving arises grasping (confirmed and habitual craving); from grasping arises becoming (the life-impulse); from becoming arises birth once more;h and from birth come decay and death," thus closing the circle. The formula of Dependent Origination in this way summarizes the causal relations of three cycles, a past, a present and a future life, with craving as the motivating factor.

"Thus it is, Ānanda, that craving comes into being because of sensation" (Mahā Nidāna Sutta). But for the sensation to exist there must already be mind and body, and that mind and body itself must have been brought about by prior craving, so that the sequence of cause and effect extends infinitely into the past. This is precisely the idea which Dependent Origination presents; it is a system of related conditions rather than of temporal sequence, and actually stands for two modes of causality, serial and contemporaneous. The divisions of past, present and future may be placed indifferently at either of the two points where a new arising takes place; that is, at 'mind and body' or at 'birth'. But the points at which it can be brought to an end are, as we shall see later, the two dominant psychological factors, 'craving' and 'ignorance', which are contemporaneous and mutually supporting.

The question of a first cause does not enter into the Buddhist view of the cycles of becoming (*Saṃsāra*), nor of the universe. When the process of incessant arising and passing away is seen as a complex of interrelated conditions, any theory of a primal cause becomes irrelevant. In the logic of causality there can be no absolute beginning, for each cause is seen to be the effect of a preceding cause. So a Creator God must himself have had a creator; if he had not, the argument for his existence on the basis of causality collapses. The idea that there must have been a beginning in the ultimate sense rests upon a defect in human understanding, as certain modern philosophers have pointed out. We are brought to the position stated in the *Visuddhimagga*, that:

No God nor Brahmā here is found,
Creator of Saṃsāra's round;

Empty phenomena flow on
Subject to cause and condition.

From another standpoint it can be said that the act of creation is taking place from moment to moment, as in the Bergsonian system of creative evolution. The prime mover is the craving impulse, which may be regarded as the basic energy of the universe.

This does not mean that the universe in its present form had no beginning. It came into existence in accordance with natural law (*niyāma*), but it did not originate out of nothing. It is not the first or only system of its kind, but is one of an infinite cyclic series, of which no beginning can be found. As one cosmic system comes to an end another one comes into being.

Science offers several tentative theories as to how the present universe began, the two most widely accepted being based on the expanding universe hypothesis and the steady state cosmology respectively. Its 'beginning' can be placed with a fair amount of certainty at about 5,000 million years ago. But whether it started with a tremendous cosmic explosion or in some other way, Buddhist cosmic analysis holds that the matter, or energy, of which it is formed, derives from that of a previous universe, and that it was set in motion by the kamma of the beings belonging to that former system. The evolution (*samvaṭṭa*) and devolution (*vivaṭṭa*) of world systems follow a course parallel to the process which governs sentient life. When a cosmic system comes to an end, the matter of which it was composed disintegrates and its atomic units become dispersed or compressed in space in a uniform distribution. For aeons it lies dormant, but in course of time the suspended energy becomes active once more, and the physical laws of attraction and repulsion come into play. Clots of matter begin to form, and from them the island universes emerge and take shape. After a further lapse of time, organic evolution begins, and runs its course to the end of the cycle, when the cosmic structure again disintegrates and the entire process is repeated. In this fashion evolution and devolution follow one another in a ceaseless round, all the time bound up with the kamma, or volitional energy, generated by living beings. And since all willed action is motivated by desire it is in literal fact the force of craving that perpetually renews and sustains the process.

Concerning the genesis of craving, the *Abhidhammatthasaṅgaha* VIII.I says:

> Through ignorance a being fails to understand the impermanent and 'substanceless' nature of existence as it truly is. He enjoys the things of the world, taking them to be real and lasting, and so creates a craving for them. On account of his cravings he seeks to obtain one and avoid the other. This leads to the continuity of his life-process, a chain of struggle for living. His craving and grasping do not end with the destruction of the physical body, but keep the struggle on in another birth.
>
> His good and bad activities (*saṅkhāra*) of one life determine the type of his birth, his mental disposition and all his resultant consciousness in the subsequent one. This gives rise to the mental and physical aggregates in the new life according to its own nature. Depending on the mental and physical aggregates he acquires the six fields of sense-cognition. Depending on the six fields of sense-cognition he gets contact with the object of sense. The contact produces sensation; the sensation gives rise to craving, and craving to grasping. Grasping continues the life-processes. It does not cease with the death of the being, but flows on in the next birth. Thus he starts a new life again; he becomes old and dies, experiencing all kinds of grief, lamentation, suffering, anxiety and despair. Perpetually he moves on and on in the round of birth and death so long as he is in the bondage of ignorance.

Man's failure to comprehend the universe is due to the primal nescience (*avijjā*) which to a greater or lesser degree governs all conceptual thinking. Since *avijjā* is linked with *taṇhā* it deepens as the mental defilements caused by craving increase, lessening as they are reduced. It is an invariable rule in the Buddhist system of causal relations that two or more factors are required to produce a given result. As we have seen, in the genesis of a living organism the mental energy produced in a past life combines with the physical processes of biology to form a sentient being. Similarly, in the genesis of world systems the total thought-energy of beings from the past activates the physical substance of the universe to bring about a new cycle of evolution. All these processes, therefore, are partly mechanistic ones, to the extent to which they depend upon purely physical laws, and partly are subject to variability through their dependence on mental causes and the intervention of will. To will is to desire, and so desire is really the chief determining factor; if it were not present at all the automatic processes of nature would take control and the universe would run its course to the end as a lifeless mechanism.

The constant pattern of interdependence is shown in the arrangement of the factors in Dependent Origination, where those that are conditioned by past causes alternate with others that are subject to modification by the act of willing. Thus, in the section relating to past causes, Ignorance gives rise to volitional thought and action (*saṅkhāra*), the Ignorance factor being a continuing influence on the thought and action. Then, at the time of death a thought-moment arises which constitutes the rebirth-linking consciousness, its nature being determined by the volitional thought and action which preceded it. So past kamma shapes future tendencies, the rebirth-linking moment of consciousness carrying these tendencies into a new life just as the germinal seed carries in its chemistry the pattern of the future plant—a pattern that may, however, be altered in some respects by subsequent events. The new mind and body thus brought into being is naturally equipped with the sensory apparatus and the fields of sensory perception appropriate to it. From these come its contacts with the external world and the sensations accompanying them. So far, the connections have represented two belonging to the order of past causality, Ignorance and the volitional mental formations, and five which are their resultants, from rebirth-linking consciousness to sensations. These last five, therefore, are conditioned by the kamma of the past.

But at this point the element of free will comes into play, for while sensations are predetermined as to their nature, the mental responses to them are not. Although ordinarily the response to a pleasant object is desire, which may prompt some action, if the moral sense tells us that the action is a bad one, the will can prevent it. Even the desire itself can be reduced, suppressed and controlled by an act of will or by diverting attention to something else. Consequently, the dependent connections which follow from this point, that is, craving, grasping and becoming are not predetermined. They represent the active side of the picture, in which man shapes his individual destiny. It is necessary to stress this point because it is often mistakenly believed that the doctrine of kamma is fatalism. Nothing could be further from the truth; Buddhism emphasizes above everything else the moral responsibility of the individual and the power that is his to create his own destiny. So in the last two connections, birth (rebirth) and decay and death, we find summarized the future resultants of the causes generated in the craving-grasping-becoming series.

Considered from the standpoint of temporal sequence, Dependent Origination is thus divided into three sections, relating to past, current and future life. These three have two major divisions: the active order of becoming (*kammavaṭṭa*), in which causes are generated, and the passive order (*vipākavaṭṭa*), which stands for the results of those causes. Ignorance and volitional mental formations belong to the active order, whilst birth and decay and death belong to the order of passive resultants. The middle section, that which deals with the current life, includes both the passive and the active orders. The five links from consciousness to sensation are passive resultants; but the remaining three, craving, grasping and becoming, represent the active, and creative process.

Again, at the beginning, ignorance and volitional mental formations are a summary of the active and causal process in the past; at the end, decay and death summarize the passive resultant series as it follows in the future. Thus the circle closes on itself in perpetual, self-sustaining operation, a cause-effect complex, the links of which can be considered either as a temporal sequence or as existing concurrently in the form of mutually supporting factors.

Understood correctly, the process of Dependent Origination does not postulate either absolute causal determinism nor absolute freedom of will. It describes an interplay of conditions which is ultimately subject to the individual's freedom of choice between good and bad courses of action. It is by this choice—the anguish of decision, which is itself a form of dukkha that life imposes on all morally responsible beings—that each individual determines for himself and by himself the nature of his rebirth. Whether it shall be in a state above the human condition or in one below it, or, if it is a human rebirth, whether it shall be a happy or an unhappy one, depends entirely on the actions—of body, speech and mind—

that are being performed here and now. It depends, in short, on the degree to which craving is brought under control. And, as we shall presently see, Buddhism offers a means whereby craving can be entirely eradicated, and the process of Dependent Origination brought to an end for good.[7]

But before moving on to the third stage of the inquiry, which is concerned with the possibility of escape from the round of rebirths, another function of craving is worthy of notice: that is, the part it plays in organic evolution.

We have already noted that apart from the Buddhist interpretation, life appears to be devoid of ethical values and purpose. Yet in the evolving pattern of organic structures it seems to display a strong directional trend. From extremely simple unicellular organisms nature has evolved highly complex forms, equipped with delicate sensory apparatus and a brain capable of rational thought. But this has been accomplished only over a long period of trial and error involving many failures, and by employing methods that are both wasteful and productive of the most extreme suffering, such as would have been eliminated in a better designed plan. So on a general survey the system seems to be in a certain sense directed, yet at the same time blundering and inept. There is sufficient order to suggest a creator; but an omnipotent and benign Intelligence could certainly have accomplished the work in better style.

Science fights shy of teleological theories and concentrates attention on the means by which natural effects are produced; and so we have hypotheses such as that of natural selection, backed up by the observed facts of genetics, biochemistry and kindred sciences, which go some way towards explaining the *modus operandi* of evolution but do not offer any suggestion as to the 'why' of the process. The moving force behind or within it remains a mystery, and the paradox of a plan, apparently well-conceived as to its biological results but very badly executed, and without any purpose except that of evolution for evolution's sake, has come to be considered so insoluble as to discourage further speculation.

7. For a proper understanding of this important subject the reader is recommended to study *Wheel Publication* No. 15, *Dependent Origination* by the Ven. Piyadassi Thera.

An entirely fresh light is thrown on the problem, however, by recent studies that have been made of the electrical activity in the brain, as registered by the electroencephalogram. These have established definitely that the neural impulses and the processes of cognition are associated with electrical impulses.

Now, if the brain functions by means of electrical energy—or, what is equally likely, by some other form of energy that acts in the same way as electricity—and is able to move the mechanism of the electroencephalogram solely by impulses generated in the brain cells, we have strong reason for supposing that mental activity is capable of spreading from its source in much the same way as do radio waves. It is in fact a radiating energy comparable to others that are perceptible to us, such as light and sound, and others—imperceptible, such as cosmic radiations. This would at once explain such diverse phenomena as hypnotism, telepathy and various forms of extrasensory perception. But the possibilities it opens up become still wider when we apply the hypothesis to organic evolution, and clearer still when we connect it with the Buddhist concept of craving as an actual force, generated by the mind and capable of operating on and through the physical substance of the universe.[8]

The psychology of behaviourism holds that desire, manifesting as the 'will-to-live,' is the basic motivating urge in all forms of life that have analyzable mental reactions. The desire may be unconscious, revealing itself in instinctive patterns of behaviour, or it may be fully present to the conscious mind. When it lies beneath the surface of consciousness it functions as the Freudian 'id' and the 'libido' of Jung; that is, as the energy resident in all instincts. It may also be called the primordial life-urge; but whatever name may be given to it, in reality it is the force of craving—precisely that *taṇhā*, which the Buddha declared to be the root cause of rebirth.

8. Over fifty years ago the late U Shwe Zan Aung wrote: "To recognize that thought is a radiation is, I submit, a great thing in itself. Who can say that this may not one day lead some discoverers to devise an instrument exploiting some substance, yet unknown, which is sensitive to thought, and so to measure our thought 'waves' and their duration?" (*Compendium of Philosophy*, p. 284.)

Every volitional act is motivated by some kind of desire; consequently, thought itself is practically inseparable from desire in the mind still dominated by ignorance. And it is the thought-impulse that radiates outwards in the last moment of consciousness which gives rise to another psycho-physical organism, thus renewing the sequence of cause and effect in a fresh life-continuum. Throughout the creative process the urge that maintains this perpetual renewal of energy is the desire to experience conscious life, 'seeking, now here, now there,' for satisfaction.

In the first stages of evolution the individualized yet impersonal currents of craving, generated in the past, operate upon the physical substance of the universe and out of inorganic matter give birth to the first single-cell protozoa. From there the life energy proceeds to build up and elaborate, by the familiar trial and error methods we have noted, more and more complex and specialized forms, the craving-impulse being transmitted through the currents of 'rebirth' and the laws of genetics by parallel and complementary processes. Wherever the necessary chemical constituents of life exist together with the suitable conditions, life in some form manifests itself; and this principle obtains, as Buddhism has always taught, throughout the innumerable worlds that exist simultaneously in the universe.

So out of material from various sources, we are able to construct a picture that is teleologically satisfying and fully in conformity with the known facts. To summarize: it was under the domination of the craving-urge that the rudimentary forms of life evolved into the complex structures of the higher animals and man. More and better sensory organs were needed to satisfy the unconscious craving for sense-experience, and so the vital urge worked through the processes of biological evolution to produce them. Life is not the work of a conscious creator, with his object fully in view; it is the result of a blind, groping force, transmitted from one living being to another in the course of rebirth. Hence the many 'mistakes' thrown aside in the course of evolution—animals, which, through over-specialization or some other cause, became unfitted to their environment and consequently died out.

Science as yet has no valid theory to account for the purposive factor in evolution, nor for the persistence of instinctive behaviour patterns in those birds and animals which perform quite complicated operations such as nest-building, seasonal migrations and so forth, without the necessity of learning. Neither can it decide the much-disputed question of whether acquired characters are genetically transmitted, many geneticists feeling compelled to deny it, against the evidence of observation, solely on the ground that no biological mechanism can be found answering to the requirements of such transmission. Here again Buddhist doctrine comes to the rescue, for it shows how both instinctive behaviour and acquired characters can be transmitted by the re-arising again and again of the same current of identity—that is, 're-birth'—within the same species, the same ethnic or cultural group and even the same family. For whatever tendencies are acquired and cultivated in one life, whether of animal or human being, will make themselves apparent in subsequent lives, until some fresh impulse of kamma diverts the life-current into a new channel.

Buddhism teaches that the distinction between human and animal life is not one of kind, but of quality. Man is not a distinct and special creation; he merely represents the highest peak to which organic life has reached on this planet. Man alone has the power of moral choice, whilst animals are merely suffering passively the results of past activities dominated by lust, ill-will and delusion. In other words, they are the products of former bad kamma. Their individual life-currents remain on a low level until the particular mental tendencies that produced them have run their destined course. When the results of the bad kamma are exhausted some residual good kamma from a former human life, of which all beings have a latent unexpended potential (*katattā-kamma*), comes into play and the life-current emerges on a higher level once more. This process can be understood only by discarding the idea of an individual self-entity, call it soul or what one may, and thinking instead in terms of the current of 'becoming' which Buddhism insists is all that constitutes the rebirth-continuum. By thus bridging the gulf that appears to exist between the human and animal worlds, the Buddhist doctrine of rebirth and kamma gives to life that organic unity which scientific thought demands. At the same time it shows that the universe, despite its seeming purposelessness, is in reality the manifestation of moral and spiritual law.

Thirty-six streams of craving are recognized in Buddhist psychology; eighteen of them internal (*ajjhatta*), depending upon subjective concepts, and eighteen external (*bāhira*), associated with subject-object relationships.[9] But every type and degree of craving contributes to the sum total of the grasping which fastens living beings to the wheel of rebirth. This is especially true of the lower forms of craving connected with the unwholesome mental concomitants: lust, ill-will and delusion. So we find in the Aṅguttara Nikāya (III 33): 'Wheresoever beings spring into existence, there their deeds will ripen; and wherever their deeds ripen there they will gather the fruits of those deeds, be it in this life, or be it in the next life, or be it in any future life.'

And in the Saṃyutta Nikāya comes the solemn affirmation:

> There will come a time when the mighty ocean will dry up, vanish and be no more. There will come a time when the mighty earth will be consumed by fire, perish and be no more. But yet there will be no end to the suffering of beings who, fettered by ignorance and ensnared by craving, are hurrying and hastening through this round of rebirths.

Dukkha Nirodha Ariya Sacca

The Noble Truth of the Cessation of Suffering

The Buddha's Enlightenment was attained in three stages. In the first watch of the night he acquired the knowledge of previous states of existence, the memory of which arose as the fruit of intense mental absorption (*jhāna*). In the second watch he obtained the knowledge of the manner in which beings pass from one state of existence to another in accordance with their deeds. At this point he had discerned the truths of suffering and of moral causality as it operates through kamma. At the conclusion of the last watch he penetrated to the knowledge of the underlying causes of existence, the process of Dependent Origination. He then understood both the origin of conditioned existence, with its root in craving and ignorance, and the means by which the process could be brought to an end.

And in the last watch of the night, out of compassion for living beings, by fixing his mind on Dependent Origination and meditating on it both in order of becoming and in order of cessation, at sunrise he obtained supreme Enlightenment. And then he uttered these words of triumph, such words as countless myriads of Buddhas have spoken in the past:

> Vainly have I wandered through many births, seeking the builder of this house. Painful indeed is repeated birth. Now, O Builder of the house, you are seen! Never again shall you build. All your rafters are shattered, the ridgepole cast down. My mind has attained the unconditioned; the cravings are extinguished.
>
> (Dhp 153–54)

The house is the body, the builder is craving, passions are the rafters and the ridgepole is ignorance.

> For, through the complete fading away and extinction of craving (*taṇhā*), clinging to existence (*upādana*) is extinguished;

through the cessation of clinging the process of becoming (*bhava*) is extinguished; through the extinction of becoming, rebirth (*jāti*) is extinguished, and through the extinction of rebirth, decay and death, grief, lamentation, suffering, sorrow and despair are extinguished. Thus comes about the extinction of this entire mass of suffering.

'And thereby comes the cessation and overcoming of bodily form, of sensation, perception, mental formations and consciousness; this is the cessation of suffering, the end of disease, the overcoming of decay and death.'

(SN 12:1)

The cessation of suffering is Nibbāna, in Sanskrit Nirvāna, a word formed from the negative prefix *nir* added to the root *vā*, which has the original meaning 'to blow.' In its Buddhist sense Nibbāna means the cessation of the process of becoming, as when a fire goes out from lack of fuel or because of ceasing to blow on it. The fire is the threefold conflagration of lust, ill-will and delusion; when it ceases to burn because the fuel is withheld, the life-affirming impulses come to an end and there is no more rebirth. As experienced by the Arahat during the remainder of his natural life term it is *saupādisesa-nibbāna*—the state of Nibbāna in which the mental and physical aggregates still exist, but are no longer associated with clinging. It is absolute peace, tranquility and fulfillment:

No anguish is there for him who has ended his journey and is freed from all grief, who is emancipated in every way and has destroyed all attachments. There are no more wanderings (in saṃsāra) for such a one, who like the earth, has no resentment, is firm in character like a city gatepost and as pure as a deep pool free from mud ... Calm is the mind, calm the speech and calm are the actions of him who, rightly understanding, is wholly liberated and at peace.

(Dhammapada, Arahatta-vagga)

When the Arahat reaches the end of his life, the final cessation of his life-process (*samuccheda-maraṇa*), he attains *anupadisesa-nibbāna*; that is, the absolutely unconditioned Nibbāna in which none of the factors of individualized personality remain. It is not the annihilation of a being, because in the true sense no being has ever existed; there has been only a process. Nibbāna is the cessation of the process, the extinction of the aggregates of clinging that formerly gave rise to the phenomenal life-continuum. It is the only state in which suffering cannot find a foothold.

In the Dhammacakkappavattana Sutta the Buddha declares:

> This, Bhikkhus, is the noble truth of the cessation of ill: the complete cessation, giving up, abandonment of that craving, complete release from that craving and complete detachment from it.[10]

Here, in the basic statement of Nibbāna from the Buddha's first Discourse, we have the psychological state presented in terms that are ethically meaningful; they relate to an attitude towards the world and towards the contents of sensory perception. But what of the *nibbānadhātu*—that is to say, Nibbāna considered in its own nature?

In that, its ultimate aspect, it is defined as *asaṅkhata-dhātu*, the Unconditioned, because it is not subject to change or conditionality; it is unitary, in the sense that it is not compounded, as are all phenomenal things. But to give it a precise definition in positive terms is not possible. All the terms of reference we use in thought and communication are founded upon things and ideas belonging to the realm of conditionality, so that we have no means of formulating an idea that is not related, by comparison or contrast, to some other idea. The whole content of our experience is a complex of relationships. Thought swings continually between the opposites—light and dark, heat and cold, good and bad. All these are relative values representing oppositions or degrees of contrast, none of which has any real meaning apart from that relatedness. Since nothing in the world of sense-experience has any character except in relation to something else, the only way to regard the sensible world is as a sphere of merely relative reality. It is certainly real on one particular level of awareness, the one on which consciousness normally functions (although, it must be noted, its nature as to details is not altogether the same for any two

10. Soma Thera's translation from *The Buddha's First Dis-course*, Bodhi Leaves No. B. I.

individuals), but on other possible levels of consciousness it must of necessity be quite unreal perhaps even non-existent. The physicist sees the universe in terms of electronic forces, the mathematician reduces it to mathematical formulae; and while both have to deal with the world as though it really is what it appears to the ordinary man, their picture of it on the level of their work is something quite different. They have to live simultaneously in a world of the senses, taking it to be just as their sensory faculties report it to be, and in another world of the intellect, in which they know that the sensory picture is not a true one. The information we receive has a kind of validity, but in the ultimate sense the picture formed from it is a product of sensory legerdemain. The 'solid' objects we see and feel consist more of space than of matter. This fact is demonstrated by the structure of the smallest atom known, that of hydrogen. In the hydrogen atom the distance of the electronic orbit from the nucleus is, relative to its size, twice the distance of the earth from the sun a matter of 96,000,000 miles. On comparison, 'solid' matter contains more space than our solar system. What we cognize through the senses, therefore is not the 'thing as it is' but a relative aspect of it—relative, that is, to our own particular mode of consciousness. To say that the physical world as it appears to us is unreal is false, because it exists as a fact in our consciousness, but to say that it is real, as an external and objective reality, is even further from the truth.

This being so, it is clear that any thinking about Nibbāna must be done without concepts, if such thinking were possible. The fact that it is not possible has given rise to some unfortunate misunderstanding. Because he consistently refused to give any positive definition of Nibbāna, and also declined to commit himself on such points as whether the world is eternal or not eternal, and whether the Arahat continued to exist in Nibbāna or not, the Buddha has been called an agnostic. His reply to such questions was that they were wrongly put. They are in fact based on misconceptions regarding the reality or non-reality of the objects discussed and the terms of reference used in respect of them. Any reply given in positive or negative form would be about equally misleading. If this life were 'being' in the true sense, Nibbāna would be non-being—annihilation. But that is not the case. On the other hand, if this life were utterly unreal it would amount to non-being, in which case Nibbāna would be absolute Being. If anything, this comes somewhat nearer the truth; yet it is not quite true. This life is not 'non-being,' for, the experience of suffering is real; and Nibbāna cannot be called Being because it is not characterized by any of the features which we associate with 'being', such as the awareness of individual identity. It is devoid of selfhood. The other questions are open to similar objections; they are inadmissible because they refer to states and predicates that have no real validity. The Buddha refused to answer them not because he did not know, but because he did not wish to falsify. One important point, however, is very definitely maintained: there is no place in the system for a Creator-god. The Buddha expressly condemned the idea of an over-ruling power, as leading to fatalism and inaction.

The questions that are called 'undetermined' (*avyākata*,) as well as that concerning the 'undeclared' (*anakkhāta*) nature of Nibbāna, are placed in their correct perspective by the Buddhist recognition of two kinds of truth; that is to say, conceptual or relative truth (*sammuti-sacca*) and absolute truths (*paramattha-sacca*). Conceptual truth embraces the sphere of relativity, its validity being conditional upon accepted modes of relationship, and also to a great extent on the laws of semantics. Thus when the Buddha said: (*attāhi attano nātho*) "Self is the lord of self" (Dhp 160), he was using the word "self" (*attā*) in its indispensable semantic role, as a word without which no thought of phenomenal personality can be expressed. In somewhat similar fashion we are constrained to say "It is raining," although we should find it difficult to define whether by 'it' we mean a cloud, the sky, or the sum of meteorological conditions. The personality, since it is a compound of ever-changing aggregates, a current of transition, has no noumenal existence. In the ultimate (*paramattha-sacca*) view, it is descriptively a current of events in the space-time continuum; while beyond the realm of description it does not exist in any sense. It is a merely conventional reality. It is necessary to reiterate this point because upon it hangs not only the Buddhist view of life but the concept of the ultimate goal.

It follows that a question framed in terms of relative reality cannot be answered in the same terms to give an answer that embodies absolute truth. In the ultimate sense, *paramattha-*

sacca cannot be expressed at all; even the analytical descriptions of phenomena are only approximations to it, arrived at by eliminating the cruder misconceptions belonging to relative truth. It is that kind of 'descriptive' *paramattha-sacca* which is contained in the Buddhist ethico-psychological system, the Abhidhamma, where states of mind are dealt with, unattached to any concept of a persisting entity, in a manner that foreshadowed the trends of present-day dynamic psychology. There we find thought without a 'thinker' and action without an 'actor', both thought and action being no more than aspects of the life-flux of consciousness, just as they are in the philosophy of Henri Bergson.

Nibbāna cannot be described; it can only be realized. And in its realization the problems connected with it, and with the nature of being in general, are not so much answered, as found to have been really non-existent all along. They are unreal constructions, born of the mistaken belief that ultimate truth can be understood through conceptual thinking bound to the realm, and the terms, of sense-data. It is for this reason that the brave attempts of philosophers, profound and intricate though they may be, have never succeeded in giving a final and completely satisfying account of reality.

Notwithstanding the essentially incommunicable nature of the nibbānic experience, however, there are a great number of descriptive words applied to it in the Pāli texts—words that have easily-understood value meanings and which convey the ideal of release from saṃsāric conditions in non-philosophical language charged with the poetry of aspiration. Nibbāna, besides being the Deathless is the Further Shore (*para*), the Ageless (*ajara*), the Happy (*siva*), the Permanent (*dhuva*) and so on. But finally and always it is *anakkhāta*, the Undeclared, and *asaṅkhata*, the Unconditioned. Seeking for the cause of cause we find only effect. The final Nibbāna is the point at which cause and effect become identical, and by cancelling one another out, annihilate space, time and all the categories of thought.

> O Bhikkhus, of all the states, compounded or uncompounded, Liberation is the best—namely, the expulsion of pride, the relief of thirst, the uprooting of attachment, the cutting off of the round of birth and death, the extinction of craving, emancipation, cessation, the going out of worldly desire. (A II 34.)

There is no lack of positive affirmation as to the reality of Nibbāna. It is found wherever the Buddha contrasts the timeless and unchanging *asaṅkhata-dhātu* with the world of birth, decay and death, as he does in these words from the Udāna:

> O Bhikkhus, there is an Unborn, Unmade, Unoriginated, Unformed. Were there not such a state, Unborn, Unmade, Unoriginated, Unformed, there would be no escape from that which is born, made, originated, formed. But since, O Bhikkhus, there is indeed this state of the Unborn, Unmade, Unoriginated and Unformed, there is truly an escape from the born, made, originated, and formed.

It is in such assurances as this that the reality underlying the third of the Four Noble Truths—the cessation of suffering as a positive goal—is brought most vividly before the mind.

Dukkha Nirodha Gāmini Patipadā Ariya Sacca

The Noble Truth of the Way to the Cessation of Suffering

> And what, O Bhikkhus, is the Noble Truth of the way that leads to the cessation of suffering? It is the Noble Eightfold Path, namely, Right Understanding, Right Intention, Right Speech, Right Action, Right Livelihood, Right Effort, Right Mindfulness and Right Concentration.

The fourth Noble Truth outlines the practical means by which Nibbāna is to be realized; but before announcing it the Buddha cleared away certain misconceptions which were current at the time and which had proved a serious hindrance to the quest for truth. In the first discourse after his Enlightenment, that delivered to the five disciples who had deserted him when he abandoned the path of self-mortification, he explained that there are two extreme courses to be avoided: on the one hand, that of sensual indulgence, which is "base, low, vulgar, impure and unprofitable," and on the other, the practice of extreme physical asceticism, which is "painful, impure, vain and unprofitable." In contrast to these stands "The Middle Path, which the Enlightened One has discovered; the Path which enables one to see and to know, which leads to peace, to discernment, to full knowledge, to Nibbāna. Free from pain and torture is this Path, free from lamentation and anguish; it is the perfect path" (SN 56).

From the standpoint of modern psychology the Buddha's condemnation of extreme ascetic practices goes deeper than appears in the actual words he used. In certain forms of yogic asceticism still practised today there is an element of pathological self-hatred, perhaps also a masochistic pleasure in the experience of pain. Whatever the motive may be, such practices result in an inordinate preoccupation with the body, which instead of releasing the mind only fastens it more securely to its physical base. Around these manifestations of inverted sensuality there tend to gather constellations of obstructive ideas, such as that of a soul or spirit-entity distinct from the body and warring against it, the belief that the flesh is the enemy of the spirit and therefore a fit object of hatred, for which the spirit must be continually devising fresh tortures to bring it into subjection. Much the same attitude is found in the flagellations, the hair shirts, the prolonged fastings and the courting of martyrdom in early Christian asceticism. The body was the ever-present enemy; but an enemy is someone important, especially when one cannot get away from him. By being so regarded the body took on an independent life, and that a malignant one. Very often it hit back, with unpleasant psychological consequences.

But Buddhism eschews violence, to oneself as much as to another. The body must be brought under control, certainly, but by different methods. It is not itself the seat of the passions, but only the vehicle for them. It is in the mind that the citadel of craving must be stormed, not in that poor ox, the body, which only obeys its driver.

The Noble Eightfold Path, therefore, is a way of life that begins with the mind and ends with the mind transcended. Its first requirement is Right Understanding, which means an intellectual grasp of the nature of existence. "What now is Right Understanding? Truly, it is to understand suffering, the cause of suffering, the extinction of suffering and the Way to its extinction" (DN 22). Elsewhere it is explained that it also means the understanding of the law of moral causality, the roots of meritorious and demeritorious action. In the Saṃyutta Nikāya it is also said that when one understands that body, sensation, perception, the mental aggregates and consciousness are all impermanent (and hence subject to suffering and devoid of selfhood), in that case also one possesses Right Understanding.

"What now is Right Intention? Truly it is intention that is free from greed and lust, free from ill-will, free from cruelty." It is of two kinds: Right Intention concerned with the things of this world, which expresses itself in good actions bringing good worldly results; and Right Intention directed towards the higher path of purification, which has Nibbāna as its fruit.

"And what now is Right Speech? Truly it is to avoid

lying, and adhere to the truth; to abstain from tale-bearing and to promote harmony instead of dissension; to abstain from harsh language and cultivate gentle, courteous speech; and to avoid vain, irresponsible and foolish talk, speaking always in reasoned terms on subjects of value, such as the Dhamma of the Enlightened One."

"And what now is Right Action? Truly it is to avoid the taking of life, to avoid theft and misappropriation, to avoid sexual intercourse with women under the protection of father, mother, brother, sister or relatives, married women, women under the ban of the king, engaged women and women who are the temporary wives of others." "Now, avoidance of killing, of theft and sexual intercourse with the prohibited classes of women is called mundane Right Action; it results in good worldly results (in this life or another). But the turning away from these things, the complete rejection of them with a pure mind intent upon the Path to deliverance—that is called transcendental Right Action and has its results in the paths and the fruits of purification."

"And what now is Right Livelihood? Truly it is to reject wrong means of livelihood and to live by right means." Here, wrong livelihood means gaining a living by slaughter or any other way detrimental to the welfare of sentient beings.

"And what now is Right Effort? Truly it is the Four Great Efforts (*sammappadhāna*): the effort to avoid, the effort to overcome, the effort to develop and the effort to maintain." The first is the effort to avoid the arising of evil, demeritorious states that have not yet arisen; that is to say, the arising of attachment on the presentation of sense-objects to the consciousness, from which greed and sorrow result. The second is the effort to overcome evil and demeritorious states that have already arisen through such causes. The third is the effort to develop good and beneficial states of mind conducive to enlightenment. The fourth is the effort to maintain these states when they have arisen, by perseverance, energy and endeavour.

"And what now is Right Mindfulness? Truly it is the contemplation of the body, of sensations, of the mind and of mind-objects." There, the disciple dwells in contemplation of the body, of sensation, of mind and mind-objects, 'ardent, clearly conscious and attentive, putting away worldly greed and grief.' This refers to the four stations of mindfulness which is described as "the only way that leads to the attainment of purity, to the overcoming of sorrow and lamentation, to the end of pain and grief, to the entering upon the right path and the realization of Nibbāna." (Mahā Satipaṭṭhāna Sutta).

"And what now is Right Concentration? Truly it is the absorption of the mind, the fixing of the mind upon a single object; this is Right Concentration." The objects of concentration are the Four Stations of Mindfulness, and its prerequisites are the Four Great Efforts. "The practising, developing and cultivating of these things constitute the development of Concentration."

Each of the eight sections of the Path has a very precise meaning, a meaning that is related logically to the Buddhist philosophical and psychological system as a whole. Thus, Right View is something more definite than simply "having good thoughts." It stands for an intelligent grasp of the realities of life, in outline if not in detail. At the other end of the Path we come to Right Concentration, which signifies the transcendental state of consciousness, in which the truths that were formerly apprehended only by the intellect, and imperfectly, become the object of direct intuitional experience. It is only when this is attained that Right View itself is perfected. The eight sections of the Path are not to be taken seriatim or progressively, but are to be cultivated together, for the perfection of one can come only through the simultaneous development of each. Just as in the case of the links comprising the formula of Dependent Origination, the members of the Eightfold Path do not stand in a solely temporal cause-effect relationship to one another; they are to be considered as mutually-supporting factors also. Right Concentration develops and lifts on to a higher plane the knowledge that started as Right Understanding, and so the end is adumbrated in the beginning.

The path is conventionally divided into three parts: *Sīla* (Morality), *Samādhi* (Concentration) and *Paññā* (Wisdom). Right Speech, Action and Livelihood belong to *Sīla*. Right Effort, Mindfulness and Concentration to *Samādhi*, and Right Understanding and Intention to *Paññā*. A detailed discussion of Buddhist ethics is not possible in the compass of this work; it is sufficient to note that morality in Buddhism springs directly from the central concept of its philosophical system, the ultimate non-reality of self. The 'bad' or unwholesome deed is one that is self-centred and self-regarding, and so governed by greed or lust, animosity and delusion. The 'good' and meritorious is that which is selfless and inspired by benevolence and insight. Buddhist morality is not an arbitrary code of behaviour, tenuously attached to a theological system of doubtful worth, and subject to the exigencies of time and circumstance; it is rooted in principles that are universal and undeviating because they belong not to the changing world of events but to the inner world of psychological motive, which is a constant of human nature.

Where do craving and attachment come to an end? The Buddha's reply was that they come to an end where they arise—in the contact between the organs of sense and their respective objects, the things seen, heard, smelt, tasted, touched and conceived in the mind. When sensations are observed as bare experience, as empty phenomena having no relation to an experiencing 'self' and without awakening the discriminative responses, desire for them is cut off at its source. A process of dissociation takes place. So, in 'contemplation of the body' bare attention is directed to the body, considering it impersonally as a compound of physical elements unattractive in themselves as for instance, a hair in a dish of food. By analyzing its constituents and dispassionately noting their repulsive aspects, attachment to the body is weakened and sooner or later, according to the degree of concentration achieved, it is eliminated. The body, instead of being viewed as an inferior and inimical 'self' is in this way seen to be precisely what it is: matter in momentary process of decay and corruption, the product of physical laws and past kamma.

The subjects of meditation, or more properly mental cultivation (*bhāvanā*), are of various kinds suitable for different temperaments, but they all have one object, the realization of the voidness of phenomena, the essential voidness of the observer and the thing observed, which can only be arrived at by intense mental absorption. Now, this voidness (*suññatā*) becomes fully comprehended when the jhānas, or states of absorption, have themselves been transcended:

"No longer giving attention to that (jhānic) consciousness he should now advert repeatedly in this way: 'There is not,' or 'Void, void,' or 'Secluded, secluded,' and so give his attention to it, contemplate it and strike at it with thought and with applied thought." Thus, "The bhikkhu who is devoted to the defining of the four great primaries immerses himself in voidness and eliminates the perception of living beings. Since he does not entertain false notions concerning (different kinds of beings), because he has abolished the perception of such beings, he conquers fear and dread, delight and aversion; he is not exhilarated by agreeable things nor depressed by disagreeable ones; and as one having great understanding he either attains the deathless or secures for himself a happy rebirth."

(Vism X. 33, Vism XI. 117.)

Between the state of delusion bondage and suffering and that of complete release lie the paths and fruits of attainment, marked by the progressive elimination of ten fetters. They are: 1. the delusion of selfhood, 2. doubt, 3. belief in the efficacy of ritual observances for deliverance, 4. sensual craving, 5. ill-will, 6. craving for form-existence, 7. craving for formless existence, 8. conceit, 9. restlessness, 10. ignorance. One who has destroyed the first three is known as a Stream-winner; he has entered the current of emancipation and his destiny has become fixed. He cannot be reborn in any sphere lower than the human, and if he does not attain full emancipation earlier he is bound to do so within the course of seven lives at the most. When, in addition, the next two fetters are weakened he becomes a Once-returner, who will not have to endure more than one rebirth in the sensuous sphere. At the time of completely destroying all the first five, which are known as the grosser fetters, he becomes a Non-returner, who will not be born again in the spheres of sense.[11] With the breaking of all the ten fetters he attains the state of Arahat. He has then realized the paths and fruit of the holy life, and for him the painful round of rebirth has come to an end. These four stages

11. The sensory spheres (*kāma-loka*) are the planes of existence which include the human world.

of the Noble Person (*ariya puggala*) are sometimes separated by intervals, sometime they follow immediately after one another but at each stage the 'fruit' or attainment follows instantly upon the realization of the path in the series of thought-moments. When the thought-moment of insight flashes forth, the meditator knows beyond all doubt the nature of his attainment and what, if anything, still remains to be accomplished.

When, by the total eradication of lust, hatred, and delusion (*lobha-kkhaya, dosa-kkhaya*, and *moha-kkhaya*) the arahat gains Nibbāna, he obtains with it the type of enlightenment known as *sāvaka-bodhi* (the Disciple's Enlightenment) that goes with his attainment. That is, he fully understands the causes of existence and how they have been counteracted, and he experiences an extension of his faculties consequent upon the breaking down of the delusion of selfhood, which normally acts as a barrier to the mind, isolating it in the personal realm of sensory experience. But the enlightenment of a Supreme Buddha is of a higher order and of illimitable range. Over and above the knowledge pertaining to Arahatship he acquires *sabbaññutā*, the perfect understanding of all things. This, he gains, as the result of his determination formed in a previous life and realized through the cultivation of transcendent virtue, to become a Fully Enlightened One, a World-teacher for the welfare of all beings; for without that completeness of knowledge he could not set in motion the Wheel of the Law. But by the nature of things, the greater part of his knowledge is not communicable to others. Nor is there need to communicate it. In speaking of natural phenomena the Buddha used the language and ideas of those whom he was addressing, and to whom any other ideas would have appeared bizarre and incredible. One does not speak of the general theory of relativity to a person who can barely understand Euclid. When he was questioned as to whether he had taught all he knew to his disciples the Buddha replied with a simile. Taking a pinch of dust on his nail he asked which was greater—the pinch of dust he was holding or the remainder of the dust on the ground. The obvious answer was given, whereupon he said: "Just so much greater is the knowledge of the Tathāgata than that which he has taught."

From this, attempts have been made to prove that the Buddha had an esoteric teaching which he reserved for a select body of disciples. But the meaning is made clear by what follows: "Nevertheless, everything necessary for complete emancipation the Tathāgata has taught." And again, "The Tathāgata has taught the Dhamma without making any distinctions of esoteric and exoteric doctrine. The Tathāgata has not the closed fist of a teacher who keeps some things back." The things the Buddha knew but did not teach were such as did not conduce to liberation, and had no bearing on the task of guiding others across the ocean of Saṃsāra.

He did not encourage metaphysical speculation, knowing it to be profitless. He did not offer theories. "The Tathāgata holds no theories" is a phrase that occurs frequently in the texts. Having 'seen the truth face to face' he had discarded views based on mere reasoning and imperfect knowledge. Reason is a good guide—none better so far as it goes—and certainly nothing that is contrary to reason should be accepted as true; but the point of departure for the ultimate destination is where reason unaided can carry us no further. It is there that the *adhi-citta* or higher mind takes over and completes the journey. Until such time as it is allowed to do so the ratiocinations of the discriminating, conceptual mind remain to some extent a hindrance.

Yet knowledge can be pressed into the service of wisdom, and today we are perhaps in a better position to understand the truths the Buddha taught than were our ancestors in the days before science anatomized the physical world. The scientific method, the mental discipline of relating thought to known facts, has its value. The Buddha was the first to apply it to the search for absolute truth. Beginning with the observed fact of suffering he sought out its causes and their antidote by analysis of the factors of existence. The result was the Four Noble Truths which summarize the Dhamma. And just as science offers its discoveries for empirical verification, so the Buddha offered his teaching, not as a theory, a religious dogma or a visionary's dream, but as a demonstrable truth which anyone can verify for oneself. When he opened the gate of the Deathless he did not give the key to one man or any group of men. He left it wide open to all, for each to enter by one's own effort.

Unquestionably, the Dhamma is "profound, subtle, discernible only by the wise," but in the language of the Buddha wisdom does not mean academic learning. It means the ability to see things clearly. In this, a child is often wiser than a philosopher. It was a childhood experience of meditation that gave the Buddha the first glimpse of the way he was to take. Age, experience, erudition—these things may be accompanied by wisdom or they may not. The innocence of childhood may be just a simple, animal ignorance, or it may be accompanied by insights brought from former lives. But at any age, the man who is in full possession of his faculties, whether he be learned or illiterate, has the means by which he can find out the true nature of life and can tread the path to Nibbāna. For him the gate of the Deathless stands open still.

Buddhism and the Age of Science

U Chan Htoon

Two Addresses

delivered by

Thadu Maha Thray Sithu

U Chan Htoon
Formerly Judge of the Supreme Court of
the Union of Burma

WHEEL PUBLICATION NO. 36/37

Foreword

The two lectures which are here reprinted were delivered by the Honourable Justice U Chan Htoon when he was invited to represent Buddhism at two religious Conferences in the United States: the Sixteenth Congress of the International Association for Religious Freedom, held at Chicago, and the Conference on Religion in the Age of Science, held at Star Island, New Hampshire, U.S.A., in August 1958.

The Sixteenth Congress of the International Association for Religious Freedom, which was convened by the University of Chicago, August 9–13, 1958, was attended by distinguished representatives of the five great religions of the world, Buddhism, Christianity, Hinduism, Islam and Judaism, and its purpose was "to explore various ways in which the basic needs of men and the problems of the present day world can be met by the ethical and spiritual teachings of the great world religions, with special emphasis on the importance of mutual understanding, sympathy, appreciation and active cooperation among various religions." Over one thousand delegates from many parts of America, Canada, England and Western Europe were present besides those taking an active part in the conference. The address on Buddhism was delivered by U Chan Htoon on August 12th.

The meeting at which the second of the addresses was given was the Fifth Summer Conference sponsored by the Institute for Religion in the Age of Science. It was attended by over two hundred delegates from various parts of the United States and Canada. The principal addresses were delivered by a number of eminent scientists and religious leaders, that by U Chan Htoon on Buddhism being given on August 22nd.

In preparing these addresses the chief purpose kept in mind was to show the unique role that Buddhism plays in the dramatic present day conflict between scientific thought and established religious beliefs, a conflict which impinges upon every aspect of modern life. For this, it was necessary to sketch in outline the fundamentals of the Buddhist doctrine and, in the second lecture at least, to lay particular emphasis on those features of Buddhism which distinguish it from the theistic creeds. In order to do this systematically it was thought best to construct the second lecture on a dual pattern with the first section devoted to a very brief account of the general principles of Buddhist thought. The second section deals specifically and *seriatim* with the questions concerning religion and the scientific outlook which had been framed by the sponsors of the Conference to form the basis of its deliberations. From this factual and deliberately literal approach to the problems thus posed, Buddhism emerges sometimes as a mediator between the religious and scientific oppositions and sometimes as offering solutions quite different from those proposed by either side. It also becomes apparent that many of the problems themselves are, from the Buddhist standpoint, wrongly stated. They refer to issues which arise only as a result of contemplating life from a wrong position. In the totality of its contact with both the spiritual and the mundane world Buddhism is something more than a via media; it teaches values that belong to a transcending principle, one in which the seeming conflicts between science and religion melt away before the vision of an all-comprehensive truth.

In seeking answers to those questions, which have become of tremendous importance to us at this crucial point of history when perhaps the whole future of mankind hangs on the choice between the ethical values of religion and the contingent and variable expedients of materialism, the sponsors of the Conference showed themselves acutely, even painfully, aware of the failure of traditional religious beliefs to meet the challenge. It is hoped that by offering, in the form of these lectures, a very brief statement of the Buddhist worldview, the background of Buddhist thought ,and the concept of life and the nature and destiny of man that Buddhism holds, and bringing this to bear upon the problems with which modern knowledge has confronted us, a desire may be stimulated among thinking men to make a further study of the Dhamma. Above all it is hoped that when the ethical principles of Buddhism are recognized as being grounded in a rational view of life, they will be applied to clarify the inherent problems of the human situation in such a way that they may give to the nations of the world, as well as to individuals, a guiding light for these troubled times. The addresses were written with the conviction that the Teaching of the Buddha, which is valid for all times, all situations and all men, holds out the greatest hope for mankind. By a doctrine and way of life that surpass all others, Buddhism is capable of bringing peace of mind to this perplexed generation; and it is only through the peace of mind of the individual that peace among nations can be achieved.

The Anagārika P. Sugatānanda

Address to the Sixteenth IARF conference

I count it a great honour to have been invited to speak for Buddhism, the religion of nearly one-third of the entire human race—the religion of the majority of the people of Asia—in this Congress of distinguished representatives of the five great religions of mankind. At the same time, I am humbly aware of the magnitude of the task I have before me of presenting a picture of the Buddhist outlook and the beliefs which have shaped it; yet this I must do to the best of my ability, because the doctrines of Buddhism are inextricably woven into the pattern of Buddhist thought; and if I am to explain to you the Buddhist attitude to life and to the problems that confront mankind today, I must begin by acquainting you, at least in outline, with the fundamental tenets of this religion known to the West as Buddhism, but which we Buddhists prefer to call the Buddha Dhamma.

Before I begin, I wish to say that the sponsors of this Congress are to be warmly congratulated on their enterprise and their breadth of vision in bringing together, for mutual understanding and appreciation, the representatives of the world's leading faiths. The exchange of ideas, beliefs and aspirations, undertaken without any proselytizing design but purely for the advancement of knowledge and spiritual welfare, cannot fail to be of benefit to all who take part in it, whether as spokesmen or observers. I am convinced, also, that in the final summation it will be seen that those things wherein we are all agreed far outweigh, both in number and importance, the differences of theology and doctrine that too often obscure the real significance of human faith. We meet here, not to make converts or to establish superiorities, but to help one another towards a better understanding of certain fundamental principles we all share, and which are necessary for the right conduct of human affairs. It is therefore my sincere hope that by the unfolding of knowledge leading to wisdom, this object will be realized as the Conference progresses to its triumphal conclusion.

In order to place Buddhism in its true perspective it is necessary to begin with its historical background. Just as Christianity, Islam and Judaism share a common origin in Hebraic thought, so also Buddhism and Hinduism are to be understood as having their background in the Vedic religious thought of India. Hinduism came into being after the time of the Buddha and owes much of its development to the Buddha's teaching. Buddhism, however, antedates both Vedic Brahmanism and Hinduism, because it represents the rediscovery by the Buddha of the primal, spiritual Truth which has been taught by innumerable Buddhas in previous world-cycles. The historical Buddha, Gotama, is not a solitary teacher or prophet. He is one of an endless line of Enlightened Beings, reaching from remotest times into immeasurable cycles of futurity. Buddhist cosmology teaches that time is beginningless, that universes arise and pass away in an endless succession, obedient to the cosmic law of cause and effect, and that, in the several periods of each world cycle, certain highly advanced beings attain supreme Enlightenment and Omniscience. They become Buddhas and teach the Buddha Dhamma, or Truth, for the welfare of all beings. For this reason the Buddha Dhamma is sometimes called the *Sanantana Dhamma,* that is, primordial, eternal or timeless Doctrine. The Pāli word "Dhamma" means Law, Truth, and Doctrine. It has other significations also in different contexts, but for our present purpose the term "Buddha Dhamma" means the Doctrine taught by the Enlightened Ones, and that is the title Buddhists prefer to give to it.

Two-thousand five-hundred years ago, when the Buddha-to-be was born as a prince of a warrior clan in Northern India, religious beliefs had not hardened into dogma. Religion was conjoined with speculative philosophy, and there was a spirit of broad tolerance which embraced many schools of thought. In common with most of the ancient world, the majority of these schools accepted reincarnation as a basic fact. To thinking men it has always seemed impossible that life should come to an end with the disintegration of the physical body; and if this is so it is equally difficult to imagine that it comes into being for the first time with physical birth. Throughout nature there is a principle of continuity in change, which we are able to sense within ourselves, and it is this which has given rise to the concept of an immortal soul in man. As I shall explain later, the Enlightenment of the Buddha modified the idea of a transmigrating "Soul," but the principle of rebirth remains and is one of the central doctrines of Buddhism. It is this, together with the law of kamma, "as ye sow, so shall ye reap," which gives Buddhism its moral code. These two principles together explain all the anomalies of life and the problem of evil and suffering in the world. In India it was generally believed that the goal of the religious life was to obtain ultimate knowledge, or illumination, which most of the sects conceived to be an identification of oneself with the supreme Godhead, the impersonal Absolute, or Brahman.

There were, however, certain schools which taught nihilism and were equivalent to our modern agnostic and materialist systems. When the Prince Siddhattha renounced the world to become a religious ascetic he placed himself successively under two teachers of the Vedic and Upanishadic schools and mastered all that they were able to teach concerning union with the Brahman, both in theory and in meditation practice. He succeeded, in fact, in obtaining that identification with the highest consciousness which was considered to be the final goal of the religious experience. In after-years, when he was the Buddha, he was able to tell the Brahmins of his day that he was to be numbered among those who had known the highest spiritual state, and that he was a "knower of the Vedas" and one who had "seen Brahmā face to face."[1]

But this, he found, was not enough. Even on the highest spiritual plane the Brahmā gods were not completely liberated from the processes of life and death; they were still subject to change, and hence to uncertainty and suffering. What he desired was a state completely outside all the categories of existence and non-existence, utterly free from all the bonds of conditioned being. So, although most men would have been content to accept the highest religious norm of the time, and to have taken a place as one of the qualified exponents of these doctrines, he was not satisfied, but driven by an inner compulsion he had to seek fresh ways of attainment and a goal beyond that of the *Vedas* and the *Upanishads*.

After six years of intense striving he at last found himself in possession of the great Truth and it was then that he became the Buddha. He found that the faith he had entertained all along in

1. Tevijja Sutta, Dīgha Nikāya 13. Translated in the Wheel No. 57/58

a state of absolute liberation, a state in which the conditions of birth and death, arising and passing away, could never re-establish themselves, had been justified. This state is called "Nibbāna," and it is attained by the extinction of all the life-asserting and death-bringing qualities of selfhood: that is to say, by total elimination of all those craving instincts that bind us to the life-process, and so cause repeated rebirths in this and other realms.

The Buddhist doctrine is summarized in the Four Noble Truths, which are: first, the truth that all sentient life involves suffering; second, the truth that the cause of repeated rebirth and suffering is ignorance conjoined with craving; third, the truth that this process of birth, death and suffering can be brought to an end only with the attainment of Nibbāna; and fourth, the truth that Nibbāna can be attained by following to perfection the Noble Eightfold Path, which embraces *sīla, samādhi* and *paññā, i.e.,* morality, meditation and insight-wisdom.

In Buddhism the word *dukkha,* which we can only translate as "suffering," signifies every kind and degree of unpleasant sensation, mental and physical; it is in fact the same as the problem of pain which we find at the root of all religions and philosophies. So long as a being lives, he experiences suffering in one form or another; in the words of the Hebrew prophet, "Man is born unto trouble as the sparks fly upward." The religious instinct itself is born of the sense of sorrow and pain, for which man has tried throughout history to find either an antidote or compensation. Not only religion but science also is primarily concerned with the amelioration of suffering. But in Buddhist philosophy the fact of suffering assumes cosmological proportions, for the very life-process itself, being a process of continual change and transformation, and therefore of unrest and uncertainty, is seen as it really is, a process of suffering. In everyday speech we talk of "growing-pains," and both growth and decay, to say nothing of the incidental sickness and accidents, deprivations and grief, that are met with on the way, are indeed accompanied at every stage by suffering. From the moment of his birth man is overshadowed by death. In taking this view and insisting upon it, Buddhism is no more pessimistic than any other religion so far as the conditions of this world are concerned, for all religions are cognizant of this great problem of suffering. And it is not man alone who is thus afflicted; Buddhism takes into account the life of all sentient creatures, thereby bringing within the scope of its philosophy the entire realm of living beings, all of whom are subject to the same law of cause and effect.

The second of the Four Noble Truths goes down to the cause of this suffering process, which is psychological. Mind is the activating factor in life, and the physical bodies of living beings are only the material results of preceding mental forces which have been generated in past lives. The Buddha said, "Mind precedes all phenomena; Mind dominates them and creates them." By some process which we will be able to understand fully only when we have ourselves gained Enlightenment, the invisible force generated by the mind, when it is liberated from the body and projected outwards at death, fastens upon the elements of the material world and from them, by the natural processes of generation, moulds a new form of life. The elements are always present in the physical world, and they come together in the required order when conception takes place. It is, however, the mind—the unknown, unseen factor—that gives the new being its individuality. This mentally-generated force may be compared to the law of gravity, which operates upon material bodies without any connecting material agency, or to the force of electricity, which, travelling invisibly from its source, produces a variety of different results according to the mode of transformation its energy undergoes. Both of these dominating forces in the physical realm are indiscernible except when they come to operate on and through material substance, yet they are in a sense more real than the matter which they influence; such is the case also with the mental energy that animates living beings. And here I wish to point out, because of its importance in the present day world context, that Buddhism is the precise antithesis of materialism, for whereas materialism maintains that mind is only a by-product of matter, Buddhist philosophy shows beyond dispute that it is the mind which precedes the material formations and shapes them according to its own nature and tendencies. I wish this point to be very clear, because in it lies the answer Buddhism gives to the materialistic errors of our age. In Buddhism we try to avoid the use of the word "spirit" because this may be taken to imply some kind of enduring entity; but if "spirit" is understood to mean the current of psychic processes, as opposed to the physical process then we can say that in Buddhism it is the “spirit” which is all-important. Buddhism teaches the dominance of the mind; and in the last phase of personal evolution the mind has to dominate itself rather than, as now, being directed towards dominating external things.

But the functioning of the mind in a state of ignorance—that is, the unenlightened state—is itself dominated by craving. The deeper the ignorance, the stronger the craving, as it is in the case of the lower forms of life. As we ascend the scale we find this condition much the same in primitive man, but transformed and to a certain extent controlled in the civilized human being. By “craving” I mean that thirst for life which is manifested in seeking sensual gratification and the repetition of pleasant sensations arising from the six bases of sense-cognition, that is, the senses of sight, sound, smell, taste, touch and mental perception. These generate a continual thirst for renewed pleasures. The process of biological evolution as it is known to science today, is simply the carrying forward from generation to generation, through immeasurable ages, of this instinct of craving, and it is this which, working through biological processes, has produced the entire range of living creatures from the single-cell protoplasm to the most highly evolved and sensitized organism we know, the human being.

The craving-instinct, therefore, is the very mainspring of the life-process; it is the will-to-live and the vital urge, ever seeking fresh intensities of experience, and for this purpose equipping living forms with more and more highly specialized organs through biological selection. This process is inseparable from its parallel process of rebirth, for rebirth is not the reincarnation of a “soul” after death, but more precisely it is the continuation of a current of cause and effect from one life to another. There is nothing in the universe that is not subject to change, and so there is no static entity which can be called a “soul” in the general acceptance of that term. This idea is not peculiar to Buddhism, for it has been known to philosophers from the time of Heraclitus down to the psychologists and neurologists of our own day; but it was left for the Buddha, by means of his enlightened wisdom, to discover how this could be so and yet to perceive that this “soulless” process is in fact the basis of a continual rebirth.

A living being is the totality of five factors, one of them being material and the remaining four psychic. They are the physical body, the sensations, the perception, the tendency-formations (volitions) and the consciousness. All of these factors are undergoing change from moment to moment and are linked together only by the causal law—the law that "this having been, that comes to be." Hence, Buddhist philosophy regards a being not as an enduring entity but as a dynamic process, and all phenomenal existence is, in the Pāli phrase, "*anicca, dukkha, anattā*"—impermanent, subject to suffering, and devoid of any permanent ego-substance. When one life comes to an end the process still goes on, carried forward into a fresh existence. The volitional activities, both good and bad, of the past life then bear their results, the good deeds producing happiness and the evil ones misery.

Volitional activity in thought, word and deed is called kamma; the results are called *vipāka*, and in every life we are carrying out this dual process: we are at once the passive subjects of effects from our past actions, and the active originators of fresh kamma which in its turn will bear fruit either here or hereafter.

As I said at the outset, time is beginningless; and this implies that the act of creation is not one that took place once and for all at some particular moment selected from eternity, for it would be impossible to isolate any specific moment from a timeless eternity without past, present or future. The act of creation is rather one that is taking place continually within our selves. The idea is one that will be familiar to all who are acquainted with Bergson's theory of "creative evolution." The Buddha expressed it succinctly and with profound meaning when he said, "Within this fathom-long body, equipped with mind and sense-perceptions, O Monks, I declare unto you is the world, the origin of the world, the cessation of the world and the path to its cessation." If the human mind with its limitations cannot envisage infinity of time, neither can it form any picture of a state outside its temporal and spatial situation. Nevertheless, the third of the Four Noble Truths asserts the reality of Nibbāna, which is precisely this release from the bondages of time, space and conditioned existence.

The state of Nibbāna must not be understood as annihilation, except in the sense of the annihilation of the passions of desire, hatred and ignorance, the factors which produce rebirth in saṃsāra, the round of existences. To the ordinary man whose understanding is obscured by these imperfections, there appears to be no alternative to existence on the one hand and non-existence on the other, but the absolute, as I have already indicated, lies outside and beyond both of these illusory categories. In the Christian Scriptures it is written that "Heaven and earth shall pass away," but that something remains which does not pass away. The Buddhist does not call it God or the Word of God, because these are definitions and the ultimate goal cannot be defined in relative terms. Existence on earth, in heaven or in the states of great suffering is only temporary, for beings pass from one to the other in accordance with their deeds. Beyond all these existences there lies the ultimate, supreme, unchanging and indefinable state: the state of absolute balance, equanimity and release from the conflict of opposites.

What man in his ignorance takes to be positive and real, the world of phenomenal effects and of his own existence, is nothing of the kind. It is real in a certain sense and on one particular plane of experience, but its reality is only the relative reality of a transforming process, a coming-to-be which never actually reaches the state of perfect being.

When we acknowledge that this is indeed the case, we must grant that true reality lies in some other dimension, not only outside of time and space relationships as we know them, but also outside all that they contain of unrealized potentialities. Nibbāna cannot be described because there is nothing in our mundane experience with which it can be compared and nothing that can be used to furnish a satisfactory analogy. Yet it is possible to attain it and to experience it while still living in the flesh, and in this way to gain the unshakable assurance of its reality as a *dhamma* that is independent of all the factors of conditioned existence. That is the state the Buddha achieved in his lifetime, and which he enabled others to attain after him. He pointed the way, with the invitation, "Come, and see for yourself" (*ehipassiko*).

That way, the fourth of the Noble Truths of Buddhism, is called the Noble Eightfold Path:

Right View,

Right Resolution,
Right Speech,
Right Action,
Right Livelihood,
Right Effort,
Right Mindfulness and
Right Concentration.

For the lay Buddhist, the moral code consists of five simple precepts:

to abstain from taking life,
to abstain from taking what is not one's own by right,
to abstain from sexual misconduct,
to abstain from untruthfulness and
to abstain from intoxicating drinks and drugs.

In these five vows, voluntarily undertaken, the Buddhist layman establishes himself in basic morality, the everyday purification of thought, speech and conduct. On the *uposatha,* or fast days, he takes upon himself three or five additional precepts of a more ascetic character, including absolute chastity, making up eight or ten precepts for these regular observances. The Buddha did not enjoin severe asceticism, but only that which is necessary to free oneself from inordinate attachments; a simple, wholesome life is the Buddhist ideal, and the practice of generosity and the cultivation of universal benevolence are the cardinal virtues of his Teaching. For the Buddhist monk, however, there are 227 rules of conduct which are very precisely laid down in the Vinaya, or monastic discipline.

But ethical principles and discipline, whether for the monk or layman, are only the beginning of the Buddhist way of life. Their purpose is to make the way clear for spiritual progress through mental concentration which in Buddhism, is a very exact psychological science. It is called *bhāvanā* or mental development, and is of two kinds: *samatha-bhāvanā*, the cultivation of mental tranquillity, evenness and equilibrium, and *vipassana-bhāvanā*, which is aimed at direct insight into the true nature of reality. In the first category, the development of a mind of boundless universal benevolence towards all beings, which is called *mettā-bhāvanā*, is of primary importance. When the Buddhist prepares for meditation he first purifies his mind by generating thoughts of love and compassion for all living beings without any exception near and far, big and small, visible and invisible, and he directs these thoughts to all quarters of the universe. He does so with compassion and with altruism (joy in attainments and advantages gained by others) and then with equanimity. These meditations are performed with discursive thoughts and then with higher states of intellection. This practice gives calm and tranquillity and a more alert and poised mind, and thus helps towards the higher practice of *vipassanā.*

Buddhist meditation consists in developing the power of concentrating the mind to what is called "one-pointedness," by the exclusion of all extraneous objects or related concepts. The techniques used to this end include the practice of concentrating attention on the ingoing and outgoing breath, and development of mindfulness fixed on any of the bodily actions such as the movements of the feet in walking. In this, the object of attention is stripped of all adventitious mental associations; the arm that is lifted ceases to be "my arm," the body that is standing, sitting or lying is no longer "my body."

It is just the object of an impersonal contemplation, the instrument of movements and attitudes. By this means the mind is tamed, brought under complete control and disassociated from all false interpretations and the passions they engender. The mind, in fact, becomes depersonalized; it contemplates the physical and mental sensations as it were from the outside, detached and uninvolved. It is only when this process of mental depersonalization is completed that the mind becomes capable of perceiving the reality that lies beyond the ever-changing forms. It then becomes a keen instrument, tempered to razor-edge sharpness, with which to cut though the bonds of ignorance. To put the case in another way, the mind, which up to that point had been constructing the moment-to-moment continuum of its illusory conception of selfhood, all at once breaks the sequence of that activity, is no longer tied to it, and at once enters into a fresh realm of knowledge. When this happens, the chain of cause and effect, which is linked by the emotional and intellectual reactions, is broken; there is then no more kamma rooted in desire, and so no further projection into the future of saṃsāra. The incessant round of birth and deaths comes to an end: in the Buddhist phrase, the fire of the passions is extinguished and so Nibbāna *is* attained. One who has thus accomplished his task of liberation is called an *arahat*.

I should not conclude this short account of Buddhism without mentioning the doctrine which came to take paramount place in *Mahāyāna*, the second great school of Buddhism: the doctrine of the Bodhisatta path. A Bodhisatta is a being who dedicates himself to becoming a fully enlightened Buddha, and for this purpose renounces or postpones the attainment of Nibbāna for himself for many aeons, during which time in successive births he works for the benefit of all other living beings. In this doctrine the ideal of compassion and of service to others reaches its highest level. It has produced a rich and noble literature embodying all that is most sublime and inspiring in human thought. A Buddhist finds no difficulty in identifying many of the great teachers of other religions with those great personalities who exemplify the virtues of the self-renouncing Bodhisatta. Whosoever teaches truths that are good and enduring, who sacrifices himself for mankind and who asserts the divine potentialities of man in absolute unselfishness and love, partakes of the spirit of the Bodhisatta. A Bodhisatta is not yet fully enlightened, so he does not necessarily exhibit all the characteristics of the highest perfection, but within him there is above all else the spirit of mercy, loving-kindness and self-denial. His love encompasses all beings without distinction; and he is ready to suffer every kind of martyrdom for their benefit. He is a teacher and a guide, a loving father and the servant of all. Such was Gotama Buddha through many lives before his final enlightenment, and it is he who provides the great pattern for this ideal.

From what has already been said, certain aspects of Buddhism, as it moulds and colours the life and thought of the Buddhist peoples, must by now be clear. In the first place, Buddhism inculcates self-reliance rather than dependence upon the aid of supernatural powers. It therefore tends to promote an individualistic outlook which is characteristic of Buddhists both in their personal relationships and their national life. The rejection of all forms of authoritarianism stems from the Buddha's insistence upon freedom of will and choice, under what is nothing more than an enlightened spiritual guidance. In Buddhist society no individual is encouraged to impose his will on others; the ideal for which he must strive is to perfect his own control over his desires and impulses. In doctrine, *ex cathedra* pronouncements by religious leaders are unknown, for the sole authority is the text of the Tipiṭaka.

Buddhism requires that the freedom of the individual to determine his own destiny and to choose the kind of life he lives must never be subordinated to group interests, which seek to mould him to a standardized pattern and so deprive him of the initiative necessary for his spiritual development. For this reason the Buddha opposed caste distinctions, seeing in them an attempt to confine people in a rigid framework that would stultify their growth and prevent the full realization of their potentialities. Buddhism is democratic, but makes no attempt to achieve a classless society, considering this to be an impossible condition on account of the inherent inequalities between one man and another which are the result of personal kamma; but it classifies men according to their character and natural abilities. It is thus the antithesis of the totalitarian concept in which the individual has only a group-existence subordinate to the needs of the State. The State and its laws exist for the individual, not the individual for the State. They are merely the instruments by which men are enabled to live together in just and liberal relationships with the greatest amount of freedom consistent with a disciplined society. The problem of the exploitation of man by man is solved in Buddhism by the absolute condemnation of all forms of greed; of greed for possession, for power and for the pleasures of the senses. The worker is expected to give of his best to his employer, and the employer's duty to the worker is to compensate him generously and give him such care and protection as he would extend to his own children. The sick and needy are to be helped, and in the light of Buddhism such aid is help not only to the recipient but to the donor as well, for the law of kamma makes a reality of the truth taught in Ecclesiastes: "Cast thy bread upon the waters; for thou shalt find it after many days." A Buddhist lives, knowing that when he dies the only treasure he will be able to take with him into his next birth is the treasure he has given away. This is the only true and lasting source of worldly happiness.

Buddhism teaches us not to envy or hate the rich because

of their wealth, and not to despise the poor; they are what they are because of their previous deeds, and their destiny can be changed, for better or worse, by their actions in this present life. Buddhism therefore offers us the blueprint of an ideal society; not an unrealistic Utopia that disregards the obvious facts of human nature, but a practicable and attainable scheme for human improvement. If there is any meaning in the phrase "enlightened self-interest" it is to be found in this concept of each individual doing good for others and for himself at the same time. It may seem paradoxical that self-interest should ultimately lead to the realization that there is no reality in Self; yet such is the case when the highest form of self-interest is seen to be the denial of self for the welfare of others. By the conscious cultivation of compassion and benevolence, the Buddhist gradually weakens the bonds of self until he reaches the stage at which they, and the illusion of selfhood, no longer exist.

To view the whole of humanity in terms of rebirth and kamma must necessarily give a feeling of kinship and universal brotherhood. When a Buddhist thinks of the round of rebirths in saṃsāra, extending infinitely backwards in time and stretching into an immeasurable future, he realizes that he has lived in many parts of the world, as a member of many different races. He may at present be a Burmese but in his past life he may have been a European, a white or coloured American or an African tribesman. He cannot therefore feel that there is any real distinction in being what he now is, and ideas of superiority and of inferiority are equally out of place. He has brought with him into the world certain individual characteristics of mind, certain aptitudes and certain disabilities which are the results of past thinking and acting, and it is these, not his racial or national background, that are his real inheritance. He may congratulate himself on having earned his rebirth in a land of advanced culture, and be thankful for his past achievements that have caused him to be born where the Buddha Dhamma is taught and practised, but he cannot harbour the delusion that he has been specially singled out for these favours. They are there for everybody: prizes in the school of life that each may strive for and obtain. He cannot rest upon his laurels, but must either go forward or backward in the scale of spiritual evolution; and if he chooses to interpret this as free competition it is still competition without rivalry, for victory to oneself does not mean the defeat of someone else. On the contrary, every personal spiritual victory is one that should and can be shared with all. The Buddhist finds no difficulty in conceiving himself as a citizen of the world, a member of the great brotherhood of mankind. He acknowledges his kinship with all that breathes lives and hopes.

Faith in spiritual values is part of the logic of Buddhism. The universe is governed by a moral principle which is self-existent in its causal laws and so forms part of its essential mechanism. It is by living in the knowledge of those laws and in obedience to them that man reaches his highest fulfilment. They are not man-made laws, subject to variations according to time, place and circumstance, but universal principles which operate so long as life exists, and whether we are aware of them or not. To say that we cannot alter or escape them is superfluous; by scientific means one may resist the law of gravity for a time, but it must prevail in the end because it is a principle inherent in the structure of the physical universe. So it is with the moral law of causality. The urgent problems that confront the world today can only be solved by applying these moral and spiritual laws. But to do that, we must first of all have understanding of them. It is not enough to invent rules to fit our circumstances and justify our actions, yet this is in effect what men have been doing from time immemorial. We must approach the great mystery of life in a spirit of reverential enquiry, choosing the best guides and seeking to establish to our own satisfaction the truth behind their greatness. Only in this way can we confirm the prompting of instinctive virtue and arrive at conviction.

Religion for the man of today must be supported by reason; it must be in conformity with what we know to be facts; and where it goes beyond mere facts it must have sufficient logical probability to invite our investigation on higher levels. If we assume too much we run the risk of losing contact with reality in the realms of imagination; that is the danger of theology. If too little, we wilfully restrict ourselves to a materialistic level from which it is difficult to rise. There must be a just balance between credulity and scepticism, in order that faith may be founded on reason. In Buddhism we start with only one assumption: that there is a moral principle in life. It is a sound assumption because everything we observe confirms it. From that primary assumption everything else follows logically and we are able to discern the general pattern from the portions of it that are known to us. Everywhere we see natural effects springing from natural causes; everything changes, yet the continuity of cause and effect survives the temporary forms to which it gives birth. It is the one constant element in an ever-changing universe. Matter is energy—energy manifesting in a perpetual process of transformation. As our knowledge of the physical universe expands we find the same law of causal continuity prevailing throughout. Hence it is reasonable to conclude that the animating life-principle must belong to the same order of things. Any hypothesis beyond this is an unnecessary elaboration at this stage; it does not help us at all to assume the existence of an enduring soul when there is no evidence whatever for such an entity. The energy of kamma which forms the life continuum can produce only evil if it is used for evil, and good if it is used for good. The energy itself is neutral; it is the manner in which it is directed by volitional action that produces the moral resultants. This energy can never expend itself automatically because it is incessantly being renewed by the generator, craving. Fresh impulses are incessantly being projected to sustain and carry it forward. All our mental activities motivated by desire are perpetually renewing the current. If it is to be brought to an end it must be by a conscious effort of will, a deliberate stopping of the craving Impulses. Buddhism teaches that *lobha, dosa* and *moha*—greed, hatred and delusion—must be neutralized by *alobha, adosa* and *amoha*—benevolence, altruism and enlightenment. When this is achieved the current is cut off and there is no more rebirth. Nibbāna *is* attained.

The materialism and scepticism that are rife in the world today have their roots in the scientific attitude. Scientific facts can be proved; but for the most part religious doctrines cannot. They rest upon the willingness to believe, or the deliberate suspension of unbelief, in the faithful. In the face of scientific knowledge people are finding it more and more difficult to maintain this willingness to believe; part of their mind tells them that there is a moral and spiritual purpose in life, but they cannot reconcile any of the accepted beliefs concerning it to their knowledge and experience. Theistic religion tells them that there is a Supreme Being, who regulates the universe and that there is an immortal soul and a life after death; but there is no actual proof of these assumptions. On the contrary, the great mass of scientific evidence seems to point the other way, to a purely mechanistic explanation of life. This fact we cannot ignore when we try to assess the place of religion in modern thought.

Buddhism answers the challenge by asserting that spiritual truth *can* be proved; that it is open for every man to discover and confirm for himself. The Buddha said that it is natural to doubt, until complete confirmation is obtained through personal experience. One of the distinguishing characteristics of the Buddha Dhamma is that it is *ehipassiko*—that which invites everyone to come and see for oneself. The way to do this is by means of the Buddhist system of meditation, a technique of mental development taught by the Buddha himself and expounded in great detail in the Buddhist texts and commentaries. Its object is to break through the veils of ignorance and delusion which hide the truth from our sight, and thereby to liberate the mind. One who has attained even the first stage of this development receives absolute certainty as to the truth of the Doctrine. For him it is proved, as a scientific theory is proved, by successful practical experiment. He sees the truth, not "through a glass darkly," but "face to face." When he attains the fourth stage of purification he is completely liberated and enlightened and he can speak of the Dhamma as one who is actually living and experiencing it. His faith becomes knowledge; and Nibbāna, the state of final liberation from all sorrow, is for him the only reality.

The goal of Buddhism is very high, nothing less than absolute perfection; but there are stages of attainment on the way, and it is with these that the ordinary man is more immediately concerned. The ordinary man will ask, "What will Buddhist meditation do for me or do to me?" The answer is given by the many, who without attaining the highest path of arahatship, have yet benefited in an access of mental alertness and spiritual awareness in a wider sphere. The manifold problems of our worldly life, our social problems and problems of international relations, clamour for our attention, with an urgency greater than ever before. If we do not succeed in resolving them the consequences threaten to be disastrous to civilization, if not to humanity itself. When we look back on history we cannot say that religion—any religion—has ever, for any long period, succeeded in preventing war; but the fault lies in human nature rather than in religion. The desire for self-preservation, if necessary at the cost of others, is, in all but the most exceptional people, stronger than the appeal religion makes to the nobler side of their nature. The remedy for this can only lie in a form of religion which carries the fullest conviction; one that is impregnable against the cold blast of scientific knowledge and is philosophically comprehensive enough to include all the elements of human experience. It is only a religion of this kind which can so dominate the minds of men as to make them follow the path of virtue fearlessly, knowing that in the end right will triumph, and that there is a spiritual goal that makes their sufferings in this world bearable. Secure in this conviction, men will strive and live nobly, and the highest standards of today will become the average standards of the future. Despite all the anti-religious trends of the present day there is a growing desire on the part of great numbers of people to embrace religion. They are seeking a solid basis for faith. This is the most encouraging feature of our times, the one that offers the greatest hope for the future of mankind.

The sponsors of this Conference, and the delegates who have attended it, have in their grasp a unique opportunity for promoting spiritual values all over the world. It is my earnest wish that their labours may be richly rewarded and that we may live to see a great moral and spiritual regeneration of mankind.

May the Triple Gem of the Buddha, the Dhamma and the Sangha shed light and tranquillity on all present here. May they and all beings be happy, and may peace prevail in the world.

Buddhism—the Religion of the Age of Science

When I received the invitation to this Conference, I was deeply impressed by the thoughtful approach shown by its sponsors in framing the questions that are to be the subject of our discussion. They are searching questions—questions of tremendous import to all of us at this crucial point in the history of mankind. They are indicative of a growing awareness of the lack of spiritual values in our materialistic civilization, and of an honest and realistic attempt to get to grips with the problems of the human situation in a world that is fast losing faith in the old religious beliefs.

In view of their importance I propose to deal directly with each of the points raised, from the standpoint of a practising Buddhist. But first I must give you, as briefly as possible, an outline of the Buddhist worldview, the background of Buddhist thought, and the Buddhist concept of life and of the nature of man. This is necessary because, as you will see, Buddhism differs fundamentally from every other religious system on many points. As the pattern unfolds you will find that Buddhism gives answers to these problems that are quite different from the answers given by Western religion, while in many cases from the Buddhist point of view there is no problem at all.

Gotama Buddha, as you all know, was an Indian Prince who renounced the life of a ruler to become an ascetic, seeking spiritual realization in a life of self-discipline and contemplation. As Prince Siddhattha he was a man like ourselves; he never claimed any divine nature, inspiration or even guidance. It was not until he achieved ultimate realization and became the Buddha of this world-cycle, a perfectly Enlightened Being, that he spoke with any authority on spiritual matters. This status he achieved, also, by his own unaided efforts. The proof that he then gave in support of his claim to Enlightenment and spiritual emancipation is a proof that can be found by us today in the nature of the Doctrine he taught. He said in effect, "Come: examine, criticize and analyze my Teachings for yourself; practise the method of gaining emancipation that I shall show you. I do not ask you to take anything on blind faith; but when you have fully accomplished the method, you will see the Truth face to face, as I see it now."

That Teaching, the Dhamma, and that method, the practice of the Noble Eightfold Path, have been preserved and handed down to us by word of mouth and written texts in unbroken continuity since the time of the Buddha himself. Throughout the centuries a long line of *Arahats*—that is, Disciples who have gained the highest fruits of liberation through self-purification—attests the truth of the Doctrine and the effectiveness of the method. The Dhamma itself includes ethics, psychology, religion, and a complete cosmic philosophy that embraces all forms of life in a harmonious moral order. Whether it can also be called scientific, in the sense of being in accordance with principles that later science has revealed to us, I shall leave for you to judge when you have heard me. You will in any case agree that the Buddha in his Teaching appealed both to the reasoning and emotional sides of man's nature, and that the loftiest spiritual aspirations of mankind are to be found in the ideal he set before us.

To begin with, it must be understood that in the Buddhist system there is no place for a Creator God. There is moral law and moral order, and these principles are supreme. They are the spiritual aspect of the law of cause and effect that prevails in the physical universe. But Buddhist cosmology is based upon relativity; the related and composite nature of all phenomena. World systems, or universes, arise and pass away in obedience to natural law, but there has never been any first act of creation or any first cause. Time and relativity are a closed circle in which no point of beginning can be found. This concept has its parallel in the physical world: in former days people imagined that the horizon must indicate a rim to the earth, but as we move in the direction of the horizon it constantly recedes from us, so that at whatever point on the earth's surface we stand the horizon still spreads all around us. In the same way we mistakenly imagine that time and phenomena must in some way be bounded by a beginning. But with time and eternity it is just as it is with ourselves in relation to the physical horizon. Time, the present, is the spot on which we stand; infinity is the endless recession of such spots. Just as there is no spot at which the earth begins, so there is no point in time at which the world's causal antecedents began. It is very probable, according to the latest scientific notions, that the entire universe, or cosmos, is constructed on the same physical principle, and the fact that its nature is outside our present range of comprehension does not at all affect the mathematical indications. The relativity of space and time, a new concept to science, is and always has been implicit in Buddhist philosophy.

The moral order works through the continuum of events on the psychophysical level which we call life, the life-continuum of conscious being. That also is beginningless, an incessant flux of cause and effect. It is true it had a beginning on this earth, but that beginning was only the continuation of a series; its causal antecedents existed before, in former universes. When a universe comes to an end in the course of natural processes, the forces which constituted it are resolved into their atomic elements, but after aeons of disintegration they again reassemble and another universe gradually forms.

The cause of this cyclic process is kamma, the totality of thought-force that is being generated from moment to moment. Man's free will operates within a space-time complex that has been created by his own previous activities, having their origin in mental processes. These previous activities are called kamma; their results are called *Vipāka* in Buddhism. The kamma of the past has created the conditions of the present, while the kamma of the present is creating the conditions that will exist in the future. In the Buddhist texts it states definitely that the arising of a fresh world-cycle is brought about by the kamma of all the beings that lived in the previous one.

The idea of reincarnation, or, as we prefer to call it, rebirth, is not nowadays so unfamiliar a one to the West as it used to be. It may perhaps be said that the moral necessity for rebirth is transcendent. It is the only way in which we who believe in moral justice in the universe can account for the seeming injustices we see all about us—the thousands of cases of apparently unmerited suffering, of people stricken by incurable diseases, of children born blind, deaf and dumb, deformed or mentally-deficient, or doomed to an early death beyond human or divine aid. All these evils are due to past bad kamma. Would the words of Jesus to the man he had healed, "Go, and sin no more, lest a worse thing befall thee," apply to a child born with an affliction that could not have been brought about by any sin it had committed in this life? But if these words of Jesus did not point to a universal truth they were meaningless.

Such evils as these can be avoided in the future by generating good kamma here and now. The individual's present situation may be (but not necessarily is) beyond present remedy, but the nature of his response to it is subject to his will. He can make his future a happy one by the performance of good deeds. No man's destiny is fixed, except by his own intention. It is subject to continual alteration and change of direction. As remedy for present evils, the Buddha laid down the principles of noble conduct; the cultivation of harmlessness towards all beings, accompanied by positive thoughts and deeds of loving-kindness; the practice of charity, sexual restraint, self-discipline and mental cultivation. To avoid evil in the future we must shun evil in the present; there is no other way.

This is the reason why, we believe, science alone will never be able completely to eradicate disease and mental and bodily suffering from human life. It is also the reason why a completely equalitarian society can never be achieved; the innate differences in character, intellect and capability between one individual and another, due to past kamma, are too great. Nature will always defeat any attempts to put false values into human life.

The doctrine of kamma is the direct opposite of fatalism or predestination. While our present condition is the result of past actions, the future is being moulded by our present ones, and every man can raise himself in the scale of spiritual evolution, as well as improve his worldly position, by well-directed effort. Buddhism, in its teaching that nothing is permanent, shows that there is no constant, immutable element in the process of rebirth. The phenomenal personality is a succession of moments of consciousness, each conditioned by the ones that have preceded it, yet subject to the intervention of free-will, which can change the nature of the current of personality. The aphorism "character is destiny" is shown by Buddhism to be a deep psychological truth, for when we change our character we change our destiny with it. In truth, man has the divine power to shape his own nature and his own mode of being. He can not only improve his condition in this world but can attain higher realms. His highest destiny of all, however, is to gain his release from all forms of conditioned existence, even from the highest heavenly states, because all these are impermanent. There are altogether thirty-one major spheres of being, some of them lower than the human while others are realms of greatly refined spiritual existence; but in none of them is life eternal. After death beings are reborn in whatever sphere, human, subhuman or divine, their mental development has fitted them for but they remain there only so long as the kamma they have generated continues to bear results in that specific order of being. When that particular kamma-result is exhausted they pass away from that state and are again reborn, in whatever sphere their residual kamma conducts them to. If you will conceive these states of being as different mental planes on which our consciousness can operate while we are still here on earth, you will have formed a more or less correct picture of the spiritual cosmos. In his moods of greed, lust, hatred or violence man places himself on a low mental plane, and if it is that particular mood which manifests in his last conscious moment before death he will be reborn on the sub-human life-plane that corresponds to it. If, on the other hand, he has cultivated the higher attributes of universal love, compassion, unselfishness and detachment from material concerns, it is these qualities that will preside over his last moment, and will conduct him to the higher states of being to which they correspond. Moral law operates with mechanical precision; man cannot cheat it, but he can make use of it to advance his spiritual growth. In all this incessant round of rebirth there is no permanent "Soul" or ego-entity that is reborn; there is merely the life-continuum of cause and effect producing a succession of beings, each pursuing the line of individual causality.

In the Four Noble Truths the Buddha summarized his doctrine thus:

The life-process involving rebirth and consequent old age and death in all spheres of conditioned existence is associated with suffering. This is so because all sentient existence bears the three characteristics of impermanence, "unsatisfactoriness" and the absence of any real, enduring ego-entity.

The cause of this painful round of rebirths is craving—that is, thirst for the enjoyment of pleasure of the senses, from the lowest animal indulgences up to the most refined mental pleasure. All desires are cravings for experience and renewed experience, and it is these which promote the psychic will-to-live. Craving is thus the generator of mental energy, the strongest force in the cosmos. This craving-force is associated with Ignorance of the nature of reality.

There is a point at which craving, and the rebirth-process arising from it, can be brought to an end. At that point, craving and Ignorance are eliminated altogether, and with them the psychic elements of grasping and attaching. This cessation of the unreal life-process is called Nibbāna, the extinction of the fires of passion. It is the end of suffering and the sole unchanging reality.

The way to that final perfection is the Noble Eightfold Path of mental or spiritual development, that is: right view, right resolution, right speech, right action, right livelihood, right effort, right mindfulness and right concentration. Each of these terms has a very exact ethical and psychological significance; they are not simply vague, unformulated ideals but are minutely and systematically delineated modes of thought and behaviour. Taken all together they constitute the three essentials of spiritual development *sīla* (morality), *samādhi* (mental concentration) and *paññā* (insight-wisdom). This is the way to the cessation of suffering.

To the question, "What is human personality?" Buddhism gives the answer that it is a combined psychophysical process in which nothing is stable or unchanging. It is a flux of dependent relationships brought into being and sustained by past kamma and natural laws. A human being consists of five aggregates or *khandhas*, one of which is physical and the other four psychic. They are: *rūpa* or physical body; *vedanā* or sensation; *saññā* or perception; *saṅkhāra* or mental-formations; and *viññāṇa* or consciousness. Of these five, *saṅkhāra* is the most difficult to define because there is nothing even remotely corresponding to it in Western thought, and there is no single English word that covers all its meanings. Broadly speaking, it signifies the tendencies or characteristics that have been set in motion by past kamma; but it also includes the faculty of willing and other functions of the mind. I cannot dwell upon the subtleties of Buddhist psychological analysis now; it is a vast subject and one that, if it were to be studied systematically by competent Western specialists in psychology, would completely transform modern ideas concerning the nature of the mind. It is sufficient to say that Buddhism views living beings not as entities but as processes—or, if you like, a series of *events*—taking place within a causal nexus that gives us our concepts of time, space and phenomena. The intangible force of kamma generated in the past works through the processes of the physical universe to produce living beings; but each of these is a composite product. Just as an automobile is composed of the engine, with its various parts, the chassis, the wheels, the upholstery and so on, no single item of which by itself constitutes the automobile, but which when all put together on the assemblyline make the finished product, so a living being is formed of the various elements of mind and physical substance, not one of which alone constitutes the being. The "self," therefore, is a phenomenal product of various causes; it is not an enduring or self-existing entity. This is the meaning of the Buddhist doctrine of "*anattā*" or "non--soul." The personal ego is an illusion of ignorance, and so to attain liberation it is necessary to free the mind of self-delusion. The whole of Buddhist morality and discipline is directed towards this ultimate end.

To the question, "How did it all begin?" I can only say that there is no answer, because the question itself is merely a product of man's limited comprehension. If we understand the nature of time and relativity we must see that there could not have been any beginning. It can only be pointed out that all the usual answers to the question are fundamentally defective. If it is assumed that in order to exist a thing must have had a creator who existed before it, follows logically that the creator himself must have had a creator, and so on back to infinity. On the other hand, if the creator could exist without a prior cause in the form of another creator, the whole argument falls to the ground. The theory of a Creator-God does not solve any problems; it only complicates the existing ones.

Buddhism then, views life and the cosmos as a process—a complex of interrelated causes and dependent relationships. To find his way out of this maze, man has to develop Insight-Wisdom. This is done by cultivating the virtues, all of which are aimed at diminishing the sense of "self" and the grasping instincts associated with it. Side by side with this cultivation of moral purity there are the exercises in concentration which go by the general name of meditation. Meditation in Buddhism is not the giving up of one's mind to fantasies born of the myth-content of the unconscious; it stands for scientifically arranged and systematic mental exercises. In the course of this training, psychic powers are developed, such as clairvoyance, clairaudience, telepathy and the recollection of previous lives, but these are not the real object of meditation. They represent, in fact, another form of attachment to be overcome. Its real object is liberation. By the development of Right Concentration it is possible to break through the walls of ignorance that encompass us with illusions—to crash through time and relativity as a jet propelled aircraft crashes through the sound barrier. Once beyond this, the disciple of the Buddha finds himself face to face with Nibbāna, the Ultimate Truth in which all artificially created problems of ignorance and delusion have ceased to exist.

The Buddha was not only the Lord of Wisdom. He was also the supreme Lord of Compassion. It was out of pity for suffering humanity that he sought and found the Truth. He taught his followers to develop a heart of loving-kindness that embraces without distinction all beings. This he called the godlike state of consciousness. There are four of these *brahmavihāras,* they are: *mettā* or universal benevolence; *karuṇā* or compassion; *muditā* or sympathetic joy: and *upekkhā* or equanimity and non-discrimination. They form, for Buddhists, the ideal of what should be our attitude towards our fellow men, and, indeed, to all living beings. One who attains them in this life is already living mentally in the highest heaven, the realm of the Formless Beings whose nature is entirely of the spirit. In this way alone is it possible to realize the kingdom of heaven on earth. That kingdom is of the mind, and is entirely independent of external circumstances. Whosoever reaches it in this life will, if he does not go on to the final goal of all, Nibbāna, be reborn after death in the spiritual sphere corresponding to his attainment.

It is in the light of this view of the world that I now ask you to consider the answers I am going to give, as a Buddhist, to the problems confronting religion in this age of science.

Does man in a civilization pervaded by the ideas of science still require beliefs that inform him concerning his own highest goals?

The purpose of science has always been to examine the physical universe and discover the laws by which it operates. Its function in civilization has been to transform the life of man by the development of technical means of better living, the conquest of disease and in general the mastery of man's physical environment. It is not primarily concerned with man's purpose or goal, but in discharging its first function it has automatically laid bare certain principles that throw light on man's own nature and his origin. In so doing it has caused a great disturbance in the accepted ideas of theistic religion. From the time when Galileo discovered that the earth is not the centre of the solar system up to Darwin's first treatise on biological evolution, western religious ideas have been subjected to a series of shocks.

Nevertheless, religion despite its conflict with reason and knowledge, has survived, precisely because man does need a working hypothesis to account for his existence, his sense of moral values and his instinctive belief that there is a higher goal beyond mere comfortable living on this earth. In any case, most thinking people are now agreed that science, with all its wonders will never be able to create a heaven in this world. We have seen how, when one disease is brought under control, another source of disease arises. Bacteria which have been mastered by science proceed to transform themselves, and in the course of a few generations produce a variant of their type which is immune to the old attack; and so science has to start all over again seeking a fresh technique. I am not decrying the triumphs of science; but science as a source of knowledge seems to me superior to science as a palliative, since the benefits it has brought us have in many cases been outweighed by the dangers it has placed in our path. Disease, old age and death will always be with us; and this being so, human life will continue to be imperfect, darkened always by the shadow of grief and uncertainty.

Religion as it is understood in the West may have failed man, yet the *need* for religion still continues.

To what extent is it the function of traditional religions to interpret to man his own ultimate concerns in relation to the totality of powers, known and unknown, with which he must come to terms?

The only possible reply to this is that traditional religions can perform this function only to the extent permitted by man's present and future knowledge. It is a function that can no longer he performed through dogmas. Where traditional religion is able to assimilate new facts and hitherto unknown aspects of reality without sacrificing anything of its fundamental teachings it can continue to serve humanity as an interpreter of the "totality of powers, known and unknown" with which man must come to terms. But where dogma has been laid down once and for all as an infallible divine revelation, this adjustment is not possible. When one teaching once held to be a divinely-revealed truth is found to be false the whole edifice is shaken. This has already happened, not once but a thousand times, and there are limits to the elasticity of faith. Where most educated people are concerned those limits have already been exceeded and faith in "divine revelation" is as dead as the brontosaurus.

Buddhism, as I have already pointed out, is not a religion of "divine revelation" or of unsupported dogmas. It is the ultimate truth concerning life as discovered by one who approached the subject without any preconceived ideas, and who reached it in the only way possible, by delving into his own consciousness. Just as a scientist investigates the external world, so the Buddha investigated the internal world of the mind—or, if you like, the spirit. Everything that he taught thereafter was knowledge that is accessible to each and every one of us, if we will but follow his method of self-purification. On the intellectual side we find that there is no point at which science comes into conflict with Buddhism, nor is it ever likely to do so. The Teaching of the Buddha, therefore, can continue to perform the function indicated in this question and in the one that follows it, namely:

To what extent can the traditional religions perform this function in a community which accepts the scientific interpretation of reality?

What science interprets are natural phenomena, and science has reached the point of realizing that, since all the information we have concerning these phenomena are received through our physical senses, and the picture of the external world they present is quite different from the picture presented by physics, it is extremely doubtful whether science by investigating the external world of appearances will ever be able to bring us nearer to ultimate reality. But so far as knowledge concerning the nature of these phenomena will take us we have to accept the overall picture, including such established scientific facts as that of biological evolution. Buddhism is, I believe, the only religion which has no difficulty in accepting the theory of evolution as taught by modern biology and genetics. In one of his great sermons, the Brahmajāla Sutta, the Buddha describes how evolution and devolution take place in the course of a world-cycle, and all that he said is fully in conformity with present day knowledge. I will go even further, and tell you something that may surprise those who believe that religion is inseparable from the idea of a Creator-God. *Even if science succeeds in generating living organisms in a test-tube, or even in creating a sentient being equal to man, the truth of Buddhism is not in the least affected by it.* The reason for this is that no matter how life may come into being, whether by any of the natural birth-processes or by artificial means, it is past kamma which supplies the life-continuum, and it can operate in this manner wherever the constituents necessary for a living organism come together. There cannot be any achievement of science, no matter how revolutionary, that will ever contradict the teachings of Buddhism.

To what extent can science itself contribute to this religious function?

In the light of what I have already said it will be clear that where science is able to confirm the teachings of religion, as it does in the case of Buddhism, it changes its role from that of a destroyer of faith to that of an ally and most valuable friend. But it is useless to expect science, which confines itself to facts, to adapt those facts to the requirements of myth and dogma. It will never do so. In the struggle between religion and science in the West it is always religion that has had to give way. Buddhism welcomes science as the promoter of knowledge. More than this, it looks confidently to modern science to bring about that change of outlook which is essential if man is to realize the higher spiritual truths. We claim for the Buddha that he was the only religious teacher to bring scientific methods of approach to bear on the questions of ultimate truth.

What among the traditional religious beliefs remains effective?

This can only be answered from the viewpoint and experience of each of the representatives, speaking for one's own creed. As regards Buddhism, all its doctrines remain valid, and therefore all remain effective.

Is there some way in which the incompatible and competing claims among different systems of religious belief can be reconciled or reduced to a commonly acceptable denominator so that a rational mind can accept them?

Various attempts have been made throughout history to reconcile different systems of religious belief, but none of them has been successful. To quote only one instance, Sikhism began as an effort to reconcile Hinduism and Islam. Circumstances decreed, however, that in a matter of a few generations the Sikhs were to become the greatest opponents of Islam in India. Syncretism in religion sometimes enriches human thought, but more often than not it ends in confusion and failure. The modern attempts in this direction, such as Theosophy, have never attracted any large following because their efforts at reconciling the irreconcilable lead to a result that is even less acceptable to a rational mind then the original doctrines.

The reasons for this are perfectly clear; each theistic religion claims that its doctrines have been revealed by a "Supreme Being—God. These "revelations" contain different accounts of "creation," different interpretations of the "Supreme Being's" nature and intentions, and different versions of man's position in relation to "God" and his destiny after death. Arising from these conflicting doctrines there are widely differing systems of morality. Since none of the "divine revelations" can be altered in any fundamental way (except, presumably, by a fresh "divine revelation) the dogmas will always remain an insuperable obstacle to religious unity. Even between the various Christian sects there are deeply-rooted antagonisms although they all claim to take their inspiration from the same scriptures. Each theistic religion will always maintain that its own God is the only true deity, and will condemn the beliefs of all others. In the Semitic religions this is particularly marked; it began in Biblical times with disputes between the followers of various tribal gods, and it has carried on to the present day. There is absolutely no hope of these religions ever combining. Where such religions are concerned, tolerance of the views of others only comes when religious indifference sets in.

In Buddhism there are many reasons why tolerance of the religious views of others is enjoined as a necessary virtue. In the first place, Buddhism does not teach that any individual is eternally damned because he happens not to be a Buddhist. Followers of other religions may be reborn after death in heavenly states, if they have been virtuous during their lifetime. Suffering or happiness comes about as the result of actions (kamma), not as the result of having blind faith in any particular creed. There is no "salvation by faith" in Buddhism. Furthermore, Buddhist *mettā* or universal benevolence, extends to all beings, whatsoever their creed, race or colour. Buddhism is not a "divine revelation" which claims absolute faith and unquestioning obedience; it is a system for discovering truth and reality for oneself, and therefore invites reasoned criticism and objective analysis. History bears witness that Buddhists have always been able to live peacefully side by side with those of other faiths, so long as those faiths do not produce fanatics with whom it is impossible to live. Buddhist tolerance has been carried so far that for many centuries past it has ceased even to be a proselytizing religion.

Or, is only one of them valid? If so, how can it be established in the minds of all men?

If each of us did not personally believe that his own religion is the only valid one, he would not go under the banner of that religion. He would call himself an agnostic, a rationalist or a materialist.

The only way in which the validity of any religious belief can be established is to put it to the test of realization. First the question must be asked, "Are its doctrines compatible with reason and experience, and with the knowledge we have gained concerning the nature of the universe and of life? Secondly, does it offer us a way in which we, individually, can verify its claims in a manner which places it beyond all dispute?"

Here I must ask you to take note of the fact that not once throughout history, has any one of the supposed "Creator-Gods" given man a revelation of so final and conclusive a character that all men would be forced to accept it. On the contrary, all that the "revelations" have done has been to cause further dispute, and too often religious persecution.

What I have already said provides the answer to the first of my questions, so far as Buddhism is concerned. Buddhist philosophy is fully in accordance with reason and experience; it agrees with the general picture of the universe given by science and it does not ask us to believe in anything outside the normal order of nature. To my second point, the answer is that Buddhism does provide each of us with a means of verifying it for himself, through the practice of a scientific system of mental training and meditation which culminates in *vipassanā* or direct insight.

Jesus of Nazareth said, "By their fruits shall ye know them." We recognize the *Arahats* or Purified Ones of Buddhism by their spiritual and moral nature. If the whole of humanity were sufficiently developed intellectually and spiritually, all men would acknowledge a truth so completely demonstrated. But as I have said before, human beings are on different levels, due to their past kamma, and it is not likely that all men at the same time will ever be able to recognize truth with the same clarity. When the Buddha first gained full Enlightenment he felt doubtful whether any human beings would be able to understand the truth he had discovered, so utterly different was it from any of the accepted ideas of his time. But almost immediately he realized that there were some few "whose eyes were but lightly covered" with the dust of ignorance, and he determined to teach the Dhamma for their sake.

For our own age, however, there is one ray of hope. It comes from the fact that the majority tend in the long run, to follow the leadership of the intellectuals. If a sufficient body of intelligent men can be convinced of the reality of the spiritual truths, apart from all irrational dogmas and all sectarian associations, we might yet see a great religious revival and restoration of moral values in the world. It would be sufficient if each man would follow the religion of truth so far as he is able to comprehend it.

Or, is it impossible for man to be rational about religion?

Here, honesty compels me to be very blunt. Man can be rational about religion only when his religion is itself rational. If religion has up to now been associated with irrationality it is because the faith it demands is of a kind that can only be fed by unreason. To what else can "the willing suspension of disbelief" lead? The disgust felt by rationalists at the excesses of religious fanaticism is perfectly natural. So also is the reaction against irrational religion which has taken the form of scientific materialism. The sad fact, however, is that if the irrational elements are removed from most of the traditional religions there is very little left. This is the reason for the failure of religion in the western hemisphere.

What May Science Offer for Religious Belief?

What do the psychological sciences offer for the cure of sick souls, and the social sciences for the cure of a sick society?

To what extent are the psychoanalyst and the social worker the heirs of the priest and preacher?

Why are the psycho-social sciences so ineffective in performing these religious tasks?

These three questions must be taken together, since they form three aspects of a single problem.

The psychological sciences have had a limited success in the treatment of sick minds but they are still in the experimental stage. In many cases they fail to relieve the tensions and inner conflicts that come through the lack of a spiritual anchorage in our turbulent and distracted society. There is now a tendency for medical science to fall back on drugs—"tranquilizing tablets" and sedatives—for the relief of neuroses. Psychological science has not yet got down to the cause of man's psychic unrest, and until the cause is found and removed there can be no permanent cure. The methods of psychological treatment are lengthy and laborious, and results can never be guaranteed. Further, they are beyond the reach of most income groups. It is more than doubtful whether psychological science as it is practised in the West today will ever succeed in restoring man's confidence and inner harmony as does a firmly-held religious conviction. It can never be a substitute for that deep inner awareness of spiritual values, and that sense of security in a dangerous world, which religion gives.

The social sciences are concerned only with man's environment and external conditions. They bring happiness only to the extent to which they are capable of improving these conditions and within the limitations of the individual's response to them. They do not touch the inner, subjective life of man. It is there that he needs comfort and assurance, a refuge from the ever-present threat in the *sturm und drang* of life. Accidents, disease, the failure of the faculties, and finally old age and death are not to be prevented by the social sciences, so that they, too, can never be a substitute for religion. Man, who is something more than an animal requiring only creature comforts, needs to be informed concerning his purpose and destiny, and the need is so strong in him that for centuries he has been ready to accept even the most improbable theories in the name of religion, rather than nothing at all. Science has made it more difficult for him to do so, but has not been able to provide a satisfactory replacement for the beliefs it has destroyed.

What do the medical and biological sciences have to offer? Can the new medicine men bring peace of mind and loving spirit more effectively via the drugstore than the old rites did? Can we have personal salvation through surgery and pills?

These questions are all statements of the same problem in different terms. The "old rites" being no longer effective for modern man, he has had to have recourse to the drugstore, and possibly what it gives him is psychologically on a par with what his ancestors got from their religious rituals. Temporarily, one may be as effective as the other, but neither gets down to the basic cause of psychological unrest, which is desire. But whereas most of the traditional religions do at least urge man to curb his desire, our modern commercial civilization increases it while giving the illusion of satisfying it. The individual from his earliest years is taught to be competitive and acquisitive, and these qualities are exalted to the status of virtues. But it is not everybody who can be successful in competition, or who can acquire more wealth than his neighbour, and when there is no other objective in life set before a man he suffers from a feeling of frustration and personal inadequacy if he is one of the failures. At the same time, the failures of necessity outnumber the successful. In a materialistic society, the man who has failed materially is the equivalent to the man who was damned under the old religious dispensation. What has science to offer him? Nothing but empty palliatives. It is from this that we get mental disorders, psychosomatic sicknesses, neuroses, alcoholism and crime.

There is only one remedy—knowledge and understanding. By this I mean that man must understand the laws that govern his being. If circumstances seem to be against him, he should understand why they are against him, and why it is that his neighbour appears to be more favoured than himself. He can then endure the circumstances without being cast into despair, and he can work confidently to improve his prospects for the future. It is this rational understanding that Buddhism gives us through the knowledge of kamma and rebirth. It is a source of strength and an incentive to moral endeavour. In every way it is far superior both to the priest and his rites, and to the new medicine man with his drugstore remedies. By showing man that he is truly the master of his fate, and can transcend the errors of the past, it makes every day a day of spiritual regeneration and hope. The real and lasting psychological treatment is that which a man gives to himself, by self-understanding and self-mastery. This is the basis of Buddhist psychology, which is aimed at removing the causes of misery through the attainment of wisdom and insight.

For better crops is it more effective to take our gifts to the geneticist and chemist than to the altar?

Most educated people today would place their reliance on the scientists. And in this particular field they would be right. Religion, as Buddhists understand it, has nothing whatever to do with good crops. If the fields have not been tended diligently and fertilized as they should be, no amount of supplication at the altar will produce better crops. And if the cultivator's past kamma is bad, no amount of science will prevent blight, unseasonable weather or sickness from ruining his work. In this, as in all else, cause and effect, are the deciding factors, but it always takes more than one cause to produce a given result. To trust entirely in the altar, the scientist, or one's own labour, or in a combination of all three, might equally prove a mistake. I make this point expressly to impress upon you the fact that Buddhism gives answers that are different from those of the scientific materialist, the theistic religionist and the common sense "men-in-the-street" in equal degree. But any farmer, knowing from his own experience how often what appears to be sheer "chance" has ruined his crops, despite all his precautions, will be bound to agree that the Buddhist explanation fits the facts better than any other.

Can biological science do anything to prevent social disorder and injustice?

Short of interfering with the natural biological processes to such an extent as to amount to a remaking of man—that is, artificially creating a new type of humanity—there is surely not much that science can do about social disorder and injustice. Operations on the brain might make law abiding citizens out of criminals and potential criminals, but even if these doubtful techniques were to be brought to perfection there would still remain the problem of administering them. They would involve a heavy moral responsibility in interfering with an individual's personality and free will. Such operations could only be carried out on a large scale in a totalitarian society where individual rights had ceased to exist.

The problem of injustice raises this question to its highest factor. Biological science could only prevent injustice by making all men equal and producing a general uniformity in human nature. This is already theoretically possible, in that certain techniques are being developed by which mass-produced thinking tends to iron out the differences in outlook between one person and another. It may become possible in the future to direct mass thinking to such an extent that human beings lose their individual identity and become like the units of an ant community, controlled from a brain centre radiating thought-influences as required by the State. Injustice only exists where there is awareness of it; if it vanished as a human concept it would for all practical purposes cease to exist. But there is a wide gulf between what is theoretically possible and what is possible in practice. Man's attempts to interfere with the law of kamma, which is what in reality lies behind inequality and seeming injustice, have always failed. By democratic laws man may give equal opportunities, but no means has yet been discovered of making all men equal in intellect or character. The most fundamental injustices are those which are inherent in human nature itself. Why is one child born with a brilliant intellect while another is mentally deficient? The biologist may think he has the answer when he speaks of the characteristics inherited through the genes, but he is only describing a process; he is not explaining why that process takes place. To say that the genes have combined in a certain way to produce a given result is not the same as explaining why they have so combined and not in any other way. Buddhism does not deny the process, but it points to kamma as the underlying cause. Science might try to impede the working of kamma, and perhaps succeed in diverting it up to a point, but the end-result for humanity would be disastrous. It is not in man's nature to live in a state of ant-like uniformity because in such a condition he could never fulfil his highest potentialities.

I have said that if man's sense of injustice were obliterated, injustice would cease. But a much better solution to the problem is for mankind to realize that there are two kinds of injustice: human injustice, which can be remedied and natural injustice, which is only injustice in appearance. A visitor to a prison, knowing nothing of the offences for which the convicts had been sentenced, but seeing only their present wretched condition, would denounce it as a terrible injustice. So it is with persons who in this life are handicapped in some way, apparently for no fault of their own. The man who knows nothing of kamma is like the ignorant visitor to the prison; he sees only injustice in their present condition. But one who understands the law of cause and effect as it operates from birth to birth sees the workings of a just moral principle. He knows that there is no unmerited suffering. At the same time he knows how this suffering can be avoided, by adhering to the moral law. This understanding can eliminate the crushing sense of injustice under which many people labour, far more effectively than anything that can be expected from biological science.

Do the physical sciences answer our prayers for greater comfort and safety amid the hazards of the earth? But, are not all the benefits brought by scientifically based engineering more than offset by the dangers coming out of the laboratories of the nuclear and other scientists? And, what avail all the comforts if we are left depressed by the suggestion that the cosmos is indifferent to human value, and is a cosmos where our warm hopes are doomed to the ultimate cold of the death of our sun and all life? Can the physical sciences console or transform the hearts of men?

Every achievement of science, from the internal combustion engine onwards, has brought in its train as many perils as it has provided comforts. Everything science has given us is a potential cause of injury or death. People are killed by automobiles and airplanes; they are electrocuted by labour-saving devices; and death frequently comes to them via the surgeon's knife or the doctor's hypodermic syringe. These mishaps are called accidents, but there is also the misuse of scientific discoveries due to man's greed, hatred and ignorance or disregard of moral laws. In every direction nature thwarts science either by natural hazard or else through man's own imperfect nature. Life must always be a balance of opposites; there is nothing that has not its evil as well as its beneficial aspect. It is useless to look to science to give man increased happiness, unless science is applied in full knowledge of the spiritual laws. Even if that were to come about, it would only be the intentional misuse of science that would be eliminated; the accidental mishaps would still remain. And they would still require explanation.

We must accept the fact that the cosmos is indifferent to human values. The physical universe gives no indication whatsoever of the existence of a beneficent deity or of a purpose. The Buddhist is not disturbed by this fact. The life-process is a blind, groping force of craving, which in itself has no purpose except the satisfaction of desire. This life-process, involving rebirth after rebirth, is called in Buddhism *saṃsāra*. It has no higher purpose than the satisfaction of craving for sentient existence in one form or another. This is a very important and fundamental point on which Buddhism is in agreement with science and completely at variance with the theories of theistic religion. In Buddhism the only higher purpose in life is what man puts into it. This higher, spiritual purpose is the extinction of craving, which brings rebirth to an end.

The goal of Buddhism is the supreme goal of Nibbāna, which lies outside the saṃsāra or cosmic order. There alone is absolute peace to be found. Within saṃsāra all is strife, an unremitting struggle for existence; that is the very essence of what we call living. The "pleasure-principle" of modern psychology and the "struggle for survival" known to biological evolution are both facts which have always been recognized by Buddhism. Yet at the same time moral order is inherent in the law of cause and effect. If a man is crushed by it, as in a blind, impersonal and indifferent machine, it is because he himself is blind to the moral law and misuses his free will. The law of cause and effect is pitiless and inexorable. All the more reason, therefore, for man himself to cultivate pity, for he must put into saṃsāric life the higher qualities which it lacks. Whatsoever of divinity there is in life is of man's creation. By self-purification, eliminating the worldly instincts of lust, ill will and delusion, man can make himself into a god. The higher planes of saṃsāra are inhabited by such beings, *visuddhi-devas*, or "gods by purification." The arahat while alive on this earth is also a *visuddhi-deva*, enjoying the bliss and unbroken peace that can come only when all the worldly attachments are severed. The attainment of this state is the purpose which we ourselves can put into an otherwise purposeless round of existences. The cosmos does not impose any purpose on us; we are free to choose what our purpose shall be. We have the choice of two paths; either to go on being reborn for the satisfaction of sensual craving, with all the suffering that rebirth brings in its train, or to extinguish the fires of passion and gain the supreme and unchanging state of Nibbāna. Conditioned existence is impermanent, subject to suffering and devoid of self-reality. Therefore it is not real in the absolute sense. The supreme reality lies outside and beyond saṃsāra. Nibbāna cannot be described, for the simple reason that there are no words or concepts that we can derive from our experience of life in the sphere of relativity to apply to it. It can be experienced, but it cannot be described.

Nevertheless, the Buddha used certain terms to convey some idea of what Nibbāna means. He called it *asaṅkhata,* the unconditioned; *pāra,* the other shore (beyond saṃsāra); *ajarā,* the ageless; *amata,* the deathless; *dhuva,* the permanent; *ṭhāna,* the refuge; and *leṇa,* the shelter. But for that which has no qualities, since qualities mean relative values, there can be no exact description. It is sufficient to know that because there is this saṃsāra, which is impermanent, subject to suffering and void of reality, there must be that which is permanent, free from suffering and real in the ultimate sense. It is that reality which we mean by Nibbāna. It is not, as some people have imagined, a negative concept. It is beyond both negative and positive, for negative and positive are opposite poles of a relativity-complex. Neither is absolute because each depends upon the other for its existence. The cosmos exists by virtue of such opposites; hence it must always have good and evil mixed, each of them being relative to the viewpoint of the illusory "Self." Nibbāna being freedom from self-delusion, is also free from the opposites created by man's egocentric viewpoint.

The Buddhist is not dismayed by the prospect of the ultimate cold of the death of our sun. The Buddha taught that universes, or world-cycles, arise and pass away in endless succession, just as do the lives of individual men. Certainly our world must at some time come to an end. It has happened before, with previous worlds, and it will happen again. But so long as their kamma and vipāka life-continuum carries on, the beings now living in this world continue to be reborn in other spheres and other universes. All these states of being are impermanent; only Nibbāna is unchanging. The physical sciences can never console or transform the hearts of men. Only wisdom and understanding have this power; one who understands the nature of the universe and of life can face reality without fear. Knowing that all compounded things must pass away, he views even the destruction of universes with equanimity. His kingdom is not of this world.

Is the contribution of the several sciences to religion a negative one?

Should we frantically scratch among the old beliefs for some comfort and hope, and hold fast to them no matter how illogical and irrational they are, in the light of the scientific system or belief that we prefer to hold for resolving our other problems?

Can we be irrational and survive?

Scientific knowledge has shown itself not only negative towards dogmatic and "revealed" religion, but positively hostile to it. If it were not so, these questions would not be asked. It is man's awareness that his old religious ideas have broken down under the impact of science that has brought about this heart-searching quest for truth on some different level.

In the case of Buddhism, however, all the modern scientific concepts have been present from the beginning. There is no principle of science, from biological evolution to the General Theory of Relativity, that runs counter to any teaching of Gotama Buddha. Einstein himself wrote that if there is any religion which is acceptable to the modern scientific mind it is Buddhism. Yet it is doubtful whether even Einstein quite realized the extent to which modern science confirms the teachings of Buddhism. Only one who has both studied and meditated upon every aspect of the Buddha Dhamma can fully appreciate the light that it throws upon the problems that science itself has raised. In fact, Buddhism continues where science leaves off; it carries scientific principles to higher planes of realization. It shows that the laws of physics are the counterpart of spiritual laws and that there is a common meeting ground for both.

If physics says that the apparently solid universe is not in reality composed of solid substance at all, but is actually a flux of electronic energy, Buddhism said it first. If the scientific philosopher says that our senses deceive us in presenting this insubstantial series of nuclear events in the guise of solid, enduring matter, Buddhism anticipated him by saying the same thing and making it the basis of the Buddhist analysis of phenomena. If the psychologist, neurologist and biologist say that there is no indication of an immortal soul in man, they have made the discovery two thousand five hundred years after the Buddha. If science says that there is no ground for belief in a Creator-God, it is merely confirming an essential doctrine of Buddhism. But if the most advanced thinkers believe, as they now tend to do, that in some way mind, or mental activity, is the activating force behind the phenomena of life, they have hit upon one of the eternal verities which Buddhism has always proclaimed. For the Buddha said: "*Mano pubbaṅgamā dhammā, manoseṭṭhā manomayā.*" "Mind precedes all phenomena; mind predominates them and creates them." It is man's mental activity which creates them; and that act of creation is going on from moment to moment. Kamma is mental volition: the will-to-act followed by the action. If the mental volition is of an immoral order the resulting states of consciousness are fraught with suffering because of the reaction. But if the mental volition is of a moral type and the action is a good and beneficial one, the resulting states of consciousness are happy. In other words, good actions bring as their result good conditions and the pleasurable consciousness associated with such conditions.

Thus we create the world, making it good or bad for ourselves by the process of kamma and *vipāka*. Truly, life is exactly what we make it for ourselves. Therefore Buddhism tells us not to look to any external agency for salvation, but to rely entirely upon our own efforts. It is the science of the mind, which teaches us how to harness the tremendous power of mind for our own benefit and that of all beings. It is for this reason that Buddhism places such great importance on its profound system of psychology: the Abhidhamma means the "highest law" and this system gives a minute analysis of all the states of consciousness; it is the complete path to self-understanding and self-mastery. Abhidhamma goes much further than modern Western psychology because it deals with basic principles of the mind and relates the mental processes to the universal system of moral values. It is precisely here that Western psychology fails, for the psychoanalyst of the West is not concerned with moral values; in fact, he doubts whether they have any existence outside man's imagination. He is unable to give guidance on questions of right or wrong. But Buddhism explains the relationship between mental activity and ethical laws, showing that morality is an integral part of the pattern of cause and effect which is set up by our mode of thinking and the actions produced by it.

Science is concerned with discovering the causes of phenomena. So also is Buddhism; but Buddhism goes further in revealing how these causes can be moulded to produce better results. In placing mind at the centre of all phenomena, Buddhism is the opposite pole of materialism; yet its picture of the physical world corresponds exactly with that of modern science. This in itself is a remarkable fact which should claim the attention of all intelligent persons. That the Buddha was able, by direct insight, to fathom the nature of the universe, without any of the aids of modern science, two thousand five hundred years ago, is the proof of his Enlightenment. No other religious teacher in the world's history has achieved this. Where the physical sciences will never be able to console or transform the hearts of man, Buddhism does both. It satisfies the intellect and the heart in equal measure, and it gives hope founded upon a rational and verifiable faith. To the Buddhist there is no question of having to decide between faith and reason. For us, followers of the Supreme Buddha, faith is reasonable, and reason confirms faith.

Or, is it possible to re-examine the human situation in the fuller light of the spectrum of knowledge, to establish a picture of man and his opportunities in the cosmos that is hopeful as well as honest?

This is precisely what Buddhism enables us to do. Accepting all the facts of science, even those most disturbing to man's complacency and egoism—seeing human life, just as science does, a mere fraction of the vast mass of phenomena cast up by the cosmos—it yet places the highest possible value on human life and human endeavour. It shows that man, despite his seeming insignificance in this tremendous cosmic process is really the master of it, if he can become the master of himself. Pascal saw that man is greater than the blind forces of nature because even though he is crushed by them he remains superior by virtue of his understanding of them. Again, Buddhism carries the truth further: it shows that by means of understanding man can also control his circumstances. He can cease to be crushed by them, and can use their laws to raise himself. The Buddha said, "Behold, O monks, within this fathom-long body, equipped with sense-perception and mind, I declare unto you is the world, the origin of the world, the cessation of the world and the way to its cessation." The mastery of the external world is not in the external world, but in ourselves.

Has there not been revealed to us, if we will but look at the newer truths or beliefs yielded by the sciences, that man finds himself indeed a creature created by the cosmos, and thus ordained by it, and so endowed by that creator with a mind which can in its finite way learn to appreciate the whole, and to enter creatively and consciously into the grand scheme of development in which the infinite cosmos is engaged?

Here is a wonderful mass of contradictions, such as Buddhism could never have produced. Man, created by the cosmos, which is blind, impersonal and mindless, cannot have been endowed by that mindless cosmos with a mind. The cosmos being mindless, how could it give its creation a mind? And if the mind is finite, how can it ever appreciate the whole, and "enter creatively and consciously into the grand scheme of development" of a cosmos that is infinite? What, in any case, is that "grand scheme of development"? Where is there any evidence of a purpose in the cosmos beyond the blind, groping force of craving which I have already mentioned? We have seen that science pictures a cosmos that is indifferent to man; what possibility, then, is there of his being able to co-operate with whatever scheme it may have? The reply of the scientist to this would be merely that the question is another example of man's petty conceit. Why should man suppose that his efforts one way or another are of any interest to the cosmos? Here, it is obvious the word "cosmos" is being used simply as a substitute for "God." A cosmos with a purpose becomes the same as the theistic idea of "God." But whereas the theistic idea of a scheme evolved by "God" gives man individual hope—the hope of a personal immortality—the idea of a scheme being worked out by the blind, impersonal forces of a cosmos which clearly cares nothing for the units of the human race holds out no such promise. Those who can derive hope from the contemplation of a remote futurity when the cosmos will have perfected humanity, but they themselves will have totally ceased to exist, may be satisfied with this concept, but it will never be a source of inspiration to better living for the majority. The individual ants composing an ant army may be content to form a bridge across water for their fellows with their own drowned bodies, but human beings are not ants. The average human being desires that his own life should have a meaning and a goal, and not be just a stepping-stone towards a doubtful goal for his remote descendants. In any case, the ultimate perfection of humanity by biological processes is now more than doubtful. Science has shown that evolution simply does not work that way; it produces retrogression as well as progress. Some species have entirely disappeared from the earth. Have we any guarantee from science that man will not vanish also—perhaps with the aid of science itself?

The answer to this question can only be an emphatic "No." This view of life will never fulfil human aspiration or give comfort and support to suffering mankind. But now we come to the final query.

What thrilling and life-giving and hopeful beliefs are possible from an honest contemplation of the new revelations of reality?

We can derive thrilling, life-giving and hopeful convictions from contemplating the "new revelations of reality" in the light of Buddhism. No other way is possible. There are no "new" truths, and there is certainly nothing in the new revelations of science that is not already in the Teaching of Gotama Buddha. By way of summing up I will repeat:

Buddhism does not depend upon any of the commonly accepted religious dogmas which science has exploded, such as that of a Creator-God, an immortal soul, a supernatural scheme of salvation, or a particular "revelation" made at one specific point of history and one special geographical location to a select person or group of persons. It does not maintain that man is a special creation marked off from the rest of living beings by having an unchanging, undying element that has been denied to others. It does not require any myths, such as that of "original sin" to explain the presence of evil and suffering in the world.

These are the negative aspects of its agreement with science. The points of agreement are many. They include the view that all phenomena, including life, are a flux of energies; the correspondence between biological evolution and spiritual evolution; the truth that craving, or the "life-urge," is the motivating factor behind the processes of evolution; the fact that ours is not the only planet capable of producing and supporting life; the truth that mankind and the animals differ from one another only in a qualitative sense, as one species differs from another, not in essential kind; and the view that although the cosmos is itself mindless, the operative force behind it is an activity corresponding to mind.

The Buddhist explanation of the cosmos is that, as I have indicated, it is man's own mental activity which creates the cosmos; every successive world-cycle is brought into being and supported by a combination of natural causes—the physical causes known to science, and the kamma of beings who have lived before. Buddhism, like science, is based on cause and effect.

Herein lies the greatest hope for mankind. Buddhism gives a positive and rational motive for moral endeavour and spiritual aspiration such as cannot be found in any other religious system. It asserts the supremacy of moral law without resorting to supernatural causes. It shows that there is no injustice in the causal law, yet at the same time gives us the knowledge that in extending compassion to those who are suffering the results of their past misdeeds we are advancing the higher spiritual laws. Even though we cannot undo the past kamma of ourselves or others, we can yet help to mitigate the suffering it may have brought, or provide some compensation for the handicap, such as blindness or deformity, which is its present result. In so doing we are originating good kamma which will produce beneficial results in the future. Thus Buddhism teaches the cardinal virtues of *mettā*, universal benevolence, and *karuṇā*, compassion. It is man himself who puts pity into a pitiless universe. And the highest effort and highest aspiration of all is that which is directed to the attainment of Nibbāna. Man need not despair of all worldly improvement, since such improvement is within his reach by obedience to the moral laws; yet even though earthly conditions were to be rendered hopeless by human greed, hatred and ignorance, there is still a temporary refuge in the higher planes of existence, and a final, unchanging certainty in Nibbāna, the Eternal peace—which, however, must be won by individual effort in self-purification.

That is the message of hope I bring in the name of Buddhism to the delegates to this conference. The Supreme Buddha's Teaching is for all times and all men. It is capable of bringing peace, happiness and prosperity to our troubled world. As the humble spokesman of millions of Buddhists I earnestly entreat that all men of understanding and good will here present will weigh in their hearts the things I have said and form their own judgement as to whether they are true, reasonable and good. The Buddha himself did not ask more than that.

May all beings be happy!

The Lamp of the Law

Excerpts from Gurulugomi's
Dharmapradīpikā

Translations by

Soma Thera & Piyadassi Thera

WHEEL PUBLICATION NO. 38

Introduction

In the early forties when the second world war was being waged in all its fury, two bhikkhus lived away from the haunts of men in the quiet solitude of a forest hermitage (*Samarasiṃhārāmaya*) at Telijjavila in South Ceylon (now Sri Lanka), passing their days in quiet contemplation and study. A book that interested them much was a Sinhala treatise on the Dhamma, Gurulugomi's *Dharmapradīpikā*; so great was their fascination with the lucid exposition that they decided to put into English selected excerpts from that celebrated work. One of them, the Venerable Soma Thera, is no more. Meeting ends in parting (*saṃyoga viyogantā*).

Dharmapradīpikā, which may aptly be translated as Lamp (*pradīpikā*) of the Law (Dharma), is a sort of commentary on the *Mahābodhivaṃsa*, the "Chronicle of the Tree of Enlightenment," written in Pāli by that erudite author, Upatissa Mahā Thera.

Judging from the style of language, it can be said that the *Dharmapradīpikā* was written either toward the end of 12th century CE or beginning of the 13th century. As our author himself says in his other work, *Amāvatura*, the "Perennial Spring," *Dharmapradīpikā* is a work dealing with the doctrine (*Dhamma*) of the Buddha while *Amāvatura* speaks of the life of the Buddha.

Gurulugomi explains with skill and taste two hundred and five Pāli quotations, or rather terms, from the *Mahābodhivaṃsa.* Some of the explanations are terse, but many others are written at length. These elucidations are not written in unvarying tone, but have change and variety. While making clear the Dhamma terms he introduces charming and informative stories from the Buddhist Canon, and adorns his work with copious, suitable quotations, both verse and prose, from the Pāli and Sanskrit. Though it is easy to trace the origin of the Pāli quotations, scholars have found it difficult to trace some of the Sanskrit verses to their original sources. Some are from the works of Āryaśūra, Śāntideva, Harṣa and the logician, Dharmakīrti.

Gurulugomi is renowned as one of the rare masters of Sinhala classical diction and style. His translations have the verve and freshness of something vitalisingly original. His elucidations are smooth, natural and convincing. His descriptions, even of the most unlikely things, have vigour, and can hold the reader's attention. Though he is not known to have written any work of poetry, his *Amāvatura* is a prose-poem of deep feeling, lucid and dignified.

Dharmapradīpikā testifies to the range and quality of the author's knowledge of Pāli and Sanskrit wisdom, his dexterity of choice, and his grasp of the subtleties of the Buddha's teaching. Though it bears the title of a scholium to a book of religious history, it is also intended to be a handbook of instruction on practical points of doctrine.

It may be stated that this is a free translation to which a few quotations from other sources also have been added.

The Buddhist Publication Society merits a word of praise for making this translation available for the large number of their readers, at home and abroad.

Piyadassi
Vajirārāma, Colombo 5,
Ceylon (Sri Lanka)
November 1961.

The Vision of Suffering

Vibrant with compassion for sorrowing humanity, the Wise Being working for perfection, thought, "Without a perceptible starting-point is the wandering on through birth and death (*saṃsāra*); fearful are the states of misery; hard to get at is human life, and in the other remaining kinds of existence good cannot be wrought out well. My forebears accumulated much wealth but flitted hence taking not a copper with them; nor did they ever return to enjoy their treasure. Alas! They have been destroyed; they have missed the luck of getting the best out of a good rebirth." In this manner, great beings in search of enlightenment view existence and making a gift of their possessions to the world depart for the homeless state of lone endeavour in self-mastery.

What is wandering on (*saṃsāra*)? Penetrating into the centuries and the millenniums with his unclouded knowledge, the Master knows the non-perceivable as such; he knows the limits of knowledge. Through the assured understanding of clear insight into the limits of the knowable, he has declared that a first beginning and a last end of beings faring on in the interminable sea of birth and death cannot be known, cannot be perceived. Wandering on (*saṃsāra*) is just the succession of the mental and bodily aggregates (*khandhānaṃ paṭipāṭi*) of birth-bound beings whirled between the imperceptibility of the beginning and the imperceptibility of the end.

In this wandering on, this journeying in incalculable time, the suffering borne by beings is colossal. How can one reckon all one's sorrows, life after life, through partings from the beloved, through union with the unloved, through death of dear ones, and through the loss of one's own health, and wealth, limbs and life?

In this sweeping on of life's stream, hard it is, says the Master, to find another who has not been one's own mother, father, brother, sister, son or daughter. Ay, every man might well have been bound to every woman, and every woman to every man, in this long trail of woe!

Where in the whole wide earth could be found a spot unpolluted of the dead? Somewhere in beings' endless flux some one might well have lain dead anywhere on the earth's face. To the Brahmin Upasālhaka, who was searching for virgin ground, for ground where no corpse had been burnt, the Master said,

> "Just on this spot have been burnt the very
> Corpses of Upasālhakas as many
> As fourteen thousand; there isn't any
> Place on earth that's not a cemetery."

Every brand of suffering does one undergo through rebirth in the diverse planes of becoming. And there is nothing in the world but suffering to one who sees life aright; for everything including the highest and most intense form of pleasant sensuous experience, is impermanent, fleeting, passing away. Therefore did the foremost of mankind's truth-speakers declare: *all that is experienced is suffering.*[1]

And in view of this absolute pain-laden nature of sentient existence the Master urges on his disciples the need for the complete renunciation of it, thus: "Beginningless is the wandering on through the round of rebirth; not to be known is the start of beings enmeshed by ignorance, gulled by craving; running on, speeding on through interminable births and deaths: and in this way, for long have you felt sorrow bitter and sharp, and made the graveyards bigger and bigger. Because of that should you turn away from all *karma* formations (*saṅkhārā*), cut them off, and become free of them."

Rare is Human Birth

During secular stretches of wayfaring in life, very, very rarely does one get human birth: "It is as if a man should cast into the wide ocean a yoke with a single hole in it, and that yoke should be carried hither and thither by the wind's impetuosity—now westward, now eastward, now northward and now southward. And say that a blind turtle comes to the surface once in a century. What do you think, O monks, will that blind turtle shoot its head through that yoke-hole?"

"If Lord, after the passage of a long period of time it succeeded, then it would be a marvel."

"Quicker, O monks, will be the passing through of the head of that turtle through that yoke-hole, than the getting back to the human state of a man fallen into an existence of misery (*apāya*)."

Fully hard it is to accumulate merit when experiencing great suffering in states of misery: as an animal trembling with fear of death, at the time of seizure, by net, fish-snare and the like; as a draught-animal prodded by pointed goad and so forth; as a ghost tearful of face, subject to insatiable hunger and unquenchable thirst, with a mere skin-and-bone body and exclaiming ever and anon, "Alas, what woe!'"

Thus owing to extreme suffering in the states of misery, and owing to intense delight and self-indulgence in the happy worlds of the shining ones, one does not accomplish well doing in both those sorts of becoming, those being unfit for such accomplishment.

But in the human state, through the conjunction of a fair measure of pleasant living, and the fellowship of the good, the door to merit is open. If one suffers as a human, there is every chance of that very suffering becoming a supportive condition for growth in insight, for the gaining of confidence in the truth.

In the fashioning of the sword of wisdom which destroys ignorance and the passions, suffering and pleasant living are like the water and the fire to which the smith resorts in forging a weapon and bringing it to efficiency and the right firmness. Human birth with its "tolerableness" becomes a suitable ground for producing skill. Yet if beings bear human form and have the nature of denizens, of states of misery, that is, of those tormented in hell, in the ghost plane or in the animal plane, then such beings do not accumulate skill. Three are the kinds of unfortunate beings in human guise and they may be known thus: the first by their readiness to kill and to commit all kinds of violence; the second by their lack of energy and consequent depression and misery; the third by their extreme sensuality, lack of independence of character, and by their transgression of the limits of decency.

Then, to which kind of human is it possible to get skill? Only to that kind which has established itself firm in human righteousness. And what is that righteousness? The state of being endowed with shame and fear to do evil; the settled reliance on the fact of moral causation, that is, that good action produces good consequences, and evil, bane; the knowing of what is, and what is not, conducive to one's own weal; compassion toward other beings; plenitude of the heart's upsurge to realize the good and the true according to actuality; the shunning of the action-course of unskill (*akusala*); the practice of the action course of skill (*kusala*).

One established in this manner enters the place of merit; for him the way to the acquisition of worth is open; he grows in good. He becomes pure.

II
On Liberality and Virtue

Liberality is the first among the ten perfections (*pāramī*),[2] the four beneficent actions (*saṅgaha-vatthu*),[3] and the three great kinds of merit (*puñña-kiriyā*);[4] it is a quality that all Bodhisattas possess in abundance, and a treasure of the Buddhas.

Givers are of three kinds: those who give away the coarse, and keep for themselves what is fine; those who share with others what they have, be it coarse or fine; those who give away what is fine and keep for themselves what is coarse. The first are those who give as to a servant, the second as to a friend, and the third who give as a master in a lordly way.

Wealthy folk who stint in giving are like rain clouds that do not empty themselves on the thirsty earth. Like clouds that burst over some particular area, in some folk tract, are they who give of their abundance to some particular person, sect or denomination. And those who give to all without distinction of caste, creed,

---

2. The *pāramī* are ten essential qualities of extremely high standard, initiated by compassion, and ever tinged with understanding, free from craving, pride and false views, that qualify an aspirant for Buddhahood. They are: *dāna*—charitable giving; *sīla*—virtue or purity of conduct; *nekkhamma*—renunciation; *paññā*—wisdom; *viriya*—unflinching energy; *khanti*—forbearance; *sacca*—truthfulness; *adhiṭṭhāna*—resolution, *metta*—loving-kindness; *upekkhā*—equanimity.

3. *Dāna*—generosity; *piyavacana*—pleasant speech; *atthacariyā*—selfless service; *samānattatā*—equality.

4. *Dāna*—liberality; *sīla*—morality; *bhāvanā*—meditation.

colour, race or any other restricting consideration, are like those clouds which pour down their fertilizing contents on all parts of a country and nourish all vegetal life.

A giver should be happy and satisfied at every stage of giving. Pleased and contented should his heart be while going to make a gift, while actually making the gift and after. Only in such circumstances does the full benefit of giving accrue to the giver.

Fivefold is the advantage of such giving: one becomes dear to many, wins the company of the good, one's fame spreads, one fulfils a duty of the household-life, and lastly one fares well after death.

Timely giving is of five kinds: the giving to guests, to those on the point of making a journey, to the sick, to the famine-stricken, and to the virtuous.

Gifts are properly given when they are handed over with respect, with dignity, not casually, and when they are given with belief in the effect of the gift, i.e. its moral efficacy.

Liberality should be practised not only with regard to human beings. Our dumb and forlorn fellows of the animal kingdom too must experience our liberality. All who are capable of benefiting by our gifts should be made partakers of our liberality.

Virtue

The giving of material gifts and alms, however, blesses only a few. But he who cultivates virtue blesses all sentient beings. He makes to all beings the gifts of fearlessness by his stainless conduct.

Therefore, the Master taught thus: "Here, O monks, a disciple of the Pure Ones giving up killing is restrained as regards killing ... giving up theft is restrained as regards theft ... giving up sexual wrong is restrained as regards sexual wrong ... giving up untrue speech is restrained as regards untrue speech ... giving up drink is restrained as regards drink, and thereby blesses all sentient beings with the gift of security, non-hate, and harmlessness."

That kind of conduct which brings happiness and ease of mind, which never gives room for remorse and repentance to come up, which leads to a good destiny and is the basis of the good life here and now is called virtue.

Killing

One abstains from killing other beings because one knows how dear life is to oneself; so infers that it must be the same for others. All happiness of men in this world depends on their lives. So to deprive them of that which contains all good for them is cruel and heartless in the extreme. Is it, therefore, a wonder that those who destroy others' lives bring on themselves the hate and ill will of those they slay?

Further, it is said in the books that those who kill will be struck by deadly weapons often in this life, and come to a terrible end generally. After this life the *kamma* of their ruthless deeds will for long push them to states of woe. Should such destroyers of life be born in prosperous families with beauty and strength and other happy bodily attributes, still their *kamma* will dog them to an early grave. Therefore it is said:

> "Tho' born to treasure, grain and pleasure all
> Tho' dowered with the love-god's grace of cast,
> Who take away the lives of others' fall
> To early death unwilling; sure's such blast."

Neither in the sky, nor in mid-ocean, nor in a cleft in the mountains is that place to be found on earth, abiding wherein one may escape from (the consequences of) one's ill-deed.

But those who refrain from the slaughter of beings, who are as it were protectors of all living sentient things, who give all other beings the gift of security are like mighty trees that shelter and shade man, bird and beast, with their myriad foliage.

Even though their lives be in grave peril, and death with all its terrors confronts them, they stand firm in their determination to save from harm all other forms that pulse with sentience.

In Āryasūra's *Jātakamālā*, the "Garland of Birth Stories," we read that once when the *Bodhisattva* was hard pressed by enemies in hot pursuit, rather than get beyond reach of his pursuers by crushing an eagle's nest full of eleven eaglets, he turned back and went towards his enemies in order to save the small unfledged birds, saying to his charioteer:

> "So turn back the car; better for me to die
> Struck down by dreadful titan-clubs that loom,

Than live in blame; ashamed, as sure I must,
If I those timid fledglings send to doom."

And he who thus abstains from slaughter of all kinds becomes himself fearless, calm and serene, pleasant of presence, beloved of all beings human, divine, and ghostly. Such a one truly approximates to the sage in character, for "Ever does the sage guard the things that breathe," "*niccaṃ muni rakkhati pāṇine.*"

Theft

Things which belong to another, things of which another is the master, are never wrongly taken by him who walks according to the Dhamma. To take things wrongly from others, violently or by compulsion or by deceit, is against all standards of decency and gentlemanly conduct. Says an olden book: "*paradravyaharanaṃ ātmadravyasya vināśahetu*"—the wrongful taking of others' substance becomes the cause of one's own loss of goods. And again: "*Na cauryātparaṃ mṛtyuypāśaḥ,*" worse death-trap there is none than robbery. For who robs and spoils others becomes subject to the king's punishment and the people's indignation, to endless suffering and tribulation. Therefore should one avoid this evil action of wrongly taking others' property as one would avoid poison, fire, and fearful, deadly snakes. Who keeps the rule of abstaining from theft gains much in inner and outer well-being. He lives a happy life and fares well after death.

"Free from the gyve, the lash, the stick, the knife,
Free from the wrath of king, men's ire and blame,
Free from the loss of wealth, of limb, and life,
Full free from theft, the good gain, bliss and fame."

Misconduct

He who abstains from sexual wrong is blessed with a heart that is ever at peace and serene, and a body possessed of strength and energy at all times. He is moving on towards higher ways of life, and nobler states of thought.

"Who chastely lives wins beauty, strength,
And good men's praise and boon of health;
His mind is clear and fit to tread

The Path to Truth; and he is wed
To noble thought, to kindly deed,
And speech that's pure; he sows the seed
Of virtues rare; makes all to sprout,
And blossom. Then rich fruit brings out."

But sad is the fate of him who goes wrong sexually. He soils his own mind-flux and that of others. Therefore it is written by the poet:

"The matrix sure of every bane,
The bringer to states of dreadful pain,
Free love is. Dākini's the name
Of wife not thine. Think not on such dame."

False Speech

Who abstains from false speech wins the trust and confidence of many, and is honoured by those who know him. It is an abstention pre-eminently practised by the *Bodhisattvas*, the beings who are in search of perfect enlightenment. Of them it is said that they never utter untruth, in any circumstances whatsoever. The speaker of truth is free from fear and trembling in the midst of assemblies. He is ever courageous and firm, and unshakable even when confronted with the greatest hostility. He is strong with the strength of a mighty host in full panoply, because his heart is crystal-clear, pure and speckless. He is always pleasant and gentle, courteous and helpful, restrained and patient, a speaker who delights and calms others with the effortless eloquence of truth. Such a one may truly say of himself:

"Pure is my heart for all that's true I think,
Clear, my mind; there no dark lies slink.
Clean my speech, rid of things that soil,
A smooth soft kindly flow of limpid oil."

The liar is everywhere discredited. Who is shameless enough to speak untruth, he has no virtue in his heart. There is no wrong that a deliberate liar cannot perpetrate. So say the books.

If one who has taken on the life of the homeless monk utters untruth, then by that very utterance one makes one's "monkhood" empty. "Empty, O Rāhula, is the life of that monk who shamelessly utters untruth," says the Master urging on his beloved son the importance of true speech in the holy life.

Further, it is said that the liar comes to get a bad destiny hereafter. He becomes dull, stupid, hideous of presence, repellent to others, and passes on to states of becoming where he loses the power of speech.

Intoxicants

One abstains from intoxicants in order to keep the mind free from confusion. Drink and drugs are destructive of right thinking, that is, thinking based on non-hate, non-violence, and renunciation. He who takes intoxicants becomes angry, cruel, infatuated. Therefore, the follower of the Buddha, knowing well the disadvantages of wrong thinking which follow intoxication, does not taint his mind with the poison of drink which burns out the germinal power of the seeds of good in his mind. Speaking of the evils of drink, Āryaśūra in his *Jātakamālā* says:

> "O lord of men, how canst thou e'er partake
> Of that drink by which good qualities fully break,
> Which stuns all worth, doth violence to good name,
> Blurs mind's vision and drives out all shame."

Such is the treasure of virtue which men wishing for happiness should increase and protect. It is the right expedient for winning all good things here and hereafter.

All inner wealth has virtue for source. Like a rich mine which yields countless jewels virtue gives endless delight to the good man.

Virtue is the ground from which one takes off to the high place of perfect holiness.

Virtue is the charmed weapon to slay the passions, and the coat of mail that wards off all the blows of Māra.

Virtue makes life pleasant, imbues it with power and vitalizes and refreshes it.

Virtue is like the cool, cleansing, fertilizing rain.

The virtuous attain to the splendour of great renown, wealth and honour.

The man of virtue is always mindful and completely aware. At the moment of death he is free from all confused thinking and is calm and composed.

Because of these things that go along with virtue one fosters it, guards it, and protects it with the single-minded devotion of a mother protecting her only child, the apple of her eye.

III
Renunciation

Now, a man endowed with the treasure of virtue begotten of his confidence in the Blessed One, sees the disadvantages of sensual pleasures, remembers how the Teacher impressed on his disciples the need for giving up sensuality—the low, common, worldly thing—by comparing it to a bare bone, a piece of flesh that produces strife, a flaming torch, a pit of fiery coals, a dream, borrowed goods, a fruit tree laid low when one is on it eating the fruits, and turns away from the world's way. That man is like a mighty elephant speeding out of a burning wood. Stirred by the world's ill, he hastens out of the confined life of the house to the life of homelessness, free and open as the spreading sky, with just one aim in view: perfection.

Then away from all disturbing worldly influences the giver-up of home lives the lonely life of the recluse according to the enfranchising precepts of restraint (*pātimokkha-saṃvara-sīla*).

He observes the precepts meticulously, seeing danger even in the smallest fault.

Seeing a form, hearing a sound, perceiving an odour, tasting a flavour, feeling some tangible thing, or cognizing an idea, he is not moved either towards or away from any object of consciousness. He maintains perfect equipoise putting afar all likes and dislikes. He subdues his heart. This control, this guarding of the doors of sense (*indriya-gutta-dvāra*) he practises with zest.

He is moderate in eating (*bhojane mattaññū*). He takes his food right carefully, reflecting according to the Dhamma, all the while he eats. He knows that he does not eat for sport, self-indulgence, improvement of the body, or for making it appear comely, but merely for keeping the body unharmed for living out the holy life.

He is devoted to wakefulness (*jāgariyaṃ anuyutto*). Night and day he cleans his mind of all dross that may gather there.

Such a man is satisfied covering his body with a patchwork ascetic robe and stilling his hunger with what he gets into his bowl begging from house to house. He is compared to a bird. Like the wings of a bird are his bowl and robes and he goes whithersoever he lists, unhindered by the weight of many belongings, and without thought of leaving behind anything.

In all his conduct he is mindful and completely aware (*sati-sampajañña*). There is nothing done by him which is bereft of consciousness of purpose (*sātthaka-sampajañña*), of advantage (*sappāya-sampajañña*), of fitness (*gocara-sampajañña*), of actuality seen steadily in the clear light of transience, suffering and soullessness (*asammoha-sampajañña*). Doing all things, rightly and well, he grows in holiness. Of that recluse it is said:

> "Who is freed in mind of all that is vain;
> Not fickle; wise, with senses under rein;
> He verily shines in his robe of rags,
> Like lion in its cave midst the mountain crags."

This searcher of the highest weal practises the burning out of the passions, the true *tapas*. He thinks: Others may harm, but I will become harmless; others may slay living beings, but I will become a non-slayer; others may wrongly take things, but I will not; others may live unchaste, but I will live pure; others may utter falsehood, I, however, will speak the truth; others may slander, talk harshly, indulge in gossip, but I will talk only words that promote concord, harmless words, agreeable to the ear, full of love, pleasing to the heart, courteous, worthy of being borne in mind, timely, fit, and to the point; others may be covetous, I will not covet; others may mentally lay hold of things awry, but I will lay mental hold of things fully aright. Energetic, steeped in lowliness of heart, unswerving as regards truth and rectitude, peaceful, honest, contented, generous and truthful in all things will I be. I will cherish mindfulness and wise penetration that is fully aware of the truth at all times, and will not be moved by the evanescent or grasp at it. Thus, he never acts slavishly like the unthinking herd.

Progressing in this way, shedding all dust by the intensity of practice that becomes keener and keener, he develops the path of mental absorption (*jhānamagga*) by casting out the hindrances.

Seated in cloister cell, at the foot of a tree, under the open sky, or in some other suitable place, he fixes his mind on a subject of meditation (*kammaṭṭhāna*) and by struggle, and unceasing effort washes out the impurities of his mind-flux and gradually reaches the first, the second, the third and the fourth absorption, and enjoys the benefit of his high attainment. Lastly with the power of concentration he has won, he turns his mind to the understanding of actuality in the highest sense, and when he knows that, clears himself of all defilements by the roots.

With that final clearing out he reaches the state where dawns for him the Light of Nibbāna, the calm beyond words, the "unshakability" beyond all thought, the freedom that is beyond all deeds, the sure and secure ground, the splendour that is imperishable, the happiness of stillness, of relief and perfect peace immeasurably deep and pure which can be overturned by nothing and by none, the highest truth.

That is the very crown of the homeless life; its greatest fruit. That is the thing for the sake of which young men of good family leave home for the homeless life. By that fruit all birth, old age and death are brought to an end, the pure life of holiness is lived out, all that must be done is done, and the world holds nothing more for one.

IV
The Heart of the Holy Life

He who wishes to put out the fire of anger holds fast to restraint and control and never separates from the genial company of love. *Mettā,* that super-solvent among virtues, which causes all disharmony and luridity of mind to disappear.

Love

Ever is the loving one—*mettavādi*—one who draws in the claws of retaliation and revenge in him. For him, all that irritates and makes for anger is as it were nonexistent. He holds himself well in, under the greatest provocation.

"Seeing well, he seems to be one blind;
Hearing well, he seems not ware of sound;
Knowing, he seems a fool of some kind;
Powerful, he seems to weakness bound."

Effacing himself, expunging his propensities and tendencies to anger, he cools his heart with the water of love's unfailing spring and sprinkles all whom he contacts with the selfsame soothing potency.

Intact is the strength of one who keeps his heart in obedience to reason and strays not to ways of ill will, aversion and hate. He hurts not himself; he hurts not others. He is a blessing to himself and to all else. He becomes beloved of all. His paths are made smooth. None envy him. Nobody is against him. Nobody grows jealous of him. He wings through life like a swan through the blue sky unhindered, an object of delight to all eyes.

Where such a loving one dwells, there all is at peace; for the loving one never interferes with others' rights, with others' freedom, with others' lives, in any way. He helps others in pleasant, kindly acts, endearing, encouraging, energizing and vitalizing all with his benign nature.

If in a woodland haunt such a loving one stays,

> "The tigress seeing the lean young deer
> Gives it suck as tho' it were its cub;
> And serpents sun-struck for shelter steer
> To the shade of pea-fowls' wings: mice do rub
> Against the sides of deadly snakes for play
> And through the fearful coils make their way."

says the poet, and continues thus:

> "In forest glade anywhere does one such stay
> Who spreads forth love grown great night and day
> And by his thought all hatred does allay
> In brute breast, homage him I pay."

Through love does the Blessed One tame all beings. It is with love that he overcame the hosts of Māra in the terrace of enlightenment. All violence and ferocity can be overcome with love; it is the magic wand to quell the waves in men's unruly hearts.

Other kinds of spiritual emancipation are not equal to the sixteenth part of the emancipation of the heart through love. Through love one adds to the fund of human happiness, one makes the world brighter, nobler and purer and prepares it for the good life better than in any other way. There is no ill-luck worse than hatred, it is said, and no safety from others' hostility greater than the heart of love, the heart in which hate is dead.

Therefore, says the lovable Śāntideva:

> "How many I slay my foes as welkin vast!
> Aye, if hate in my heart is slain my foes don't last."

And again showing a way to overcome the thought of hate he in his own inimitable way says:

> "Overlooking the missiles that hurt if I rate
> At him who hurled them moved by force of hate,
> Right better would it be to hate hate, which wove
> The thought, which him to act of hurling drove."

If one has developed love truly great, rid of the desire to hold and to possess, that strong clean love which is untarnished with lust of any kind, that love which does not expect material advantage and profit from the act of loving, that love which is firm but not grasping, unshakable but not tied down, gentle and settled, hard and penetrating as diamond but unhurting, helpful but not interfering, cool, invigorating, giving more than taking, not proud but dignified, not sloppy yet soft, the love which leads one to the heights of clean achievement, then, in such a one can there be no ill will at all. So our books say that if one should say that he has developed mental emancipation through love, and has still hate in his heart he should be told, "Not so! Speak not thus ... Do not misrepresent the Blessed One ... Surely he would not say this was so!"

The power of love as illustrated by the life of the Buddha can be seen in many a story told of him. Among the best is that of Roja, the Mallian, who in order to escape a fine imposed on persons of his clan who did not visit the Buddha, undertook a visit to the place where the Buddha was living once, and then was drawn to the Master as a cow to its calf even before he saw him. That was an instance of the psychic power of love (*mettā-iddhi*). The taming of the drunken elephant, Nālāgiri, of the demon Ālavaka, the saving of Paṭācārā, Kisāgotamī and many another, of helping the greatly worried and dejected Culla Panthaka, Nakulapitā and so forth are all examples of our Teacher's love.

Love is an active force. Every act of the loving one, is done with the stainless mind to help, to succour, to cheer, to make the paths of others easier, smoother, and more adapted to the conquest of sorrow, the winning of highest bliss.

The way to develop love is through thinking out the evils of hate, and the advantages of non-hate; through thinking out according to actuality (*kamma*) that really there is none to hate, that hate is a foolish way of feeling which breeds more and more of darkness that obstructs right understanding. Hate restricts; love releases. Hatred strangles; love enfranchises. Hatred brings remorse; love brings peace. Hatred agitates; love quietens, stills, calms. Hatred divides; love unites. Hatred hardens; love softens. Hatred hinders; love helps. And thus through a correct study and appreciation of the effects of hatred and the benefits of love, should one develop love.

Patience

A Perfect One is a patient one. Patience is of the essence of all holy living. Without this quality one cannot persevere in good, one cannot maintain oneself in harmlessness, in non-anger, in kindliness; one cannot help others; one cannot become fit for full enlightenment.

Therefore does the Bodhisattva cultivate this virtue of patience at all times, in all circumstances, whatever befalls.

In the past birth stories of the Master we read that he bore up with unsullied heart dreadful punishment inflicted on him and with his dying breath blessed his torturer (*Khantivādi-jātaka*, No. 313). So deep set was this quality in him that even when reborn as an animal he displayed tremendous endurance and forbearance when put to severe pain.

The patient one becomes dear to all, beloved of all; he becomes freed of many faults. At death he is well-composed.

Patience and forbearance, says the Master, comprise the aim of a recluse.

> "Bearing up is the best ascetic way,
> Forbearing, the ceasing best, Buddhas say."

And further, it is said:

> "Who bears with a heart that's from anger free
> The gyve, the scourge, the rack, the stake, that one,

For whom his patience can an army be,
That one's a man who unto worth has won."

It is because folk are impatient of others that discord is rife in the world. Violence, spoliation, bloodshed, all these, source from hatred, the child of impatience. The patient one is ever forgiving, ever restrained, ever ready to overlook others' shortcomings and to forget injuries done to him. He cannot cherish revenge. He knows:

"Time-honoured is this law which says: 'Never ended
Is hate by hatred here: but by non-hatred.'"

Therefore is it said:

"Just as the fragrant sandalwood tree
Perfumes the axe which lays it low,
So the good man, willer of world's weal,
Angers not though struck by cruel blow."

V
The Buddha

Four incalculable aeons ago, our Buddha, as an ascetic full of knowledge and compassion, meeting the Perfectly Enlightened One, Dīpaṅkara, turned away from the Nibbāna that lay within his grasp as though it were saṃsāra. Thereupon entering the difficult track of suffering he completed the Perfections and was reborn in the Tusita realm. At the entreaty of the *Devas* and *Brahmas* of tens of thousands of world-systems he thereafter took human form at Kapilavatthu and in the maturity of manhood left home life for the homeless state. Then setting great energy afoot, seated in the pose of meditation under the Tree of Enlightenment, conquering Death, he attained omniscience.

His Virtues

The Perfectly Enlightened One who is called omniscient is endowed with boundless virtues. Inconceivable, incomparable, incomprehensible is the Perfect One's beauty of form; so also the charm of his speech and the splendour of his wisdom. Therefore, he is beyond measure of thought, the reach of words, the range of similitude, the grasp of knowledge. Though a Perfect One lauds his peer's virtues a whole aeon long, still would those virtues be unexhausted. Though put into the vast ocean, the capsule of a mustard seed, a crock, a pot, can take in only so much water as each can hold. In the same way those who enter into the ocean of Buddha-virtue can know only so much as the ability of each one of them allows. They cannot know that virtue in all its fullness.

Some of the virtues of a Perfect One are common to worldlings and to his pure disciples. Others are peculiar to him. Grass is the common food of herbivorous animals but when it is eaten and digested by the Gandhahatthi, "the fragrant elephant," it produces a fourfold aroma. So also the grace of form and the mental qualities of absorption, supernormal powers and the like passing into the Buddha flux become unique.

As the precious fat of lions does not keep in vessels not golden, so the ten powers, the four confidences and the like which are exceptional, abide not in a flux other than a Buddha's.

The beauty of form of an Omniscient One comprises the thirty-two marks of the superman and the eighty lesser characteristics that go along with them.

The charm of the speech of an Omniscient One is the instruction given with the voice endowed with the eight factors: clarity, intelligibility, agreeableness, worthiness of being listened to, smoothness of flow, the state of being confined to the intended audience, depth, resonance.

His Wisdom

And in the pointing out and the laying down of the disciplinary rules, the distinguishing of the mundane and the ultra mundane planes, of relatedness, and the refutation of the views of alien sects, the Buddha's powers of speech spread strong as the lion's roar.

The splendour of the wisdom of an Omniscient One is that it penetrates to the very end of all that is worthy of being known in a thing. It resembles a red-hot iron which burns through to the bottom of a heap of dried leaves on which it is applied.

In the word of Venerable Sāriputta, the Elder, "Greatly wise, indeed, is the Blessed One, broadly wise, pleasantly wise, expeditiously wise, keenly wise, penetratingly wise; he is wise in skilful analysis, a realizer of the fourfold analytical knowledge, an arriver at the four confidences, a possessor of the ten powers, a man-steer, a man-lion, a man-elephant, a man-steed, a human burden-bearer, infinitely wise, infinitely majestic, infinitely glorious, rich, opulent, a leader and a tamer of men willing to be tamed; who makes others think aright, who makes others see Truth, who makes others glad.

Indeed that Blessed One is the creator of the uncreated path, the producer of the unproduced path, the revealer of the unrevealed path, the perceiver of the path, the knower of the path, the expert on the path. Knowing, he knows; seeing he sees. He is as it were the eye incarnate; wisdom incarnate; the Dhamma incarnate; purity incarnate. He is the speaker, the best speaker, the giver of deep sense, the donor of the deathless, the lord of the Dhamma. And naught there is that the Tathāgata knows not, perceives not, realizes not, experiences not, by his wisdom.

To the extent of things worth knowing stretches the wisdom of the Enlightened One. All things become objects to him when he adverts, when he wills, when he attends, when he thinks. Open to him are all beings' inclinations, tendencies, behaviour, and dispositions. He knows beings who are slight of passion and those heavy of passion; also known by him are those possessed of controlling faculties that are keen or soft, fine or coarse.

Blessed, worthy, fully-wake, endowed with wisdom and virtue, is the Tathāgata. Rich with the ten powers, the four confidences and innumerable such attributes is the Body of the Dhamma, which the Master realized.

Rid of greed, hate, and ignorance, he is blessed; endowed with many lucky qualities, he is blessed; seeing deep into the nature of things through penetrative analysis, he is blessed; spewing forth all passion, all wayfaring in saṃsāra, he is blessed.

Worthy is the Blessed One because he is free from defilement, because he has destroyed the foes of the passions and broken the spokes of saṃsāra's Wheel of Becoming. Suited is he for the receiving of offerings because he does not do evil even in secret.

Realizer of the Truth without the aid of a teacher is the Enlightened One who has understood the Dhamma unheard of before. One who reached the very peak of the ten powers is he; one who has made others attain to the Truth. Through omniscience, through seeing everything with the eye of knowledge, through radiating measureless worth, through being numbered among the eradicators of evil, through separation from all soil, through assured freedom from the triple fire of lust, ill will, and ignorance, through treading the Sole Way to emancipation, through attainment of Uttermost Perfection, he is the Enlightened One.

The Ten Powers

The Master is the possessor of the ten powers, to wit: the knowledge of what is and what is not a particular cause; the knowledge of the effects of action in the three divisions of time, past, present, and future; the knowledge of the exact nature of wayfaring in the future to which every volition leads; the knowledge of the world comprising aggregates, elements and sense-bases; the knowledge of every being's dispositions; the knowledge of the hearts of others in regard to the controlling faculties of confidence, mindfulness, energy, and so forth; the knowledge as regards the falling away from and development of the different kinds of absorption, emancipation, concentration, and attainment, and the emergence from them; the knowledge of past births; the knowledge of beings passing away and reappearing life after life; the knowledge of the final extinction of the cankers.

The Four Confidences

The four confidences of the Master are: the calm, courage, and certainty consequent on the absolute impossibility for any recluse, Brahmin, god, Māra, or Brahmā to disprove that the Tathāgata is supremely enlightened as regards those things mental about which he says that he is supremely enlightened (*Sammā-sambuddho*); the calm, courage, and certainty consequent upon the absolute impossibility for any recluse, Brahmin, god, Māra, or Brahmā to disprove that the Tathāgata has eradicated those cankers which he says he has destroyed utterly (*khiṇāsavo*); the calm, courage, and certainty consequent on the absolute impossibility, for any recluse, Brahmin, god, Māra, or Brahmā to disprove what the Tathāgata says are obstacles on the Path to Deliverance; the calm, courage, and certainty consequent on the impossibility for any recluse, Brahmin, god, Māra, or Brahma to disprove what the

Tathāgata says are things leading out of the swamp of saṃsāra to the firm ground of Nibbāna.

The Possessor of Vision

The Enlightened One is the possessor not only of the fleshly, the physical organ of sight, but of the divine eye by which the death and rebirth of beings, their faring on according to kamma is seen, the eye of wisdom by which all things in the three divisions of time are sensed aright, the enlightened eye by which the character and faculties of beings are understood and the all-seeing eye of omniscience.

> "Nothing at all in the world is unseen
> By the Tathāgata; unknowable by him is naught;
> In all the wide world is there aught
> Knowable? Sensed by him has all that been."

Amongst all the jewels of the world the Enlightened One is the most excellent. The brilliance and glow of all worldly gems fade before the effulgence of the Buddha-sun which dispels the darkness of men's abysmal ignorance. Therefore do gods and men hail him as the Teacher par excellence the illuminator of the clouded heart and the mist-veiled mind. Further is he called Teacher because he taught the way out of the world's ills, and pointed the path across the floods of passion to the haven of Uttermost Safety.

* * *

Purification of Character

Bhikkhu Vimalo
(Germany)

WHEEL PUBLICATION NO. 39

Purification of Character

By Bhikkhu Vimalo

In the Aṅguttara-Nikāya[1] the Buddha describes three kinds of defilements: coarse, medium, and subtle. The coarse ones are: wrong action (*kāya-duccarita*), wrong speech (*vacī-duccarita*) and wrong thinking (*mano-duccarita*); the medium ones are: sensual, hostile, and aggressive thoughts (*kāma-, byāpāda-, vihiṃsā-vitakka*); the subtle defilements are: thinking about relatives, country, and not being despised (*ñāti-, janapada-, anavaññatti-paṭisaṃyutta vitakka*).

It is not possible to get rid of these unhealthy inclinations without first making their driving forces conscious. Buddha called these driving forces (be they conscious or unconscious) *cetanā* and said, "Intention, O monks, I call *kamma*" (*cetanā 'haṃ, bhikkhave, kammaṃ vadāmi*).[2] *Cetanā* may be translated as will, volition, intention, inclination, drive, striving, direction, tendency, or motivation. In the *Sutta-piṭaka* several types of *cetanā* are distinguished, namely, the driving forces of our action (*kāya-sañcetanā*), speech (*vacī-sañcetanā*), and thought (*mano-sañcetanā*);[3] *rūpa-, sadda-, gandha-, rasa-, phoṭṭhabba-sañcetanā*,[4] the reaction to sense-objects, or interest in them (Freud's cathexis, i.e. the investing of an object with libido); and *dhamma-sañcetanā*,[5] the reaction to ideas, memories, imagination and their *cathexis*. Lastly there is our attitude towards ourselves (*atta-sañcetanā*) and towards others (*para-sañcetanā*).[6]

When one speaks of making unhealthy inclinations conscious, it is *cetanā* above all that is referred to. The goal of *Satipaṭṭhāna*, or practice of mindfulness, consists in emerging from the predominantly unconscious condition in which most people live, into a state of being fully conscious, without conflict, repression or self-deception.

The Buddha said, "When the mind is wrongly directed, then action, speech, and thought are wrongly directed," (*citte byāpanne kāya-, vacī-, mano-kammaṃ byāpannaṃ hoti*).[7] In other words, when our attitude towards ourselves, and others, is distorted, it influences all our activities. One should try, therefore, to get to the root of one's problems and not be satisfied with superficial solutions.

In order to overcome the various undesirable character traits a profound knowledge of oneself is imperative. Through *satipaṭṭhāna* insight may be gained, not only into our mutually conflicting tendencies, conscious or unconscious fear and self-defence, resistances or self-justifications, but also into our attitude and reaction to these inclinations. Depth psychology shows that character is largely formed in early childhood. Many traits, together with basic attitudes and unconscious claims (*cetanā*), are acquired at that time, as the child learns to fit in with his environment, in particular with important personalities, and develops his character in such a way as to obtain the greatest security for himself in the given circumstances. Even if they should later prove themselves harmful these attitudes are retained, since they afford a certain security in dealing with life.

It is not enough, however, to recognize what has led to the formation of certain character traits in the past. One must also understand why they persist at the present time. Many an unhealthy inclination continues because there is an advantage or a satisfaction connected with it. The person who is not prepared to give up this advantage seeks for some subterfuge or justification. All resistances must be examined, since they oppose a possible change. They consist for example in justification, unwillingness to make an examination, forgetting, and not seeing things in their correct context. Burying one's head in the sand and pretending not to see anything that cannot be reconciled with one's ideal image (*asmi-māna*) is certainly not consistent with Buddhist mind training. Nietzsche gives a lucid account of this process: "'I did it,' says my memory. 'I couldn't have done it,' says my pride and remains inexorable. In the end, memory yields."[7] "Whoever considers clarification as the essential process of human life knows that the way to it leads through suffering, and that those who wish to avoid suffering will miss clarification."[8]

7. A I 262
8. F. Nietzsche: *Beyond Good and Evil*, 68.

If insight penetrates sufficiently deep, it gradually brings about a change of heart as the mental conflicts are overcome; it is in this way that right effort (*sammā-vāyāma*) and the right attitude of mind (*sammā-saṅkappa*) grow stronger. "Nobody divided within himself can be wholly sincere."[9] The right mental attitude can only arise when one surmounts the inner conflict, and is no longer driven by neurotic needs[10] (*micchā-vāyāma*) for power, perfection, independence or affection.

When the Buddha wanted to investigate inner hindrances he often asked himself, "what is the cause, what is the reason ...?" (*ko hetu, ko paccayo...?*). He says in the Satipaṭṭhāna Sutta[11] that one should examine how feelings, states of mind and *dhammas* arise (*samudaya-dhammānupassī, vedanāsu, citte, dhammesu viharati*). The same applies to the five hindrances (*yathā ca anuppannassa kāmacchandassa byāpādassa,* etc. *uppādo hoti, tañ ca pajānāti*).[12] The 61st and 151st Suttas of the Majjhima Nikāya give a thorough explanation of this meticulous examination (*dhamma-vicaya*). In these Suttas the Buddha says that one should examine what one does, says or considers, not only before, but also during and after the action or thought concerned. Master Eckhart has this to say about awareness: "This 'seeing' serves two purposes: it scotches what is mischievous and makes us forthwith remedy our faults. Many a time I have laid it down that great workers, great fasters, great vigil-keepers, if they fail to mend their wicked ways, wherein true progress lies, do cheat themselves and are the devil's laughing stock."[13]

Whoever wants to advance to the higher stages of Buddhist mind training must first get the better of the "human, all too human" and for this courage, determination, and honesty with oneself are needed.

9. F. Kuenkel: *Einfuehrung in die Charakterkunde*, p.153
10. K. Horney: *Our Inner Conflicts*, p.163 (Norton, New York).
11. D II 292, 299, 301; M I 56, 59, 60; cp. S III 14: *Samādhisutta.*
12. D II 301, M I 60; A I 272
13. *Master Eckhart*, transl. by C. de B. Evans (Watkins, London), vol. I p. 135.

I

(1) It often happens that the compulsive nature of unhealthy activities is broken when one looks into the forces which drive them: whether it is a question of occasional petty theft or deceit or of more serious transgressions, or violence, sexual misdemeanours or heavy drinking. Self-reproaches (*kukkucca*) often do not help at all. Someone may occasionally indulge in small frauds because he is avaricious and wishes to save money, or because he finds it humiliating to ask for anything; or various objects of acquisition are used as substitutes for love and affection. He may perhaps commit these offences out of defiance or the desire for revenge. With regard to the third *sīla* that is concerned with sexual misconduct, we should not forget that the attitude towards sex varies in different cultures, as Ruth Benedict,[14] Margaret Mead[15] and other anthropologists have shown. The various Buddhist countries differ markedly in their marriage customs. It is one aspect of *satipaṭṭhāna* to become aware of the cultural influences, which form the background of a person's whole outlook on life, and conditions him in many ways. There are great differences between East and West in this respect. Some forms of cultural conditioning are difficult to overcome because they are absorbed early in childhood and are later taken for granted and never questioned.

What is essential in keeping the *sīlas*[16] is the right attitude of mind—an attitude, which does not look upon others as simply the tools of unbridled egotism.[17] "Therefore we may briefly say here, that he who voluntarily recognizes and observes those merely moral limits between wrong and right, even where this is not secured by the state or any other external power, thus he who, according to our explanation, never carries the assertion of his own will so far as to deny the will appearing in another individual, is just. Thus, in order to increase his own well-being, he will not

14. Ruth Benedict: *Patterns of Culture.*

15. Margaret Mead: *Sex and Temperament in Three Primitive Societies: Male and Female.*

16. i.e. the basic rules of morality.

17. Cf. S V 353, Dhp 129, 130; *attānaṃ upamaṃ katvā.*

inflict suffering upon others, i.e. he will commit no crime, he will respect the rights and the property of others.

"We see that for such a just man the *principium individuationis* is no longer, as in the case of the bad man, an absolute wall of partition. We see that he does not, like the bad man, merely assert his own manifestation of will and deny all others; that other persons are not for him mere masks, whose nature is quite different from his own; but he shows in his conduct that he also recognises his own nature—the will to live as a thing-in-itself (*Ding an sich*), in the foreign manifestation which is only given to him as an idea. Thus he finds himself again in that other manifestation, up to a certain point, that of doing no wrong, i.e. abstaining from injury. To this extent, therefore, he sees through the *principium individuationis*, the veil of *māyā;* so far he sets the being external to him on a level with his own—he does it no injury. If we examine the inmost nature of this justice, there already lies in it the resolution not to go so far in the assertion of one's own will as to deny the manifestations of will of others, by compelling them to serve one's own."[18]

(2) Buddha described lying (*musā-vādā*), slander (*pisunā vācā*), harsh talk (*pharusā vācā*), and gossip (*samphappalāpā*) as wrong speech (*vacī-duccarita*).[19] The person who tells lies should try to discover how far he is dependent on the good opinion of others. Intimidation and too strict an upbringing often result in the child's not daring to admit that he has done something forbidden, since he is afraid of losing love. (As the dependence on other people's affection—Karen Horney[20] calls it the neurotic need for affection and approval—is very common, it is useful to examine it more closely in all its ramifications.) There is neither freedom nor love as long as one needs the affection of others (A person who is dependent on other people's affection has rarely any love for them). If someone wants to impress others and lies in the process, it can often be traced back to humiliation. Lying serves a compensatory purpose

18. Schopenhauer: *The World as Will and Idea*, 3 vols.; transl. by R.B. Haldane and J. Kemp; Routledge & Kegan Paul, London, 1883; tenth impression 1957; vol. I p. 478.

19. A II 141

20. Karen Horney: *Self Analysis* and *The Neurotic Personality of Our Time* (Norton, New York).

(*vacī-sañcetanā*),[21] that of erasing the previous disparagement and substituting recognition for it.

Speaking badly of others (*para-vambhanā*) and praising oneself (*attukkaṃsanā*), especially when it develops into a character-trait, is frequently nothing more than self-justification, an attempt to avoid self-hatred (*ajjhattaṃ byāpāda*).[22] As long as a person lacks the courage to investigate his conflicts and will not give up superficial solutions, so long will lack of self-confidence and inferiority-feelings (*hīno'ham asmi*) persist. The latter increase the necessity to compensate the lack of self-confidence and so other people are badly spoken of.

Harsh, unfriendly speech is an expression of aggressiveness. In our Western culture limits are set on aggressiveness, and one may conclude from harsh speech that this is perhaps the only outlet for repressed hostility. A person is inclined towards harsh judgments when similar impulses in himself are repressed or when many repressions are being maintained. Inner resistance to these drives is then turned outwards. Exaggerated severity leads one to suspect that it is nourished from unconscious sources.

An excessive need for conversation is frequently found in a person who cannot bear solitude. The tendency towards unnecessary talk is often present in those who had the feeling of not being wanted when they were children; they have to ingratiate themselves and to make sure that they are not rejected.

(3) The Buddha spoke of three distortions (*vipallāsa*):[23]

i. distorted perceptions, imaginings and projections (*saññāvipallāsa*);
ii. distorted mind (*citta-vipallāsa*);
iii. distorted views and prejudices (*diṭṭhi-vipallāsa*).

These distortions make us see the transitory as permanent, the painful as happy, impure as pure, and what is not self as self.

"In order to see that a purely objective, and therefore correct,

21. Cp. *Vacī-sañcetanā-hetu uppajjati ajjhattaṃ sukha-dukkhaṃ* (S II 40; A II 158).

22. S V 110

23. A II 52

comprehension of things is only possible when we consider them without any personal participation in them, thus when the will is perfectly silent, let one call to mind how much every emotion or passion disturbs and falsifies our knowledge, indeed how every inclination and aversion alters, colours, and distorts not only the judgment, but even the original perception of things."[24]

Together with attraction and repulsion, hope and fear, it is above all unsolved problems and complexes that distort perception since they are easily projected outwards. Whatever one does not wish to recognize in oneself may be seen much more clearly in others. Not only unhealthy tendencies are projected outwards but also unfulfilled ideals and the compensations for one-sided developments. Admiration and respect may in many cases be traced back to the transfer of unfulfilled ideals.

In *satipaṭṭhāna* these *cathexes* of the object, as Freud calls them, are made conscious. The Buddha says in the *Satipaṭṭhāna Sutta*, "He knows sense-organs and sense-objects and he also knows the fetter which arises conditioned by both of them" (*cakkhuṃ ... pajānāti, rūpe ... ca pajānāti, yañ-ca tad ubhayaṃ paṭicca uppajjati saṃyojanaṃ, tañ-ca pajānāti*).

This fetter (*saṃyojana*)[25] is the previously mentioned *rūpa-, sadda-, gandha-, rasa-, phoṭṭhabba-sañcetanā*; that is, interest in sense-objects as far as connected with, or followed by, defiled impulses, as greed or aversion, conceit or envy, various misconceptions, and so forth. Only when all these projections are recognized as such and abandoned can one see things with complete objectivity. Schopenhauer says:

"If, raised by the power of the mind, a man relinquishes the common way of looking at things, gives up tracing, under the guidance of the forms of the principle of sufficient reason, their relation to each other, the final goal of which is always a relation to his own will; if he thus ceases to consider the where, the when, the why, and the whither of things, and looks simply

24. Schopenhauer, op. cit. vol. III p. 134.

25. S IV 108, 164; A I 264; cp. C. G. Jung: "Interest I conceive as that energy-libido, which I bestow upon the object as value, or which the object draws from me, even maybe against my will or unknown to myself." (*Psychological Types*, p. 521)

and solely at the what; if, further, he does not allow abstract thought, the concepts of the reason, to take possession of his consciousness, but, instead of all this, gives the whole power of his mind to perception, sinks himself entirely in this, and lets his whole consciousness be filled with the quiet contemplation of the natural object actually present, whether a landscape, a tree, a mountain, a building, or whatever it may be; inasmuch as he 'loses himself in this object' (to use a pregnant German idiom), i.e. forgets even his individuality, his will, and only continues to exist as the pure subject, the clear mirror of the object, so that it is as if the object alone were there, without any one to perceive it, and he can no longer separate the perceiver from the perception, but both have become one, because the whole consciousness is filled and occupied with one single sensuous picture; if thus the object has to such an extent passed out of all relation to something outside it, and the subject out of all relation to the will, then that which is so known is no longer the particular thing as such, but it is the *Idea*,[26] the eternal form, the immediate objectivity of the will at this grade; and, therefore, he who is sunk in this perception is no longer individual, for in such perception the individual has lost himself; but he is *pure*, will-less, painless, timeless *subject of knowledge*."[27]

There are also distortions in self-observation. When otherwise clear connections cannot be seen it means that unconscious resistance is still too strong; it is most important to make this resistance conscious. As long as an impulse is repressed it is outside conscious control. A feeling of uneasiness or embarrassment *may* be an indication that a complex has been touched or that a repressed tendency is trying to break through into consciousness. Unless attention is paid to it the unpleasant feeling (*dukkha-vedanā*) remains the only indication that there is a repression. A person is practising *Satipaṭṭhāna* if he makes emotion (*vedanā*),

26. In Plato's sense.

27. Schopenhauer, op. cit. vol. I p. 231. The inclusion of this quote does not imply that all ideas expressed in it, are in conformity with the Buddhist view point; this applies in particular to the conception of the idea as an 'eternal form,' and of a timeless subject of knowledge (Editor).

mental state (*citta*), the repressed idea (*dhamma*), and repression[28] itself conscious. We read in the *Satipaṭṭhāna-Sutta,* "He knows the mind, and the dhammas, and also the fetter that arises."

Erich Fromm says in his book *Zen Buddhism and Psychoanalysis* (p. 139): "If one carries Freud's principle of the transformation of unconsciousness into consciousness to its ultimate consequences, one approaches the concept of enlightenment," and Karen Horney describes the goal of psychoanalysis as follows: "By rendering a person free from inner bondages make him free for the development of his best potentialities!"[29] The person who thinks he practises *satipaṭṭhāna* and makes good progress in Buddhist mind training, and still maintains his complexes and neurotic strivings, obviously deceives himself. Freud has shown (and anybody who has done some self-analysis can corroborate it) that repressed tendencies (*cetanā*) stay in the unconscious and persist until they are dissolved by insight. They are very little—if at all—influenced by indirect treatment. This links up with the Buddhist doctrine of Kamma, which holds that no one can escape the results of his evil actions, words and thoughts. Some profound discoveries in depth psychology have begun to reveal how this law of Kamma operates.

Citta-vipallāsa may perhaps be best explained as wrong attitude of mind. What Karen Horney calls 'neurotic trends' may also be near it. Such bad character traits as greediness (*abhijjhā*), hypocrisy (*makkha*), envy (*issā*), grudge (*macchariya*), conceit (*māna*), and self-satisfaction (*pamāda*), which the Buddha described as defilements of the mind, must be investigated to see how and under what circumstances they arise (*samudaya-dhammānupassanā*). The same holds for the inability to endure solitude or to get on well with others. Among the motivations that prompt greediness there may be the search for security, or it may be a compensation for earlier want, or a remnant of an infantile greed.

Hypocrisy is found in people with a strong need for recognition. Their principal aim is to ensure that others have a good opinion of them. Envy and jealousy may often be traced back

---

28. *dhamma-sañcetanā* (*manañ-ca pajānāti, dhamme ca pajānāti, yañ-ca tad ubhayaṃ paṭicca uppajjati saṃyojanaṃ, tañ ca pajānāti*).

29. Karen Horney: *Self Analysis*, p.21.

to the attitude towards brothers and sisters in early childhood. Psychoanalysis has shown what anyone may verify in himself and in his friends—that the attitude towards others in the early environment is easily projected on to other people in later life. Obstinacy is closely related to feelings of inferiority. People with insufficient self-confidence are often obstinate when they are with someone else who is superior to them. They assert themselves by saying no and by contradicting. It is all too often the case that a person becomes complacent and ceases to strive for something higher when he has overcome certain inhibitions and difficulties.

The Buddha says that one must not remain satisfied with what has been already achieved (*oramattakena visesādhi-gamena asantuṭṭhi*;[30] *asantuṭṭhitā kusalesu dhammesu*).[31] "For it is well known that, on this road, not to go forward is to turn back, and not to be gaining is to be losing."[32] "Why then do we not become wise? There is much to it. The most important thing is that one should go out of all things, beyond them all and their origins; this is too much for most men and so they remain within their limitations."[33]

A distinction should be made between genuine love for others and a flight from oneself, between a real need for solitude and a neurotic one. Neurotic striving for solitude is based on the incapacity to get on well with others, which often comes from a wrong attitude towards them. "If it is well with him, then indeed it is well in all places and with all people. But if it is ill with him, then it is ill in all places and with all people."[34]

Mutually contradictory unconscious claims on others, for example the wish to dominate them and at the same time be loved by them, make it difficult, if not impossible, to establish satisfactory relationships. These claims are bound to bring up resistance in others. This rejection again strengthens the fear of defeat: a person either moves further and further away from others and makes up in

30. A IV 22
31. A I 50; D III 214
32. *The Complete Works of Saint John of the Cross*, transl. by E. Allison Peers; Burns Oates & Washbourne Ltd. p. 51.
33. Quint: *Meister Eckhart*, p. 203
34. ibid. p. 58

fantasy and daydreams for what reality denies him, or else feelings of insecurity and inferiority already in existence are strengthened and show themselves in awkward behaviour. This insecurity, together with compensatory feelings of superiority, is felt by others and rejected. So the whole cycle begins again: the tension between inferiority feelings and the need for recognition increases, and suffering becomes more acute.

In these vicious circles one can see clearly how the law of Kamma operates. The Enlightened One said, "*Kamma* is *cetanā.*"

So long as one does not change these wrong attitudes to oneself (*atta-sañcetanā*) and others (*para-sañcetanā*), one must suffer. We may remember here the first verse of the Dhammapada: "If a man speaks or acts with an evil thought, sorrow follows him even as the wheel follows the foot of the ox which draws the cart." To bring these unconscious claims into the clear light of consciousness is not easy and it demands long practice of *satipaṭṭhāna* and development of intuitive understanding. "I grant you this needs effort, application, careful cultivation of the interior life and good sound sense and understanding whereon to stay the mind in things and with people. This is not learnt by flight, by one who runs away from things, who turns his back upon the world and flees into the desert: he must learn to find the solitude within where or with whomsoever he may be."[35]

Prejudices, distorted views (*diṭṭhi-vipallāsa*), conceptions of good and evil, are often taken over uncritically from parents or those in authority.

It is a part of *satipaṭṭhāna* to make these sometimes completely unconscious attitudes conscious and to restrict self-centredness. As a rule the stronger the feelings of inferiority the higher the ideal of oneself will be, and hence the possibility of understanding the *anattā*-doctrine of the Buddha will be similarly limited. Only he who removes the tension between inferiority feelings and the need for recognition can understand, "This is not mine; this am I not; this is not my Self."

35. *Meister Eckhart*, transl. by Evans, vol. II p. 9.

II

In the 20th Sutta of the *Majjhima Nikāya* the Buddha explains how unhealthy thoughts should be overcome: 1. by attending to a healthy idea; 2. by seeing the danger in unhealthy thoughts; 3. by not attending to unhealthy thoughts; 4. by cutting off this mental activity; 5. by forcefully suppressing these thoughts. Above all, one should try to gain insight into those states of mind, which always lead to the arising of sensual, hostile and aggressive thoughts. In addition one should endeavour to practise meditation and awareness and to develop those factors, which exclude or at least weaken unhealthy thoughts. According to the Buddha, it is essential for the overcoming of sensuality that higher happiness and serenity be found;[36] in freeing oneself from animosity one develops *mettā*;[37] in abandoning aggressive thoughts one develops compassion.[38] The Buddha said that if one practises *satipaṭṭhāna* correctly these unhealthy thoughts are gradually extinguished.[39]

(1) In the *Salla-Sutta*[40] the Buddha says that the ordinary person knows no other escape from unpleasant feelings except sensual pleasures. Painful feelings, threats to the ego-ideal, and inner conflicts may lead to the arising of sensual thoughts.

There are many ways of forgetting suffering, such as alcohol, sex, forced activity or distraction. Such a flight from unpleasant feelings is not a permanent solution, since the conflicts persist as long as they are not deeply investigated. By practising patience a person may learn to bear unpleasant feelings without immediately seeking sensual pleasures or other escapes.

Repressed sensuality may break through in daydreams and fantasy, and gives them their force and compulsiveness. A person acts out in fantasy what he does not dare to put into actual effect, owing to his inhibition. If one looks for what is common to all these fantasies the insight gained into unconscious

36. See *The Wheel* No. 21: *The Removal of Distracting Thoughts* (*Vitakkasanthāna Sutta; MN 20*) Buddhist Publication Society, Kandy
37. M I 91 & 504.
38. A III 291; D III 248, 280.
39. S III 93.
40. S IV 207

driving forces and compensations may cut the ground from under them. Repressed sensuality, and negative attitude towards it, may often be traced back to early childhood. As long as these repressions persist, unconscious *anti-cathexes* will be maintained, unproductively consuming energy. Repression of drives is not a lasting solution, since they remain in the unconscious. Those who practise Buddhist mind training should learn gradually to put conscious control into effect, instead of submitting to a fear of these tendencies that leads to repressions. Freud says:

"The laws of logic—above all the law of contradiction—do not hold for processes in the *id*.[41] Contradictory impulses exist side by side without neutralising each other or drawing apart; at most they combine in compromise formations under the overpowering economic pressure towards discharging their energy ... In the *id* there is nothing corresponding to the idea of time, no recognition of the passage of time, and (a thing which is very remarkable and awaits adequate attention in philosophic thought) no alteration of mental processes by the passage of time. Conative impulses, which have never got beyond the *id*, and even impressions which have been pushed down into *id* by repression and are preserved for whole decades as though they had only recently occurred.

They can only be recognized as belonging to the past, deprived of their significance, and robbed of their charge of energy, after they have been made conscious by the work of analysis."[42]

(2) Many people unconsciously expect from others love, pity, admiration, fear or submission. A few examples suffice to show the connection between unconscious claims, often of a compensatory nature, and resistance or open hostility. The person for instance who has a neurotic need for independence conditioned perhaps by previous coercion and injustice, will set himself against any outside influence. Another may strive for intellectual superiority and becomes angry if his ideas are not accepted. If anything taboo is touched upon, such as a complex, the emotional reaction is particularly strong. Unconscious resistance to repressed impulses

41. The *id* is "the sum total of crude, unmodified instinctual needs." (*New Ways in Psychoanalysis* by Karen Horney, p. 184).

42. Sigmund Freud: *New Introductory Lectures on Psychoanalysis*; chapter on 'The Anatomy of the Mental Personality.'

turns outwards and directs itself against the person who dares to disturb it.

This anger may also be repressed, especially when one recognizes that love and hate of the same person are incompatible, or when a loss of love is feared if free rein is given to anger. Repressed aggressiveness shows itself in daydreaming and fantasies of killing and destroying, but in most fantasies there is some displacement or compromise-formation, so that the aggression is turned against other people or objects. It may also be projected outwards, in which case all the animosity which one does not dare recognize in oneself is seen in others. The next step, so well described by Karen Horney,[43] is that one finds thunder, animals and other objects dangerous and threatening. Hate, aggressiveness and fear of retaliation are displaced from their original object on to a neutral one.

While unconscious claims are made on others it is impossible for the person to feel genuine goodwill (*mettā*) towards them. If he fears rejection he is incapable of loving, since his deep inner insecurity bars the way; nor can he love while he strives for power and is concerned to arouse envy, admiration or sympathy.

In the Aṅguttara-Nikāya[44] the Buddha describes various ways of overcoming ill-will. He advises the practice of *mettā*, sympathy (*karuṇā*), or equanimity if animosity arises; one should remove one's attention from it, or consider that each person will experience the results of his own *kamma*.

The more the *mettā*-meditation is practised, and the right attitude of mind developed, the less will animosity and aggressiveness be able to find a foothold. He will feel compassion instead of anger for those who are overwhelmed by their angry impulses. He preserves his equanimity since he regards unwelcome experiences as a practice in patience and self-discipline. Because he has made conscious the influence on his own mind of both the conscious behaviour of others and their unconscious attitude,[45]

43. Karen Horney: *The Neurotic Personality of Our Time*. Cp. also Freud's analysis of the 'Little Hans' in his *Collected Papers*, vol. III.

44. A III 158

45. *ajjhattaṃ ca bahiddhā ca cittānupassanā* (D II 216); cp.: *pare vā taṃ kāya-, vacī-, mano-saṅkhāraṃ abhisaṅkharonti, yaṃ-paccayā 'ssa taṃ uppajjati*

he does not get excited. He remains objective and realizes that the behaviour of others is not his business. If he becomes angry this will hinder his own development and will increase the force of unhealthy impulses in others.

(3) "Freedom from vengeance is to me the bridge to the highest hope, a rainbow after continual storm."[46] Whoever harbours thoughts of vengeance would do well to examine closely his ambition, feelings of inferiority and need for recognition. In people who were often humiliated when they were young, the search for revenge and the tendency to belittle others are frequently stronger than the wish to advance themselves, especially when fear of defeat is involved. Fear of failure restricts the ability to make a decision and the consequent feelings of inadequacy are compensated by aggressiveness and putting others in their place.

Such is often the purpose of sarcasm. Habitual sarcasm and irony destroy the character: in the end one is like a fierce dog, which has not only learnt to bite but to laugh as well."[47]

If one does not understand why thoughts of revenge arise from slight causes, one should try to discover what is common to all these different reactions, remembering that it may be a question of compensation. In this way a complex or a 'sore point' may be discovered. It is necessary, above all, to look for the cause when our reaction is stronger than the occasion warrants (*ko hetu, ko paccayo*).

III

The Buddha described the more subtle defilements of the mind as thoughts of relatives (*ñāti-vitakka*), country (*janapada-vitakka*), and the thought of not being despised (*anavaññatti-patisaṃyutta vitakka*).

(1) In the case of thoughts about relatives we should not forget that in the Buddha's time the bonds of family in India were incomparably stronger than they are in contemporary Western Europe. Perhaps the problem for 'modern' man exists in the form of strong attachments to father, mother, brother or sister. For

---

ajjhattaṃ sukhadukkhaṃ (A II 158; S II 40).

46. Nietzsche: *Also sprach Zarathustra.*

47. Nietzsche: *Menschliches, Allzu Menschliches.*

example a man who as an only child, or the youngest, had a strong link with his mother, may marry a considerably older woman who then takes the place of his mother. Another who has developed still stronger and more exclusive attachments to his mother may find it impossible to enter into any sort of relationship with the opposite sex. He will probably declare that he has a 'natural' inclination to asceticism. Freud's explanation would sound a little different and might mention an unsolved Oedipus complex and fixation of the libido.[48] Wherever it is a question of an exclusive attachment to a single person, accompanied by jealousy, one should see if it is perhaps a fixation or compensation.[49]

(2) Thoughts of country and home may occur if one lives in a foreign country and suffers from homesickness. To live abroad for a time may at least help one to see the relative nature of one's customs and habits. National pride, which some consider as the most stupid sort of pride, falls into this category.

(3) One cannot avoid the impression that in our Western culture, in which so much stress is laid on competition, the fear of failure—so far from being one of the weaker fetters—has assumed an almost neurotic force. A person may have developed this fear through unpleasant early experience; he may have been an unwanted child, or his brothers and sisters may have been given precedence over him. If he also has great ambition he will generally try to avoid superior people. He will surround himself with people who do not arouse inferiority feelings in him, and he will—in a somewhat compulsive fashion—unconsciously evaluate everyone he meets:

"I am superior" (*seyyo'haṃ asmi*); "I am inferior" (*hīno'haṃ asmi*); or "we are equal" (*sadiso'haṃ asmi*).

48. "A person whose experience is determined by 'his fixation to his family,' who is incapable of acting independently, is in fact a worshipper of a primitive ancestor cult, and the only difference between him and millions of ancestor worshippers is that his system is private and not culturally patterned." E. Fromm, *Man for Himself*, p.49 (New York).

49. "Love which can only be experienced with regard to one person demonstrates by this very fact that it is not love but a symbiotic attachment" (ibid. p.130).

The inability of such people to live together with a superior person lies in the fact that they must make up for the painful experience of the past, and must prove to themselves that they are in no way inferior. They cannot bear any reminder that their inflated self-evaluation, which is a compensation for past humiliation and the resultant feelings of inferiority, rests on self-deception.

These people all too easily project their self-hatred outwards and are convinced that others see them as they see themselves, with all their unsolved problems, complexes and contradictions. In order to avoid a fresh rebuff they wait for others to take the initiative, and they approach someone who interests them only after they have assured themselves they will not be cold-shouldered. When they are recognized they easily overvalue the person who, at least momentarily, releases them from the torturing doubt about their own worth.

Since they cannot bear that others think badly of them, they are often insincere. It is essential for their well-being that others have a good opinion of them; they cannot bear the thought of being despised. The recognition of others cannot for long liberate them from their insecurity for they may have a profound doubt whether their strivings are genuine. This doubt arises because the driving forces (*cetanā*) of their actions are registered in the unconscious, despite all their deceptive manoeuvres and the splendid mask they show to the world.

Fear of defeat drives others to collect possessions, offices and titles or to pursue power and security. As long as feelings of inferiority are the motivation, the pursuit takes on a compensatory and compulsive character and even success can only relieve unhappiness and insecurity for a short time. "Really poor in spirit is the man who prefers to do without all unnecessary things ... And best is he who knows how to dispense with what he has no need of."[50]

The wish not to be despised may show itself in resisting any influence and criticism, particularly when the compulsion towards independence and perfection is present. A person who has these characteristics to a serious extent easily develops into a tyrant.

50. Meister Eckhart, op. cit., vol. II: p. 39.

Equanimity with regard to praise or blame cannot be attained while a person is dependent on the opinions of others and possesses only slight self-confidence. Self-confidence arises when repressions are lifted and the split between incompatible tendencies overcome. Then one sees: "This is not mine; this am I not; this is not my Self."

Nāgārjuna says, "Because the arising of all dharmas is conditioned all dharmas are empty" (*apratītya samutpanno dharmaḥ kascin na vidyate; yasmāt tasmād asūnyo hi dharmaḥ kascin na vidyate*).[51] "All things are empty and are not only made such by wisdom" (*na prajñā asūnyān bhāvān sūnyān karoti; bhāvā eva sūnyāḥ*[52] *yan na sūnyatayā dharmaḥ sūnyān karoti; api tu dharmā eva sūnyāḥ*).[53] "Therefore then, Subhūti, the Bodhi-being, the great being, after he has got rid of all perceptions, should raise his thought to the utmost, right and perfect enlightenment. He should produce a thought which is unsupported by forms, sounds, smells, tastes, touchables, or mind-objects, unsupported by *dharma*, unsupported by no-*dharma*, unsupported by anything."[54] "Whoever searches for something or strives after it searches and strives for Nothing, and he who asks for something receives Nothing."[55]

51. *Mādhyamikā Kārikā* 24 19.
52. *Samadhirāja Sūtra.*
53. *Kāsyapa-parivarta Sūtra.*
54. Edward Conze: *Buddhist Wisdom Books*; Allen & Unwin, Lond.
55. Quint: *Meister Eckhart*, p. 211.

Purification of View

Dr. C. B. Dharmasena
MB. B.S. (Lond.)

WHEEL PUBLICATION NO. 40

Purification of View

by Dr. C. B. Dharmasena, MB.B.S(Lond).

How blest from passion to be free,
All sensuous joys to leave behind;
Yet far the highest bliss of all
To quit the illusion false—'I am.'[56]

The inner tangle and the outer tangle,
This generation is entangled in a tangle.
And so I ask of Gotama this question:
Who succeeds in disentangling this tangle?[57]

There is hardly any need to stress the hopelessness of the tangle that the present generation has found itself entrapped in through its inordinate craving, for one's own requisites (inner tangle), and for requisites belonging to others (outer tangle). Today we are in greater need of an answer to the above question than the generation that lived in the time of the Buddha. The Blessed One, the perfect physician for mental ills, specifically those concerned with the 'I' and 'mine,' and with 'we' and 'our' provided the answer to the above question in the following stanza:

When a wise man, established well in Virtue,
Develops Concentration and Understanding,
Then as a Bhikkhu ardent and sagacious,
He succeeds in disentangling this tangle.[58]

Development of understanding or *paññā* referred to above is divided by the Buddha into five stages, the first of which consists of purity of view or *diṭṭhi-visuddhi*, the subject matter of this essay. This implies the vision according to reality that what is

---

56. Solemn utterance of the Buddha at the foot of the Mucalinda tree after his attainment of Buddhahood. Translated by H. C. Warren in *Buddhism in Translations* § 9, from Vinaya Piṭaka, Mahā Vagga I.3.

57. Vism §1 (quoted from Saṃyutta-Nikāya I 13).

58. Vism §1 (quoted from Saṃyutta-Nikāya I 13).

commonly referred to as a living being consists merely of mental and material (corporeal) phenomena, i.e. mind and body, or *nāma-rūpa,* and is void of an ego.

Modern Conception of Matter[59]

Until the beginning of the present century our conception of the material world was one in which all things including our own bodies were made up of various permutations and combinations of 92 different kinds of atoms, meaning indivisible units, static and unchanging. But during the twentieth century it has been found that atoms, despite their name are no longer the indivisible and static units they were once supposed to be, and they are themselves complex structures composed of still smaller and more fundamental units moving at incredible speeds, and separated from each other by distances enormous by comparison with the minuteness of the size of these units themselves. We are told that the composition of the atom is comparatively simple, and consists of three kinds of 'elementary particles' or building bricks, the proton, the neutron, and the electron.

However the actual arrangement of these 'elementary particles' within the atom is complex, but a simplified picture consists of a central core or nucleus made up of a varying number of protons and neutrons, whilst electrons equal in number to the protons within the nucleus are disposed around the nucleus in 'shells,' at a very much greater distance from the centre. Different combinations of these elementary particles form all the 92 naturally occurring elements from which all things including our own bodies as already mentioned are made.

The modern conception of the *properties of matter* in terms of atomic physics is that these 'elementary particles,' the protons, neutrons and electrons occupy an infinitesimally small volume compared to the remainder of the empty space within the atom. The difference in the various qualities displayed by different objects of matter is a property not of the mass possessed by these minute elementary particles, but of the forces between them,

59. Most of the statements in this paragraph has been taken from *What is Atomic Energy?* by K. Mendelssohn.

firstly that of attraction between dissimilar charges of the negative electrons and the positive protons, secondly of the *tremendously powerful forces of repulsion* between protons of similar (positive) charges, and thirdly of the still obscure phenomenon of 'exchange forces' due to change between protons and neutrons of the recently postulated 'mesons,' whereby the strong forces of repulsion between the protons are more than counterbalanced, and result in the *strong cohesion of* the atomic nuclei. Lastly the properties of matter are greatly modified by the particular arrangement of the protons and neutrons within the nucleus, and of the electrons in the varying number of shells of the electronic cloud, particularly in the 'open' outermost shell, where most changes take place owing to its varying degrees of 'unsaturation.' Further Einstein has demonstrated that mass and energy are equivalent. The property called mass is simply concentrated energy. In other words, matter is energy, and energy is matter, and the distinction is simply one of temporary state.[60]

Buddhist Conception of the Properties of Matter

What is thus outlined in the language of popular science of today was described by the Buddha in the ordinary or conventional language of his time so as to be understood by the educated people of his day. The Buddha described a living being as made up of mind and body or *nāma-rūpa*; the latter, i.e. the body, he described as being made up of four primary qualities or 'elements'[61] and of the 'space element,' or *ākāsa-dhātu*.

The importance of the four primary 'elements' lies not in their tangibility, but in their qualities and in the forces inherent in them.

One cannot conceive of an object, animate or inanimate existing apart from its qualities, and in reality one should not say that an object *has* this shape, this colour or this odour; but the object *is* this shape, this colour or this odour. Material bodies are nothing but groups of qualities coming together in different ways

60. *The Universe & Dr. Einstein* by Lincoln Barnett.

61. MN 140, Dhātuvibhaṅga Sutta. MN 28, Mahāhatthipadopama Sutta. MN 62. Mahā-Rāhulovāda Sutta. Vism II.31–38, 81–92, 109.

and proportions that constitute them and exist in and with them. Such a group of qualities is called a *kalāpa.*

The *earthy quality or element,* or *paṭhavi-dhātu,* derives its name from the word *paṭhavi,* which means earth; it refers to qualities possessed by earth, e.g. of hardness (and of its opposite softness, for if something is less hard than something else, the first may be described as soft by comparison), of density, of heaviness and its opposite lightness, and of roughness and its opposite smoothness. The function of the earthy element is to act as a foundation for the other three elements.

The *watery quality* or *element,* or *āpo-dhātu,* from *appoti* to flow, refers to the quality that a fluid has to spread out and diffuse. If a small quantity of the watery element diffuses and penetrates amidst solid particles such as clay, cement, or flour, the loose particles of the latter will be bound together into a lump. The function of the watery element therefore is that of cohesion, or binding the three remaining elements together.

The *element of heat* or *the fiery element,* or *tejo-dhātu,* has a powerful control over the three remaining elements, varying their consistence even to the extent of converting a solid to a liquid or a gas. To this 'element' belong the properties of anabolism or building up and maturing, and of catabolism or breaking down, ageing and disintegrating, and in the case of living beings, of keeping them warm and of digesting the food they ingest.

The *airy element,* or *vāyo-dhātu,* has two important characteristics, firstly that of motility; and secondly that of distending, of being prevented from collapse, of repulsion, of being blown out, or causing to be blown out. The above description of the airy element may be compared with the following statement: "The tendency of any gaseous atmosphere is to dissipate away into space."[62] All material things must possess all the four 'elements' or qualities at one and the same time; no three of these elements can exist without the fourth being present simultaneously. Each quality or element is so intimately connected with the remaining three that together they appear as objects. Each 'object' thus merely consists of the coming together of the four primary

62. *The New Outline of Modern Knowledge* by Alan Pryce-Jones. Chapter on Astronomy by Sir Harold Spencer Jones.

elements, in groups of qualities or *kalāpas*, the difference in the appearance of objects being due to the vastly different proportions in which the primary elements blend. Generally when one element predominates in comparison with the remaining three elements it is conveniently, and conventionally, spoken of as an object belonging to that element, e.g. solid, liquid, or gas.

The *space element*[63] has the characteristic of delimiting matter. Its function is to display the boundaries of matter. It is manifested as the confines of matter, or as the state of gaps and apertures. It is on account of it that one can say of material things that 'This is above, below, around.'

It is solely on account of this space element that the tiniest parts of one's body are, or the body as a whole is, able to move about freely, and to function properly; without the presence of the space element no movement or activity or function is possible.

To summarise: the main property of the earthy element is that of stiffening and acting as a foothold for the other three elements, and of the watery, airy and fiery elements that of cohesion, of distending or causing motion, and of maturing respectively.

The Buddha time and again, and in numerous ways, and with varying analogies suited to the intelligence of his audience, and the circumstances under which he spoke, emphasised the lack of a permanent ego in living beings including man. Says the Buddha, "Just as when the component parts such as axles, wheels, frame, poles etc. are arranged in a certain way, there comes to be the mere term of common usage 'chariot',[64] yet in the ultimate sense when each part is examined, there is no 'chariot'; and just as when the component parts of a house[65] such as wattle, clay, timber, creepers, and grass are placed so that they enclose a space in a certain way there comes to be the mere term of common usage 'house,' yet in the ultimate sense there is no house—so too when a space is enclosed with bones and sinews, and flesh and skin there comes to be the mere term of common usage a 'being' a 'person,'[66] yet in the ultimate sense there is no being as a basis for the assumption of 'I am' or 'I'; in the ultimate sense there is only mind and body."

63. MN 140, and Vism XIV.63.
64. MN 28; Vism XVIII .28.
65. Vism XVIII .28.
66. Vism X .43 & XVIII.28; MN 28.

No doer of the deed is found
No being that may reap the fruits
Empty phenomena roll on,
This is the only right view.[67]

In modern terminology, the same thought may be seen in the following lines from *The Universe and Dr. Einstein* by Lincoln Barnett. "However theoretical systems may change, and however empty of content their symbols and concepts may be, the essential and enduring facts of science and of life are the happenings, the activities, the events. Within the framework of modern physics one can depict a simple physical event or happening, such as the meeting or collision of two electrons—two elementary grains of matter, or two elementary units of electrical energy—as a concourse of particles or of probability waves, or as a co-mingling of eddies in a four-dimensional space-time continuum. Theory does not define what the principles in this encounter actually are. Thus in a sense the electrons are 'not real,' but merely theoretical symbols. On the other hand the meeting itself is 'real'—the event is 'real'."

Immaterial States

Now, for the immaterial states taught by the Buddha, and made evident to us through any act of cognition or consciousness, e.g. the four groups or *khandhas*—feelings, perception, mental formation (*saṅkhāra*), and consciousness (*viññāṇa*), which are inseparable and which may be spoken of under the one term mentality or *nāma*. The five modes of cognition through the five bases (exclusive of the mind-base), eye, ear, nose, tongue and body have now to be appreciated.[68]

The eye and a visual object constitute materiality (*rūpa*), the visual (eye)—consciousness, which arises by their coming together, constitutes mentality (*nāma*). Similarly, the ear and sound constitute materiality, and the ear-consciousness, which arises by their coming together, constitutes mentality;

67. *Path to Deliverance*, Nyanatiloka, paragraph 176.
68. Vism XIV.54–57

The nose and odour constitute materiality, and the nose-consciousness, which arises by their coming together, constitutes mentality;

The tongue and taste constitute materiality, and the tongue-consciousness, which arises by their coming together, constitutes mentality;

The body and tangible object constitute materiality, and the body-consciousness, which arises by their coming together, constitutes mentality.

"If an ear-consciousness (mentality) arises owing to the presence of a sound and the ear-base (materiality), one is inclined to think of it as 'I hear it'; in the ultimate sense however this is incorrect for if these two be identical when at death the mind (ear-consciousness in this example) disappears, the body should disappear at the same time; and again the mind must remain so long as the body remains.

But neither of these is true; the reason is that in the ultimate sense there is only mind and body (*nāma-rūpa*), and no 'being' or person, which are only terms of convenience."[69]

Says the Buddha:[70] "Even the ignorant, unconverted man, O Bhikkhus, may conceive an aversion for this body which is composed of the four elements, may divest himself of passion for it, and attain freedom from it: for the increase and the wasting of this body which is composed of the four elements, and the way in which it is obtained (conceived), and afterwards laid away (at death) are evident. But, O Bhikkhus, what is called the mind, intellect, consciousness—here the ignorant, unconverted man is not equal to conceiving aversion, is not equal to divesting himself of passion, is not equal to attaining freedom, because, O Bhikkhus, from time immemorial the ignorant, unconverted man has held, cherished, and affected the notion 'This is mine; this am I; this is my ego.' But it were better, O Bhikkhus, if the ignorant, unconverted man regarded the body which is composed of the four elements as an ego, rather than the mind. And why do I say so? Because it is evident, O Bhikkhus that this body which is composed of the

69. *Diṭṭhi Vipassanā*, Ven. Mohnyin Sayādaw, p. 20.

70. H. C. Warren, *Buddhism in Translations*, Ch. 18, from Saṃyutta-Nikāya (12:62).

four elements lasts one year, lasts two years ... fifty years, lasts a hundred years and even more. But that which is called the mind, intellect, consciousness keeps up an incessant round by day and by night of perishing as one thing, and springing up as another."

Interdependence of Mind and Body (nāma-rūpa)

Time and again the Buddha laid stress on the interdependence of these two factors. Here is the analogy of the *two sheaves of reeds* that are propped one against the other:[71] "Each one gives the other consolidating support, and when one falls the other falls; so too mind and body occur as an interdependent state, each of its components giving the other consolidating support, and when one falls owing to death the other falls too." And again the analogy of the marionette:[72] "Just as a marionette is void, soulless and without curiosity, and while it walks and stands merely through the combination of strings and wood, yet it seems as if it had curiosity, and interestedness; so too, this mind and body are void, soulless and without curiosity, and while it walks and stands merely through the combination of the two together, yet it seems as if it had curiosity and interestedness. This is how it should be regarded." Furthermore, "The mind has no effective power; it cannot occur by its own efficient power. It does not eat, it does not drink, it does not speak, it does not adopt postures. The body is without efficient power; it cannot occur by its own efficient power. For it has no desire to eat, it has no desire to drink, it has no desire to speak, and it has no desire to adopt postures. But rather it is when supported by the mind that the body occurs. When the mind has the desire to eat, the desire to drink, the desire to speak, the desire to adopt a posture it is the body that eats, drinks, speaks, and adopts a posture."[73]

71. Vism XVIII .32.
72. Vism XVIII. 31.
73. Vism XVIII .34.

Concepts of Compactness and Continuity

Despite all that has been said so far, and despite all that one has learnt on numerous occasions it is no easy matter to loosen—much less to get rid of, even temporarily—the notion of an ego that is so deeply ingrained within each and every one of us. In the first instance, the notion is so widely held and mental apathy for the effort necessary in the search for an alternative explanation precludes one from taking the trouble to question its validity. Further, appearances are so very plausible that the idea of an ego is readily accepted just as the view that the sun rises and sets 'because the sun revolves round the earth' used to be accepted at one time not so long ago. Further, because of the concept of compactness,[74] we take phenomena in their entirety; hence the characteristics of 'not self' e.g., the absence of an ego, does not become apparent, until resolution of the compact into the various elements is given attention; and because of the concept of Continuity the characteristic of impermanence does not become apparent, until continuity is disrupted by discerning that phenomena rise and fall, and that nothing remains static even for the minutest fraction of a second. The Buddha has given us an apt illustration in the difference between our attitude to a cow and its meat.[75] Whilst feeding a cow, bringing it to the slaughter house, keeping it tied up after bringing it there, and seeing it slaughtered and dead, the butcher does not lose the perception of 'cow' so long as he has not carved it up and divided it into parts: but when he has divided it up and when he sits down to sell it he no longer retains the perception of 'cow,' and in its stead the perception of meat occurs; he does not think 'I am selling cow,' or 'they are carrying cow away,' but rather he thinks 'I am selling meat' or 'they are carrying meat away'. So too this Bhikkhu, whilst still a foolish ordinary person does not lose the perception 'living being' or 'man' or 'person' so long as he does not by analysis of the compact into its elements review the body however placed, however disposed as consisting of elements. But when he does review it as consisting of elements, he loses the perception of 'living being,' and his mind establishes itself upon elements.

74. Vism XXI. 3–4
75. Vism XI. 30

The corrective to these concepts of compactness and continuity in the corresponding terminology of modern physics is well illustrated by the following analogies. We are told,[76] "The nuclei of matter in an armour plate are as separately placed as a collection of apples separated from each other by a distance of about three miles, and yet the armour plate appears to be impregnable." Again[77] "It is beyond belief, but scientific proof shows that if it were possible to assemble atoms into a mass the size of an average marble such as children play with, the weight of the marble would be four hundred billion pounds"; and again[78] "Electrons circle round their nuclei with enormous velocity, and atoms and molecules themselves rush about with incredible speed. The speed of the molecules in the air for instance is about one thousand miles per hour." In these circumstances no movement can possibly be noticed by our senses even with the aid of the most powerful instruments, since these speeds occur within such a very limited space as is available within molecules of matter.

Knowledge and Understanding

We have so far made a study and gained some knowledge of the vision according to reality showing that what is commonly referred to as a living being consists merely of mind and body or *nāma-rūpa*, and is void of an ego. We have merely attempted to acquire the theoretical knowledge required for gaining purification of view, which is the first of the five stages towards the attainment of understanding. But we are yet a long way, a very long way, from the actual understanding of purification of view. The Buddha has spoken of *three grades of wisdom*[79]: by learning (*sutamaya paññā*), by reasoning (*cintāmaya paññā*), and thirdly by meditative development (*bhāvanāmaya paññā*). This last grade is the one by which alone higher truths can be grasped, and to which alone the term understanding or insight may correctly be applied. Understanding is a very precise form of realization, and never a

76. *What is Atomic Energy?* by K. Mendelssohn
77. *More Modern Wonders and How They Work* by Captain Burr W. Leyson.
78. *What is Atomic Energy?* by K. Mendelssohn
79. Vism XIV.14.

vague kind of mystic vision. Says the Buddha,[80] "The *dhamma* one has learnt and mastered must be tested by intuitive wisdom; these things that are not so tested their meaning does not become clear. Some foolish men master the *dhamma* simply for the advantage of reproaching others, and for the advantage of gossiping, and they do not arrive at the goal for the sake of which they mastered the *dhamma*. They are like the man who catches a large snake by its tail or by its body, and not by its neck, and because of his wrong grasp is stung by the snake," or they are like the "cowherd who counts others' kine, for they do not share in the blessings of a recluse."[81]

Aldous Huxley illustrates clearly the difference between knowledge and understanding when he states:[82] "Understanding can only be talked about, and that very inadequately; it can be passed on; it can never be shared. There can of course be knowledge of such an understanding, and this knowledge may be passed on. But we must always remember that knowledge of understanding is not the same thing as understanding, which is the raw material of that knowledge. It is different from understanding as the doctor's prescription for penicillin is different from penicillin. Understanding is as rare as emeralds, and so is highly prized. The 'knowers' would dearly love to be 'understanders'; but either their stock of knowledge does not include the knowledge of what to do in order to be 'understanders,' or else they know theoretically what they ought to do, but go on doing the opposite all the same. In either case they cherish the comforting delusion that knowledge, and above all pseudo-knowledge are understanding."

Our generation has undoubtedly grown rapidly in knowledge and in intelligence, but can we say that we have grown in Understanding? Is not this 'inner tangle' and this 'outer tangle', referred to in the opening paragraph of this essay, of our own making? If we hope to disentangle this tangle are we prepared firstly to make a study of the basic teaching of the Buddha, and once we have begun to appreciate its fundamentals, perhaps at

80. MN 22.

81. Dhp 19.

82. *Adonis and the Alphabet and Other Essays*, Aldous Huxley. Ch. 2—"Knowledge and Understanding."

first with a few reservations, are we prepared to undertake the training, arduous and prolonged, that is essential, in the words of Huxley, from being 'knowers' to become 'understanders'? Buddha the perfect physician for mental ills has given us the prescription, and it is left to us to have it dispensed by studying his teaching, and most important of all to start taking the medicine ourselves by putting his teaching into practice. The illness is of a very serious nature although often showing little or no symptoms to the unwary and the thoughtless. It is 'infectious,' deep-rooted and extremely chronic. Moreover, it is beset with many complications, and the patient is a danger to society.

The treatment *is* difficult, and is so prolonged that for the preponderating majority of us, for want of an adequate trial, it will have to be spread over many, many lifetimes before a cure can even be reasonably expected. However a beginning must be made sometime, and fortunately an amelioration of the symptoms may be noticeable shortly after one commences the treatment in proportion to the enthusiasm with which it is followed. This will infuse fresh enthusiasm and hope as to the final efficacy of the treatment. From the point of view of society however it is most fortunate that the benefits of the treatment are spectacular and immediate. It is as if the patient who is suffering from violent maniacal fits is calmed down within a few days of the commencement of the treatment, although a cure may be ever so remote; it is as if a patient with an infectious disease requiring prolonged treatment is rendered non-infectious from the very outset of the treatment. This aspect of the Buddha's teaching ought to make a firm appeal to all those who control the affairs of their community or their country, and should create an enthusiasm in the minds of those in a position to mould international relationships. For is their any doubt that it is the greed to satisfy the 'me' and the 'us', so deep-rooted within us, and the ill-will resulting from any obstacles in our path in the attainment of that satisfaction, both of which are the result of ignorance, that are the causes of all our entanglements—the jealousy and rivalry, the suspicion, fear and anxiety, and man's inhumanity to man, that we see all round us? What other cause is there for all this misery, for the obstacles to our economic and our spiritual development, and for the meanness and the degradation resulting from the exploitation of man by man? A knowledge of the Buddha's teaching, and much more even a far off glimpse of its understanding, will convince those who hold the destiny of their country in their hands, that so long as they avoid the ugly features of greed, of lust for power, and of exploitation of one nation by another, they may safely concede to nations who wish to develop their nationhood along any lines, and through any stages of nationalism peculiar to their own genius, the right to do so. In this way the minds of national leaders may be infused with the ultimate ideal of a world brotherhood of nations.

Understanding the Practice

The conversion of knowledge into understanding and final deliverance rests on a systematic development and perfection to a minimum but definite extent of each of the seven stages of purification in successive steps. It is not possible to bypass any of these stages. It will thus be seen that purification of morality is the first essential requisite, and purification of concentration the second before one can profitably embark on the five final stages of purification of understanding, which commences with the stage of purification of view.

Purification of morality or *sīla-visuddhi* is

> "To refrain from all evil,
> To do good."

"Refraining from all evil," is not a mere negative and physical phenomenon of abstaining from wrong action and wrong speech. It is based on the internal restraint of a clear conscious and guiding mind: and for the layman this consists in the abstention from bodily and vocal misconduct, 'unskill' in action and speech.[83] The first includes killing or inflicting injury, acquisition either by stealing, fraud, threat, or violence, sexual misconduct, the use of intoxicants and undesirable modes of livelihood. The second consists of lying, harsh speech, slander and frivolous talk. In order 'to do good' one develops characteristics directly opposed to unskillful acts and speech already enumerated, for instance, the practice of loving-kindness (*mettā*), compassion (*karuṇā*), liberality

83. *Pañca Sīla* (the five precepts).

(*dāna*), the practice of restraint of the senses (*indriya-saṃvara-sīla*) with constant mindfulness, self-possession and detachment, the practice of truthfulness, of kind and helpful talk, a golden silence where speech is not indicated and the practice of the difficult art of rejoicing at the good fortune of others (*muditā*). By 'refraining from evil' one has the great reward amongst other things, in the Buddha's own words, of freedom from remorse, of a sense of ease without alloy, and of tranquillity and facility to concentrate.[84] Besides these daily practices one practises from time to time for periods of one or more days at a time and as frequently as possible other rules of morality,[85] such as celibacy, abstention from all food after the hour of twelve noon, abstention from dancing, music, shows and other amusements, from the use of cosmetics, perfumes, garlands and adornments and lastly abstention from the use of lofty and comfortable seats and couches. These periodic practices are meant to develop control over one's sexual appetite, and the craving for food, and to lessen one's inordinate craving for the floating pleasure of the senses. They further stimulate one's enthusiasm for the more satisfying and stable enjoyment of voluntary renunciation and of detachment.

Purification of Concentration (citta-visuddhi or samādhi)

This is the second of the seven stages of purification. It is profitable unification of the mind on a single object, whereby the mind remains undistracted, unscattered, pure and tranquil—a preliminary condition absolutely necessary as a foundation either for developing insight, i.e. *vipassanā* (understanding), or for the acquisition of the various *jhānas*. The latter are super-sensual states of perfect mental absorption, in which the fivefold sense activity has ceased, and where perfect unification of the mind is associated with various *jhāna* factors, which in the fourth or highest *jhāna* of the *rūpa* world consists of the finest *jhāna* factor of equanimity (*upekkhā*) alone, unmixed with any of the less refined factors

84. A V Ch. 1.

85. E.g. The eight precepts, consisting of the five precepts, with the substitution of strict celibacy for abstention from sexual misconduct, and with the addition of the three abstentions mentioned as regards food, amusements, and comfortable seats.

associated with the earlier *jhānas*. This fourth *jhāna* is also known as the *pādaka* or foundation-*jhāna*, as it is the foundation from which may be developed either the *jhānas* of formless existence (*arūpa jhānas*), or the supernormal powers or *abhiññās*, e.g. various psychical powers—the ability to read the minds of others, the remembrance of past lives, the divine ear and the divine eye.

It is left to one's own wish to decide the stage in mental concentration at which he would desire to begin developing understanding (*vipassanā*), for it is not essential for final deliverance to develop mental concentration (*samādhi*) to the lofty heights mentioned above. On the other hand it must be clearly borne in mind that mental concentration can never be by-passed altogether, as some would have us believe, before one may profitably embark on meditative development of understanding (*vipassanā-bhāvanā*). When one is able to prevent the attention from jumping from one thought to another, and to keep it steady on one line of thought, and when the strain of such concentration on a single line of thought no longer exists, one is ready to embark on meditative development of understanding. The *Visuddhimagga* has summarised for us the instruction given by the Buddha in forty subjects for meditation for the development of concentration,[86] giving us the choice of selecting one to two or three subjects suited to our temperament, and to the circumstances and surroundings under which we are placed for carrying out the practice. No attempt is made in this essay to enumerate these, much less to describe them even briefly.

A good friend and teacher to guide one in the choice of a suitable subject for meditation, and to help one from time to time with advice and encouragement during the course of one's meditation, is invaluable, but failing such a person, one may rely on a careful study of the written word. Next, as to the choice of a suitable place for meditation, a room where one can lock oneself up for half an hour daily free from intrusion, and from noise, is the most practicable. As for a *suitable time* for meditation, a brief half hour, when one is not too tired either physically or mentally, and when the necessary privacy and freedom from noise is available should be chosen. Once such a time is chosen the practice of meditation

86. Vism XVIII .23.

should be carried out regularly every day at the same time, either reckoning by the clock, or relative to some other regular event of the day, say within a specified number of minutes from waking up, or some specified period of time either before or after dinner. The aim of such regularity in the practice is the formation of a habit of meditation, a habit as regular as that of taking meals, for habit regulates one's life. This calls for thought and rearrangement of the day's program, which in turn means some inconvenience, which however is negligible in relation to the benefits to be gained from regular meditation. The formation of a habit of meditation will convert a practice that was at the beginning irksome, into one of pleasant anticipation and privilege. The duration of these practices will vary considerably depending on circumstances, and on the degree of one's enthusiasm. However for the layman living in a town under present-day conditions, and occupied in earning a living, a regular half-hour per day once or preferably twice daily is perhaps what ought to be aimed at, with longer periods at intermittent intervals. One cannot reasonably expect marked benefits from meditation undertaken for periods much shorter than half an hour. However, regular ten minutes or even five minute periods are of benefit in the sense that it will ultimately infuse enthusiasm into the meditator sufficient to want him to extend the duration of his meditative practice. It is important to adopt a comfortable position to which one can, without much difficulty, get accustomed to. The essential point is to keep the spine erect so that one may not be fidgety, or sway one's body. For a brief period just prior to sitting down for meditation one should forget all business interests, and personal likes and dislikes and prejudices. This is conveniently done either by a brief period of quiet reading from a portion of the *dhamma*, or of worship of the Buddha (*vandanā*). Lastly, one has to cultivate patience and enthusiasm if one is not to be discouraged by one's lapses in not maintaining the regularity of one's meditative practice in the early stages.

Bhāvanāmaya Paññā

This connotes meditative development of understanding. Purification of view, as already mentioned, is the vision according to reality, that what is commonly referred to as a living being, consists merely of name and form or *nāma-rūpa,* and is void of an ego. The meditative development of this view may be done in one of several ways.

Meditation on the Body

Taking the body first, materiality may be discerned in one of several ways—by way of the 18 elements (*dhātu*); by way of the 28 properties of materiality (*mahābhūta* and *upādāya-rūpa*); by way of the corporeal groups (*kalāpas*); or lastly by way of the four primary elements (*mahābhūta*). By way of the last mentioned, one may discern materiality in his own person by meditation either with constituents of the body in brief, or with constituents by analysis in detail, taking each of the thirty-two parts separately, one by one.[87] Meditation on the body, with constituents in brief is done in the following manner: "In this body all parts whose predominant quality is that of hardness or roughness are said to belong to the *earthy element.* Every such solid part of one's body—e.g. head hair, body hair, nails, teeth, or skin, flesh, sinews, bone, marrow or mesentery, every solid organ such as kidney, liver, spleen, or brain, every hollow organ such as stomach, intestines, or the heart, and all the solid contents of hollow organs such as undigested food in the stomach, or excrement in the intestines—is made up of a multitude of groups or *kalāpas* of all the four primary elements or qualities coming together in a certain manner, and in varying proportions. The four primary elements are widely separated from one another by the element of space (*ākāsa-dhātu*), which makes it possible for the former to be in a continual state of movement, of change, and of activity; and which enables the primary elements to function properly. In each solid part of one's body the earthy element predominates; hence it appears as a stiffened solid. These groups of the earthy element are, on the one hand held together by the small quantity of the watery element present, 'flowing out' amongst

87. MN 140; Vism VIII .44; and XI .47–82.

these groups and binding them, whilst on the other hand they are prevented from collapsing by the quality of distension possessed by the airy element. Further these groups of the earthy element are maintained, matured, removed, and renewed by the fiery element. The earthy element present in the solid parts throughout one's body is in its fundamental characteristics in no way different from the earthy element present in solids outside one's body. Just as the solid element present in a tree or a rock does not represent a living being, even so what is called hair, teeth, or bone or any other solid part of one's body is a particular component of one's body, without thought, morally indeterminate, void, and not a living being."

One next meditates, in a similar manner on all the fluid parts of one's body thus: "In this body all parts whose predominant quality is that of 'flowing out,' and subsequently of 'holding together', the other qualities are said to belong to the *watery element.* Every such fluid portion of one's body, e.g. bile, blood, oil of the joints, or other secretion, sweat, tears, spittle, urine or other excretion, is made up of a multitude of groups or *kalāpas* of all the four primary elements or qualities coming together in a certain manner, and in varying proportions. In every drop of fluid in one's body the watery element predominates; hence it appears as a liquid having the quality of flowing out, or spreading out. The small quantity of the earthy element present gives the liquid the necessary foundation or 'substance.' Each drop of liquid present in one's body is prevented from collapsing by the quality of distension possessed by the airy element. Further each drop of fluid is secreted, maintained, altered, and matured by virtue of the fiery quality or element present. The watery element present in each drop of fluid in one's body is in no way different to the watery element present in liquids outside the body. Just as the watery element present in a pond, or well, or a river does not represent a living being, even so what is called bile, or blood, sweat or urine or any other liquid part of one's body is a particular component of one's body, without thought, morally indeterminate, void, and not a living being."

One next meditates on the 'fiery' and the 'airy' qualities in one's body thus: "The fiery quality in one's body has the function of warming (*santāpana*), of ageing (*jīrāpana*), of burning up or breaking down (*pariḍayhana*), and of digesting (*pācaka*). It maintains this body, keeps it warm, ensures its proper appearance and prevents it from putrefying."

"In this body all parts whose predominant quality is that of distending and preventing from collapse, of motility, and of lightness belong to the airy element. Every such gaseous portion of one's body, e.g. up or down going winds, wind both inside and outside hollow organs in the chest and in the abdomen, wind in gaps and apertures such as the ears or the nostrils, is made up of a multitude of groups, or *kalāpas,* of all the four primary qualities coming together in a certain manner, and in varying proportions. In each gaseous portion of one's body the airy element predominates; hence it appears as a gas having the quality of distending, of motility and of lightness. The small portion of the earthy element present gives the gas the necessary foundation or 'substance.' These gases are held together by the watery quality present, and they are maintained, by the fiery quality. The airy quality present in the gases in one's body is in its fundamental characteristics in no way different to the airy element present in gases outside one's body. Just as the airy element present in the atmosphere does not represent a living being, even so what is called up or down going winds, or wind in the lungs or in the intestines, or in any other part of one's body is a particular component of one's body, without thought, morally indeterminate, void, and not a living being."

One may profitably do the above meditation in stages, as it has to be done when the meditation is carried out in detail, where each of the thirty-two parts of the body are taken up separately one by one. Firstly, one *learns by heart* the summary of the meditation as given above, or suitably modified. Secondly, there is the verbal recitation[88] of what has been learnt by heart. "This shall be done even if one is a master of the Tipiṭaka, for the meditation subject only becomes evident to some through recitation." Thirdly, when one is proficient in the verbal recitation, one should do the recitation mentally.[89] "Just as it was done verbally, for the mental recitation is a condition for the penetration of the characteristics of the primary elements." Fourthly, when one becomes proficient in both the verbal and the mental recitation, one commences the actual meditation itself.

88. Vism VIII. 49.
89. Vism VIII. 57.

Instead of doing the meditation in the above manner, one may do it in terms of recent atomic physics. One may make one's own summary from the facts gathered from this essay, and from other sources. This summary should embody the following facts: that everything in the universe, including our own bodies, is made up of one or a combination of two or more of the 92 elements or atoms, in varying combinations; that these atoms themselves are complex in structure, and are made up of three elementary particles or building bricks, the protons, the neutrons, and the electrons; that, of these, the first two are placed within a central core or nucleus, and that the electrons are disposed at great distances from, and around the nucleus; that the size of these elementary particles, in comparison to the space in which they are disposed, is infinitesimally small; that the difference in the qualities displayed by different objects is a property not of the mass possessed by these minute elementary particles but of the forces of attraction, and of repulsion between them; that these minute elementary particles are not static, but are constantly moving at incredible speeds; that the property called mass is simply concentrated energy. One would then conclude thus: "The elementary particles, e.g. the protons, the neutrons, and the electrons present throughout one's body, are in no way different to the protons, neutrons, and electrons present in solid objects, liquids or gases outside one's body. Just as the protons, neutrons, and electrons present in solid objects, liquids or gases outside one's body do not represent a living being, even so the protons, the neutrons, and the electrons, present in one's body are without thought, morally indeterminate, void, and not a living being."

One meditates in this way—either in terms of the four 'primary elements' or in terms of the three elementary particles that go to form the atom—regularly, with enthusiasm, and with increasing confidence, for months, for years, or for a lifetime until one is quite sure of discerning materiality (*rūpa*), in one's body. If and when one has thus become quite sure of discerning materiality in this way, and not until then, should one undertake the task of discerning immaterial states (*nāma*).[90]

90. Vism XVIII .23.

Meditation on the Immaterial States

This meditation is based on the formula given in the paragraph on immaterial states above, and is carried out thus: "The eye and a visual object constitute materiality (*rūpa*); the eye-consciousness, which arises by their coming together constitutes mentality (*nāma*): besides the eye, the object that impinges on the eye, and the resulting eye-consciousness there is no 'being,' or 'person,' which are only terms of convenience. The ear and sound constitute materiality. The ear-consciousness, which arises by their coming together, constitutes mentality. Besides the ear, the sound, and the resulting ear-consciousness there is no 'being' or 'person,' which are only terms of convenience." Similarly one carries out the meditation for the nose and odour, and the resulting nose-consciousness; for the tongue and taste, and the resulting tongue-consciousness; and for the body and tangible object, and the resulting body-consciousness. Further "through the mind-element (*mano-dhātu*), and mind-object (*dhamma*) there arises the mind-consciousness-element (*mano-viññāṇa-dhātu*); besides the mind-element, the mind-object, and the resulting mind-consciousness -element there is no 'being' or 'person,' which are only terms of convenience."

In addition to the above one runs one's mind through everything that has been described in the remaining portion of this section, on immaterial states, through the section on interdependence of mind and body, and through the section above on the concepts of compactness and continuity.

The above meditation undertaken for discerning the immaterial states will have to be carried out with diligence, with enthusiasm, and with regularity, and for an ever increasing duration of time daily for years or for a lifetime until one gains purity of view—that "correct vision of mind and body, which after defining mind and body by these various methods, has been established on the plane of non-confusion by overcoming the perception of a being, is what should be understood as "*purification of view.*"[91]

91. Vism XVIII. 37.

Buddhism and Peace

K. N. Jayatilleke
M. A. (Cantab), PhD. (London)
Professor of Philosophy
University of Ceylon

WHEEL PUBLICATION NO. 41

Buddhism and Peace

While fellow-scientists have been able to come together and discuss their common problems without bitterness or acrimony, the idea that people of different religions can meet and discuss topics of mutual interest is of more recent origin. This is unfortunate since it is the religious men who profess to stand for the ideals of truth and love, who should have given a lead in this matter to the others. I need not go into the historical reasons for this, but I am glad that this organization among others has in recent times succeeded in extending its hand of fellowship beyond sectarian boundaries.[1]

What Buddhism has to say on the theme of peace and the concepts of truth, freedom, justice and love is, I believe, particularly appropriate to our times. This view, I also believe, would be shared by most of you in respect of your own religions. This raises a number of problems. Are we all saying the same thing? Or are we saying a number of things which complement and supplement one another, each of us contributing some aspect of truth regarding these concepts, values and ideals? Or can it be that only one of us (or none of us) is right and the rest are wrong? Or is it the case that our talk about these things is devoid of meaning and has only an emotive significance for us and some of our hearers? We cannot hope to solve all these problems, but I believe that discussions of this sort can go a long way to help us see one another's points of view and clarify our own views about them.

It is evident that there is a common content in the higher religions. All these religions profess a belief in a Transcendent Reality, in survival, in moral responsibility and moral values, and in a good life, despite the differences when we go into details. The Christians and Muslims seek communion with God, the Hindus seek union with *Brahman*, and the Buddhists seek to attain Nibbāna. It is equally evident that on matters on which they disagree they cannot all be true—unless it can be shown that the disagreements are purely verbal. Christianity believes in one unique Incarnation; Hinduism in several. To Islam the very idea is blasphemy. To the Buddhist it depends on what you mean. Now, what I have to say on the concepts of peace, truth, freedom, justice and love in Buddhism belongs partly to the common content and partly to the disparate element, which distinguishes Buddhism from other religions. It would be necessary for me to point out both, if I am to give a clear picture of the account given of these concepts in Buddhism.

Peace is a central concept in the religion of the Buddha, who came to be known as the "*santi-rājā*" or the "Prince of Peace." For, on the one hand the aim of the good life, as understood in Buddhism, is described as the attainment of a state of "Peace" or "*santi*," which is a characteristic of Nibbāna or the Transcendent Reality. On the other hand, the practice of the good life is said to consist in "*sama-cariyā*" or "harmonious (literally: peaceful) living" with one's fellow beings. It was this doctrine, which gave "inward peace" (*ajjhatta-santi*,)[2] and resulted in "harmonious living" (or "righteous living"—*dhammacariyā*—as it is sometimes called), which the Buddha for the first time in the known history of mankind sought to spread over the entire earth when he set up, as he claimed "the kingdom of righteousness" (*dhamma-cakkaṃ*, literally, rule of righteousness) or "the kingdom of God" (*brahma-cakkaṃ*).[3]

The Buddha, who in the earliest texts is said to have been "born for the good and happiness of mankind" (*manussaloka hita-sukhatāya jāto*[4]), first trained sixty-one of his disciples to attain the highest spiritual goal in this life itself and then sent them out, requesting that no two of them were to go in the same direction. They were "to preach this good doctrine, lovely in the beginning, lovely in the middle and lovely in its consummation." It is necessary to stress the importance of this training which was intended to bring about the moral (*sīla*), intuitive (*samādhi*) and intellectual-spiritual (*paññā*) development of the person. For it was only those who had attained the "inward peace" who were considered fit to preach, since according to Buddhism "it is not possible for a man who has not saved himself to (help) save

2. Sn 837

3. "*Brahmā*" means here "the highest" or the "most sublime" without theological connotations.

4. Sn 683

another."[5] Those who went out on such missions were to train themselves in such a way that "if brigands were to get hold of them and cut them limb by limb with a double-edged saw," they should not consider themselves to have done the bidding of the Buddha, if they showed the slightest anger towards them.[6]

The practice of "*mettā*" or compassionate love was thus an essential part of the training. The worth placed on love in Buddhism may be gathered from the following remark of the Buddha: "None of the good works employed to acquire religious merit is worth a fraction of the value of loving-kindness."[7] The word *mettā* is the abstract noun from the word *mitra*, which means "friend." It is, however, not defined just as "friendliness" but as analogous to a mother's love for her only child. "Just as a mother loves her only child even more than her life, do thou extend a boundless love towards all creatures." The practice of the "highest life" or the "God-life" (*brahma-vihāra*) is said to consist in the cultivation of compassionate feelings towards all beings, sympathy (*karuṇā*) towards those in distress who need our help, the ability to rejoice with those who are justly happy (the opposite emotion to that of jealousy, envy, etc.) (*muditā*) and impartiality towards all. The person who has successfully developed these qualities is said to be "one who is cleansed with an internal bathing" after bathing "in the waters of love and compassion for one's fellow beings."[8]

When the Buddha's disciple Ānanda suggested to him that half of the religion of the Buddha consisted in the practice of friendliness, the Buddha's rejoinder was that it was not half but the whole of the religion. It was this emphasis on compassion which made it possible for Buddhism to spread its message over the greater part of Asia, without resorting to military force or political power. It is the proud boast of Buddhism that not a drop of blood has been shed in propagating its message and no wars have been fought for the cause of Buddhism or the Buddha. It was able to convert people to its view by its reasonableness and the inspiring example of those who preached it.

Differences of opinion there were with regard to the interpretation of the texts among the Buddhists themselves, and

5. M I 46
6. M I 129
7. *Itivuttaka*, 19–21
8. M I 39

this was inevitable in a religion which gave full freedom of thought and expression to man. But these differences did not result in fanaticism and an attempt on the part of one party to persecute the other. History records the fact that those who subscribed to the ideals of Mahāyāna or Theravāda Buddhism were able to study side by side in the same monastery. In world conferences of Buddhists, Mahāyānists and Theravādins come together despite the known differences in their views. Another aspect of this practice of compassion on the part of the Buddhists is the fact that they were the first in history to open hospitals in India, Sri Lanka and China for the medical treatment not only of human beings but of animals as well, thus translating into action the saying of the Buddha that "he who serves the sick serves me."[9]

The effect that this doctrine of compassion had on the Buddhist emperor, Asoka, may be seen when he says, "All men are my children, and, as I desire for my children that they obtain every kind of welfare and happiness both in this world and the next world, so do I desire for all men." Here was a king, unique in history, who on his conversion to Buddhism gave up military conquest as an instrument of policy not after defeat but after victory. Asoka had conquered an area almost the size of Europe, but he did not extend his conquest to the southernmost part of India or try to annex Sri Lanka, although he could have easily done so.

The Rock Edict XIII contains a personal confession of his remorse at the sight of the suffering and carnage which his military campaigns involved. When he embraced Buddhism, he indulged in spiritual conquest saying that "the reverberation of war drums" was now replaced by the "reverberation of the drum of the dharma." It appears as if Asoka was trying to emulate the example of the righteous "universal monarch" (*cakkavatti-rāja*) as depicted in the Buddhist texts. The Buddha had said that "it was possible to rule a country in accordance with dharma without resorting to harsh punitive measures or engaging in military conquests."[10]

The "universal monarch" who is called a "king of righteous-

9. *Vinaya Piṭaka*, *Mahāvagga* VIII. 26.

10. S I 116. According to Buddhist tradition, there are periods in the world cycles when human beings are at the peak of moral and intellectual development, and at such times a world ruler (*cakkavatti*) is able to govern in righteousness, without the use of force.

ness" (*dharma-rāja*) governs his country as a model state in which there is both economic prosperity as well as the practice of righteousness. The idea and fame of this Just Society spreads over the earth until the entire world follows its example and comes under a single rule "without the necessity for arms or the sword" (*adaṇḍena asatthena*). In any case he seems to have been impressed by the sentiments about war expressed in the Buddhist texts. The Dhammapada says:

> "Victory breeds hatred,
> for the conquered sleep in sorrow;
> casting aside victory and defeat,
> the peaceful one dwells at ease."[11]
>
> "The conqueror gets someone who conquers him."[12]
> "Hatred does not cease by hatred—
> hatred ceases by love—
> this is the eternal law."[13]

The *Mahāyāna* work, the *Suvarṇabhāsottama Sūtra*, contains a plea for peace and concord between "the 84,000 kings of India."

The Buddha not only preached against war but actually intervened on one occasion to prevent a war—the first practical lesson in *ahiṃsā* in the field of politics. Two tribes, the *Sakyas* and the *Koliyas*, who lived on either side of a river were making warlike preparations to destroy each other because they could not agree on dividing the waters for their use. It is on this occasion that the Buddha intervened and brought about a settlement after asking the warmongers what they considered to be of greater worth—water or human lives! It is these acts of compassion of the Buddha, who gave up a kingdom to show humanity the way to enlightenment, which made one of his contemporaries say of him, "I have heard it said that God is compassionate but I have seen with my own eyes how full of compassion the Blessed One is." It is not surprising therefore that in the *Mahāyāna*, the Buddha should be conceived of as the Incarnation of the "highest compassion" (*mahā kāruṇika*).

11. Dhp 207
12. S I 85
13. Dhp 5

The idea of compassion has its origins in pre-Buddhistic thought. It is first met with in the *Chāndogya Upanishad*, where it is said that one should practise *ahiṃsā* (non-violence) towards all creatures with the sole exception of holy places[14]—in other words animal sacrifices to God were permitted. The concept of *ahiṃsā* also finds a central place in Jainism, where the Jain ascetic goes into extremes in practising this virtue. But it was Buddhism which made *ahiṃsā* basically a virtue to be practised in human relations and introduced the new word "*mettā*" (the abstract noun from *mitra*, friend) to denote this concept. But the object of one's *mettā* (compassion, love) is not only human beings but all beings both higher and lower than the human, and it came to mean the completely selfless but boundless compassion of a Buddha.

The concept of "beings higher than the human" is unintelligible except in the background of the Buddhist cosmology. According to the Buddhist conception of the cosmos, there are an innumerable number of world-systems. The Buddha says, "As far as these suns and moons revolve shedding their light in space, so far extends the thousand-fold world-system. In it are a thousand suns, a thousand moons, thousands of earths and thousands of heavenly worlds. This is the thousand-fold minor world-system. A thousand times such a thousand-fold minor world-system is the twice a-thousand middling world system. A thousand times such a twice-a-thousand middling world-system is the thrice-a-thousand major world-system."[15] This is a conception that partially coincides with the modern physicist's view of the cosmos, with its hundreds of galactic systems or island universes, whether we accept the interpretations of Bondi and Hoyle or Ryle.

The compassion of the Buddhist is to be extended not only to the humans and animals on our earth but to the beings in all these worlds. All beings within the cosmos, however low their state of evolution may be, are said to have the capacity to evolve up to the very highest state; and however high their stature may be, are said to be subject to death so long as they remain within the cosmos—both these facts teach us the same lesson, namely, that it is each one's duty to help his fellow beings and that no one has any right or valid grounds to despise another.

14. *Chāndyogya Upanishad* 8, 15

15. A I 227, 228; IV 59, 60

At the human level the need for mutual help is much greater. Buddhism taught the doctrine of the equality of mankind at a time when human inequality was taken for granted. We find here for the first time the biological argument that mankind was one species. The Buddha says, "Know the grasses and trees ... the marks that constitute species are for them and their species are manifold. Know the worms and the moths and the different sorts of ants, the marks that constitute species are for them ... As in these species the marks that constitute species are manifold, so among men the marks that constitute species are not found ... Not as regards their hair, head, ears ... Difference there is in beings endowed with bodies, but amongst men this is not the case—the difference amongst men is nominal (only)."[16]

The Hindu conception of society was static and was dominated by the idea of caste. This was given a divine sanction by being considered a creation of God: "God created the fourfold castes with their specific aptitudes and functions."[17] Against this was the dynamic evolutionary conception of society as pictured in early Buddhism. The Buddha countered the arguments that the hierarchical fourfold division of society was fundamental by pointing out that in certain societies (e.g. among the *Yona-Kambojas*, i.e. certain Persian states), there were only two classes, the lords and the serfs and that even this was not rigid for "sometimes the lords became serfs and the serfs lords."[18]

While the theists at that time urged that men were created unequal by God, the Buddhists turned the arguments of the Theists against them. Aśvaghoṣa, a *brahmin* convert to Buddhism, writes in his *Vajrasūcī* (circa 1st century BCE) in a polemic against caste that the fatherhood of God should imply the brotherhood of man. He says, "Wonderful! You affirm that all men proceeded from One, i.e. God (Brahmā); how then can there be a fourfold insuperable diversity among them? If I have four sons by one wife, the four sons having one father and mother must be all essentially alike." We also find moral and spiritual arguments for equality to show that all people, irrespective of caste, race or

16. *Suttanipāta*, Tr. Fausböll, *Sacred Books of the East*, Vol. 10, pp. 111–113
17. *Bhagavad Gīta*, IV. 13
18. M II 157

rank were capable of moral development and the highest spiritual attainments. The Buddhist idea of fellowship or *mettā* is thus founded on the conception of the oneness of the human species, the equality of man and the spiritual unity of mankind.

The Buddhist undertaking to refrain from killing is not a negative precept and has its positive side when fully stated, viz. "One refrains from killing creatures, laying aside the stick and the sword, and abides conscientious, full of kindness, love and compassion towards all creatures and beings."[19] A Buddhist layman has to follow a righteous mode of living (*sammā ājīva*) and this meant that certain professions were not open to him. According to the texts five trades are forbidden: he should not engage in the sale of arms (*sattha-vijjā*), the sale of human beings or animals (*satta-vijjā*), the sale of flesh (*maṃsa-vijjā*), the sale of intoxicating drinks (*majja-vijjā*) and the sale of dangerous and poisonous drugs (*visa-vijjā*).[20] The order of monks were exhorted to practise the following, which are said to promote unity—to be compassionate in their behaviour, their speech and their thoughts towards one another and to have all things in common.[21]

I said that the ideal in Buddhism was to attain a permanent state of mind described as the "inward peace" not in the remote future but in this life itself. This is not a passive apathetic state of quietism as some Western critics of Buddhism have thought. For the passage from our finite self-centred existence to Nibbāna is pictured as one from bondage to freedom (*vimutti*) and power (*vasi*), from imperfection to perfection (*parisuddhi, parama-kusala*), from unhappiness to perfect happiness (*parama-sukha*), from ignorance to knowledge (*vijjā, aññā, ñāṇa*), from finite consciousness to infinite transcendent consciousness (*ananta-viññāṇa*), from the impermanent to the permanent (*nicca*), from the unstable to the stable (*dhuva*), from fear and anxiety to perfect security (*abhaya*), from the evanescent to the ineffable (*amosadhamma*), from a state of mental illness to a state of perfect mental health, etc. It is a peace that passes understanding for it is the result of what is paradoxically described both as the extinction

19. D I 4
20. A III 208
21. M I 322

of one's self-centred desires and the attainment of an ultimate reality. Let me explain. According to Buddhism, the springs of action are six-fold, comprising the three immoral bases of action (*akusala-mūla*) and the three moral bases of action (*kusala-mūla*), viz.

Immoral bases

1. a. *rāga* (craving): *kāma-rāga* or *kāma-taṇhā*, the desire for sense gratification; *bhava-rāga* or *bhava-taṇhā*, the desire for selfish pursuits
   b. *dosa* (hatred): *vibhava-taṇhā*, the desire for destruction
   c. *moha* (delusion): erroneous beliefs.

Moral bases

2. *arāga-cāga* (charity)
   adosa-mettā (love)
   amoha-vijjā (knowledge)

Toynbee has said that the Buddha failed "to distinguish between self-devoting and self-centred desires."[22] But the distinction between the two is so marked in Buddhism that the former (the Moral bases) are not even called "desires." "Desires" or "thirsts" are threefold—(1) the desire for sense-gratification (*kāma-taṇhā*), (2) the desire for selfish pursuits (e.g. self-preservation, self-continuity, self-assertion, self-display, etc. (*bhava-taṇhā*), (3) the desire for destruction (*vibhava-taṇhā*). These desires continually seek and find temporary satisfaction (*tatra-tatrābhinandinī*) though ever remaining unsatisfied and provide the fuel for the process called "the individual." They are said to be narrow and limited (*pamāṇa-kataṃ*),[23] while their opposites—charity and love—are boundless (*appamāṇa*).[24] Now, the Buddha urges only the total extinction of these self-centred desires (i.e., 1 a & b) and the complete elimination of ignorance or delusion (i.e., 1–c). This is done by gradually cultivating and developing the

22. Toynbee, Arnold, *An Historian's Approach to Religion*, Oxford University Press, 1956, p. 29
23. M I 297
24. loc. cit.

opposite traits of charity, love and knowledge until the mind at all its levels is finally purged of all such self-centred desires and considerations.

The mind is said to be "divided into two compartments" (*ubhayato abbhocchinnaṃ*),[25] the conscious and the unconscious. As long as it is affected by the threefold desires, there is an influx of defiling impulses (*āsava*) into the conscious mind, and it is in a state of tension and unrest. Now, diseases are classified as twofold, bodily disease (*kāyiko rogo*) and mental disease (*cetasiko rogo*). It is said that we suffer from bodily disease from time to time, but that mental illness is continual until the final state of sainthood is attained. This is the concept of the healthy mind as understood in Buddhism—a state in which the self-centred desires are utterly extinguished and the mind enjoys an "inward peace," which is said to be one of indescribable happiness.

Toynbee has said that this goal "looks intrinsically unattainable"[26] since desires cannot be given up without cultivating the desire to give them up. This criticism has already been forestalled and met in the Pali Canon itself. The self-centred desires are to be eliminated by depending on desire (*taṇhaṃ nissāya-taṇhaṃ pahātabbaṃ*)[27]—namely the desire for Nibbāna. But this latter master-desire, it is pointed out, is not on the same footing as the first-order desires, for unlike the self-centred desires, which continually seek gratification from time to time without being permanently satisfied, the master-desire would achieve final satisfaction and be extinguished with the eradication of the self-centred desires and the attainment of Nibbāna, which coincides with it. This is the "inward peace" spoken of in the in the Buddhist texts. It is a word full of meaning but it has meaning only to those who have experienced it, partially or fully. To others it is devoid of meaning in the same way in which the formulae of a physicist would be devoid of meaning to one who does not understand his subject.

This brings us to the problem of meaning and truth in Buddhism. The two are related for before we can say that a statement is true or

25. D III 105
26. Toynbee op. cit. p. 64
27. A II 146

false, we are obliged to ask whether it is meaningful or significant. It is to the credit of the Buddha that he was one of the first thinkers of the East or West to discuss the problem of the meaning of statements, particularly of the statements of religion. We cannot go into this in detail, and we may state briefly that, according to the Buddha, a statement is meaningful if it is in principle verifiable in the light of experience, sensory or extra-sensory. A statement should also have a basis in a person's experience before he can meaningfully assert it, so that the same statement may be meaningful in one context and meaningless in another. Meaningful statements may be true or false. Truth is said to have the characteristic of "correspondence with fact" (*yathābhūtaṃ*). If I believe that there is a next world, and it is the case that there is a next world, then my belief is true[28] and otherwise false.[29] Truth must also be consistent; it is said that "truth is one and there is no second truth."[30] But consistency is not enough, for it is possible to have several internally consistent systems of thought, mutually contradicting one another. For this reason any religion based on pure (a priori) reasoning (*takka*) is said to be unsatisfactory, for, even if the reasoning is sound (*sutakkitaṃ pi hoti*)[31] and internally consistent, the theory may be false if it does not correspond with fact.

While Buddhist tolerance is partly derived from its emphasis on compassion, it also has its roots in its attitude to truth and its general conception of man. If men did wrong, it was because they were ignorant rather than sinful, and it is, therefore, our duty to enlighten the ignorant and reform them rather than punish them for their wrong-doing. Ignorance again cannot be replaced with knowledge by imposing one's beliefs on others, even if they were true. People have to grow up and discover the truth themselves, and the most that others can do (even the Buddha) is to help them to do this. Far from being detrimental, the scientific outlook was considered to be essential for the moral and spiritual development of man; and our critical faculties should be exercised to the fullest extent in the discovery of religious truth. The Buddha tells a questioner, on more than one occasion,

28. M I 430
29. M I 402
30. Sn 884
31. M I 520

> "You have raised a doubt in a situation in which you ought to suspend your judgment. Do not accept anything because it is rumoured so, because it is the traditional belief, because the majority holds it, because it is found in the scriptures, because it is a product of metaphysical argument and speculation, because of a superficial investigation of facts, because it conforms with one's inclinations, because it is authoritative or because of the prestige-value of your teacher."[32]

Even his own teaching was no exception, and the Buddha did not demand a blind faith or allegiance for it. "One must not," he says, "accept my Dhamma (teaching) from reverence but first try it as gold is tried by fire."

The sincerity and frankness on which a truly religious life should be grounded demanded healthy criticism and continual self-examination, and the importance of such an outlook is nowhere so well emphasized as in the following exhortation: "If anyone," says the Buddha, "were to speak ill of me, my doctrine or my order, do not bear any ill-will towards him, be upset or perturbed at heart, for, if you were to be so, it would only cause you harm. If, on the other hand, anyone were to speak well of me, my doctrine and my order, do not be overjoyed, thrilled or elated at heart, for, if so, it would only be an obstacle in your way of forming a correct judgment as to whether the qualities praised in us are real and actually found in us."[33] There is a distinction drawn in the Buddhist texts between a "rational faith" (*ākāravati-saddhā*) in what is verifiable and worth trying out and a "baseless faith" (*amūlika-saddhā*) in unverifiable dogmas—the former is commended and the latter condemned.

Buddhism parts company with other religions in holding that moral and religious truths (with one exception) are not different in principle from scientific truths. Paradoxical as it may seem, it was the Buddha—i.e. a religious teacher—who was the first in the history of thought to state formally the two principles of causal determination, namely that A and B are causally related, if whenever A happens B happens and B does not happen unless A has

32. A I 191
33. D I 3

happened. The theory of causation is central to the understanding of Buddhism. The Buddha tells us "the causes of things that arise from causes" and adds that "he who understands causation understands the Dhamma and vice versa." Causation, however, is not strictly deterministic since the mind (with its acts of will) can often divert and direct the operation of causal processes and the mind is said to have the capacity to act with degrees of freedom according to its state of development. The Buddhist concept of causation, therefore, stands midway between Indeterminism (*adhicca-samuppāda*: Skt. *yadṝccha*) on the one hand and strict determinism (*niyati*) on the other.

There were three forms of determinism prevalent at the time to which Buddhism was opposed—one was natural determinism (*svabhāva-vāda*) which held that everything that happens is due to the innate constitution of things; another was karmic determinism (*pubbekata-hetu*, Skt. *purātana-karma-kṝtaṃ*), which held that everything that happens to an individual was due to his past *karma*; lastly, there was theistic determinism (*issara-nimmāna-vāda*), which held that all that happens was due to the fiat or will of a personal God who has created the universe and sustains it.

In the universe there operate physical laws (*utu-niyāma*), biological laws (*bīja-niyāma*), psychological laws (*citta-niyāma*) and moral and spiritual laws (*dhamma-niyāma*). While the natural scientists tell us about the first three, the Buddha discovers and reveals the latter. It is said that, whether the Buddhas appear or not, these laws operate and we are subject to them. All that the Buddha does is to discover (or re-discover) them. What is thus discovered is said to be verifiable by each and every one of us, by following the path that leads to their discovery. It is a contingent fact that the moral and spiritual life (i.e. the religious life) is both possible and desirable in the universe in which we live. If the universe were different from what in fact it is (e.g. if indeterminism or strict determinism were the case, if the soul were identical with the body or were different from it, if there were no Transcendent Reality), then the religious life might not have been possible and would not have been desirable.

One of the spiritual truths stated in Buddhism is the law of *karma*. As understood in Buddhism it merely states that there is an observable correlation between morally good acts and pleasant consequences to the individual and morally evil acts and unpleasant consequences. It does not state that all our present experiences are due to our past *karma*. This is in fact emphatically denied, where it is shown that many of our experiences are due to our own actions in this life or to causal factors (such as the weather, our state of physical health), which have nothing to do with our *karma*. The law of *karma* as stated is a causal correlation, which guarantees the fact of individual moral responsibility. It is said to be a correlation that is observable and verifiable by developing one's faculty of retro-cognition, i.e. the ability to recall one's past lives. This faculty and others are said to be within the reach of all of us to develop by the practice of meditation. What evidence is there to believe in rebirth? Since rebirth or "reincarnation" is said to be a meaningful concept and a logical possibility,[34] the problem is whether it is the case or not.

Briefly, the evidence today is of two sorts: (1) there are cases of spontaneous recall of previous lives, especially on the part of young children, which have been verified and claimed to be found true. There was a recent case in Sri Lanka reported in *The Ceylon Observer* of 19 January 1951;[35] (2) there is also experimental evidence. People under deep hypnosis are able to recall not only the lost memories of this life but of previous lives as well[36]. Several interpretations are possible of these experimental data, but I believe that the simplest and best hypothesis to account for the data I have seen so far is that of rebirth. It is hoped that with more and better experimentation on this verifiable theory of survival, we shall be able to know the truth about it before long.

While the *Upanishadic* thinkers interpreted the mystic experiences that they had as being due to the grace of God,[37]

---

34. See Ayer, A. J., *The Problem of Knowledge*, Penguin Books, 1957, pp. 193, 194

35. Cf. "The Case of Shanti Devi," *The Illustrated Weekly of India*, 15 December 1935; also, "The Problem of Rebirth," *The Milwaukee Sentinel*, 25 September 1892, reported by Ralph Shirley.

36. See a recent study by Dr. Jonathan Rodney, *The Explorations of a Hypnotist*, Elek Books, London, 1959, where the experiments are varied so as to eliminate hallucination.

37. *dhātuh prasādāt, Katha Upanishad* 2.20

Buddhism explains these experiences as due to the natural development of the mind. For Buddhism they result from the operation of causal processes relating to religious experience. They are, however, not considered subjective and are held to be of great value, though Buddhism does not subscribe to the metaphysical and theological interpretations given to them in the Upanishads and the rest of mystical literature in the East and West. One of the prerequisites for developing these experiences, which give meaning to the religious life, is the absolute moral integrity of the individual.

I have tried to illustrate what I meant by saying that for Buddhism spiritual truths were on a par with scientific truths. There is, however, one "experience," if it may be called an experience, which is beyond the empirical, phenomenal and causal. This is the experience of Nibbāna, which is called "the Truth" (*sacca*). This illumination is said to be comparable to that of a man born blind obtaining sight after a physician has treated him. It is described as a flaring up of a great light (*ālokā udapādi*) and is said to coincide with the extinction of the fires of greed, hatred and delusion, and the attainment of the peace that causes understanding. It is not a conditioned causal experience, since Nibbāna is said to be the Unconditioned (*asaṅkhata*), the Uncaused (*akataṃ, na paṭicca-samuppannaṃ*) and the Timeless (*nibbānaṃ na vattabbaṃ atītan ti pi anāgataṃ ti pi paccuppannan ti pi*), not located in space (*na katthaci, kuhiñci*). To say that one exists (*hoti upapajjati*) in *Nibbāna* or ceases to exist (*na hoti, na upapajjati* are both said to be wrong.

The question was put to the Buddha in his own life-time: "The person who has attained the goal—does he cease to exist, or does he exist eternally without defect; explain this to me, O Lord, as you understand it." The Buddha explains, "A person who has attained the goal is beyond measure; he does not have that with which one can describe him."[38] Elsewhere, the Buddha explained that the question is meaningless. It is the concepts with which we are familiar that make us ask it. We can only conceive of two alternatives—the annihilation of the individual at some point of time or his eternal duration in time. The Buddha illustrates what he means with an example. If someone, who has seen a fire in

38. *yena naṃ vajju taṃ tassa natthi.* Sn. 1076

front of him go out, were to ask in which direction the fire has gone—northern, southern, eastern or western—it is a question which cannot be answered, since the question itself is meaningless. Wittgenstein takes the same example to illustrate the same point: "Thus it can come about that we are not able to rid ourselves of the implications of our symbolism which seems to admit of a question like 'Where does the flame of a candle go when it is blown out? Where does the light go? ...' We have been obsessed with our symbolism. We may say that we are led into puzzlement by an analogy, which irresistibly drags us on."[39]

The Buddha classified questions into four types, (1) questions which can be answered categorically, (2) questions which can he answered only after analysis, (3) questions which must be answered with a counter-question, and (4) questions which have to be put aside as meaningless. The question whether the saint exists in Nibbāna or not, is said to be meaningless, although there is a psychological urge and a linguistic reason for asking it. Another set of questions which the Buddha set aside as meaningless were the questions, "Is the soul identical with the body?" and "Is the soul different from the body?" Having discarded as an empiricist and a "verificationist" the concept of the soul or substance as meaningless these questions too are meaningless since they contain a meaningless concept. The traditional explanation says that these questions are like asking whether "the child of this barren woman is fair or dark." It was not agnosticism which made the Buddha discard these questions but a realization of their very nature. It is not that there was something that he did not know but that he knew only too well what he was talking about. Where language failed, the Buddha literally followed the dictum: "Whereof one cannot speak, thereof one must be silent," but his silence was more eloquent than words. To those who had attained Nibbāna, no explanation was necessary; to those who had not, no explanation was possible.

The Buddha was very meticulous in the use of language. He often reformulated questions or removed ambiguities in words before answering them in order to remove misleading implications. He claimed that he was not a dogmatist (*ekaṃsa-vādo*) but an analyst (*vibhajja-vādo*). The truth of Nibbāna or the ultimate reality is thus

39. *The Blue and Brown Books*, Oxford, p. 108

strictly inexpressible, but all else that belongs to the realm of moral and spiritual truth can be stated and stated precisely.

The final state of "inward peace" is also a state of perfect freedom (*sammā-vimutti*), for the mind then ceases to be conditioned by the load of its past and the desires raging within it. It becomes master of itself. In the state of normal everyday consciousness we are finite conditioned beings. According to what the texts say, we are conditioned by what we inherit from mother and father, by the store of unconscious memories going back to our childhood and our previous lives, by the desires and impulses which agitate within it and by the stimuli which come from the "six doors of perception," i.e., the data of the five senses, our environment and the ideas that we imbibe and respond to. But, despite the fact that the ordinary man is thus largely conditioned by his inner nature and environment, he has a certain degree of freedom to act within limits.

During the time of the Buddha there were violent disputes about this problem between two schools of thought. There were *akiriya-vādins* who denied freewill because they were determinists in some sense or another, and in the opposite camp were the *kiriya-vādins* who upheld freewill. The Buddha held that man was possessed of a degree of freewill, while not denying that he was largely conditioned. What is meant by attaining salvation in Buddhism is the attainment of full freedom from our relative state of bondage. This is possible because of the very fact that we possess a degree of freewill and the processes of sublimation and de-conditioning are causal processes, which can be understood and directed by the mind. It also means that man's salvation lies in his own hands and that he cannot and should not depend on an external saviour. As the Dhammapada says:

> By ourselves is evil done
> By ourselves we pain endure
> By ourselves we cease from wrong
> By ourselves we become pure.
> No one saves us but ourselves
> No one can and no one may
> We ourselves must tread the path
> Buddhas only show the way.[40]

---

40. Dhp 165

The Buddha says that there are four false religions and four unsatisfactory religions in this world.[41] One of the four false religions is that which denies causation and asserts that "beings are miraculously doomed or saved" (*natthi hetu natthi paccayo sattānaṃ saṅkilesāya ... visuddhiyā*).[42] Buddhists pray that "all beings may be happy" (*sabbe sattā sukhitā hontu*); but they do not pray for salvation either to the Buddha or to anyone else. When our salvation depends on what we ourselves do with our freewill, prayer is superfluous and is nothing more than a pious wish or hope. The Buddha compares a person who prays to God for salvation to one who wishes to cross a river and get to the other bank, but hopes to achieve this by incessantly calling on the other bank to come to him.[43]

Religious truths, with the exception of the truth about *Nibbāna*, are thus "statable." They are all verifiable and have meaning only to those who verify them. There is individual moral responsibility and, therefore, justice in the universe. Freedom we have in a limited sense, which makes it possible for us to attain Freedom in the absolute sense. Seeking our own salvation may appear to be a selfish pursuit, but it is a paradoxical fact not only that we can attain this only by living in a completely selfless manner but that the goal itself is one in which our self-centred individuality is lost in a state "beyond measure." Selfless charity (*cāga*), compassionate love (*mettā*) and enlightened behaviour (*vijjācaraṇa*) is what we have to develop in attaining this goal.

The Buddhist monk does not cut himself away completely from society. His isolation is intended to provide him with the leisure to develop his mind and spiritual vision. He is thus in a position to speak from direct experience about the nature of spiritual truths and give guidance and advice to his fellow beings. He is one who is expected to specialize in his field of inquiry as much as the physicist specializes in his. The development of the mind is a full-time job, and the findings of these explorations are of no less interest and value to society than the findings of the natural scientist working in his laboratory. Both have something to offer to society; and monasticism, if understood rightly, has a big part as yet to play in the moral and spiritual regeneration of mankind.

41. *Majjhima Nikāya, Sandaka Sutta*

42. M I 516

43. D I 244, 245

There is no easy solution to the problem of how we can have peace on earth and goodwill among mankind. The West believes that their military potential is keeping the Communist monster at bay, while the Communists in turn are convinced that their military might prevents the Capitalist demon from swallowing them. Each side is certain that war is the lesser evil to being dominated by their opponents. The great powers are working for peace by forging the weapons of war and talking about peace for propagandist purposes. But the real alternative to peace today is the destruction of mankind. What is really happening is that, while half the world is spending colossal amounts of money on armaments, the other half is dying of starvation, malnutrition and disease in an age when all this can be prevented if the resources are available and goodwill is present. People and governments tend to do what is expedient rather than what is morally good. Can we say that in such a world, people have much faith in moral and spiritual values? There is hope in the possibility that the very fear of the dire consequences of the next war may prevent it. It would be too much to hope for a great power to have the moral courage and the spiritual strength to disarm unilaterally without fear of the consequences, but for those who love humanity more than themselves or nations there seems to me to be no other alternative but to work unreservedly for pacifism.

Appendix

(A)

The following are some of the sentiments expressed about peace and compassion in the *Dhammapada,* a Buddhist anthology included in the canon.

"He abused me, he beat me, he defeated me, he robbed me"—
the hatred of those who cherish such thoughts is not appeased. 3

"He abused me, he beat me, he defeated me, he robbed me"—
the hatred of those who do not cherish such thoughts is
appeased. 4

Hatred never ceases by hatred in this world.
Hatred ceases by love—this is the eternal law. 5

The world does not know that we must all come to an end here.
Quarrels cease when there are those who perceive this truth. 6

The noblest victor is he who would conquer himself
rather than defeat a hundred thousand men in battle. 103

Better, indeed, is the conquest of self than of all other folk. 105

Happily do we live without anger among those who are angry.
Let us live without anger amongst angry folk. 197

Victory breeds hatred; the vanquished live in sorrow.

The peaceful ones live in harmony
giving up both victory and defeat. 201

Conquer enmity with amity; evil with good;
conquer miserliness with charity and falsehood with truth. 222

The followers of Gotama whose minds are constantly bent
on *ahiṃsā* day and night, awake clear and alert. 300

(B)

The following is an extract from the *Cakkavatti-sīhanāda Sutta*, which gives an account of the evolution of human society. Speaking of the future, it says that there will be a gradual loss of values due to economic causes, resulting in a cataclysm. The aftermath would see a new humanity emerging from the remnant and creating the Just Society with a change of heart and a change of system. The allusion to the decrease in the life span of human beings is, perhaps, not to be taken literally.

> "Thus as a result of goods not accruing to those who were destitute, poverty becomes rife; from poverty becoming rife, stealing increases; from the spread of stealing, violence grows apace; from the growth of violence, the destruction of life becomes common; from the frequency of murder both the span of life in those beings and their comeliness waste away ...
>
> "Thus as a result of goods not accruing to those who were destitute, poverty becomes rife; from poverty becoming rife, stealing ... violence ... murder... lying ... evil speech ... adultery ... abusive and idle talk ... covetousness and ill-will ... false opinions ... incest, wanton greed and perverted lust ... till finally lack of filial and religious piety and lack of regard for the head of the clan grow great ...
>
> "There will come a time when the descendents of those humans will have a lifespan of ten years. Among humans of this lifespan, maidens of five years will be of marriageable age. Among such humans these kinds of savours will disappear: ghee, butter, oil of *tila*, sugar, salt. Among such humans *kudrusa* grain will be the highest kind of food. Even as today rice and curry is the highest kind of food, so will *kudrusa* grain be then. Among such humans the ten moral courses of conduct will altogether disappear, the ten immoral courses of action will flourish excessively; there will be no word for moral among such humans—far less any moral agent. Among such humans they who lack filial and religious piety and show no respect for elders—'tis they to whom homage and praise will be given, just as today homage and praise are given to the filial-minded, to the pious and to those who respect their elders.

"Among such humans there will be no such thoughts of reverence as are a bar to intermarriage with mother or mother's sister or mother's sister-in-law or teacher's wife or father's sister-in-law. The world will fall into promiscuity, like goats and sheep, fowls and swine, dogs and jackals.

"Among such humans keen mutual enmity will become the rule, keen ill-will, keen animosity, passionate thoughts even of killing, in a mother towards her child, in a child towards its mother, in a father towards his child and a child towards its father, in brother to brother, in brother to sister, in sister to brother. Just as a sportsman feels towards the game that he sees, so will they feel.

"Among such humans there will arise a war lasting seven days, during which they will look on each other as wild beasts; dangerous weapons will fall into their hands and they, thinking 'this is a wild beast', 'that is a wild beast', will with these weapons deprive one another of life.

"Then to some of those beings it will occur, 'Let us not just slay anyone; nor let just anyone slay us! Let us now, therefore, betake ourselves to dens of grass or dens in the jungle, or holes in trees, or river fastnesses, or mountain clefts and subsist on roots and fruits of the jungle.' And they will do so for those seven days. And at the end of those seven days, coming forth from those dens and fastnesses and mountain clefts, they will embrace one another and be of one accord, comforting one another and saying, 'Hail, O mortal, that thou livest still! O happy sight to find thee still alive!'

"Then this will occur to those beings, 'Now only because we had gotten into evil ways, have we had this heavy loss of kith and kin. Let us, therefore, now do good. What can we do that is good? Let us now abstain from taking life. That is a good thing that we may take up and do.' And they will abstain from slaughter and continue in this good way. Because of their getting into this good way, they will increase again both as to their span of life and as to their comeliness. And to them thus increasing in life and comeliness, to them who lived but one decade, there will be children who will live for twenty years.

"Then this will occur to those beings, 'Now we, because we have gotten into good ways, increase in length of life and comeliness. Let us now do still more good. Let us abstain from taking what is not given, let us abstain from adultery, let us now abstain from lying, let us now abstain from evil speaking, let us now abstain from abuse and from idle talk, let us now abstain from covetousness, from ill-will, from false opinions, let us now abstain from the three things—incest, wanton greed and perverted desires; let us now be filial towards our mothers and our fathers, let us be pious towards holy men, let us respect our elders, yea, let us continue to practise each of these good things.'

"So they will practise these virtues. And because of the good they do, they will increase in length of life and in comeliness so that the sons of them who lived but twenty years will come to live forty years ... Among such humans there will be only three kinds of disease—desire, hunger and decay. Among such humans the earth will be mighty and prosperous, the villages, towns and royal cities will be so close that a cock could fly from each one to the next."

The just society as depicted in the Buddhist texts is one in which there is equality, economic prosperity and the practice of the good life. The person who is instrumental in bringing about such a society is called the *Cakkavatti-rāja* or "the universal monarch." It appears as if Asoka was trying to emulate the example of such an ideal monarch. His Rock Edict No. XIII portrays his Buddhistic attitude to war and his attempt to found a state on Buddhist principles.

"The country of the Kāliṅgas was conquered by King Priyadarsi, Beloved of the gods, eight years after his coronation. In this war in Kāliṅga, men and animals numbering one hundred and fifty thousand were carried away captive from that country; as many as one hundred thousand were killed there in action and many times that number perished. After that, now that the country of the Kāliṅgas has been conquered, the Beloved of the gods is devoted to an intense practice of the duties relating to the Dharma, to a longing for Dharma and to the inculcation of Dharma among the people. This is due to the repentance of the Beloved of the gods on having conquered the country of the Kāliṅgas.

Verily the slaughter, death and deportation of men, which take place in the course of the conquest of an unconquered country, are now considered extremely painful and deplorable by the Beloved of the gods. But what is considered even more deplorable by the Beloved of the gods is the fact that injury to or slaughter or deportation of the beloved ones falls to the lot of the *brāhmaṇas*, the *śramaṇas*, the adherents of other sects and the householders, who live in that country and among whom are established such virtues as obedience to superior personages, obedience to mother and father, obedience to elders and proper courtesy and firm devotion to friends, acquaintances, companions and relatives as well as to slaves and servants. And if misfortune befalls the friends, acquaintances, companions and relatives of persons who are full of affection towards the former, even though they are themselves well provided for, the said misfortune as well becomes an injury to their own selves. In war, this fate is shared by all classes of men and is considered deplorable by the Beloved of the gods.

Excepting the country of the *Yavanas*, there is no country where these two classes, viz. the *brāhmaṇas* and the *śramaṇas*, do not exist; and there is no place in any country, where men are not indeed sincerely devoted to one sect or another. Therefore, the slaughter, death or deportation of even a hundredth or thousandth part of all those people who were slain or died or were carried away captive at that time in Kalinga, is now considered very deplorable by the Beloved of the gods.

Now, the Beloved of the gods thinks that, even if a person should wrong him, the offence would be forgiven if it is possible to forgive it. And the forest-folk who live in the dominions of the Beloved of the gods, even them he entreats and exhorts in regard to their duty. It is hereby explained to them that, in spite of his repentance, the Beloved of the gods possesses powers enough to punish them for their crimes, so that they should turn from evil ways and would not be killed for their crimes. Verily the Beloved of the gods desires the following in respect of all creatures, viz., non-injury to them, restraint in dealing with them and impartiality in the case of crimes committed by them.

So, what is conquest through Dharma is now considered to be the best conquest by the Beloved of the gods. And such a conquest has been achieved by the Beloved of the gods not only here in his own dominions but also in the territories bordering on his dominions, as far away as at the distance of six hundred *yojanas*, where the *Yavana* king named Antiyoka, four other kings named Turamāya, Antīkini, Makā and Alikasundara are also ruling, and towards the south, where the Cholas and Pāṇḍyas are living as far as Tāmrapaṇṇi. Likewise, here in the dominions of His Majesty, the Beloved of the gods—in the countries of the *Yavanas* and *Kāmbojas*, of the *Nābhakas* and *Nābhapanktis*, of the *Bhojas* and *Paitryanikas* and of the *Andhras* and the *Paulindas*—everywhere people are conforming to the instructions in Dharma imparted by the Beloved of the gods.

Even where the envoys of the Beloved of the gods have not penetrated, there too men have heard of the practices of Dharma and the ordinances issued and the instructions in Dharma imparted by the Beloved of the gods and are conforming to Dharma and will continue to conform to it.

So, whatever conquest is achieved in this way, verily that conquest creates an atmosphere of satisfac-tion everywhere both among the victors and the vanquished. In the conquest through Dharma, satisfaction is derived by both parties. But that satisfaction is indeed of little consequence. Only happiness of the people in the next world is what is regarded by the Beloved of the gods as a great thing resulting from such a conquest.

And this record relating to Dharma has been written on stone for the following purpose, viz., that my sons and great-grandsons should not think of a fresh conquest by arms as worth achieving, that they should adopt the policy of forbearance and light punishment towards the vanquished even if they conquer a people by force of arms and that they should regard the conquest through Dharma as the true conquest. Such a conquest brings happiness to all concerned both in this world and in the next. And let all their intense joys be what is pleasure associated with Dharma. For this brings happiness in this world as well as in the next."

Note:

The Greek (*Yavana*) kings mentioned in this inscription, may be identified as follows:

Antiyoka	—	Antiochus II Theos of Syria and Palestine (261–246 BCE)
Turamāya	—	Ptolemy II Philadelphus of Egypt (285–247 BCE)
Antīkini	—	Antigonus Gonatus of Macedonia (276–239 BCE)
Makā	—	Magas of Cyrene (c. 258–250 BCE)
Alikasundara	—	Alexander of Corinth (252–244 BCE) or Alexander of Epirus (272–255 BCE)

Assuming that this inscription was contemporaneous with the rule of all these five kings, it may be dated between 252–250 BCE or 258–255 BCE. The similarity of the Dhamma with the doctrines and practices of the pre-Christian Essenes (s.v. *Encyclopaedia of Religion and Ethics*) of Syria and Palestine and the Therapeutae (s.v. *ibid.*) of Egypt suggests that they were a result of Asoka's missions, in the light of what this inscription states. The Essenes and the Therapeutae seem to have adapted the Jewish scriptures to adopt Buddhist beliefs and a Buddhist way of life.

Early Western Buddhists

Extracts from *The Buddhist Review*,
1909–1914

Selected and presented by
Francis Story

WHEEL PUBLICATION NO. 42/43

Early Western Buddhists

Buddhism made its first real impact on the Western mind in the early years of the present century. The way had been prepared for it by the Pali and Sanskrit translations of Max Muller, Fausböll, Warren, Rhys-Davids and a number of other oriental scholars. In Europe, some familiarity with the broad outlines of Buddhist thought had been created by Schopenhauer. In England, Sir Edwin Arnold's fine poem, *The Light of Asia*, had given thoughtful readers an insight into the beauty at the heart of the Buddhist ideal. For the first time there was an interest in Eastern philosophy that was more than academic. It came about partly as a reaction against the constricting materialism of nineteenth century scientific views, and partly as a revolt against traditional religious teachings which science had shown to be inadequate (where they were not altogether false).

Many people found an escape from the clash between two equally rigid modes of thought (the religious and the scientific) in the mysteries of theosophy, with its loosely syncretic structure and the liberty it allowed for semi-scientific speculation. At that time the ferment caused by the new scientific ideas was at its height, and the popular construction placed on Darwin's theory of evolution had not yet sunk down to the level of general acceptance it occupies today. A need was felt for some religious or philosophic view that would reconcile the material and spiritual aspects, a theory that would embody the idea of a progressive evolution, of life straining upwards from the primeval slime towards a glorious and godlike fulfilment. If this concept could find some sanction in the mysterious and romantic religions of the past, so much the better, no matter what contradictions might be involved. Man, as perhaps never before, was becoming conscious of himself as part of the pattern of an evolving cosmos. The prevailing mood was reflected in the theosophical leanings of such dissimilar writers as August Strindberg and Pierre Loti, as well as in several of the English poets. Among the philosophers there were some who, like Mac Taggart of Cambridge, were in the groove of neo-Pythagorean thought to the extent of accepting reincarnation as a law of life.

Everywhere the old shackles were being cast aside. The currents of a fresh movement were making themselves felt not only on the intellectual level but also in aesthetics. It was the era of new experiments in painting, sculpture, music and poetry. The art of the Fauves, the Dadaists and the Cubists competed with the music of the new composers Stravinsky, Bartok and Honegger, as to which could make the most decisive break with tradition in the shortest time. In every sphere the idols of the past were being asked, in not very respectful terms, to show their credentials.

Amidst this upsurge of creativity and intellectual vigour there was at the same time a growing feeling of political insecurity not so much in respect of the internal structure of society (which in most of the European nations at that time presented a deceptive appearance of stability), but in international relations. The mounting tensions which were to break in the First World War were already making themselves felt, and, as we shall see, the anxiety they caused found an individual expression in the writings of some of the first European Buddhists.

This was the *mise en scène* against which the ideas of Theravada Buddhism were first presented to the West, in the language of the West. It may seem inappropriate to speak of the articles in such periodicals as *The Buddhist Review* as "early" writings on Buddhism by "early" Western Buddhists, but historical perspectives sometimes bear little relation to the actual length of the periods they cover. Since the time when these writings first appeared, close though it is to the present, great and radical changes have taken place in the life and thought of mankind. A considerable amount of history has been telescoped into a brief half-century, and it has brought about a great deal of rethinking on some of the fundamental issues. Many of the most adventurous ideas of those days have become commonplace in our time. What is of interest to us today is the manner in which the early Western Buddhists applied the new ideas to their own situation, the characteristic colouring they gave to Buddhist thought, and the degree to which they had assimilated the principles of their adopted creed.

It is interesting, for example, to note the resistance many of them put up to the romantic theories of theosophical syncretism. Sometimes their interpretation of Buddhism leaned, if anything, rather too heavily on its purely rationalistic side. But they avoided that most seductive of all the conceits that the pseudo-scientific religious eclecticism of the time favoured: the optimistic belief that man's spiritual course is an inevitable upward progression. Those of them who correctly understood the parallel between the law of *kamma* and that of biological evolution grasped the truth that every law, whether physical of psychological, must be capable of working to the detriment, as well as to the advantage, of the beings subject to it. In this they were more realistic than those among their contemporaries who held that once the human state had been attained in the course of evolution there could be no falling back to inferior conditions. Comforting as that "esoteric" theory may be, it is no more in accord with the principles of evolution than it is with the real teaching of the Buddha.

In these early writings there is, in fact, surprisingly little attempt to tamper with the Pali texts and their meaning. The writers seemed happy to accept Buddhism as they found it. It was as well for the continued validity of their ideas that they did so, for (since they wrote) the world has witnessed events which leave little room for supposing that man, collectively, is on the path to perfection by virtue of a law that permits him only to advance. Truth is angular and non-conformist; it does not obey popular fashions.

That there were among the first Western Buddhists some minds which were fearless, and in a sense revolutionary, cannot be doubted by anyone who goes through the pages of the early Buddhist publications. These were people who were not afraid to label themselves with the name of a religion which was still looked upon with distrust by the majority. It is not easy these days (when some knowledge of Buddhism has become part of the equipment of every educated man, and when books on the subject are easily accessible to all) for us to reconstruct the attitude, compounded of ignorance and not a little fear of heathenish superstitions, which was that of the ordinary man towards Buddhism at that time. The present writer well remembers, even so late as the nineteen-twenties, a serial story, "False Gods," published by a London evening newspaper which purported to be based on the Buddhism of Tibet. It was an example of the most lurid and improbable fiction, in which sinister Lamas moved and had their being enshrouded in Gothic-Himalayan mystery, and worked out their evil designs to the peril and distress of respectable upper-class English families. That was the era when the editors of British Sunday newspapers (taking time off from their lucrative task of crime-reporting, varied by frequent orgies of moral indignation), every so often lashed out at the new menace of Buddhism, which, according to their mood, was either a species of black magic or (to quote one of them from memory) an "attractive cult for blasé Londoners in search of a new thrill."

It cannot be denied that there were some questionable personalities vaguely associated in the public mind with the early Buddhist movements, but the dabblers in the occult, make-believe magicians and other picturesque poseurs were not Buddhists in any sense; most of them were not even on the fringe of any genuine Buddhist activities. Had the self-appointed journalistic guardians of public morality taken the trouble to glance at the articles in *The Buddhist Review*, and noted the names of the contributors, they would have found it difficult to sustain their prejudice. Even the most bigoted could not fail to recognize the earnestness, sincerity and intellectual integrity of these pioneer Western Buddhists, to whom the later progress of Buddhism in the West owes so much.

The First Issue Editorial

There is no better way to begin our symposium of extracts from these Western writings than to quote some passages from the editorial, signed J.E.E. (J.E. Ellam) which introduced the first issue of *The Buddhist Review* in 1909. He wrote:

"The most striking phenomenon of our times, a process which has been going on for more than a decade, is the growing confusion in the Religious Thought of the West. With the weakening of theological dicta has proceeded an indifference to the higher, more spiritual aspects of life, together with tendencies towards gross superstitions which find their expression in diverse, and most unhealthy forms of heterodoxy. It is not necessary to specify these; indeed, it would be against the Buddhist spirit to do so. The Buddhist method is now, as it has ever been, to refrain from the condemnation of other modes of thought, but simply, gently, yet with emphasis, to set forth its own teachings, and to leave them to plead their own cause at the bar of human reason and experience.

In psychology, in the sphere of the mind in the realms of the spiritual, Buddhism moves at ease, confident of its knowledge, confident of its logic, to state clearly, fully and conclusively its solutions of those problems which have vexed the minds of men from time immemorial, solutions which were presented satisfactorily to the acute mind of the Orient two thousand five hundred years ago, and which, finding a mentality, an intellectual standard, in the West only now capable of adequately grasping them, are about to be presented, as we think to the great benefit of this and coming generations. And those who are helping in this great work will, in the future, come to be regarded with the same feeling of gratitude, with the same reverence, which we accord to those who stimulated the Renaissance from the dark ages of Medieval Europe. There is, thus, no hostility or even rivalry between the Buddhist Movement and the conventional forms of religion in the West. Buddhism is the friend of all, the enemy of none. Animosity, if such there be, can only proceed from one side, but it is certain that it will never be returned in kind. For those who are uneasy in their doubts and questionings, who lack a sure guide to peace of mind, who are bereft of the consolations of Faith in the higher sense, Buddhism has a Message: strong, sure, convincing. For those who are satisfied with any other belief, creed, philosophy (call it what they will), Buddhism has no other feelings save of sympathy, of kindliness, of fellowship united with a desire for helpful co-operation, provided only that their efforts are for the benefit, the well-being, the uplifting of humanity to higher ideals of life, of thought, of action, and of the duties of Common Brotherhood throughout the world."

Buddhism and Ethics

In the same issue, the essentially tolerant and progressive spirit of Buddhism is also stressed by Mrs. C. A. F. Rhys-Davids in the article, "Buddhism and Ethics":

"Here is a doctrine that takes us back as far as the days of the very beginnings of Hellenic Science. For this doctrine, it is claimed that it might have served, not to check or to ignore the discoveries of Copernicus and Bruno, Galileo and Newton, Darwin and Spencer, but to stimulate and inspire them. Not a guide that they might have adhered to from convention only, or appealed to now and again to reconcile the lay world with their discoveries and conclusions, but an oracle that would have spurred them on in their quest for Truth.

"Well, it is one thing to talk about achievements of modern science and advance of modern thought, and another thing to claim for this age in general that it is imbued with the scientific spirit, or that the views and conduct of the average man or woman are governed thereby. This state of things is but in its infancy. But it is born, and is growing. Hence any movement of thought will have, more and more, to cope with the scientific spirit, and will stand or fall largely by its sanction. And hence all who call themselves Buddhists, or who are interested in spreading a knowledge of Buddhist doctrine or, at least, the spirit of that doctrine, should look into this claim that is made for it. Those, again, whose interest lies in tracing the growth of human ideas, can in no wise feel indifferent to the real extent to which the ancient mind of India anticipated a standpoint slowly and painfully won to by the intellect of Europe.

"The fact that early Buddhism and modern Science express belief in a universal law of Causation in terms so similar leads inevitably to the further inquiry as to how far there is historical evidence that the evolution of this belief among early Buddhists was parallel to the corresponding evolution in Europe. The lack of continuity and of chronological certainty in the literatures of ancient India hinder and complicate such an inquiry. But there does survive a body of Brahmanical literature, an accretion of various dates, known as the Sixty Upanishads of the Veda, in which a form of Pantheism called Ātmanism or Vedantism is set forth, with mainly archaic views on what we term First, Final, and Occasional Cause. And we have the Pali Canon of the Buddhists, coinciding, it is thought, in date with the middle period of these sixty books, and repudiating this Ātmanism, whether macrocosmically or microcosmically conceived.

"To what extent Buddhism, as a lay, anti-Brahmanic, anti-sacerdotal movement originated the rejection of Ātmanism, or carried on a wider and older tradition of rejection, it is not possible to say. But the fact that the founders of Buddhism did, in leaving the world for the religious life, take up this Protestant position on the one hand, and on the other make a law of ritual causation their chief doctrine, suggests at all events a profound psychological crisis."

In such passages as these we see Mrs. Rhys-Davids at the height of her powers, when she was contributing the best of her scholarship to the Buddhist cause. The profound psychological crisis to which she refers is a recurring condition. Perhaps, indeed, every major change in the human situation is brought about by an insupportable paroxysm of the mind. Progress is the name we give to a collective crisis that has taken the right turn.

Buddhism and Science

In the same issue, the article, "Buddhism and Science," by E.J. Mills, D.Sc., F.R.S., deals with the still-disputed subject of Anattā (Egolessness), in connection with rebirth. It contains the following passage:

"Now, nothing is more clear than that evolution is an essential constituent of Buddhism. It is necessarily a part of its doctrine of rebirth and heredity. A qualitative result-character alone survives death; and this is reborn with a new set of *skandhas*, in accordance with the karma of that instant.[1] There may be but very little distinction between the old 'character' and the new. On the other hand, there may be a very great deal. It is within our power, as Buddha and Huxley both say, to influence our environment and ourselves very greatly. And it is clear that the next link in the pedigree may be so different, on occasion, as to be to all intents and purposes a new species. This gets rid of much of the difficulty about time in Darwin's theory. But we must not forget the instruction of the Buddha that the new link may, if we so condition it, be worse than before; there is a "way up" as well as a "way down" as Heraclitus says. The new species may be a new reversion. This is a horrible thing to contemplate; but of its truth there can be no doubt whatever. A modification of this doctrine was adopted (I need not say), and probably from Buddhism—into the Christian scriptures."

1. Death-proximate kamma, the last thought-moment that precedes rebirth consciousness. *Ed.*

The reference here is of course to the Christian doctrine of eternal damnation: the state of torment or eternal deprivation. But Buddhism teaches that nothing in the sphere of causality can be eternal. While all things are subject to retrogression and degeneration, there is always hope, amounting to certainty, of a future opportunity to recover the lost ground. The eternal damnation threatened by theistic religion, and believed in literally for so many centuries, had by its inherent brutality become so discredited that many people still professing theistic creeds had abandoned it. In deference to the more enlightened and humane view, the pulpits no longer thundered out the horrors and terrors of the life to come. Yet what is the meaning of salvation, if damnation is no longer believed in? The progressive weakening of religion as a moral influence was bound to follow on the removal of its punitive aspect, for relatively few people, even amongst the most civilized of mankind, are sufficiently advanced to choose the good for its own sake, and in all circumstances, on purely humanistic and ethical grounds. This is so even when (which is rarely the case) they can be positively certain as to what constitutes the right course of action without guidance from religion. Aside from this, there is no discernible justice in a system that offers rewards for doing good, without exacting some kind of retribution for wrong-doing. The early Western Buddhists were quick to see that Buddhism saved the moral order by substituting for eternal punishment a system of automatic causal balance between good and ill, in which the measure of suffering resulting from wrong action is exactly equal to the force of the deed that produced it, neither more nor less.

Transmigration in East and West

This theme is the subject of an article by another scientific writer, Ernest R. Carlos, M.A., B.Sc., who wrote in *Transmigration in East and West*:

"If, as many believe, one single life decides the whole course of the future, why is one life here for a few weeks, and another for seventy or eighty years? For one thing, there is in the first case less risk of eternal loss. But the question is: 'Does this life matter or does it not?' If it does not, why are we here at all? If it does, then evidently the child who took his departure after three weeks did not reap the full benefit of life, and if life has value, if we are to learn from it, where is the logic in sending into eternal bliss a life which scarcely deserves it? Moreover, if we are to strive for perfection as enjoined by our Teacher, it seems utterly unthinkable that one could arrive at perfection in a single life. Again, it would be unjust for one to have a greater opportunity than another, and if we consider the wide gulf existing between the primitive savage and the enlightened civilised man, we must admit that it would be to the great advantage of the former, were he to return a few more times, instead of shooting off straightway into eternity 'with all his imperfections on his head.'[2]

"The idea first occurred to man partly from the desire for justice, and partly from the deep and overwhelming feeling of pain which the manifest transience of earthly life produces in the human breast. That the idea did arise is not strange. The final law of creation is said to be Love. But the sin and suffering bequeathed to our race, through no apparent fault of ours, makes us regard life as a ceaseless struggle in which the strongest win and the weakest go to the wall. Why are some born rich and others poor? Why are some endowed with the seeds of intelligence and high mental qualities, while others have minds that the best education can make nothing of? We see royal souls, men in whose faces we may read high sentiments of love and self-sacrifice, whose characters are pictures for admiration, and others whose very countenances are strange, criminal and even inhuman.

"What answer can be given to the criminal, who, in reply to our exhortation to love justice and kindness says, 'How can I help being so? Blame him who has put me in bad surroundings. I was born in a slum, brought up by drunkards, heard little more than curses and filthy language in my youth, and was taught nothing that was noble. Can you wonder that I am wicked? I was not so fortunate as you, who, through no merit of your own, were placed among refined people full of tenderness, giving you everything you wanted, and offering you no daily temptations to steal. I had not your education, why blame me? Blame my

2. One may question the advantages of civilization without weakening the argument. *Ed.*

environment.' Justice demands that every man should have an equal opportunity, and Reincarnation gives this opportunity. It furnishes the answer to problems which religious dogma cannot deal with, and which material science is not ready to face.

"Hume states that this theory 'is the only system of immortality that philosophy can hearken to,' and many people are startled at the statement that the belief in Immortality demands a belief in Rebirth. What begins in time must necessarily end in time, and it is impossible to conceive of anything eternal in its onward duration, and, at the same time, having a beginning. There can be no 'beginning' to eternity. If the soul was specially created for this body, why should it continue to live when this body dies? Its purpose is fulfilled. The materialists who hold that the 'I' arose with the body, and will end in death, are certainly the more rational. Life eternal must be life for ever, and it is unthinkable that, from an infinite history in the past, the soul enters this world for its first and only physical experience, and then shoots off into an endless spiritual existence.

"The Christian holds to the belief in original sin and future punishment, and it is difficult to conceive how one man can be responsible for a sin in which he had no share. If, however, we are indeed those who, in their first contact with matter did sin, then we can understand how man is born in sin. As to future punishment, it is not difficult to look thereon as a punishment in a future bodily existence, especially as it is now becoming very unfashionable to believe in Hell. Isaac Disraeli says: 'If we accept the belief of a future remuneration beyond this life for suffering, virtue, and retribution of successful crimes, there is no system so simple, so little repugnant to our understanding, as that of Metempsychosis. The pains and pleasures of this life are, by this system, considered as the recompense or punishment of our actions in another state.'

"To say that Science requires Reincarnation to complete the theory of evolution is to make a very bold statement, yet she could with advantage add this one to her other hypotheses. The struggle for Existence is not a complete explanation of the nature of Man. Professor Huxley once remarked, 'It seems that man, a fragment of the cosmos, has set himself against the law of the cosmos. He advances by self-surrender and not by the survival of the fittest; he develops by self-sacrifice.' If we look upon those whom humanity has always regarded as the blossoms of the race, we find their lives are one long self-sacrifice. But self-sacrifice, charity, love, sympathy, and the surrender of all one has do not conduce to the struggle for existence. Man advances by self-sacrifice; that is the True Law. Such people, however, die out. One who risks his all must eventually perish, and the social virtues and more human attributes tend to kill out their owners, leaving the more selfish and the more brutal to live. Such lives must return doubly reinforced with that spirit of self-surrender which makes for moral growth.

"In heredity it is hard to explain why a good father should have a wild and immoral son, why a genius is born of mediocre parents, or why there should be but one genius in a family (if character is determined merely by physical forces). Science gives us no definite explanation of this and other matters. Professor Weissmann's theory, that moral and intellectual qualities acquired during life are not transmitted to the offspring, is held by the majority of scientific men. If all the high qualities of a man are not handed down from father to son, through the body, how are we to explain human progress, unless, side by side with the continuity of protoplasm, we have a continuity in the development and unfolding of spirit? It seems strange first to imagine that Nature should end her masterpiece (Man) with total annihilation at death, and even then should not devise some means whereby he can transmit to his offspring the qualities he has acquired. If such qualities were transmitted by the body we should have a material basis for progress; but as they are not, we must presume that the bond of union between the various stages lies in something else. Kant recognized the difficulty when he said:

> 'All the natural qualities of a creature are intended to unfold themselves completely and suitably, and it would take an immeasurably long life for a man to learn how to make a perfect use of all his natural qualities. It would take an unending series of generations for the one to hand over its enlightenment to the other, in order that the germ of our species may at last arrive at that degree of development which shall be perfectly adapted to the fulfilment of its design. How

it may be with the dwellers on other planets and their nature, we know not. Perhaps in these every individual may attain his appointed design in life. With us it is otherwise, and only the species can hope for it.'

"Kant saw the hopeless nature of the question, and took refuge in the abstract idea of species. He had only to lift the veil and see how a man might make more and more perfect use of all his natural powers sooner than he expected, if each personality added its experience to a reborn 'Intelligent Character.'

"Reincarnation is no doctrine of pessimism. Selfishness is necessary for pessimism and has produced it, but where there is a certainty of progress, of the possibility of perfection, there can be no pessimism. To say with the Buddhist, 'Painful is the wheel of rebirth.' is no more pessimistic than the Christian desire or union with God. Both wish for liberation from the body which confines the Eternal Man. The doctrine rightly understood brightens life, in that we look upon this body as a garment and the world as a school. Sorrows and troubles are brushed off as only touching the accidental and not the eternal. The heresy of separateness must disappear, and we must look on all as brothers.

"Progress is the Law of Life. 'Man is not man as yet.' And Emerson was right when he said, 'We wake and find ourselves on a stair. There are other stairs below us which we seem to have ascended; there are stairs above, many a one, which go upward and out of sight'."

'Upward and out of sight' is a phrase of deep import for the mind at last awakening to a sense of life's continuity and its unimaginable goal. But was the way of evolution to be exclusively a spiritual and personal one, or did it require a complementary effort along the lines of worldly progress? Was there to be any involvement with the mundane concerns of others in the life we share, for better or worse, on this planet ruled by physical needs? There were those, as there are today, who asked themselves these questions with some perplexity and uneasiness of mind.

Buddhism and Social Problems

An attempt was made to answer these questions by Alexandra David (afterwards Mme Alexandra David-Néel), in the article "Buddhism and Social Problems". The article, which here follows in full, was very ably translated by Francis J. Payne, and appeared in the July-September issue of 1910:

"Among the questions of a practical nature which we have to face is one whose examination forces itself upon us without our being able to put it aside: 'What attitude are we going to adopt towards the social problems, which are, at this moment, the chief preoccupation of the whole world?' It is impossible to be unaware of them, and it is also impossible to dismiss them. Unless we are content to remain a small closed circle of scholars and dilettanti, finding a refined pleasure in handling the subtle thought of ancient Buddhism, and seeing therein but an intellectual exercise, we shall come into collision with the outside conditions of social life. Before us will arise men who will be oppressed not only by mental pain, but by the most commonplace material suffering. What shall we do? Shall we answer them that the Doctrine of the Buddha is only made for the wise, that it despises the pain of the flesh, and the tears of those whose horizon does not extend beyond the limits of coarse sensation and earthly longings?

"On the morrow of the day when, for the first time, he has perceived within himself a flickering and pale reflection of the Great Light, stopped at the threshold of the Path, and seeing the enormous intellectual effort necessary to walk therein, there is not a single disciple who has not repeated the words which the Mahāvagga ascribes to our Master:

> 'To this people who are given to desire, intent upon desire, delighting in desire, the law of causality and the chain of causation will be a matter difficult to understand; most difficult for them to understand will be also the extinction of all *saṅkhāras*, the getting rid of all the substrata [of existence], the destruction of desire, the absence of passion, quietude of heart, Nirvana. This doctrine will not be easy to understand to beings that are lost in lust and hatred. Given to lust, surrounded by thick darkness, they will not see what is abstruse, profound, difficult to perceive, and subtle.' (Mv I 5)

"Where the Master hesitated[3], the disciple may well have a touch of despair.

"That moment was a decisive one in the history of Buddhist preaching. To live it again individually is one of the most difficult tests that we have to overcome.

"One question which confronts us is very distinct and very grave: Shall we imitate the Pharisee of whom the Gospel speaks, and, congratulating ourselves in a proud thanksgiving on the superior quality of our brain, attempt to realize an egotistic salvation, turning our eyes away from the miserable mob of mediocre intelligences? Or rather, sincerely grieved and compassionate at the misery of our brothers, but seeing therein no remedy, shall we remain inactive before their suffering? Finally, choosing a third solution, shall we approach suffering, even that which seems to us paltry, even that which appears low or deserved, the puerile suffering of childish minds, that of coarse beings, of the wicked, and strive to conquer them all?

"Two motives will prompt our answer: Can we bring efficacious help to the multitudes who seek social emancipation and material well-being? And, ought we to give it to them?

"Let us consider the first point.

"Amongst the most usual objections urged against Buddhism is this: It is a philosophy for instructed minds. It looks with haughtiness above life, it teaches its vanity and, more than its vanity, the non-reality of its existence. Its language is not within reach of that majority of beings who feel strongly the impression of their personality, who see nothing but that personality, who dream only of it, and who aim only at its material needs and suffer cruelly in all their feelings.

"The most thoughtful writers, those who have shown the greatest sympathy for Buddhism, have recognized that nothing in the Buddha's teaching, such as the texts handed down to us, can present him to us as a leader of the masses. That is understood. Although we have to consider that the disdain shown by our Master and the early Buddhists for the distinctions of caste (the foundation of Hindu society and much more tyrannical

3. Doubting whether it would be possible to make others understand the Dhamma. *Ed.*

in their effects than the present distinctions between capitalists and workers) marks their apostleship with a truly revolutionary character, we shall not try to misrepresent the personality of the Buddha by making him a stirrer of crowds, an apostle of social claims. We have no need of such subterfuges. Neither shall we seek to disavow the saying: 'The doctrine is directed to the intelligent man, not to the fool.' Whoever he may be that pronounced it, we recognise it as quite truly in accord with the Buddhist spirit.

"Deliverance, under whatever particular aspect we regard it (spiritual, moral or social deliverance; deliverance of the individual or of nations), is not a gift but an acquisition: a bitter and laborious acquisition of the intellect. Now what doctrine is better able than Buddhism to guide man towards intelligence?

"If we have hesitated, a thoughtful examination of Buddhist teaching will give confidence. We are better armed than anyone to approach the victims of our modern communities. We have something better than sentimental manifestations of piety or the problematic compensations of Paradise to offer them, for we possess the sovereign formula of social emancipation and material deliverance purely earthly, as well as that which opens before us the unfathomable horizons of Nirvana.

"When the Buddha proclaimed that *the cause of suffering is ignorance,* he uttered an eternal truth, a truth infallible on every plane of existence. His voice tells us the way. We may agree that our philosophic discussions, and even the fundamental questions of impersonality and the impermanence of the formations, cannot be presented at the first onset to popular audiences, but there is a gospel which we can offer them, and it is this: Suffering can be destroyed; it can be destroyed by us; it can only be destroyed by ourselves; our ignorance alone creates it.

"These are not vain declamations. There is nothing more scientific in spirit than this modern credo; nothing which is more capable of a practical result.

"Sociologists may discuss learnedly the processes of the formation of our contemporary communities, they may point out the causes which have produced the terrible inequality of conditions among the individuals who belong to them, or find fault with the growth of capital or its relations with labour. There is one plain fact above all these considerations: the ignorance of the masses alone has permitted their subjection.

"The wretched masses, in turn a pitiful herd of beasts of burden or unchained brutes, pass through the horrors of sanguinary revolts. They stretch their arms towards the gods who never yet have taken pity on them, towards men who betray their confidence, towards vague ideals of Justice and Liberty. And all in vain, because the irresistible Law of things pursues its course: he who is deceived, he who sees beings and things falsely, shall expiate, by suffering, the unskilfulness of his error.

"Let us teach the people to think, to reason, to become by their mental development the authors of their own deliverance. Let us put into their hearts, not childish enthusiasms and inauspicious venerations, but the worship of Knowledge, the liberator and purifier. Such is the way to intervene in the social problems of our time which Buddhist teaching suggests to us. That teaching places in men's hands a lever capable of transforming the base of society:

> Believe only in that which you yourselves have recognised as true and reasonable. Believe nothing on the authority of another. Fulfil only the acts which you have analysed and which have appeared to you conformable to reason, to your welfare and that of others. Be ye a light unto yourselves.

"These lessons are in our old books. Can we not see their enormous import? What a profound difference there is between a society based on such principles and ours, in which arbitrary regulations, antiquated laws inadequate for our present needs, credulity, superstition and erroneous notions of all kinds predominate. So, without resolving to dogmatise on special questions of authority, property, labour, and so many other things, we can, whilst preaching the liberation of thought and the supremacy of reason in accordance with the Buddhist spirit, prepare men to find for themselves in all these problems normal and healthy solutions according to the surroundings and the various degrees of evolution of those who will work them out and will contribute most powerfully to their well-being and the continuance of their mental progress.

"To destroy ignorance does not exclusively mean to soar with already superior minds into the subtlest regions of the Dharma. Alas! Are not most of us still lisping its first lessons? To destroy ignorance, even in the religious sense in which we wish to consider it here, may be to teach an ignorant one to read, to deliver a popular scientific lecture before an unlearned audience, to stimulate humble brains to reflection and reasoning.

"Need we insist further? We think it superfluous. We have seen that if Buddhism does not furnish us with definite social formulae, it has a thoroughly clear-sighted conception of evolution, and of the necessary changes that its progress demands in human relations and institutions. And more. Buddhism possesses, in the highest degree, the consciousness of the necessity of free individual development. Individuals' dreams of happiness are fitted to their mentality; their mentality depends upon the nature of the elements which enter into the perpetually moving and changing aggregate-forming which is called personality; and the meeting and union of these elements is determined by the great law of Karma. From this conception Buddhism concludes that we do not have the power of organising the details of the happiness or welfare of men whose mentality differs from our own. But it aims still higher and sees more widely in us, permitting us to show to all the sure way by which each one will be able to accomplish his dreams of happiness, and the criterion which serves to test the materials which he proposes to use to build it up with, in order that, believing he builds the place of his rest, he will not make for himself a new Gehenna.

"It might be useful to deal with this first point; we hesitate to touch on the second. Ought we to render aid to those who suffer, when the cause of their suffering is altogether material and their dreams of happiness hover solely in the circle of earthly longings? Our sisters and brothers will pardon us for daring to put such a question. Has a single one of them ever experienced the slightest doubt on the subject? It is not a ceremony, a profession of faith, which hallows us and makes us true Buddhists, but simply the opening, in our hearts, of overflowing and universal compassion, which through the centuries permits us to commune with him who was above all and above everything (the Great Compassionate One).

"Is that classic meditation which consists of embracing in succession each quarter of the world, then the whole world, in an intense feeling of love (with the ardent desire of using oneself for the good of the beings which compose it) a simple amusement?

Is that a fantastic recreation? Do we not rather see the indication of the definite goal towards which this rapture tends, namely, to throw ourselves as untiring combatants into the struggle against suffering?

"Christians have the legend of the Saviour who gave his life for the deliverance of humanity. We have others which open before us more widely the vast expanse of charity. Who, then, can forget this story? The land is wasted with drought and famine. In the forest which the terrible Indian sun has burnt up, the Buddha is walking. He is in one of his many existences which preceded his deliverance. He is yet but a pilgrim on the path which leads to Bodhi. On the other side of a thicket a tigress dying with hunger lies amidst her expiring young ones. Too weak to attack the man who is passing, she turns her eyes towards the prey which is escaping from her. A supreme longing lights them up; a memory of the joyful frolics in the cool nights, a vision of murmuring springs, the maternal instinct in despair and a passionate attachment to existence, all these flash at the same time in her look. The Buddha[4] stops, contemplates the miserable creature for a moment, weighs his deed, and then, quite calmly, turns from the path to this lowly animal pain, and delivers up his body for food. The very exaggeration of this symbolical act is a lesson to us. Who would dare to unfeelingly pass by human anguish asking for bread and the little joys of earth, and afterwards call himself a follower of a doctrine which pushed its dream of compassion so far?

"And if we tried, in spite of all things, to avoid the imperious duty of removing suffering from our unfortunate brothers, pretending that our mission consists solely in the preaching of complete Deliverance and not in lightening the burden of social miseries, should we not immediately be stopped by the indissoluble union in man of the mental and the physical element? Do we not know that any boundary betwixt the two is purely arbitrary? Does not experience prove to us the impossibility of directing, towards the summits of Buddhist doctrine, the thoughts of those men whom industrialism reduces to the state of living tools, whom it leaves at the gate of the factory or the mine, enfeebled, brutalised, incapable of the smallest cerebral effort? Should we

4. Read Bodhisattva. *Ed*

not prove that our apostleship was illusory and hypocritical if we contented ourselves with repeating in their ears, which fatigue has rendered deaf, the words of deliverance? Is not our mission to prepare for them by our efforts a more human life in which their mentality can progressively evolve, until they are permitted to conquer by themselves that which no saviour can bring as a gift: Redeeming Intelligence. 'Go ye now, and wander for the gain of the many, out of compassion for the world.' Thus has our Master spoken; let us not discuss the meaning of this command, but GO even as he has bidden us."

Since the time when Mme Alexandra David-Néel wrote these words, industrial conditions in the West have substantially improved. In general, there is more abundant leisure, and education is more readily available to those who desire it. The problem in some countries now is rather that large numbers of people have more leisure than they are capable of using beneficially for themselves, despite the opportunities for cultural advancement that have been offered to them. Yet her words are still true for countless numbers of the under-privileged all over the world, and so they still have meaning for us today (perhaps a more urgent message than when she wrote them). Buddhists, particularly in those parts of the world where they are in control of the material resources, should never allow to fade from their minds the occasion when the Buddha declined to preach the Dhamma to a hungry man until that man had been fed; it contains a lesson that is too often overlooked.

It should be remarked that, in the story of the Bodhisatta cited by Mme Alexandra David-Néel above, if turning "from the path to this lowly animal pain" is intended to mean turning away from the path to Bodhi in order to assuage a purely physical need of someone else, the interpretation is not quite correct. The act of self-renunciation was performed to *advance* the Bodhisatta on the way to Supreme Buddhahood; for, unlike the Arahat, the aspirant to the highest office of all (that of the World Teacher) has to practice such sacrifices of the self (if not literally in this way, at least in ways no less rigorous and difficult, through many successive lives). This constitutes the Pāramitā by which he acquires the powers of one who is fitted to turn the Wheel of the Law. As the *gātha* explains:

"This body of flesh I wear
Just for the world's welfare."

Seen in this light, it was not merely to provide a passing alleviation of suffering that the ultimate sacrifice was made, but in order to gain the insight, and the extraordinary power of teaching, which would bring to a total end the suffering of innumerable beings in a later time. That power, bought at so heavy a price, is the goal that ennobles an act which might appear somewhat extravagant if considered as the sacrifice of a human life merely to afford a temporary relief to the pain of a wild beast.

It must be understood as part of an arduous process of self-transcendence, the final object of which is the perfection of mind and of faculties found only in a Supreme Buddha. Whether the Jātaka is taken literally or symbolically, the truth it teaches is this: the necessity of complete renunciation of the illusory concept of selfhood, and the inflexible resolution of a Bodhisatta.

The Value of Buddhism to the Western Mind

The question of where Buddhism stands in relation to the mundane concerns of day to day life was also dealt with by Victor E. Kroemer in the article, "The Value of Buddhism to the Western Mind" (1912), from which the following is an extract:

"We have to live in the Western world, and adjust our lives according to its civilization. But there is nothing to prevent our meditating on the principles of Buddhism, or the glorious philosophy that the Buddha propounded. And the effect on the individual of an understanding of this philosophy, and of meditation on its principles, is to give one a poise, a stability, an insight into causes and effects, into the meaning of all that happens in the world, that can come from no other source. It keeps the mind calm and collected in all circumstances, makes the body the instrument of the self, trains the mind to think only those thoughts that are good and pure and beautiful. And it has this advantage over all else that is taught in the West (especially at the present time when all kinds of freak cults are being followed and sought after): its principles are based on eternal verities, they have stood the test of time for 2,500 years, and they are as fresh and practical today as they ever were (and are likely to be so until a new Buddha arises to restate them in the course of ages).

"What is the use of seeking solutions for problems in directions that only intensify the causes by destroying the effects, when in philosophic Buddhism we have a clear statement of all the causes which produce all the troubles and sorrows of existence? The cause of sorrow is desire, the cessation of sorrow is attained by conquering love of self and lust of life. Apply this to any Western problem, and there is the antidote. People will continue to have sorrow as long as their minds are centred in the causes that produce sorrow, and will be released from sorrow when the causes of the cessation of sorrow are found and practiced. True, sorrow in the larger sense is an outcome of manifested existence, and here again the antidote to sorrow lies in the cessation of birth and death, the overcoming of the desire for manifested existence.

"So to the Western Mind, Buddhism shows the purpose of all existence, the object of our life here, and the goal to which all is tending. It goes behind the veil of illusion into the reality beyond, and teaches fundamental and basic principles derived from the Buddha's enlightenment and insight into the working of the scheme of things. And in Buddhism, in whatever form it ultimately comes to the West, lies the solution of all the social problems, all the unrest, that exist in the Western World. The blending of the East and West will give to the West philosophy, and to the East self-government and economic progress, and in the unity of both of these lies the salvation of the world. That is our firm conviction and our best belief. We pay our reverence to the Teacher who gave us this great light so many years ago, and trust that his principles and philosophy will evermore increase in the West."

The Concept of Personal Evolution

The strong appeal made by the Buddhist concept of personal evolution is apparent from the frequency with which it appears in the writings of the early European Buddhists. The following is an excerpt from an article by Hodgson Smith: "The Life and Teachings of the Lord Buddha" (1910):

"In looking at the world around and within, the Buddha saw a gradual process of evolution. He did not shut His eyes to what had before so saddened Him: the struggle for existence, the incessant warfare which goes on between plant and plant, and animal and animal for the means of subsistence. But with His illuminated vision He saw, as the result of this struggle, evolving life, which needed a succession of higher and higher forms for its expression. He lived at a time when superstition was rife, when men thought that their conditions and character depended upon the gods, who could be persuaded to help or hinder as they were worshipped and sacrificed to by their followers. In the Tevijja Sutta we find a very curious account of the practices of some of the religious teachers (Brahmans) of the day, and if these were performed by them, what must have been the state of the mass of the people!

"These teachers got a living by divination from marks on the body; by auguries; by the interpretation of dreams and omens; by divinations from the manner in which cloth and other things have been bitten by rats; by sacrifices to the god of fire; by offerings of food and of liquids ejected from the mouth; by bloody sacrifices; by teaching spells for preserving the body, for determining lucky sites; for protecting fields; for luck in war; for protection against ghosts, goblins, and so forth; by guessing the length of life; by pretended knowledge of the language of beasts; by foretelling future events; by predicting earthquakes; by pretending that the eclipse of the moon or of the sun will have such and such effect; the rising of the sun, moon, or planets, cloudy or clear, will have such and such an effect; by teaching spells to procure prosperity, or to cause adversity to others; to remove sterility; to produce dumbness, locked-jaw, deformity, or deafness. All these the Buddha stigmatised as low arts and lying practices, and turned the attention to the great law of cause and effect.

"All that is, is the result of antecedent causes. This is recognised by us now in the material world, but the Buddha proclaimed it as operative not only in the material but in the emotional, mental and moral worlds. This great law of cause and effect is a just law, bringing to each one of us, neither more nor less than we ourselves have earned. For to the Buddhist as to the Hindu, this law of cause and effect is not limited to the present life or to the life beyond the grave, but continues through all our cycles of lives; is, indeed, a universal law. It is true it is operative here and now. As we think, so we tend to become, thought being the most important factor in the building of character. While desire brings us to the place where it may obtain satisfaction, action has a gradual but sure effect upon our circumstances. We know this by reflection upon our own life and observation of the lives of others.

"We can see, in our own case, how the nature of our thoughts during our present life has gradually built up our character, a character as varied as our thoughts and feelings; and our desires have brought us opportunities, first in one direction and then in another; our acts, being the outer expression of our thoughts and desires, have more or less modified our circumstances. Of course there is no real separation between thought, feeling and action, but only a predominance now of one and now of the other; the whole man thinks and feels and acts. What we recognise in ourselves we also observe in others, and there is every reason to think that birth and death are but incidents in the working of this law of cause and effect.

"Thus the Buddha taught that each life was the result of all lives before it along one particular individual line. I have had one line of past lives, you have had another; therefore our present characters differ because our past has been different, and we are each the result of the whole of our past. As my physical body is the result of one series of ancestors, and your physical body is the result of another series, so my character is the result of one series of lives, and your character is the result of another series. The doctrine of reincarnation of *character* is the complement of the evolution of the body. "Each life the outcome of our former living is." Just as we now are, so we have made ourselves by our past thoughts, desires and acts. We are our own architects and our own builders, and, if the building is not to our liking, we can set to work to alter and improve.

"Here we all are, then, according to the teaching of the Buddha, revolving upon this wheel of birth, decay, death, life elsewhere, and then re-birth in other surroundings, but very generally the old attachments under new forms. Gradually the character evolves. It slowly acquires aptitudes and faculties, and at last learns to discriminate why it is bound on the Wheel of Change. The Buddha saw that it was desire that brought the man back time after time to the round of earth-life, and He proclaimed to all who would listen a way to cast off the fetters binding the man. The great cause of human misery the Buddha saw to be 'Ignorance', and, in order to dispel this ignorance and lead men to become wise, He taught the Four Noble Truths, and the Noble Eight-Stepped Path."

Why Look Back?

The reaction against a materialistic outlook which saw in religion nothing more than the reflection of man's uncertainty and fear in the face of natural powers that he had not yet succeeded in understanding or controlling to his own satisfaction, is brought out in a thoughtful article by Jeno Lenard on "Buddhism in Modern Western Thought" (1912). By bringing Buddhism into comparison with the theistic creeds to which this form of explanation more suitably applies, the writer shows both an essential difference and an organic development in the religious consciousness, both of which mark Buddhism off from what may be termed the religions of compensatory myth. His conclusions may be summed up in the following extracts.

"One of the outstanding characteristics of the present day is the renaissance of religious thought and feeling. The so-called positive religions (Christianity with its two hundred and forty sects; Judaism and Mohammedanism; the various scientific religions, such as Haeckel's Monism, Professor James' Pragmatism and Ostwald's Energetism; and finally that unique religion which stands in solitary grandeur in a class by itself: Buddhism) are showing renewed force and activity. Philosophy is studied, Ethical Societies and Free Thought organisations flourish, and on all sides we see this mighty forest of the human intellect budding forth with the vigour of awakened spring.

"The primary objects of interest are the abstract questions which lie at the very roots of morality and ethics. In those sections of the community where the first consideration of existence, the economic, is more or less satisfactorily settled (but even where the question of one's daily bread absorbs the bulk of thought and reflection), the questions 'Why?', 'Whence?' and 'Whither?' still arouse considerable interest. Undeterred by the blatant flamboyancy of materialistic energy, religion (that is to say, the problems of morality and ethics and metaphysics) maintains its even course.

"In religion, as in every other sphere of human inquiry, growth and development follow the great law of evolution, and we find ourselves confronted with an ever-increasing stream of differentiations. Indeed, this progress has reached such a pitch that it is almost impossible to secure even such a general view of the field of speculative philosophy as could be taken as a fair representation of its outlines and general tendencies. Of course all persons of culture and education may examine such systems as they care to, and pick and choose according to their disposition and fancy; but we desire to bring 'these varying units into groups of species, and scientifically to compare their merits one with the other'. Which, then, is the standpoint from which we can gain a clear and impartial view?

"Truth is the test by which all science (empirical or otherwise) stands or falls, and should constitute a platform which will give us a firm and solid standing.

"We will take empirical, experimental, scientific truth as being the nearest approach to absolute verity which human insight, thought and knowledge can attain; and will see how far these various religions harmonise with what we know, from research and experience, to hold good as truth.

"Religions are born almost daily before our eyes in the laboratories of German, English, American, and French Universities and Scientific Institutions; in the centres of intellectual culture; in the studies of independent and more or less officially persecuted savants like Ostwald, Haekel, Mach and Bergson; and in the minds of the toilers with their new religion of human solidarity: the Gospel of Socialism.

"The connection between Buddhism as a living modern system of thought and Agnosticism, Free Thought and Modern Science has often been discussed, both in Buddhist circles and in this Review. Nothing gives stronger impetus to the study of Buddhist Modernism than the ever-spreading knowledge that there is a connection between Buddhism and all these spheres of intellectual energy, and that by this connection each and all gain mutual support.

"Isolated individual efforts to clear away the must of centuries are strong in themselves, but lack that forceful solidarity which only a religion can give. Buddhism is a religion which fulfils the requirements of the innocent heart of the child, the critical intelligence of the man, the sweet charm of the maiden, and the mature serenity of the matron. There is only one religion which makes this universal appeal, which is the hallmark of philosophic genius, and that religion is the system of Gotama the Buddha.

"'Why look back twenty-six centuries?' is a question that is often asked. Why should we not look forward to the genius of our own day? The answer is simply because we have no such living universal religious genius. For the same reason we go back to Euripides, Sophocles, Shakespeare, and Goethe for the greatest tragedy; to Homer for the perfection of epic poetry; to Euclid, Aristotle, Plato, Dante, Schiller, and Beethoven for the greatest achievements in their respective spheres. It is conservatism in the best sense of the word, and is wholly in accordance with what we consider best in our own day: the Middle Path.

"There are more Buddhists than we dream of. It matters not whether those who lead a noble life of refined ethics really call themselves followers of the Buddha, whether they belong to any Buddhist society, whether they have ever even heard the name of the Buddha (who never asserted that whosoever believes in him shall enjoy eternal bliss, and whosoever has unfortunately never heard of him shall be for ever lost). Buddhism has no need of monks or pagodas, or of compulsory teaching, so long as day by day the leading ideas of Buddhism gain ground simply by reason of their own merits.

"Evolution and Periodicity are the lights of Science and of Buddhism. The idea of doing good is gradually becoming divorced from belief in a special retribution after death in Heaven and Hell. The world is beginning to do good for its own sake. The law of absolute causality is spreading far and wide, and the idea of an omnipotent being, god, trinity, or power, distributing eternal bliss or punishment, is fading away from an intellectual world.

"Like a wave of Idealism breaking against the sordidness of Materialism, new prophets preach the law of selfless love (of *metta*, not *kāma*[5]) of looking up and away from the heart's desire for material and transient things (*anicca*) to the nobler, happier life of selflessness (*anattā*), and the cardinal truth of human life, the life of Suffering (*dukkha*).

"We know how to classify, how to name and judge these things, because we are humble pupils of our teacher; what he taught was not transient dogma but absolute verity, and it has

5. *Kāma*, that is, desire for pleasure; not *kamma*, deeds, character. (Ed.)

passed down to us through fifty generations. The light has been blurred at times by priest and peasant; the dust of centuries lies thick on many of its tenets. But with our intellect we may clear away the dross from the pure gold, which shines as brightly now as it once gleamed forth beneath the Bo tree. Let all of us who enjoy its splendour be thankful for our privilege; let us wander forth and preach the Good Law wherever there are ears to hear; let our aim be to establish the Kingdom of Righteousness, the Kingdom of the Good Law."

Peace or War?

It has already been mentioned that the increasing possibility of a European war formed part of the background against which these articles were written. By 1912 the probability had become so strong that it could not be ignored by any writer who claimed to speak for his generation and its problems. So we find *The Buddhist Review* in that year featuring an essay by Marr Murray on "The Basis of Peace." The extracts that follow show how the writer interpreted the situation in the light of his Buddhist convictions.

"For our present purpose we will take two things as granted: first, that War with all its attendant horrors is bad, cruel and debasing, and therefore, undesirable; and second, that Peace with its joys, being the opposite of War, is most excellent and desirable. Assuming this much, we propose to search out some method by means of which War may be utterly annihilated, and its place taken by perpetual Peace with its infinite vista of progress.

"It is obvious that some method is necessary. The human mind is so constituted, that it is affected by no innovation that is not persistently presented in some systematic and coherent manner. Every age has had its thinkers to weave their dreams of peace into visions of Republics, Utopias and Arcadias. But none of these disjointed efforts has borne fruit, for the simple reason that the soil has not been prepared for their reception. Mankind is a garden, and its finest blooms cannot come until the whole has been carefully cultivated in the right way. That is the object of our search: the right method of cultivation for the delicate blossom of Peace.

"In the history of the human race, how have the truly great, lasting changes (as distinct from the merely temporary) been effected? Let us take one or two of the outstanding landmarks and examine them. The art of Greece, the standard of aesthetics for all time, could have arisen in no other age and amongst no other people. It is the result of blending a religion, laden with the fragrance of the beauty of Nature, with a democracy full of keen intellectuality. The rise of Christianity was based upon the yearning for liberty and happiness of a democracy crushed beneath the tawdry load of a decadent and bestial materialism. The growth of Science, the wresting from Nature of her secret wonders, is founded upon the innate curiosity and thirst for truth of a people who had outgrown their gods and were making new ones. These three far-reaching changes were democratic in the fullest sense of the word. They depended in no wise upon the whims of princes or the wisdom of legislatures; their foundation was the temperament of the people. That same foundation will, and must, serve for the coming of World Peace, the most sublime of all the dreams that have ever enriched the brain of man.

"What is War but the direct result of the sensual glorification of the ego? Victory, lordship, empire, and the rest of them prove upon examination to be composed of nothing but the gross lust of the great 'I am,' decked out with the flimsiest of tinsels. And like all lusts, they serve but to pile misery upon misery. World Peace must therefore arise from the subjugation of the ego, from the higher thinking and higher doing of humanity; in other words, an advance in morality must be the forerunner of Peace. Morality is no exception to the law of rhythms. It does not sweep onward at a level speed, but has its alternate phases of progress, stagnation, decadence, and renewed progress. It is like a climber towards the light: it climbs up a space, then, proud of its accomplishment, it relaxes its efforts, it makes no progress and finally slips down a little. A new effort is made, and with a burst of energy the lost ground is regained and the advance continues.

"The method which we seek, then, is the stimulus which will urge morality to make the necessary leap forward. We have to find that system of blended ideas which will induce an ethical enthusiasm in mankind and permanently elevate its temperament. In other words, we have to find the right religion.

"All religions, no matter how absurd and foolish they may appear, whether we believe in them or disbelieve in them, have one fundamental excellence. That excellence may be, and often has been, obscured in a greater or lesser degree by excrescences. Nevertheless it is there at the very roots. This excellence is comprised in the two words 'Be Good,' which is the one fundamental message which every religion seeks to instil into the heart of humanity. According to the broad methods by which religions seek to teach this simple lesson they may be divided into two classes. There are first of all those in which the theistic conception of the cosmos is predominant. They wander away from the present life, the regulation of which is their raison d'être; and dabble in the supernatural, in the origin of the universe and in the prospects of some life on the other aide of the grave. The second class is devoted wholly to the problems of this present life. Their whole energy is devoted to the alleviation of actual existence and not frittered away on vain and visionary theories. As regards the creation of the universe and what follows death, this second class of religions maintains the purely agnostic view. It says frankly that we do not know, cannot know, and, moreover, that there would be no gain if we did know. The first class of religions, the theistic, comprises every religion from the Animism of the savage to the Christianity of the European, except one. Buddhism forms the second class, and stands alone, unique in the history of ideas.

"Let us examine the first class of religions, and ascertain how much they can be expected to do towards preparing humanity for the establishment of World Peace. We know that they mean well, they intend to make men good. The point is how far can and do they fulfill their intentions, if at all? We must observe, however, that national morality is but the reflection of the morality of the individuals composing the nation, and it is useless to expect a cessation of war, that is to say, national strife, unless individuals cease first of all to strive amongst themselves. The individual ego must be thoroughly subdued before we can hope to check the national ego.

"Keeping this in mind, we will examine the first class, the ideas current throughout by far the greater portion of the globe. All theistic concepts deal with the supernatural; at the best, they are but guesses at the unknowable. Suppose yourself placed in a garden surrounded by a very high and unclimbable wall, so that you could never hope to see anything of the world beyond. You might spend the whole of your life (and more) in making guesses, each different from the preceding one, as to the exact constitution of the surrounding country which you can never hope to see, and so can never prove which guess was right and which wrong. It is not necessary to dwell here upon the idiotic waste of time such a procedure would entail, except to notice the infinite number of guesses that are possible, and the hopelessness of verifying any one of them. That hopelessness is increased a thousandfold when, instead of guessing at concrete possibilities (such as the landscape hidden by a garden wall), we seek to make guesses at what lies on either side of life, at the unthinkable, the infinite, the absolute, and the eternal. Here, then, we have a fundamental disadvantage inherent in any theistic concept. It is capable of infinite variations, all equally plausible. Somebody has only to make a fresh guess, to satisfy a few people that he is right, and a new sect comes into existence. Another person makes a slightly different guess, a new sect arises, and so the process goes on, entailing an ever-increasing number of sects and creeds, each sure of its own supreme excellence, full of ecstatic enthusiasm, anxious to convert all and sundry, and profoundly jealous of its rivals. What more fruitful source of strife could be desired?

"True, the fundamental excellence underlies all these variations, but how can that excellence be realized when ideas are presented in such a wrangling mob? To carry weight with humanity at large they must be presented with consistent homogeneity, otherwise they are received with suspicion and lose the greater part, if not all, of their force.

"And then, as regards morality, it tells mankind to be good, but what reason does it give for being so, in preference to submitting to the gaudy allurements of evil? It simply says, 'Be good and you will go to heaven; be wicked and you will go to hell.' Now this may be a potent form of argument with a child, when heaven is the near prospect of a jujube and hell the equally imminent prospect of punishment, but it can hardly be said to be an argument likely to have any lasting results with men and women. Even with the child it has no lasting effect, as the first opportunity for mischief proves. These are the things which really count in a religion, and although we admit that current systems mean well and have the highest motives, they have not, unfortunately, the strength, to fulfil their proposals. Theism is in the same position as a man who might say, when remonstrated with for supplying a wheel barrow instead of a motor-car, 'I really meant it for a motor-car.' We want a religion that will permanently raise the standard of mankind. If it cannot do that we have no use for it.

"From an examination of the inherent characteristics of the theistic system of urging man to be good, we therefore find that, instead of teaching with any success the simplest ethical virtue (love of one another), it ought, if our examination has been correct, actually attain the opposite effect of perpetuating strife. Actual observation will prove how far we have been correct in our deductions.

"Before we will subscribe to the pessimistic view that humanity is incapable of any approach to perfection in this life, we will see if we cannot find a really successful religion, something that will not only tell men to be good, but will make all men good and *keep* them good. What are the characteristics of such a religion? Obviously it will have none of the defects we have already found in the current ideas of the Western world. It will be non-theistic, that is to say, will belong to the second class of religions. It will require neither priests nor ritual. It will deal wholly with this present life on this very earth. Its heaven will be the ground which all men tread. It will offer something now instead of problematical visions. And, finally, it will make a simple, dignified appeal direct to the common sense of every man on the face of the earth.

"There is only one religion which fulfils these conditions, and that religion is Buddhism. It is what may be called a pure and unadulterated religion. It deals only with positive facts and not with hypotheses, and the result is that Buddhism alone of all religions welcomes all progress and all true knowledge. Whereas the ideal of the opinions current in the West is necessarily an unquestioning faith based upon comparative ignorance, no advance of knowledge can mar the truth or undermine the authority of Buddhism. It says to mankind: 'You are unhappy; the reason of your unhappiness lies in the base desires of your heart. Be purged of those desires, and you will be happy beyond your brightest dreams. Your actual present life will be a heaven or a hell; the choice rests with you alone. Nothing can save you from the hell that follows on the heels of base doing and base thinking; nothing can take from you the heaven which is the immediate result of right doing and right thinking. The simple Eightfold Path is the one road to bliss, and every man may walk upon it without the need of any guiding hand.' Peace must be founded on the temperament of mankind. A system is necessary to raise that temperament, and, of all the systems which have arisen, Buddhism with its Noble Eightfold Path alone holds out any hope to the world."

In their stand against war the Western Buddhists linked hands with the rationalist and humanitarian, but they had their own reasons for the position they took. They realised that the final price of non-violence in a violent world is sacrifice. Where others were prone to shirk the logical conclusion of the pacifist path, they were fully aware of it and accepted it. But to accept it is a decision that can be made only by each individual for himself. To one who has fully attuned his mind to the Teaching of the Buddha, the final objective of the Unconditioned and Deathless state must always take a more important place than considerations of personal survival in a world dominated by delusion and pain. But at the same time, no one has a right to impose this view on others who are not ready to embrace it, nor should he condemn them if they (in his view, short-sightedly) prefer to fight for their existence and the survival of those they love. The anguish of choice is with us all the time, and each man must face and decide the issues for himself.

Buddhist Attitude to Death

In the same year as the preceding article (1912), we find the Buddhist attitude to death expressed in an article by Joseph Bryce. "An Opponent of Buddhism" is a refutation of Saint-Hilaire, and most of the essay is beside our present purpose. But the following extracts are of interest in this connection:

"Those terrible fears to which the thought of annihilation often gives rise, in the minds of those whose faith has been nurtured upon the hope which the soul-theory is said to afford, are wholly unknown to the Buddhist. 'There is this remarkable fact in Buddhism,' says the author of *The Soul of a People*, 'that nowhere is any fear expressed of death itself, nowhere any apprehension of what may happen to the dead'. Buddhism is a creed of life and conduct. Its followers have always been happily free from that morbid, unhealthy tendency which broods over the fate of the hypothetical 'soul'. Whatever the natural change we call death may signify, it argues a misconception of the psychology of Buddhism to give it the materialistic interpretation which the term 'annihilation' implies. If the notion of a Universal Spirit into which the human soul is absorbed be absent from Buddhism, it nevertheless recognises the existence and continuance of the life of humanity, which is not a theory, but a truth which any cultured mind may apprehend. As all that constitutes our real selves, our thoughts and ideas, our emotions and aspirations, have their roots in the thought-life of humanity in the past, in like manner will our lives become re-incarnate in the life of humanity in the future. Even Christian philosophy regards it as a noble thing for a person to sacrifice his personal interests to the well-being of his fellow creatures: to lose, as it were, the sense of self, and become identified with the larger life of the whole human race. It, too, regards the passions and desires as inimical to high spiritual attainments, but the end and object of all its sacrifice and striving is individual reward in another life. That sharp distinction, however, between life and death which the soul-theory has created is nowhere to be found in Buddhism. Nirvana, the peace which follows the entire subjection of evil desires, the absolute control and mastery of our thoughts and actions, can be attained here and now. That peace, which the troubles of this transient life are unable to disturb and the whispering voice of evil allurement cannot touch, is an ideal that in the life of the Buddha we find translated into actual experience. Nirvana is not attained either by crucifixion of the flesh or retirement from the world, but by the direction of our energies into right channels, and the absorption of our individual desires and our life's activities into the higher life and larger demands of the human race (in the realisation of the oneness of life). But this identification with the life and higher aspirations of humanity knows no severance, no cessation.

"Since the days of Saint-Hilaire, when men were accustomed to speak with confident dogmatism upon such subjects as the existence of God and the immortality of the soul, a great change has taken place in the general intellectual attitude towards such assumptions. And if we examine the trend of mental and social efforts today, the modern spirit which is leavening religious thought, we shall find our human activities and ideals are being weaned from the hope of a 'life beyond the grave', and are being directed to the present betterment and elevation of mankind. We see the best and noblest spirits of our time, without the hope of that future reward which was held to be a necessary inducement to a godly life, labouring unselfishly for a higher ideal, content with the satisfaction which a virtuous and intellectually active life always brings.

"Criticism of the Buddhist view of life and the Universe has spent itself against an impregnable rock. Modern thought (by a somewhat slow process, truly, but not the less surely) and the humanitarian activities of our age, are gradually gravitating towards the rational position adopted by the Buddha long ago. The whole structure of the supernatural, which has stood as a barrier to intellectual and moral progress, is crumbling away before the certainties of scientific knowledge. But the glories of Buddhism lie in the marvellous unity of its conceptions. The conclusions of physical science, of psychological investigation, and the attainments of moral truth, are all combined into one complete system in the philosophy of Gautama, and applied in a practical way to the business of life, in a manner that is unequalled in the history of any other faith. Upon this comprehensive nature of its fundamental doctrines and ideals rests the claim of Buddhism to meet the needs and aspirations of man, and its doctrine of universal brotherhood knits into a living whole the hopes, feelings and sentiments of our common humanity."

By September 1914 the distant mutterings of war had burst out over Europe into the crash of drums and the thunder of heavy artillery. Overnight, the world had been plunged into a black frenzy of hate, a shrieking chaos in which all but a few voices of reason and temperance were drowned. For the Western Buddhists, who had turned to the Teaching of compassion and restraint out of a compelling sense of its necessity, the war was a critical test of the values they had chosen.

As individuals they reacted in different ways, for the issues to be decided were not so clear cut as those of the conflict that was to follow twenty-five years later. Some refused to fight in a war that they felt could have been averted by curbing the activities of a few international financiers and armaments manufactures. Others accepted the situation in which as laymen they found themselves, and went to war with the rest. As it was in England, so it had been in Germany, where there was also a promising Buddhist movement, inspired by the writings of Paul Dahlke and led by Karl Seidenstucker. From the year 1905 the latter had been editor of a German Buddhist magazine which was the first of its kind in the West.

The new era, which was to grow into our present nuclear nightmare, had arrived at puberty and was being initiated into manhood with the traditional rites of savage humanity. Or, like a nice, civilized English boy at his first kill in the hunting field, it was having its face tastefully blooded.

In the midst of this idiotic carnival of destruction, this most preposterous beginning to a century of progress, the tiny "I" was carefully guarded. In a street of South London, one of the first to take the Yellow Robe, the Bhikkhu Ānanda Metteyya, was fighting quite a battle of his own, a personal war against poverty and increasing sickness. By day he worked on inventions which he hoped would bring much-needed money for the movement, and in the evenings lectured on the Dhamma (when his health permitted) to a small group of earnest students. It must have been one of these, C.R.J., who wrote in *The Buddhist Review* of September that year the article that follows, entitled "The Fruits of Meditation."

The Fruits of Meditation

"The central truth of the Message of the Buddha is the doctrine of the possibility of deliverance from all sorrow. It is this which appeals to the minds of Eastern and Western people alike: the giving and the finding of happiness (the cause for satisfaction and peace) in every event that chances upon us and in every detail of our environment. This indeed is the *summum bonum* of this optimistic religion: happiness and the beyond of happiness (infinite, unspeakable peace). In the Mahāmaṅgala Sutta this idea is followed out through many stanzas. Satisfaction is found in ordinary and everyday occurrences, intercourse with friends and opportunities for helping kindred. This satisfaction is no different in kind from that offered by some apparently more exalted external destiny that provides an opportunity of doing good from a prominent position, or discovering some transcendental truth.

"An example of this occurs in the following stanza:

To support father and mother;
To cherish wife and child;
To follow a peaceful calling;
This is the greatest blessing.

Unselfishness provides the reward
in the household life,
And bestows it in the homeless one:

Self-restraint and purity;
The knowledge of the Noble Truths;
The realization of Nirvana;
This is the greatest blessing.

"But this acceptance of life never comes as the result of apathy or indolence. Nor is it the result of resignation to the will of some higher power. It has to be gained by earnestness, built up by untiring energy. Says the Lotus of the Good Law:

"The wise man is indefatigable; not even the thought of fatigue will arise in him. He has no listlessness and so displays to the assembly the strength of charity."

"... The satisfaction and the enlightenment that Buddhism offers is built up of seven elements: energy, recollectedness, penetration, lofty enthusiasm, tranquillity, concentration and even-mindedness. By the acquisition of these elements or factors it is possible, the doctrine affirms, to suppress in life all the varying causes that give rise to sorrows (whether great or small) and to amass such a store of good, of wisdom, as to be utterly beyond the reach of evil destiny. Nor is this an incredible teaching when one considers what it is that furnishes an evil destiny with its opportunities for injury. When we examine the nature of the things and events that have caused us trouble, have they not been almost invariably the fruit of faults we have harboured, idle cravings, sloth, a hasty or unforgiving temper? But if the trouble is beyond these causes, does it not often spring from a refusal to acknowledge natural laws as being inevitable in their working? Nor is the necessity for exercising all the elements of enlightenment any the less when the deed a man is engaged in performing is one to which he would ascribe a Buddhist motive.

"There are some who say, "The keynote of Buddhism is renunciation." This is only the case if renunciation is based on enlightenment. Throughout the Jātakas there are very numerous instances of great renunciations; of the giving up of wealth, of favourite steeds, of wife and children, even of life itself—and this to people who were not worthy to receive such gifts. But all this, though of very great moral value, *could not,* by itself, bring about purification, and, consequently, the renunciations that the Buddha had made in the past were not taken as a precedent after he had attained enlightenment. Thus, when his cousin, Devadatta, ambitious for leadership, asked the Buddha to resign in his favour, the request was declined. There are some whose destiny leads them to carry out the principle of renunciation, even though their deeds can ripen no visible fruit, as, for example, by giving time, money, effort, to the first stranger who asks for them irrespective of the merits of the case... Such sacrifices have value in rooting out the false, illusory self, but they yet fall far short of that offering, which at enlightenment, is made, not to any individual, or even to any cause, but to all the world.

"Taking the seven elements of Enlightenment in the order here given, and starting with Energy, the question arises, How may this be developed? The Thera Ānanda Metteya makes use of the simile of a complicated engine in which energy generated in the boiler may be made to perform a great amount of work, or, on the other hand, owing to the defective adjustment of the parts may be largely dissipated and wasted in friction at various points. In the same way human energy may be lost through a number of leakages or *āsavas*. Through these *āsavas* the energy that should be giving value to a particular action or state of mind is being lost on vain desire, on keeping in existence something evil, on spreading error, on mental degradation. For the energy supporting the whole evil of the world, whether vice, intemperance, organised fraud, or apparently detached crimes and weaknesses, is energy leaking from the right channels. As in an irrigation system continuous leakages at a few points make wide fields less fruitful, so the *āsavas* of an individual reduce the energy for righteousness of a wide circle.

"The second element is recollectedness. This term is used to cover a very wide ground in the Buddhist system. It occurs as one branch in the Noble Eight-fold Path as Right Recollectedness. Far more must be understood by, it than self-possession or presence of mind. Self-possession is included, and presence of mind, but it further includes a consciousness that is far greater than that expressed in these. The cultivation of this quality is considered so important that it is enjoined in the disciple during his whole waking hours until he has arrived at attainment.

"It includes recollectedness of body, of states of consciousness, of duties and of environment. As regards the body, it is to be attained by keeping watch over such processes as breathing and walking—considering them merely as physiological processes involving certain muscles working in obedience to various ideas but in no wise governed by or containing a soul. Physically it includes an awareness of every action performed and the causes and stimuli that have rendered possible such an action.

"Recollectedness as regards duties is dependent on memory and on goodwill. The principal meditation for strengthening the memory is that which is concerned with remembering backward in sequential order the events of one life or of many other lives, and in a paper dealing with meditations rather than their fruits a consideration of the process of this meditation would be of great interest.

"Recollectedness considered with regard to environ-ment implies heedfulness of the particular dangers to be encountered at any time.

"Probably one of the hardest forms of recollectedness that a Buddhist has to acquire is the continual remembrance that there never can be any justification for ill will in its various degrees, from annoyance to anger and hatred. The New Testament command to forgive one's brother seventy times seven may perhaps have appeared a counsel of perfection, but the forgive-ness of an injury, when one has had time to cool down, is as nothing compared to never receiving an injury. Yet this is what Buddhism requires. It teaches that a man's troubles spring through himself, not from an external enemy. If this be realised, a host of words coined to express a sense of grievance against another vanish from our vocabulary. As Maurice Maeterlinck puts it in "Wisdom and Destiny": "Around the upright man there is drawn a wide circle of peace, within which the arrows of evil soon cease to fall; nor have his fellows the power to inflict moral suffering upon him. For indeed if our tears can flow because of our enemies' malice, it is only because we ourselves would fain make our enemies weep. If the shafts of envy can wound, and draw blood, it is only because we ourselves have shafts that we wish to throw, if treachery can wring a groan from us, we must be disloyal ourselves."

"It is in the power of every man who follows the teaching to turn any injury, abuse, deception that others may practise against him into means of helpfulness even as the fiery ashes which Mara rained down on the Buddha fell round him only as flowers.

"Over and over again do we meet with this perfect recollectedness in the history of the Buddha. A Brahman reviles him as an outcast. Instead of answering with harsh abuse, the Buddha asks the Brahman if he knows what constitutes an outcast. Having by his own magnanimity disarmed the Brahman's ill will, the Master proceeds to enlighten him as to who are really outcasts by their own deeds. Thus the occasion that appeared so unpromising bestows a follower.

"So also, when as Bodhisattva he is reclining weak and ill in a cemetery and is there tormented by a troop of badly disposed children, far from causing anger, the incident merely serves to strengthen his fortitude.

"The recollectedness which causes every event that comes charged with some burning sting to leave instead its store of honey is equally powerful in subduing the occasions for covetousness and sloth. Being born in princely circumstances, with everything favourable to a life of voluptuous self-indulgence, this does but sharpen his sympathy with the wretched, the old, the suffering. The same unselfish heedfulness that marked the outset of his mission accompanied it to the end. When a few hours before the Great Teacher's death Subhadda comes to him with a question and Ānanda would save his Master, already exhausted, from the exertion of an interview, the Buddha asks that Subhadda shall be brought in and then quickly removes his perplexity.

"Next to recollectedness comes the kindred quality penetration. As regards any phenomenon, penetration is an insight into its transitory nature, and into the immediate and remote causes of its existence. As regards persons, penetration signifies an insight into the mental state of the person at a particular time, together with a recognition of his general character. Every man carries his entire past about with him and invites each chance acquaintance to study it. One possessing insight perceives in their actual condition mind that is given to craving, or to hatred, or to delusion, as well as one that is permanently free. Likewise, he sees clearly the nature of his own mental states and actions, and the more insight he acquires, the less readily will he find himself able to dignify his faults. For many a man would find it hard to indulge in malice or enmity were he not to find a means of persuading himself that for the moment it was needful in the interests of virtue.

"The legend of Kisāgotamī and the gold illustrates the nature of insight. In this parable a merchant, because he does not use his wealth rightly, sees it transformed into ashes, and is told that the ashes will remain until some one recognises its true nature. He exposes these ashes for sale in his stall in the bazaar, but only excites the ridicule of the passers-by. Then Kisāgotamī passes by and she recognises that the seeming ashes are actually gold.

"The merchant in this fable had this advantage: that he knew the ashes had been gold and might be gold again; and so he kept a wary eye on it. How greater the tragedy of him who only realises what is life's veritable gold (wisdom, pity and love) when he sees it gathered by another! It is true that it only needs someone with more penetration to see in the ashes of a human life possibilities of the finest gold. Was it not thus that the robber Aṅgulimāla was saved by the Buddha, and that not in the sense of salvation from punishment, but made wise, compassionate, loving, by meeting a being of infinite insight who was able to look upon him without fear and without loathing.

"Penetration plays an important part in the overcoming of covetousness and of morbid ambition since it is the act of looking beyond externals. Among the disciples of the Buddha there doubtless many who, like him, renounced not only the state of prosperity and felicity which they already enjoyed, but also prospects of a career brilliant with stole and majesty. But such renunciations are not necessarily "sacrifices" in the common use of the word. The fortunate individual may have perceived that a life of peace, serenity and greater usefulness, undisturbed by cares or remorse, is a destiny that may well be chosen in preference to one of pomp and circumstance. Here, as in all things, it is the inside of the cup only that matters.

"Penetration is necessary also to perceive the eternal, the sameness, of men, things and events, beneath their apparent variety. 'Let us look upon all things as having the nature of space, as permanently equal to space, without essence, without substantiality.'

"The word "penetration" is here intended also to indicate a perfectly ripened insight into, or understanding of, the doctrine in its bearing on life. No truth ever can be fully grasped by the reason alone. And no moral truth can ever be fully expressed in words.

"The next element of enlightenment is rendered 'lofty enthusiasm' by the translator of the Majjhima Nikāya. Elsewhere, a translator has rendered the Pali *pīti* by the term 'pleasurable interest,' which helps us to understand more fully what meaning is intended. It is not so much an exceptional devotion to some worthy cause as an entire attitude of mind, a buoyancy which is able to enter into everything that destiny offers with zest and vigour.

"Solitude has always been productive of enthusiasm when enjoyed by great men. Most founders of religions have been described as conceiving their various systems in forest or desert. The enthusiasm of Buddhism, however, has nothing in common with the fanaticism which has sometimes accompanied religions nurtured in the desert (being saved by its empathy and reasonableness).

"As in olden days, so now, solitude and meditation are still the only reliable sources of fresh interest and enthusiasm. Communion with nature does not create boredom and ennui, but relieves them.

"Tranquillity or serenity is the next factor of enlightenment to be considered; and in considering it, there is borne home to us the deepening conviction that these elements of enlightenment are truly fruits (ends in themselves), even more than they are means to ends (not mere ways of getting free from sorrow, but the actual freedom itself). Especially is this apparent of tranquillity, which to us Westerners suggests nothing of the effort or accomplishment associated with some of the other factors, for example, energy. Yet Tranquillity is not, in Buddhist thought, associated with sloth. Some prejudiced travellers in Buddhist countries have seen monks seated in meditation and have seized the occasion to attribute to them laziness. But this meditation is useful, profitable. The feverish West groans for the lack of it. Without the slightest verbal inaccuracy it can be asserted that time is infinitely more profitably employed in meditation than in a hundred forms of activity directed to non-utilitarian ends (including the making of scientific instruments of warfare and battleships), which activity will cease when right meditation has shown the superiority of tranquillity. For it must be remembered that a state of tranquillity is also a state of safety provided it is tranquillity in the Buddhist sense of the word.

"Bhaddiya, a prince among the Sakyans, although he was strongly attracted to a life of ambition and glory, yet for the sake of his friend Anuruddha renounced the layman's life and became a disciple of the Buddha. While living in retirement in the forest he was heard by one of the other Bhikkhus to give utterance over and over again to the ecstatic exclamation, 'O happiness! O happiness!'

"Some of the bhikkhus who heard him reported the circumstance to the Buddha and suggested that Bhaddiya was recalling the past happiness that he had relinquished, and was discontented. The Buddha thereupon sent for Bhaddiya and inquired why he had so often uttered the expression, 'O happiness'. The bhikkhu replied:

Formerly, Lord, when I was a prince, I had a guard both in my private apartments, outside my palace, in the town and in the country. Yet though, Lord, I was thus so protected, I was fearful, anxious, guarded, distrustful, and alarmed. But now, Lord, even when in the forest, at the foot of a tree, I am without fear or anxiety, trustful and not alarmed. I dwell at ease, subdued, secure, with mind as peaceful as an antelope's. It was when calling this to mind that I cried, 'O happiness!'

"The Buddha then uttered this stanza:

'The man who harbours no harsh thoughts within him;
Who cares not whether things are thus or thus;
His state of joy, freedom from grief or care,
The very gods obtain not to behold!'

Cullavagga 7.1.20
(*Sacred Books of the East*, Vol. 20)

"Concentration, the word usually adopted for the next element, may not convey to those unacquainted with Buddhist terms much meaning. This element of enlightenment is concerned with acquiring a steadiness and fixity of the mind, just as a calf is bound to a post to prevent its wandering. The Concentration of the mind is carried through various stages; and for its attainment certain meditations have been prescribed. Though the importance of Concentration has been firmly focused on Buddhism, its attainment is not confined to those who follow this Dhamma; it is common to all the higher religions. The inward illumination which is obtained as a recognisable concomitant of Concentration is mentioned several times by Professor James in his *Varieties of Religious Experience*. It has been described also as a 'diffused glow'; as a feeling of intense peace and satisfaction; and as an intense realisation of harmony with the universe, in which all sense of separateness is for the time lost.

"Last in this series of the elements of enlightenment is even-mindedness. The principal difference between this and tranquillity appears to me to be that whereas tranquillity is a state of mind considered in its aspect of freedom from desire, aversion and fear, even-mindedness is the description of that mind considered as utterly detached from all views, utterly uninterested in all the illusions and shadow plays of existence. In the Aṭṭhakavagga 13.11 (*Sacred Books of the East, X*), this aspect of enlightenment is described thusly:

> 18. The Muni, having done away with ties here in the world, is no partisan in the disputes that have arisen; is appeased among the unappeased; is indifferent, not embracing learning while others acquire it.
>
> 19. Having abandoned his former passions, not contracting new ones, not wandering according to his wishes, being no dogmatist, he is delivered from views, being wise, and he does not cling to the world, neither does he blame himself."

"Lafcadio Hearn expresses this equanimity and what it may mean to a man of the twentieth century in his essay "Within the Circle (Gleanings in Buddha Fields)". He describes his torturing experience of realising something of the mystery of past births. Then he sees the knowledge of Anattā, the emptiness of existence, which he expresses thusly:

"Sky, sun and sea; the peaks, the plains; all splendours and forms and colours, are spectres. The feelings and the thoughts and the acts of men, whether deemed high or low, noble or ignoble, all things imagined or done for any save the eternal purpose, are but dreams born of dreams, and begetting hollowness. To the clear of sight, all feelings of self, joy and pain, hope and regret, are alike shadows. Form and the names of form are alike nothingness. Knowledge only is real. And unto whomsoever gains it, the universe becomes a ghost.

"Such understanding is not yours. Still to your eyes the shadow seems substance, darkness light, and voidness beauty. And therefore to see your former births could give you only pain.

"It is on such a detachment, born of meditation and solitude, that even-mindedness depends.

"Thus, enlightenment, that is, a Buddha, is not a gift from some Deity, is not some divine anointing; it is the fruit of meditation and action purified by meditation. The light of wisdom that each is slowly and painfully gathering is not different in kind from that great radiance which dwells in the Master's life and Dhamma. It is by this Inward Light that his followers must walk, seeking no external guide, no external saviour, whether man or God.

"Therefore the Buddha gives us this message:

Be ye lamps unto yourselves.
Be ye refuges unto yourselves.
Look not to any other refuge.
The Dhamma is your lamp.
The Dhamma is your refuge.
Look not to any other refuge."

Mahāparinibbāna Sutta

* * *

The seven factors of enlightenment (*satta bojjhaṅga*), mentioned above in "Fruits of Meditation", are more accurately rendered as 1. mindfulness, 2. keen investigation of the dhamma (mental and physical phenomena), 3. energy, 4. rapture or happiness, 5. calm, 6. concentration, and 7. equanimity. The order in which they are placed is of great importance, since each factor grows out of the one preceding it.

The enumeration of the factors constituting *satipaṭṭhāna* (recollectedness) is also at fault. The four foundations of mindfulness are: 1. body, 2. feelings, 3. state of mind (or consciousness), and 4. mind-objects.

In *satipaṭṭhāna*, mindfulness is the prerequisite for the investigation of the dhammas, or phenomena of mind and body. In the Noble Eightfold Path, it is really this mindfulness which is meant by the term *sammā sati* (right mindfulness); it is the practice of *satipaṭṭhāna* as a means to enlightenment. Its meaning of bare attention to the physical and mental phenomena, which is what gives to *satipaṭṭhāna* its distinctive quality, is not fully brought out in the term "recollectedness." The author has chosen to give it a more ethical connotation than it bears in the strictest sense. Whilst *sati* in the sense of *satipaṭṭhāna* is the real psychological basis for the realisation of impersonality (through making possible the investigation and analysis of the *dhammas*), and so produces ethically wholesome states of mind and conduct, it should not be identified with these. It stands to them in relation of the seed to plants. Yet so fully integrated is the Buddhist system of mind-development that *sīla*, or moral restraint, has to be cultivated before *satipaṭṭhāna* is attempted. It may be more accordingly said that the real flowering of moral conduct comes when the practice of *satipaṭṭhāna* has been developed. The negative qualities of morality then find their consummation in true virtue. The condition in which morality is a restraint is no longer necessary, because there is no remaining bias towards the unwholesome in thought, word or deed. *Satipaṭṭhāna*, therefore, is an instrument by which to purge one of self-delusion, and it is in this sense that it be understood as a factor of Enlightenment.

It should also be noted that the author does not give sufficient distinction to the state of mind denoted by concentration (*samādhi*). It is something more than a "diffused glow." That description more aptly applies to rapture (*pīti*), not concentration. Concentration, in the words of Piyadassi Thera (*The Seven Factors of Enlightenment*, The Wheel No. 1), is "the intensified steadiness of the mind comparable to an unflickering lamp in a windless place." It is a *fixing* of the chronically unsteady, wavering consciousness. Buddhist mental training recognises two degrees of concentration: a lower form, which is a fastening of the mental processes on a single, morally wholesome idea; and a higher concentration associated with the jhānic states. It is the latter that is meant when *samādhi* is considered as an objective of Buddhist meditation. It is an intensified, supernormal degree of the lower form of concentration, one which excludes all the distractions of sense and of spontaneous mental imagery alike.

At the time the article was written, exact information regarding the technicalities of Buddhist mind-training was not easy to come by, but the writer gives a good general outline of what is to be expected from it. In the midst of war, thoughts such as these created centres of calm and dispassion in the storm of violence that raged all around. It is by such retentions of sanity in the midst of madness that civilization is saved, again and again, in the recurring crises of history. The quiet voice that speaks out of man's higher consciousness may temporarily be drowned, but it speaks on and its message outlives the storm.

Among these early Western Buddhists a few names stand out, not only by reason of their devotion to the cause and their grasp of the Buddhist truths, but also by virtue of the literary skill which enabled them to give a vivid expression to the knowledge they had won. Some of them, like Bhikkhu Sīlacāra, were true poets; others, like Edward Greenly, J.E. Ellam and the Bhikkhu Ānanda Metteyya, were gifted beyond the average in literary expression. To them and to others of their kind we owe a deep debt of gratitude: it was they who opened the eyes of their generation to an ancient wisdom long lost to the Western world. Many of them could not be represented in this short selection; their articles are too closely integrated to allow the necessary excisions to be made without damaging their form and content. But their work remains, and will remain long after the law of impermanence has claimed their memory, a lasting memorial to minds free and untrammeled by the prejudices and conventions of the period they lived in.

Like Wind Along the Waste

It is fitting that this all too brief and inadequate glance back at the beginnings of Buddhism in the West should conclude with a few passages from the writings of one who was among the most dedicated and active in their ranks, the late Francis J. Payne. The extracts that follow are from the close of an article by him, "Like Wind Along the Waste", that appeared in *The Buddhist Review* in the year 1909:

"The human 'self' is illusive, and it requires all the persuasive eloquence of a Buddha to destroy the illusion. Man is fleeting, and, when once he grasps and lives this fact, the path of peace lies broad open before him. One state of consciousness gives place, in unerring sequence, to another. The sequence binds them together. The law of cause and effect is master. Throughout this varying scene we perceive its action, and whatsoever a man sows that shall he reap. The meaning of each deed and word is magnified a thousandfold in the light of this law. When the desire for evil is translated into action, no power above or below, within or without, can trammel up the consequence. The contemplation of this awful truth must give us pause. The evil man will not escape unpunished, the good will not go unrewarded. For punishment and reward are not dealt out at the hands of some changeful being, but are woven into the very texture of Nature.

"Why, then, be good, noble, just, and generous? Is it to please some great and omnipotent being, or, lacking faith therein, are men to 'Do good because it is good to do good'? The mind in the latter case recoils at the folly of the reasoning. Man begins to ask, 'Why not eat, drink, and be merry?' Right conduct has no foundation, for the West has ceased to believe. But the Good Law is offered. Follow the Middle Path, says the Master. All existence is pointed with sorrow. Our happy moments come like brilliant lightning flashes to illuminate the sombre grey of life; but the grey is always there. Today we are joyous. As the Angel of Desire flies by we grasp his wings and bid him stay. Wife and family, parents and material goods, are given to the heart's desire. But amid the merry peals of joy, the rippling laughter and the shouts of triumph and pride, the low-tolling bell sounds, warning men that a change must come.

"To many it has come, and all who rejoice in the present must give thought to broken hearts and grief-stricken fellow mortals. The bond of brotherhood links men one to another, and to all that breathes and suffers. None durst grasp his cloak about him, and live the selfish life. The realisation of the fleeting nature of all things is a logical, true and compelling basis for right conduct. The contemplation of sorrow led the Master to a plan to conquer sorrow, that out of sorrow might proceed happiness. He that considers his brother must adopt the faith of love. The world satiated by desire, thirsting for peace, asks for the way, and Buddhism shows the way. No demand for credulity is there. The Universe has a meaning. From life to life the weary road is trod. Each good act makes the next easy, progress is hastened, and the goal draws near. The last word in the riddle of human fate is not pessimism, but liberty, well-doing and hope."

The Contribution of Buddhism to World Culture

by

Soma Thera

WHEEL PUBLICATION NO. 44

About the Author

Ven. Soma Thera (1898–1960), lay-name Victor E. P. Pulle, was born in Colombo and was raised as a Sinhalese Catholic. Having converted to Buddhism in his teenage years, he became an active Buddhist missionary and author. In 1934 he and his close friend G. S. Prelis, later Kheminda Thera, went to Japan and, with the help of a Japanese scholar called N. R. M Ehara, translated the Chinese translation of the *Vimuttimagga* into English, which was published as the *Path of Freedom.* In 1936 the friends left Japan and went to Burma where they became Buddhist monks in Moulmein under the meditation teacher Jetavana Sayādaw. The next year they returned to Sri Lanka. During WW II he and Kheminda stayed at the Island Hermitage. Despite suffering from frequent asthma attacks he participated in missions to India and Germany and continued with writing and translating. One of the fruits of his work was the English translation of the commentary of the Satipaṭṭhāna Sutta published by the BPS under the title *The Way of Mindfulness.*

The Contribution of Buddhism to World Culture

For twenty-five centuries has the Message of the Deer Park at Benares influenced the destinies of humanity. There is ample evidence to show that the teaching of the Buddha has been something like a leaven to the mental life of mankind from the Siberian snowlands to the verdant sunny isles of the Indian sea, and from the Land of the Rising Sun to fog-bound Britain. It is not improbable that Buddhism penetrated even to the old South American civilizations in the early centuries of our era.[1] Further, it should be remembered that the two most ancient living civilizations, the Indian and the Chinese, and three of the greatest of the religions of today, Christianity, Islam and Hinduism, have been altered and improved by the infiltration of Buddhist ideas. In the light of these facts one can well imagine how colossal must be the Buddhist contribution to the fund of human culture.

"It is my deliberate opinion," says Mahatma Gandhi, "that the essential part of the teachings of the Buddha now forms an integral part of Hinduism. It is impossible for Hindu India today to retrace her steps and go behind the great reformation that Gautama effected in Hinduism. By his immense sacrifice, by his great renunciation, and by the immaculate purity of his life, he left an indelible impress upon Hinduism, and Hinduism owes an eternal debt of gratitude to that great teacher."[2]

The Buddha's doctrine, as Manmatha Nath Shastri puts it, is "the glory of India and Indians."[3] Without it, Indian culture would be a maimed thing. And the Land of the Purple Fruit, Jambudvipa, would for the world lose most of its sanctity and interest, if the Blessed One, the Buddha, had not walked in the Middle Country,

---

1. Lillie, Arthur, *Buddha and Buddhism*, T. & T. Clark, Edinburgh, 1900, pp. 205–208.
2. Desai, Mahadev and S. Ganesan, eds., *With Gandhiji in Ceylon*, Madras, 1928, p. 56.
3. Shastri, Manmatha Nath, *Buddha: His Life, His Teachings, His Order: Together with The History Of The Buddhism*, Society for the Resuscitation of Indian Literature, Calcutta, 1910, p.ii

Madhyadesa, as he did for forty-five years enfolding all within the aura of his compassion, and blazing the path of true renunciation. Realizing the significance of that ministry of the Master, C. V. Raman said, "In the vicinity of Benares, there exists a path which is for me the most sacred place in India. This path was one day travelled over by the Prince Siddhartha, after he had gotten rid of all his worldly possessions in order to go through the world and proclaim The Annunciation of Love."[4]

Again, it is the Master of Merciful Wisdom, and his love-gift of liberation for all that breathes, that grip the imagination of Edwin Arnold at Benares, the citadel of modern Hinduism, steeped though he is in the knowledge of the *Gīta* and in Vedic lore: "... it is not Hinduism which—to my mind at least—chiefly consecrates Benares. The divine memory of the founder of Buddhism broods over all the country hereabouts; and just as the walls and buildings of 'Kasi' are full of old Buddhist stones carved with symbols and legends of his gentle faith, so is the land north and south famous with the passage of his feet, and so are the religious and social thoughts and ways of all this Hindu people stamped with the impress of his doctrines. Modern Brahmanism is really Buddhism in a Shastri's robe and sacred thread. Shunkuracharya and his priests expelled the brethren of the yellow robe from India, but the spirit of Sakya-Muni's teaching remained unbanished, just as 'Greece, overcome, conquered her conqueror.'"[5]

It is impossible to overrate the importance of the work done by Buddhism for India, or, for that matter, for the world. They say that Buddhism has ceased to exist just in the country where it sprang up. Nothing, however, is more untrue,[6] according to D. R. Bhandarkar.

Many revealing statements of the above-mentioned sort could be cited from the writings both of Indians and non-Indians of note to support the contention that India is inwardly Buddhist, whatever its outer religious labels be. And labels are unimportant where a teaching like Buddhism is concerned. To the Buddha and his followers names do not matter much: "What's in a name?..."

4. *The Bosat*, Vol. 5, No. 1, 1942, Vajirarama, Colombo, p. 8
5. Arnold, Edwin, *India Revisited*, Second Edition, London, 1891, p. 223
6. *The Bosat*, Wesak, 1940, Vajirarama, Colombo, p. 95

The main thing in Buddhism is its germinal power which, penetrating silently, unhurriedly, imperceptibly into the womb of the spirit, produces the embryo of the compassionate view, the vision of life as something in urgent need of salvation from the perils that beset it. And with the development of that wisdom-view and its birth as a complete idea, is brought home to the real thinker the urgency too of a rational, practical and sane method of deliverance from all dissatisfactions, first through ameliorative action gradually, and, in the end, through the irrevocable renunciation of the self and all that it implies.

That is the view and that the method of deliverance, which the early messengers of Buddhism stood for and preached wherever they went. In this, they merely imitated the Buddha himself, who never sought to swell his ranks but to change men's hearts. We see the method of propagation as conceived by the Buddha carried out on a stupendous scale by Asoka, the pattern for all good rulers of mankind. His "conquests of righteousness in all quarters," *Dharmavijaya*, were conceived in the spirit of the broadest toleration worthy of a real follower of the Master of Compassion and carried out with full consideration for other beliefs and convictions. The people who came under the influence of the non-violent armies of Asoka's missions appear to have retained a good part of their old beliefs and ways of thought while absorbing the new teaching. The new teaching had been presented to them largely as something complementary to their earlier religious ideas, as something which was to make their lives fuller and their spiritual treasury more abundant with goods of lasting value.

This tradition, coming down from the Buddha and strengthened by the work of Asokan teachers, became settled in all Buddhist missionary activity. No decrying of other sects and no kind of coercion or compulsion has ever existed in Buddhism as they have in the missionary activities of other religions. That is how Buddhism was able to sink deep into a great variety of cultures the civilized world over, gently, without setting up useless resistances. Thus, it is said, were the conquests by the Law of Piety made "by His Sacred Majesty (Dharmasoka) both in his own dominions and all the neighbouring realms as far as Syria hundreds of leagues away where the Greek (*Yona*) King named

Antiochos dwells, and north of that Antiochos, too, where dwell the four kings severally named Ptolemy, Antiogonos, Magas, and Alexander; and in the south the (realms of the) Cholas and Pandyas, as far as Tāmrapārni, likewise, and here, too, in the King's dominions, among the Greeks, and Kambojas, the Nabhapantis of Nabhaka; among the Bhojas, and Pitinikas, among the Andhras and Pulindas ..." [7]

Buddhism was the first missionary religion of the world, both in point of time and in the excellence of its methods and results. And it is only now, more than two thousand years since the example was set, that Christianity and Islam have understood the importance of Buddhist principles of propagation of the truth, and that too, not fully, for still the fullest spirit of tolerance is not in these religions.

By the reasonableness of its ethic, its simple and direct teaching of kindliness, sympathy and strenuous exertion to make the lives of all happy and free from suffering, Buddhism is a teaching that is easy of grasp, both by peasant and by pundit. Thus, it has become a part of the world's heritage of good. "The type of consciousness," S.M. Melamed says, "that is summed up in the term Buddhism is as alive and effective today as ever. There are still millions of people in the East and in the West, who, though formally not adherents of Buddhism, still have a Buddhist outlook upon life. While this type of consciousness may express itself today in a different form than it did in the past, it yet remains a steady force in the spiritual life of man ... Even if Buddhism, as an organized religion, with all its votaries, monks and temples should disappear, the Buddhist consciousness would still remain a steady force in man's spiritual history. It will live as long as man will be overwhelmed by the phenomena of pain and suffering."[8]

The ways in which this spiritual force has expressed itself in the manifold activity of society constitute the Buddhist contribution to world-culture.

Just as Buddhism is the first great missionary religion in recorded history, so too is it the first great monastic religion of the

7. MacPhail, James M., *Asoka*, The Association Press, Calcutta, 1910, p. 74

8. Melamed, S. M., *Spinoza and Buddha, Visions of a Dead God*, The University of Chicago Press, Chicago, 1933, pp. 1–2.

world. All monasticism, Indian and Western, gets its inspiration from the Buddhists. W.M. Flinders Petrie supposed that "from some source—perhaps the Buddhist Mission of Asoka—the ascetic life of recluses was established in the Ptolemaic times, and monks of the Serapeum illustrated an ideal to man which had been as yet unknown in the West. This system of monasticism continued until Pachomios, monk of Serapis in Upper Egypt, became the first Christian monk in the reign of Constantine. Quickly initiated in Syria, Asia Minor, Gaul and other provinces, as well as in Italy itself, the system passed into a fundamental position in mediaeval Christianity, and the reverence of mankind for fifteen hundred (*sic*) bestowed an Egyptian institution."[9] There is no doubt that the Essenes and the Therapeutae were the forerunners of Catholic monasticism, and these were clearly followers of Buddhist monastic practices. "The most subtle thinker of the modern English Church, the late Dean Mansel, boldly maintained that the philosophy and rites of the Therapeutae of Alexandria were due to Buddhist missionaries who visited Egypt within two generations of the time of Alexander the Great. In this, he has been supported by philosophers of the calibre of Schelling and Schopenhauer, and the great Sanskrit authority, Lassen. Renan, in his work *Les Langues Semitiques*, also sees traces of this propagandism in Palestine before the Christian era. Hilgenfeld, Mutter, Bohlen, King, all admit the Buddhist influence,"[10] writes Arthur Lillie.

The value of genuine monasticism and of all true asceticism for the welfare of the world is great indeed. The fundamental attributes of a good monk: self-restraint, chastity, humility, self-effacement and renunciation are things that society cannot do without, and these qualities are best developed in the calm atmosphere of the monastery. The Buddhist monastic life is asceticism without self-torture and is everywhere definitely seen as the product of a progressive state of society alone. In the monastic life a man ceases to be an irritation to his fellowmen through any kind of struggle

9. Flinders Petrie, W.M., *Personal Religion in Egypt before Christianity*, Harper & Bros., London, 1909, pp. 92–3

10. Lillie, Arthur, *Buddhism in Christendom, or Jesus, the Essene*, Kegan Paul, Trench & Company, London, 1887, p. 7

and competition with them for privilege, preferment, profit or fame, and bends his energies to the accomplishment of weal for all.

Buddhism has influenced Christianity and other Western teachings in many ways, not only through the spreading abroad of the idea of monasticism. The Pythagoreans, the Neo-Platonists and the Gnostics were all indebted both to Jainism and to Buddhism. Buddhist ideas flowed freely into these teachings, and only those who want deliberately to shut their eyes to the facts can doubt or hesitate concerning the Eastern influence on the Western mind which had falsified the idea that East is East and West is West, more than twenty centuries before Kipling was born.

Buddhism penetrated westwards early. Just a century after the Buddha, his name occurs in a Persian Scripture, the *Fravadin Yasht* (16).

Clement of Alexandria knew about the Jains and the Buddhists, the *samaṇas*, recluses, and the *brāhmaṇas*, *brahmins*, and actually mentions the name of the Buddha: "There are two sects of these Indian philosophers—one called the Sramanai and the other the Brachmanai. Connected with the Sramanai are the philosophers called the Hylobioi who neither live in cities nor even in houses. They clothe themselves with the bark of trees, and subsist upon acorns, and drink water by lifting it to their mouth with their hands. They neither marry nor beget children, like those ascetics of our own day called the Enkratetai. Among the Indians are those philosophers also who follow the precepts of Boutta whom they honour as a god on account of his extraordinary sanctity."[11]

Buddhism affected Plotinian teaching profoundly, though Dr. Inge is not willing to accept it. "It is well-known," says Dean Inge, "that Alexandria was at this time (the period of Plotinus 204–270 CE) not only a great intellectual centre, but the place where above all others, East and West rubbed shoulders. The wisdom of Asia was undoubtedly in high repute about this time. Philostratus expresses the highest veneration for the learning of the Indians. Plotinus himself accompanied the Roman army to Persia in the hope of

11. McCrindle, J.W., trans and ed., *Ancient India As Described By Megasthenes and Arrian*, Thacker, Spink, Calcutta and Bombay, 1877, pp. 104–5

gathering wisdom... It is, therefore, natural that many scholars have looked for oriental influence in Neo-Platonism, and have represented it as a fusion of European and Asiatic philosophy. But, though the influence of the East upon the West was undoubtedly great during the decline of the Western Empire, it is not necessary to derive any Neo-Platonic doctrines from a non-European source. Neo-Platonism is a legitimate development of Greek thought, and of Plato's own speculations.

"In some ways it might even be said that Plato is more Oriental than Plotinus. It is another question whether Neo-Platonism was influenced in any way by the Jewish Alexandrian school, which is known to us through the writings of Philo. The resemblances between the Essenes and the Neo-Pythagoreans, and between Philo and Plotinus, are so striking that many have thought it impossible to deny a direct dependence. But it is more probable that the Greek and the Jewish Alexandrian schools developed side by side under parallel influences. Philo does not seem to have been much read by the educated pagans, who had strong prejudices against the Jews."[12] Against this view there are specialists on things Indian of the past who believe in the Greeks' and other Westerners' debt to Buddhist, Jain and other Indian thought.

Of the fifth and sixth centuries BCE, Rapson states that "at no period in early history, probably, were the means of communication by land more open or the conditions more favourable for the interchange of ideas between India and the West."[13] "This may account," according to Rawlinson, "for the influence of Indian ideas upon the development of Greek philosophy." [14]

"It is not too much," says R. Garbe, "to assume that the curious Greek (Pythagoras) who was a contemporary of the Buddha, and, it may be, of Zoroaster, too, would have acquired

12. Inge, William R., "Neo-Platonism," in *Encyclopedia of Religion and Ethics*, ed. James Hastings, Clark, Edinburgh, 1908–1926.

13. Rapson, E.J. ed., *Ancient India, The Cambridge History of India, Volume 1*, Cambridge, 1922, pp. 87–88

14. Rawlinson, H.G., "India in European Literature and Thought," in *The Legacy of India*, by G. T. Garratt, The Clarendon Press, Oxford, 1937, p. 4

a more or less exact knowledge of the East, in that intellectual age of fermentation, through the medium of Persia. It must be remembered in this connection that the Asiatic Greeks, at the time when Pythagoras still dwelt in his Ionian home, were under the single sway of Cyrus, the founder of the Persian Empire."[15]

"Herodotus, like Plato and others, attributes all wisdom to Egyptian sources ... The Greeks were deeply impressed by the great antiquity of Egyptian civilization, its lofty temples, and its closely guarded religious mysteries ... Unfortunately, it is extremely doubtful whether the Egyptians did actually believe in transmigration ... It is more likely that Pythagoras was influenced by India (re transmigration) than by Egypt. Almost all the theories—religious, philosophical and mathematical—taught by the Pythagoreans were known in India in the sixth century BCE, and Pythagoreans, like the Jains and the Buddhists, refrained from the destruction of life ..."[16]

"Alexandria in the first century CE was the second city in the Empire. In the height of her glory, she must have resembled Venice in the full tide of her prosperity. The mercantile shipping of half the ancient world tied up at her quaysides, and scholars from the four quarters of the earth met and disputed in the Museum and made use of the vast stores of literature in her great libraries. The Alexandrians were essentially cosmopolitan. They had none of the contempt for the 'barbarians' of the old Greek states, and a large proportion of the population, like the Athenians, 'spent their life in nothing else, but either to tell or hear some new thing.' A Buddhist monk from Barygaza would receive the same attentive hearing as did St. Paul at the hands of the Areopagus, and the medium was Hellenistic Greek, *lingua franca* from the Levant to the Indus. The *Milindapañhā* mentions Alexandria as one of the places to which Indian merchants regularly resorted, and Dio Chrysostom, lecturing to an Alexandrian audience in the reign of Trajan, says: "I see among you, not only Greeks and Italians, Syrians, Libyans, and Cilicians, and men who dwell more remotely, Ethiopians and Arabs, but also Bactrians, Scythians, Persians, and some of the

15. Ibid, note (Probably from *The Philosophy of Ancient India*, by Richard Garbe, The Open Court Publishing Company, Chicago 1897)

16. Rawlinson, op. cit., p. 5

Indians, who are among the spectators, and are always residing there."[17]

"Indian philosophy was acquiring a growing reputation in the Hellenistic schools of Asia Minor and Egypt."[18]

Apollonius of Tyana had visited India and conversed with Buddhists and Brahmans on a great many things and had, with those ideas got from India, changed the outlook of the Neo-Pythagoreans. Bardesanes is said to have learned many things from the Indians. He was a Gnostic teacher. He knew much about monastic life in Buddhism.

Plotinus was a fellow-student of Origen, the saintly scholar in the school of Ammonius Saccas. Of Origen, it is said that he possessed "a mind characteristic of supreme genius, the mind which anticipates the richest thought of today. He was blameless in life, unrivalled in knowledge, a pioneer in every department of study, the teacher of all that was best in the Eastern Church." It was this Origen whose teaching on the "pre-existence of souls'' was anathematized at the Second Council at Constantinople, in 533 CE. Origen believed that rebirth was "determined by its (the soul's) previous merits and demerits" (*De Principili*). He must have known what Buddhist tenets were on this subject, and Plotinus, his friend, could not have been ignorant of those tenets either. In fact, it was his great desire to know what Brahmanism and Buddhism were, stimulated perhaps by what he had already learned of them in Alexandria, that made him go with Gordian's expedition to Persia in 242 CE.

According to Max Muller, the school of Plotinus paid a great deal of attention to Eastern religions. Plotinus' idea was to revive the old religion of the Roman Empire with the addition of what appealed to him in the inspired teachings of the world. That is why, perhaps, the Buddhist-Upanishadic thought in Neo-Platonism is sometimes expressed in a strange way, though their significance is easy enough to grasp for the Buddhist. Neo-Platonism is a mosaic of Eastern and Western ideas. It is not something monolithic like Buddhism.

17. Ibid, p. 17
18. Ibid, p. 18

The closeness of Plotinian thought to the idealism of the Mahāyāna is seen in the following extract from a letter of Plotinus:

> "External objects present us only with appearances. Concerning them, therefore, we may be said to possess opinion rather than knowledge. The distinctions in the actual world of appearance are of import only to ordinary and practical men. Our question lies with the ideal reality that exists behind appearance. How does the mind perceive these ideas? Are they without us, and is reason, like sensation, occupied with objects external to itself? What certainty could we then have, what assurance, that our perception was infallible? The object perceived would be something different from the mind perceiving it. We should then have an image instead of reality. It would be monstrous to believe for a moment that the mind was unable to perceive ideal truth exactly as it is, and that we had no certainty and real knowledge concerning the world of intelligence. It follows, therefore, that this region of truth is not to be investigated as a thing outward to us and so only imperfectly known. It is within us. Here the objects we contemplate and that which contemplates are identical—both are thought. The subject cannot surely know an object different from itself. The world of ideas lies within our intelligence. Truth, therefore, is not the agreement of our apprehension of an external object with the object itself. It is the agreement of mind with itself. Consciousness is the sole basis of certainty. The mind is its own witness. Reason sees in itself that which is above itself as its source; and that which is below itself as still itself once more."[19]

The divisions of knowledge which Plotinus makes are interesting to the Buddhist. The first is opinion, the second science, and the third illumination: The first is explained as that which is gained by means of the senses. It is perception (*pratyaksa*); the second refers to inference (*anumāna*); and the third, insight

---

19. Plotinus, *Letters to Flaccus*, quoted in *Tertium Organum: The Third Canon of Thought, a Key to the Enigmas of the World*, by P. D. Ouspensky, translated from the Russian by Nicholas Bessaraboff and Claude Bragdon, Manas Press, Rochester, New York, 1920

(*avabodha*). Reason has to be subordinated to the last knowledge mentioned here. It is the absolute or final knowledge founded on the identity of mind-that-knows and the object perceived. He also speaks of evolution (*saṃvaṭṭana*) and involution (*vivaṭṭana*). How can we know the Infinite? Not by the reasoning process. Reason's business is to distinguish and define. Only by a faculty superior to reason can one apprehend the Infinite.

That can be done by entering into a state in which one is no more in a finite state. That state is the state of ecstasy (*jhāna*) or full absorption. By entering that state one becomes free of finite anxieties. Ecstasy is not a frequent occurrence even in Plotinus' case. There are different ways to ecstasy. They are: the love of beauty which exalts the poet; devotion to just one thing; the assent of science to the philosophical thinker; and, lastly, love and contemplation or prayer by which a devout soul in its moral purity tends towards perfection. The soul neither comes into being nor perishes; "nothing that possesses real being can ever perish." But souls that have lived wrongly will be reincarnated in the bodies of lower animals. The mystical ascent appears as "a progressive stripping off of everything alien to the purest nature of the soul" which cannot enter into the holy of holies while any trace of worldliness clings to it. It is called "a flight of the alone to the alone."

Plotinus gives many descriptions of the mystical trance, but he thinks that the trance is really ineffable. The vision of the One is an exceedingly rare happening. It is to be earned only by intense contemplation and unceasing self-discipline.

The ethical scheme is threefold: purification, enlightenment and unification. Good citizenship is the prelude to the course. In this system, as in Buddhism and a few other Indian systems, there is neither mediator nor redeemer.

There is nothing to prove that the teaching of Plato was founded on a system of meditation practice or *yoga* for the penetration of actuality. But Plotinus was out and out a yogi and is nearer to Buddhism than to Platonism in the higher stages of his doctrine. To ascribe the *yogic* portion of Plotinus' system, as Dr. Inge does, to the innate dualities of Platonism would require a good deal of text-torture. Neoplatonism is clearly an eclecticism; many non-Platonic elements are in it, and, among those elements, Buddhism is not negligible.[20]

The resemblances between the life of the Buddha and that of Christ have been pointed out to be too close to be casual and appear, on the other hand, to be remarkably striking, thinks H. S. Gour. Among the items he gives, the following are of importance: miraculous conception and virgin birth; Asita and Simeon; the temptation of *Māra* and the temptation of the devil; the widow's mite and the story of the poor maid, told in Aṣvaghosa's *Sutrālaṅkāra*; the Samaritan woman and Ānanda at the well; the man born blind and the blind man in the Lotus of the Good Law; the transfiguration and the effulgence that emanated from the Master's body twice during his lifetime; and the miracle of the loaves and fishes and the story in Jātaka No. 79.[21]

There is no dearth of passages in the New Testament which resemble parts of the Pāli Canon. One cannot read the Sermon on the Mount without feeling that it is an abridged version of parts of the *Dhammapada*. That is, as regards orthodox Catholic and Protestant Christian scriptures. But the position of Gnostic Christian writings is one of still closer affinity to the scriptures and traditions of Buddhism.

When we leave the domain of religion proper and pass on to the territories of art and architecture, history, drama, ethics, philosophy and social organization traceable to Buddhist influences, we find that the Order of Monks which the Buddha established was something new to India and the world. "The Buddha created a new race of men, a race of moral heroes, a race of salvation-workers, a race of Buddhas,"[22] writes Manmatha Nath Shastri. By this, the Buddha gave to the world a new conception of building up society on the basis of renunciation. "It appears," says Oldenberg, "from the very beginning to have been a society

---

20. Cf. "Neoplatonism" in *Encyclopedia of Religion and Ethics* and *Encyclopaedia Britannica* and "Plotinus" in *Encyclopaedia Britannica*

21. Gour, Sir Hari Singh, *The Spirit of Buddhism*, Luzac & Co., London, 1929, p. 435f

22. Shastri, Manmatha Nath, op. cit., p .236

governed by law."[23] There, however, was nothing coercive at the back of the law which governed the Order. It was a society that kept its laws voluntarily and which held together in friendliness for the one purpose of equipping itself for the realization of the highest good of all. That Order indeed was a power when it functioned peacefully. The power was not the property of any single person but of the body taken together. It was a great republic. The voice of the Order was a voice that got obeyed without compulsion. As a civilizing force, Buddhism has tamed the wild races and refined the tamed. The great epochs of Buddhist history, from the days of Rājagaha to that of Lhasa, have been fruitful in a lasting way.

The great architectural monuments in the form of Dagobas and monasteries and shrines, though now mostly in ruins, have still a message to the world of what can be done by men with very limited resources if only they become steady of purpose.

The beautiful statues and sculptures, the paintings and decorations that have come to us from the past, whether they be Indian, Indonesian, Chinese, Japanese, Korean, Tibetan or Mongolian, are largely witnesses of the achievements of a fortunate cycle of Buddhist history. One of those favoured periods when culture got an upward urge so far as the Buddhists were concerned, was in "the early Middle Ages, about the 7th century of our era," writes Grousset. Darkness brooded over our Western civilization which as yet guessed nothing of the approaching Romance dawn, and even extended to Byzantium where the great 'Macedonian' basileus had not yet arisen. But away in the Far East, India and China were living with an intense political, intellectual, religious and artistic life. Buddhism, in bringing them into contact with one another, had created a vast current of humanism, from Sri Lanka to the furthest isles of the Japanese archipelago. The withering of Islam, the decline of Neo-Confucianism, and the retrogression of Hinduism, which were, unfortunately, close at hand, had not yet made themselves felt. After a thousand years of meditation, Buddhist mysticism had attained to undreamed of psychic states, and Indian aesthetics had received a fresh impression from them. In China which was hospitable to new ideas and ready for innovations, Chinese force allowed itself to be softened by this gentle influence. The human spirit lived there a privileged hour, worthy of Athens or

23. Ibid, quotation

Alexandria. It was the time of the Chinese epic in Central Asia, and of the great pilgrimages to the Holy Land of the Ganges, the time of Mahāyanist idealism and the plastic art of the Gupta dynasty."[24]

The achievements in the field of learning belong to the Buddhists, through the establishment of first-class universities—at Taxilā (Takkasilā in Pali), an old educational centre; at Nālandā, where at one time there were 10,000 students of philosophy and medicine; at Vikramasīlā; at Odantapuri and at Buddha Gayā.

To the credit of the Buddhists, too, stand gigantic works of irrigation, tanks like the Kalāveva, and Minneriya of Sri Lanka, the building of arterial roads, the erection of rest-houses, and the putting under cultivation of large areas below the tanks–noteworthy acts of merit done on the "weal and happiness of all principle" of Buddhism.

The part which Buddhists played in the development of art in the India of historical times was of basic importance for the growth of Indian and Eastern spirituality. Grunwedel writes, "The art of ancient India has always been a purely religious one; its architecture, as well as the sculpture which has always been intimately connected therewith, was never employed for secular purposes. It owed its origin to the growth of a religion which has been called, in Europe, Buddhism from the honorary title of its founder, the Buddha, the Enlightened One."[25]

The Buddhists were the first historians of India. The history of one's religion, if rightly studied, can be a great help in steadying one's confidence in the Teaching and in oneself. It can also stimulate endeavour on vigorous lines for one's own and others' welfare. Further, history is nothing but the actual occurrence of change in a tangible form, in the lives of individuals, races and nations. The *Arahat* leaders of the early Buddhist Sangha realized these facts and led the way in recording the incidents connected with the rise and spread of the Buddha's doctrine. This early lead given in the *Tripitaka* was zealously taken up by the later commentators and

24. Grousset, Rene, *In The Footsteps of the Buddha*, translated from the French by Mariette Leon, George Routledge & Sons, Ltd., London, 1932, p. ix

25. Grunwedel, Albert, *Buddhist Art in India*, Translated from German by A.C. Gibson; Revised and Enlarged by James Burgess, Bernard Quaritch, London, 1901, p. 1

scholars in almost every Buddhist country, and there are many books now of the history of the religion. The writing of secular history too received an impulse through this Buddhist custom of recording things, and people became history-minded.

The oldest writing of the historical period in India now extant is the inscription on the *Piprāva* vase containing relics of the Master, which were enshrined by the Master's relatives in a relic mound. The inscription runs thus:

> Sukitibhatinaṃ sabhagiṇikanaṃ saputadalanaṃ iyaṃ salila-nidhane Budhase bhagavate sakiyanaṃ.
>
> "This container of relics of the Blessed One, the Buddha of the Sakyas, (is the gift) of the brothers, Sukiti, jointly with their sisters, children and wives."

The first royal renunciation of war in the annals of mankind is that of the Emperor Asoka, the follower of the Buddha. The first great capital cities of India in historical times were Rājagaha, Pātaliputta, Purusāpura, all connected closely with Buddhism.

Anuradhapura, Polonnaruwa, Loyang, Chang'an, Nara, Lhasa and other centres of Buddhist culture in the past are enough evidence to show the vitality of the Buddhist spirit at its best. There is every reason to believe that the idea of impermanence which has become the cornerstone of the fabric of modern scientific thought got its greatest affirmation and became widely current as a philosophic principle through the emphasis laid on it by the Buddhists. And in India, at least, the Buddhists were the first to read history as the confirmation of the Law of Transience and to value history as a means of passing on to the future the gains of the past, a factor so very necessary to keep up a high and noble tradition like the Buddhas. History, in the first sense, is just the arising and passing away of phenomena in actual practice; in the second sense, a record of the changes.

How things arise and how they pass away constitutes the kernel of all history. Though the idea of impermanence was already there in India and the West, it was the Buddha who brought out its full meaning through the formulation of the hidden truth of *anattā*, connected with the Law of Transience. By that discovery of his, he made the very fact of the fleetingness of life the basis for becoming better.

The Buddha laid hold of the fact of the fluxional nature of all things—the essence of history—and on the crest of that active conception of life as movement, passed on the waves of changing phenomena to the changeless Nibbāna. He went across the waves of suffering to the sorrowless.

Here, the Buddha is truly like a great physician, for he, like a doctor who makes people proof against a disease by the inoculation of a serum of the very kind of germs that cause that disease, introduces into the minds of those who wish to be suffering-free, the very concept of suffering, prepared in the form of the *kammaṭṭhāna*, the subject of meditation, and lets it work there till they become immune to suffering once and for all.

Like the Himālayas, say our books, is the Buddha; like the medicinal plants growing on the mountain slopes is the Dharma; and like the people treated with those medicinal plants and cured is the Ariya Sangha, the Order of the Saints.

Before the rise of Buddhism, Indian medical knowledge consisted largely in treatment with the charms and spells of the *Atharvaveda*. That was the first period of Indian medicine. With Jīvaka Komārabhacca, the greatest physician at the time of the Buddha, and the Master's own doctor who had a reputation as a specialist for children's diseases too, was ushered in the historical period of Indian medicine. He had studied at Taxilā for seven years.

"Very great improvement in medicine and surgery took place in the Buddhist period in India, because the religion of the Buddha insists on the alleviation of suffering as an important item of Buddhistic faith, and, hence, hospitals for the treatment of men and beasts alike were built in almost all the monasteries (universities) of Buddhistic India. Inscriptions engraved on rocks, pillars, etc. describe prescriptions for the treatment of diseases."[26]

The oldest and best medical treatise of India, the *Caraka Saṃhitā*, was the work of the Buddhist physician of King Kaniṣka. The *Suśruta* which we have today is not the work of the Hindu physician, but his work recast by the famous Buddhist patriarch,

26. Ray, P.C., in *The Cultural Heritage of India*, The Ramakrishna Mission, Calcutta, 1937, Vol. III, p. 445

Nāgārjuna, founder of the Madhyamika Philosophy. Of the *Caraka Saṃhitā* P. C. Ray says, "On reading the *Caraka*, one often feels as if it embodied the deliberations of an international congress of medical experts held in the Himālayan regions."[27] Of the three *Rsis* of Indian medicine, two are Buddhist—Caraka and Vāgbhaṭa. The high state of development reached by Indian medical science of today seems to date, in the main, from the Buddhist times, according to J. Jolly.

On the philosophical side, Buddhists have produced great names like Nāgārjuna, Asaṅga, Dignāga, and Dharmakirti. In the Far East, too, there were many sound scholars like Tientai and Kukai, who arose under the care of Buddhist institutions.

To the Buddhists, modern democracy owes its parliamentary procedure. Says the Marquess of Zetlund, "It may come as a surprise to many to learn that in the Assemblies of the Buddhists in India two thousand years and more ago are to be found the rudiments of our own parliamentary practice of the present day."[28]

There were many advances made in the forms of local government. These can be seen by a study of the ancient inscriptions, especially, of Sri Lanka.

Without exceeding the space allotted to the writer, he cannot even lightly mention the achievements of the Buddhists in the field of literature, drama and philosophy, on which the Buddhists clearly left their seal. Buddhism has influenced in these matters not only the ancient but the modern world too. The number of works in the West into which the Buddhist spirit has entered is very large.

And then there is the record of the monks and nuns of the Buddhist Sangha who travelled to distant lands, braving all dangers for the purpose of spreading the sweet peace-giving message of the Buddha, and died far from their homelands, happy in the consciousness that they had done their bit. Their lives and endeavours were pure and perfect. Theirs was one of the best contributions to the world's culture. Even the thought of those wonderful servants of the world can rouse in us the resolve to do as they did; to live, think and work "for the gain of the many, for the welfare of the many, in compassion for the world."

---

27. Ibid, p. 444

28. Rawlinson, op. cit., Introduction

Escape to Reality

Buddhist Essays

by

Ānanda Pereira

WHEEL PUBLICATION NO. 45/46

Life or Death?

By his own deeds the fool is consumed, as by a fire.

Dhammapada

In an address delivered at Oslo, when he was awarded the Noble Prize for Peace, that great humanitarian, Dr. Albert Schweitzer, spoke for all humanity when he said: "Let us face the facts. Man has become a superman. Not only has he innate physical forces at his command but, thanks to science and to technical advancement, he controls the latent forces of nature. But this superman suffers from a fatal imperfection. He has not raised himself to that superhuman level of reason which should correspond to the possession of superhuman strength." This is the Great Show-down. The latent forces of nature, which man now controls, will destroy man as readily as they will serve him. They are mindless and efficient, like a razor: It is for man to decide whether to shave—or cut his throat. The razor does not care. It waits, supremely indifferent. Can we raise ourselves to that superhuman level of reason necessary for our survival on this planet? Are we mature enough to realise that we cannot destroy each other any longer without destroying ourselves? A lot depends on the answers to these questions. They will make all the difference between a common home and a common cemetery.

We cannot help feeling that the scientists, with their technical advances, have thrust this problem on humanity too soon. The big decisions are not in the hands of the most mature, as they should be. Great wisdom, or what Dr. Schweitzer calls a "superhuman level," is not manifest in the public utterances of those who wield political power. At times the thinking man is aghast at the childish things the leaders say. Some of them still seem to think in terms of cavalry charges, fortresses, and waving banners when they speak of war. They still talk of war as a way of "making the world safe" for this, that or the other ideology. They seem to forget that if there is another war, on a big scale, such survivors as are left will not have time to bother with ideologies. It will be a big, dead, poisoned world, and men will have more pressing things to think about.

"All worldlings are mad," said the Buddha,[1] and we may well accept this as the simple truth. If we ever doubt it, we need only open a newspaper or switch on the radio. In whatever country the newspaper is printed, from whatever country the broadcast comes, the proof is as convincing. Nice bold type, nice clear voices, telling us in unmistakable terms that we human beings are doing everything except think. But now we *must* think. It is easy to turn away from this problem, of the survival of humanity, and seek refuge in some mental or physical dope. But this is no solution. We *must* face the facts. Humanity must grow up or perish. It must grow up fast, or perish fast. There is not much time. We must scrap all ideologies that call for the liquidation of those who do not agree with us. We must abandon the sort of nationalism that regards with distrust and hatred the people of other nations. We must think of ourselves henceforth as human beings, sharing one world. We must begin *now* or it will be too late.

How can we attain this maturity of mind? The Buddha taught the way, more than 2500 years ago. He spoke to individuals, to thinking individuals, but his message holds good for all humanity. He said, "All things are subject to change. Do not grasp. Let go- and be free."

There has never been a war but arose from greed for land, greed for trade, greed for power, greed for all the transient phenomena of life, leading inevitably to strife. Let go, and strife ceases. Think of the other fellow as a human being, with nothing to gain except your common weal, and strife ceases. Help him, and you help yourself. It does not matter what language he speaks, what political opinions he holds. You share the same planet, breathe the same air, need the same food. You cannot destroy him and survive. Your fate is linked with his.

Are You Grown-up?

If, by renouncing some slight happiness,
one may behold a larger one,
Let the wise man renounce the smaller,
considering the greater.

Dhammapada

The capacity to renounce a small, immediate happiness in order to secure some greater, more distant happiness is a mark of maturity. Few children have it, and those who do are really more mature than many adults. It means clear vision, sound judgment, and self-control, all of which are signs of a truly adult mind.

Many people go through life without ever growing up. They find it impossible to resist the temptation of immediate pleasures. Under the wise guidance and control of some mentally older person, they may forego such pleasures and pursue a line of action which yields greater happiness in the long run. But it is not of their own independent choice. Given the necessary opportunity and freedom to decide for themselves, they will fritter away their time and energy in the pursuit of the moment's pleasures, letting the future look after itself.

For such people, a theistic religion is a great help. It serves as a steadying and guiding influence. They are like children who need a wise parent, a parent who rewards virtue and punishes vice, who encourages honest endeavour and discourages laziness.

But, as Ingersoll once said, in nature are no rewards or punishments. There are only consequences. A man who plants a fruit tree, tends it carefully, and waits patiently, is not "rewarded" when at last it bears fruit. He may die before that happens, or the fruit may be indigestible for him because of some change in his personal chemistry. But the fruit appears all the same, not in order to reward him but because that is the way of nature. It is the same when a man trains a puppy badly and it grows up into a surly dog. The dog may or may not bite him, and if it does happen, it will not be a "punishment." It will merely be a consequence of bad training.

To the Buddhist, *all* phenomena are consequences, including all personal phenomena. However pleasant or painful they may be, he does not regard them as the rewards or punishments dispensed by some Supreme Being. He accepts them as the results of his own kamma, his own past actions and thoughts. He stands on his own feet and moulds his own destiny, in this and in future lives. It is a religion for adults. For this very reason, it does not appeal to those who lack mental maturity. It is too free, too unsheltered, but, to the mature, it is the only reasonable and acceptable way of life.

Accepting this doctrine of personal responsibility, the Buddhist faces life fairly and squarely. He can pursue the slight happiness offered by the world of the senses, or, if he has clear vision, sound judgment, and self-control, he can forego such happiness and seek something infinitely higher. What is this "something"? It is mental progress, clearer and ever clearer vision, sounder and ever sounder judgment, greater and ever greater mastery over self, until at last, as an Arahat, he reaches the very zenith of mental evolution and attains Nibbāna. *This* is the Way taught by all the Buddhas.

It is not an easy road or a short one. Most of us have far to go. But we must all go on that road sometime, and the sooner we start, the sooner we will reach the Goal. Let us not wait for many more lifetimes before we start. Let us not fool ourselves that if we wait patiently, trusting in some Supreme Being, our reward will be eternal bliss. Let us not hang about, like grubby children, expecting a parent or governess to wash us, undress us, and tuck us safely into bed. If we do, we shall wait indefinitely.

The Ready Ones

You yourselves must make an effort,
The Tathāgatas are only teachers.
The meditative ones who enter the Way
Are delivered from the bonds of Māra.

Dhammapada

In our last essay we said that Buddhism is a religion for mental adults. It does not sugarcoat the bitter pills of life or pretend that death is the gateway to everlasting happiness. It does not promise easy salvation in exchange for unquestioning faith in some supreme deity. It teaches self-reliance and a sense of personal responsibility.

No teacher, however wise and kind, can help those who refuse to learn. By fulfilling the ten *pāramī,* or perfections, a being who aspires to be a Buddha develops the qualities necessary to become an unrivalled teacher of gods and men. He is not "atoning" thereby for the wickedness and folly of others, although he sacrifices life itself, again and again, during this period of preparation. Nobody, however noble-minded, can atone for the faults of others. One can only improve oneself. In the case of a being striving for Buddhahood, this process of self-improvement goes far beyond the level sufficient for purely personal salvation. He wishes to help others as well. But he can only do so by teaching them how to help themselves. There is no salvation by proxy.

This may sound a hard teaching, but it is a reasonable one and it fits into the pattern of life as we know it. One cannot eat for another or learn swimming for another or keep healthy for another. Nor can one "atone" for the wickedness and folly of another. Each must pay his own debts and shape his own destiny. Even Buddhas can only show the way.

A Buddha, also called a Tathāgata, is a teacher in the truest and highest sense of the word. One cannot place a limit to the value of such a teacher. Life after life, through countless aeons, beings live in darkness. They cling to this false belief and to that. They live, die and live again, on and on, now in states of pleasure, now in states of pain. But they *do not* know how to win freedom from it all. Then, like the dawning of a glorious day, a Buddha appears. He teaches the Way of Freedom. Some leap to this Teaching and profit by it immediately. They are the ready ones, like the great Arahants of the Buddha's day. For them, a single stanza, a phrase, a word, may sufficient. Others take longer to learn. Still others do not learn at all. They are as unprepared for the Buddha Dhamma as a kindergarten child is unprepared for the Theory of Relativity.

Who are those ready ones who profit immediately by the appearance of a Buddha? According to the Buddha Himself, they are those who are meditative. Already, on their own, perhaps in many past lives they have trained themselves to think clearly. They have developed their minds. To them, the "effort" of following the Buddha's Teaching is a glad one. They do not yearn after the so-called prizes of life, the wealth, the power, the worldly advancement that others find so alluring. They see much greater worth in such things as peace of mind, contentment, and freedom. They take easily to the Way and are delivered from the bonds of Māra, the bonds of desire, ill-will, and ignorance. They win freedom.

Greatness

Higher than lordship over all earth,
Higher than sojourning in heavens supreme,
Higher than empire over all the worlds,
Is Fruit of Entrance to the Dhamma Stream.

Dhammapada

We worldlings see greatness in worldly success. To us a reigning sovereign is great, a millionaire is great, a famous actor, surgeon, lawyer, or painter is great. We measure greatness by the yardstick of worldly power or fame.

To the Buddha, greatness was something entirely different. He saw beings dying and getting reborn according to their kamma. He knew that an emperor can be reborn as a termite. He saw that, in this world of everlasting change, there is no security in worldly power, no stability in worldly fame. Death comes to the powerful and the famous just as surely as it comes to the weak and unknown. And with death there is a shedding of worldly power, wealth, and fame. Again and again it happens.

Seen against the background of eternal change, there is nothing real in worldly greatness. Even we worldlings can see things in this way if we take the Buddha's Teaching to heart and use our intelligence. But few of us do so. That is why the Buddha said, "Blind is this world. Few are they who truly see."

If, seeing things as they truly are, we refuse to grant that greatness is an attribute of worldly power, fame or success, must we conclude, that there is no such thing as greatness? The Buddha's answer was to point to the Stream-winner, the *sotāpanna,* the being who has attained the first stage of Sainthood, as that term is understood in Buddhism. "There" said the Buddha, "is one who is greater than any reigning sovereign, than any celestial being, be he even a Brahmā." And, be it remembered, there are three higher stages of Sainthood, culminating in the attainment of Final Emancipation as an Arahant.

Why is this? A Sotāpanna may well be a poor man, unhonoured and unknown. By worldly standards he may be a person of no account at all. In what lies his greatness?

His greatness lies in the security of having taken a step upward from which there can be no falling back. Never again will he have the "soul" delusion. Never again will he have doubts as to the true road. Never again will he believe in mere rites and ceremonies. Never again will he break a single one of the five cardinal precepts of Virtue. Never again will he be born in a plane lower than the human. He can be reborn, at most, only seven times more before he attains Nibbāna. He is like one who, having traversed a terrible desert, sees before him the end of the journey: The sand still burns his feet, the sun still blazes down on his head, he is tired and thirsty, but there, within sight, lie the shady trees, the cool ponds of crystal-clear water. He presses on gladly, knowing that soon he will reach his journey's end. Not for anything in the world would such a man change places with one who is wandering, hopelessly lost in the desert. That other may be a wealthy man, richly-dressed, with a large following. But he is to be pitied. He is a long, long way off from "Journey's End."

Power and Freedom

Higher than lordship over all the earth,
Higher than sojourning in heavens supreme.
Higher than empire over all the world
Is Fruit of Entrance to the Dhamma Stream.

Dhammapada

Time and time again in the beginningless succession of existences which is our life in saṃsāra we worldlings have sought power for its own sake. There is some-thing terribly fascinating about the idea of power. We wish to be "big" men. We wish to do "big" things. We wish to exercise control over our environment. Hardly any of us wishes, or attempts, to exercise control over himself.

If a wise man were asked, "What would you do if you were offered dictatorship over all the earth?" he would answer, "Refuse it of course." For the wise do not seek power, nor are they impressed by it. And yet, how many of us are wise? We seek power, imagining that it is the key to happiness. We strive for power, and if we happen to get it, we generally abuse it.

The wise seek dominance only over themselves, realising that therein lies the key to freedom. "Fruit of Entrance to the Dhamma Stream" is the first stage of sanctity, as taught by the Buddha. It is the threshold of freedom. The Stream-winner (*sotāpanna*) is beyond the reach of worldly ambition. He has done, once and for all, with the desire for worldly power.

Politicians, every one of whom is at heart a power seeker, sometimes talk of "freedom" as though it were a commodity that can be bought with votes or won in the bloody gamble of a revolution. But there is no such thing as mass-deliverance into freedom, and there never will be, whatever politicians may tell us. Humanity in the mass is fit only for what it already has, and just at present that looks like the brink of hell. Humanity in the mass may, and very likely will, plunge over the brink and suffer consequences, for a while. It has happened before and can happen again, for that is the endless story of human stupidity.

But, for the individual, there is always the opportunity to seek freedom. That was the glorious truth taught by the Buddha, and it still holds good. Freedom is not the fruit of worldly power. It is the fruit of virtue and concentration, leading to insight.

On this road of deliverance, power too comes as a by-product, a strange new power such as worldlings never dream of. But that is not the goal It is merely a sign of progress made, an encouragement to further effort. Freedom is the one and only goal. The Buddha had such power in incalculable measure, and so too did many of the arahants. They used it wisely and kindly, to help others, never to exercise dominance over them.

Generosity

They are not perished among the dead who,
Like good comrades travelling on
The jungle roads, share scanty store.
Lo! here's an ancient truth.

Saṃyutta Nikāya

Generosity is something more than giving. It is in the heart that one is generous. It springs from a feeling of comradeship, and it manifests itself in countless different ways. It is bigness of mind.

Patronage is not generosity. In generosity there is no condescension on the part of the giver or servility on the part of the receiver. It is clean and wholesome, and it leaves both parties free.

Springing as it does from a feeling of comradeship generosity goes hand in hand with sympathy. The generous person is tactful. When he hears someone tell a good story in convivial company, he does not try to cap it with a better one immediately and thereby rob the other fellow of his due share of attention. Even in giving, he is tactful. If a poor friend gives his son a cheap camera, he does not immediately buy the boy an expensive camera which will probably eclipse the earlier gift.

It is not only with material possessions that we can be generous. We can be generous with our knowledge, our skill, our energy, our time. We can also be generous in the things we think and say about others: It is easy enough to be generous in the opinions we express about those whose interests do not clash with ours and who are not in competition with us. Thus, a lawyer will readily praise a good architect or doctor or sculptor, but, as a rule, he will be much more cautious and reserved in his praise of another lawyer.

We can be generous also in our attitude towards malicious gossip. There are people who count themselves generous but who are ready to believe all the nasty things they hear about others, even their friends. They pounce eagerly on every bit of malicious gossip and pass it on, adding to it in the process. Such people cannot be truly generous. Deep down in their hearts they are mean and small. Their acts of so-called generosity are nothing more than investments, to secure the goodwill and help of others in this life and rich dividends in future lives.

When a truly generous person gives something to another, be it material help or time or information, there are no strings attached to the gift. He does *not* even expect gratitude in return. He has given, and that is the end of the matter so far as he is concerned. So he is never bitter when people, as sometimes happens, take his gifts for granted. He goes on giving. People may think that this sort of thing is unfair to the giver, but that would be a wrong view. The giver is going his own road, growing stronger and freer with each gift. If others selfishly exploit his generosity, they too are going their own road, growing weaker and less free with each act of exploitation. It is because of past deeds of one sort or the other that some people are born to wealth and freedom while others are born to poverty and slavery. We lose nothing by being generous. We gain nothing by selfishly exploiting the generosity of others.

The world would be a dark and bleak place indeed if nobody were generous. There would be no Buddha-Dhamma, for the Buddha-Dhamma is the highest manifestation of generosity, the Buddha's gift to all humanity, the gift of truth, of light, of freedom.

Praise and Blame

As a solid rock is not shaken by the wind;
Even so the wise are not ruffled by praise or blame.

Dhammapada

These words apply in their fullest sense to Arahants, but to a certain extent they are true of all wise people. Such people are not easily influenced by the praise or blame of the world. They think for themselves and go their own road.

It may be laid down as a general rule that one is seldom praised or blamed by the world for the intrinsic nature of one's actions. Take the case of a lawyer. The world at large is unable to form any opinion of his ability except by the results he produces. He may be intelligent and industrious, but, if he is unlucky enough to lose a few cases in succession, the world is apt to take a poor view of his capacity. On the other hand, if he wins a few cases that catch the public eye, his stock rises appreciably. It is the same in most fields of human endeavour.

Those with a weak character tend to accept this state of affairs without question, and to act accordingly. They crave worldly success and they work to achieve it. They know that the world cares little for genuine worth. So they buy their success with counterfeit currency as it were. They pretend to be interested in what the world at large finds interesting. They pretend to like people who can help them. They are seen at the right places, wearing the right clothes, doing the right things. And it works. The counterfeit currency is seldom examined closely or challenged. But such people never rise to be leaders, even in the sphere of worldly activities. They do not have what it takes. To be a leader, one must have the strength to walk alone at times. One must have a mind of one's own.

Of course, obstinacy is not strength. One can prevent an obstinate person from doing almost anything by commanding him not to do it. The strong do not respond to such tactics. They do not care whether others think them strong and independent or weak and docile, so they always do exactly as they choose, even when curtly ordered to do it! There is freedom in such strength.

Most of us are influenced far too much by what we think other people will think of us. We judge others by our own standards. If we are impressed by certain qualities, such as smartness, a sense of humour, or courage, we assume that others too are impressed by those qualities. So we pretend to have them. Pretence means strain, because we dare not relax and be natural for fear of being exposed for what we really are. We strain to resemble some ideal, instead of admitting frankly that it is an ideal and that we are far below it, and that we are working towards it.

The wise have a basic honesty which scorns all pretense. Therein lies their strength, and their ability to remain comparatively unmoved by praise or blame. They have ideals too, but instead of pretending to be the personification of those ideals, they work towards them with faith and patience. If the world happens to praise them, they are not unduly elated. If the world happens to blame them, they are not unduly depressed. They assess such praise or blame calmly and intelligently, questioning the competence of those who pass judgment, accepting nothing at face value. Having so assessed and questioned, they see their way clearly. Sometimes praise or blame is well-deserved and can be a useful guide. But this is not always the case. If praise or blame is undeserved, it should be ignored, just as a sane man ignores the compliments or insults of a lunatic.

Anger

Whoso, his anger, arisen like an uncontrolled chariot, checks,
Him indeed I call a charioteer. Rein-holders are other folk.

Dhammapada

All of us can recall occasions when we were angry. It is an emotion which we share with the rest of the animal kingdom, except perhaps animals like jelly-fish, slugs and worms, and for all we know even they may be furious on occasion. The world we live in is far from perfect. Things happen which, we feel, would not happen if others only were a little more intelligent and considerate, a little less greedy and selfish. When such things happen, the horse of anger takes charge of the chariot of personality, and we are well set for a period of sub-human behaviour.

It is easy to give one's anger a loose rein and let it gallop. It is easy to make it gallop faster and faster with flicks from the whip of self-righteousness. If the mad career does not end in a smash, the runaway horse tires and slows down after a while, the chariot resumes its normal rate of progress, and the charioteer feels a bit foolish. There has been, perhaps, nothing worse than an exhibition of bad manners.

But all too often such mad careers do end in smashes. In Lanka, land of the Buddha Dhamma, a depressingly large number of people are killed in quarrels every year. A striking feature of these offences is that in most cases the motive seems ridiculously inadequate. A fancied slight at a wedding party, a delay in the repayment of a small debt, a dispute over the ownership of a tree or even a fruit—such things as these have sufficed as the motive for brutal murders. Why is this?

Clearly, it is not the gravity of the motive that matters, but the character of the person concerned. If a man is childish, if he lacks a sense of humour and sense of proportion, which are really the same thing, any minor annoyance can send him along the road that ends on the gallows. The Buddha Dhamma offers people a peerless method for the building of a strong, wise, kindly character. Why is it that so many people in Buddhist lands do not have that sort of character? It must be that they have not understood the Buddha's Teaching. They call themselves Buddhists. They take part in religious ceremonies. They listen to the Dhamma upon occasion. But that Dhamma has not soaked into them and permeated them with its coolness and sanity. They are like children, happy, generous, and truly lovable at times, but horrible little brutes whenever something sends them into a tantrum. In such black moments they behave as though the Buddha had never lived, never given to humanity His message of love and understanding.

We who are mere worldlings cannot pretend to that mastery over self which was characteristic of the Buddha and the Arahants. To us, anger is a problem. But there are things we can do. There are ways of thinking which make the control of anger less difficult. To begin with, we should understand that the failure to control anger is always a sign of weakness, never a *sign of strength.* We all like to be considered strong and masterful. Anger, when it takes charge of us, does make us feel stronger and more masterful than we do normally. But this is a mere delusion, misleading and dangerous. In truth, we are, at such times, weaker and less efficient than normal. A clever boxer, if he knows that his opponent has a quick temper, will do his best to provoke a fit of temper, *because it makes his opponent more vulnerable.* Whenever we get angry we should realize that the strength we feel is not the strength of the charioteer in us. It is the strength of the runaway horse. We should immediately try to put the charioteer back in control. If we can do this, we are masters. If we cannot, we are slaves.

It is also important to reflect that nothing ever matters half so much as we think it does. There are people who take themselves so seriously that they seem to be in a state of *rigor mortis* while still alive. Such people should realize that their occasional exhibitions of bad temper are not nearly as impressive as they imagine. A man in a temper looks ugly and may even be dangerous, but he is too funny to be impressive. The wise man learns to laugh at himself at times. If he cannot, others will.

Eating

What is the one?
All beings are dependent on food.

Khuddakapāṭha

This is the first of the ten sets of questions and answers which every *sāmaṇera* (novice monk) has to learn. It is the basic truth about all living beings. From the greatest to the smallest, the highest to the lowest, all beings depend on nourishment. Stripped to its bare essence, life is a process of eating and of avoiding being eaten.

If a drop of water from any wayside ditch is examined under a powerful microscope, the truth becomes evident. One sees beings, amazingly tiny beings, each an individual, each preoccupied and actively engaged in the business of keeping alive. And what is that business? Eating and avoiding being eaten. In such an examination one may see a fight as fierce and as startling as between a shark and an octopus. One of these infinitesimally tiny beings seizes another. The other struggles to escape. There is a furious commotion, a wriggling and squirling, pauses for rest and resumptions of violence until, inevitably, the weaker is overcome and eaten by the stronger.

This process goes on continually, in every drop of water that is not sterile, in every cubic millimetre of soil that harbours animal life. Higher up the scale of life, in the visible world, the struggle goes on with unabated violence. On the land, in the water, in the air, living beings are eating and being eaten every minute, every second.

In this picture such things as kindness and gentleness are so rare as to be virtually non-existent. When the business of living, of keeping alive, lies entirely in eating and avoiding being eaten, kindness and gentleness are suicidal qualities. A gentle amoeba will not survive very long, except as the pleasant memory of a less gentle amoeba. The same thing is true of a tiger or a shark. *Taṇhā* (craving) is the dominant quality of all living beings. It means, basically, a good appetite. The greedy ones eat more and grow bigger and stronger than the poor eaters. As the risk of being eaten diminishes with the individual's size and strength, the hearty eaters stand a better chance of surviving and breeding than the poor eaters.

This is true of human life as well, though in human life the phenomenon is more complex. In primitive society a big eater has to hunt for his food. He thus has a strong incentive to be a good hunter, and more often than not becomes one. He is generally a good fighter as well and is likely to acquire more wives and breed more children than his weaker brethren. But as society evolves and grows more complex, other qualities come into the picture. Thus a poor eater may have some specialized skill, such as the ability to make things, which gives him a greater earning capacity than a hunter. But in him too the same law operates, and he stands a better chance of survival and reproduction than less capable folk

In human life as lived in highly organized societies, the big eater is replaced by the go-getter, the man who knows what he wants and is smart enough to get it. This too is a sort of eating. Power and fame take the place of food. Such people grow powerful and are held in respect by their fellows. The game of "eat and avoid being eaten" still goes on, but in a wider sense. Instead of food, men crave power, position, wealth, and what are called "good things of life." They fight for these things.

In direct contrast to all this comes the Buddha's Teaching of a process of *letting go* that leads to freedom. He taught the basic truth about all life that is dependent on food, on eating, and avoiding being eaten. But he also taught people the way to win freedom from this obscene activity, this horrible round of birth, decay, old age and death and the recurrent struggle to grab what one needs and hold what one has grabbed. Put very simply, his Teaching is one that stresses *freedom* as the one goal to which the intelligent people should aspire. *All things,* he said, are impermanent, undesirable, certain to pass away utterly, to be got rid of. Cling to nothing whatsoever in this world.

Ritual

Not in mere rites and ceremonies, nor in much learning, nor in the gain of concentration, nor in lonely abode, nor in thinking, "I enjoy the bliss of renunciation resorted to by the non-worldling," should you, O bhikkhu, rest content, without accomplishing the annihilation of ferments.

Dhammapada

Those who do not understand the Buddha Dhamma are sometimes misled by the religious practices of the Buddhist worldling. The offering of flowers at Buddhist shrines, the recurrent "taking" of the Five Precepts by the Buddhist layman, the chanting of *paritta* (recitations of protection), and the salutation of bhikkhus (monks) these and many other practices are pointed to as evidence of a highly ritualistic content in Buddhism.

This is due to lack of understanding. The Buddha has said that, just as there is one taste which permeates every drop of water in the sea, the taste of salt, so there is but one taste which permeates the entirety of his teaching—the taste of deliverance. In the stanza quoted above the Buddha has expressly pointed out that rites and ceremonies do not constitute the be-all and end-all of the way of life taught by him. The "ferments" to be annihilated are the four *āsavas*—longing for sense pleasures, longing for continual existence, false views, and ignorance. When these are annihilated a being wins free from the round of rebirth. On this road, when a being attains the very first stage of Sainthood, he loses all faith in rites and ceremonies. So it will be seen that by no stretch of imagination can Buddhism be called a religion which values ritual for its own sake.

But there is no doubt that for one who is still a worldling, one who has not attained the first stage of Sainthood, rites and ceremonies have a value. Religious ritual is a means to an end. In time of stress it can be an anchor. In time of grief it can be a solace. In time of temptation it can be a reminder that there are higher things in life than the physical appetites.

So the Buddhist offers flowers at the foot of a sacred Bodhi tree or before an image of the Buddha. While doing so he reflects on the perfections of the Incomparable One. He reflects, too, on the impermanence of the flowers he offers. With such thought, his mind grows calm and steadfast. He "takes" the five precepts recurrently, day after day, because he wishes to remind himself of these voluntary observances. He chants, and listens to *paritta* chanting because it is the truth, enshrined in the words of the Buddha himself. He salutes bhikkhus because they and the yellow robe they wear represent the highest way of life possible for a human being. Those are rituals, if one chooses to call them that. But they are not meaningless rituals. They are very definitely a means to an end. Only a superficial and unthinking observer would see a man sharpening an axe and conclude that he does so because he believes there is some ultimate good in the process.

Of course, as with many other helpful things, ritual can assume an undue importance in foolish minds. This must be guarded, or else one will be mistaking the means for the end. But, as indicated by the Buddha, this observation applies not only to ritual but also to vast learning, the attainment of concentration, the solitary life, and the bliss of renunciation. None of these is the end. All these are like rafts that carry one across a river. They are like the timbers of one single raft. When the river is crossed the raft is left behind.

Fear

Beings who see fear in the non-fearsome,
And no fear in the fearsome,
Embrace false views and go to a woeful state.

Dhammapada

According to the Buddha, there is only one thing of which we need to be afraid and of this, unfortunately, most worldlings are not afraid. It is the doing of evil. Unskilful action (*akusala kamma*) of any kind is fearsome. By unskilful action the Buddha meant such action as tends to increase greed, hatred, and ignorance, because it is by such action that we prolong and intensify our suffering, life after life, in this treacherous sea of saṃsāra. The wise fear such action and do their best to avoid it, but, to the foolish, such action often seems harmless, pleasurable, and even praiseworthy. Thus do foolish parents teach their children to "get on in the world" at all costs, ignorant of the dreadful price those children will have to pay for that temporary and utterly meaningless advance.

On the other hand, worldlings are afraid of a number of things which, to a Buddha, are non-fearsome. They fear physical danger, financial loss, sickness, un-popularity and a host of other ills which are merely part of the environment in which life is lived. According to the Buddha, such fears are stupid. "Wherever fear arises," He said, "it arises in the fool, not in the wise." He was speaking here of those beings who see fear in the non-fearsome.

A certain Brahmin once asked the Buddha whether those who resort to the lonely depths of the forest for meditation, while yet unattained to concentration, are not seized with fear. The Buddha's reply was illuminating. He said, "You have said it, Brahmin, you have said it!" He then went on to explain that those ascetics who, for one reason or another, are unprepared for the lonely forest life, *are* seized with fear. Before he attained Enlightenment, the Bodhisatta deliberately sought those "places of horror and affright" and spent lonely vigils there in order to experience and overcome that very fear. Being already a yogi of perfect purity and high mental attainment, he met and mastered the fear, soaring at last to those heights which only Buddhas attain. But he recognized the fear, saw its basis, and saw too that to the average worldling, of frail virtue and irresolute mind, it can be a very real thing.

It is true, as the Buddha said, that fear arises only in the fool. But then it is equally true that we worldlings are fools. That is why we are still worldlings. We crave for things, cling to things, hate each other for these very qualities, and are steeped in ignorance. So we experience fear. If, on occasion, we are brave, it almost invariably is for the wrong reason. For instance, the "brave" hunter, armed with the latest thing in sporting rifles, does not fear the elephant. In arming himself against a meaningless fear in the non-fearsome, he sees no fear in the truly fearsome, that is, the doing of evil. His folly is doubled.

There is only one way to get rid of fear, the way shown by the Buddha. Until that end is achieved, and Final Deliverance won, we will experience fear. But let us at least have the intelligence to recognize it for what it is—the unpleasant fruit of our own greed, our own ill-will, our own delusion.

Freedom from Fear

All tremble at punishment,
All fear death.
Comparing others with oneself,
One should neither kill nor cause to kill.

Dhammapada

The virtuous person, by reason of his virtue, gives peace of mind to those about him. He is not a menace. He will not kill others, or rob them, or corrupt them, or slander them, or get drunk and make a nuisance of himself. A person who observes the five precepts of virtue is a wholesome and pleasant neighbour.

There are those who seek to belittle these Precepts by calling them "negative." They take no thought of the positive good the virtuous precept-observer does by making his environment a happy and peaceful one for others. We sometimes forget that what most people want is not active assistance but freedom from interference. They can get along quite well on their own, and only ask to be left alone. Some overenthusiastic social workers would do well to remember this. A happy, calm environment is a precious thing in this world of strife and worry. Those who, by their lives, help create and maintain such an environment do a great service to humanity.

Ascetics carry no weapons when they retire to lonely places to meditate. And yet one rarely, if ever, hears of an ascetic being harmed by wild beasts. It is because wild beasts too are sensitive to a good environment. They sense and react favourably to an atmosphere of peace and goodwill. Indeed, there is reason to think that wild beasts are better than humans in this respect. It is not likely that wild beasts would have harmed Jesus, or Giardano Bruno.

To the Buddhists it is axiomatic that no good is ever achieved by harming one's fellow-beings. That is why the pages of Buddhist history do not stink with the blood of innocent victims, killed or tortured in the name of religion. The Buddha-Dhamma is a free and noble way of life, appealing only to the best in human nature. We do not seek to force this way of life upon others, for compulsion is the very antithesis of freedom. Nor do we claim, as certain other religionists do, that immediate conversion to Buddhism is necessary for Final Deliverance. There is time, plenty of time. There is all eternity. Those who do not accept this teaching now will do so some day. We need not worry about them, or see ourselves in the heroic role of saviours. Those others will save themselves, though not with the speed, nor by the means, that they now believe in.

The Buddhist might well ask what his attitude should be towards the follower of some other religion who tries to convert *him*. The Buddhist attitude should be one of understanding, kindliness and long-suffering patience. After all, the attempt is motivated by a friendly impulse, however misguided. And the Buddhist might well return kindness for kindness by telling the would-be converter something of Buddhism.

Nationalism

Neither in the sky, nor in the mid-ocean,
nor by entering a mountain cave,
is found that place on earth,
where abiding, one will not be overcome by death.

Dhammapada

The Buddha spoke to all men and for all time. He was born a Sakyan, in Northern India. But it is not as a Sakyan, nor as an Indian, that one thinks of him. He was too big for that.

To a follower of the Buddha, there can be no meaning in "nationalism." How can one sing "Rule Britannia" with any degree of fervour or conviction when, according to the Buddha, one will presently die, and may be reborn as a Chinaman? Nationalism is good enough for those unenlightened and short-sighted folk who cannot see the possibilities of rebirth. What is more, it is rooted in mistaken ideas of "me" and "mine."

The Buddha taught that there is nothing permanent or stable in any living being. There is nothing of which one can say, "This am I. This is mine." How then can a sincere Buddhist say "This is my country," or, "These are my people"? If we really accept the Buddha's Teaching, we cannot think of ourselves as the nationals of any particular country. We cannot, strictly speaking, think of ourselves even as human beings, because even that state of affairs is transitory. We can only regard ourselves as beings, that is, as mind and body fluxes, ever changing, subject to birth, decay and death.

In many parts of the world today, the spirit of narrow nationalism seems to be growing stronger. People tend more and more to think of themselves as members of some nation rather than as intelligent living beings. Like a dreadful cancer, this spirit of nationalism is eating into everything that is noble and generous in human nature, replacing reason, love and honesty with its own evil substance. There are some feeble-minded people who regard this as a wholesome change. But no genuine follower of the Buddha can be misled by them.

While we live this life, as humans, let us at least have the bigness of mind to see ourselves as human beings rather than as Sinhalese, Americans, Burmese, Russians, and so on, as the case may be. Let us not be so petty about our own particular national language, national dress, national customs, rites, ceremonies, and background.

The Buddha was like the sun, and, like sunlight. His Dhamma is for all men, whatever language they speak, whatever clothes they wear, whatever country they call "home." The Buddha's language was truth. He was clothed in truth, and the whole world was his home. For truth is everywhere and for all time.

Words

Better than a discourse of thousand words, imbued with worthlessness, is one significant sentence which, being heard, calms one.

Dhammapada

They pour in upon us, every time we open a news-paper, every time we switch on the radio: words, words, words. Who speaks them? Who writes them? All too often we do not even bother to find out. We have no time. But quietly, subtly, insidiously, the words we read and hear are influencing us all the time. That is why people pay so highly for advertisement space in the newspapers and time on radio commercial programmes. They know that words matter a great deal, cunningly selected words, skilfully strung together so as to work on the imagination They know that suggestive words, repeated again and again, come to be accepted as true.

And who are these people who exploit words with such care and persistence? Invariably they are people who want to sell something, be it a patent medicine or an insurance policy or a political ideology. They are all trying to put something across, and they do it in words—frightening words, inflammatory words, words that appeal to the appetites and the emotions. Rarely, if ever, do they appeal to reason and intelligence.

By appealing to reason and intelligence one encourages people to think for themselves, and that is a very dangerous thing if one has something to sell. One is on much safer ground with the emotions and appetites, and they are so many and varied that there is plenty of scope. A critical study of newspaper advertisements can be both instructive and entertaining. One is informed that So-and-so's shirts are worn by the "Best people." One is not told why, nor is one encouraged to ask. The mere information that some nebulous class of people called the "Best" habitually wear So-and-so's shirt is considered sufficient inducement for other people to wear them. And the funniest part of the business is that So-and-so is absolutely right in his estimate of human nature. His sales prove it very satisfactorily.

Then there is the appeal to fear. Insurance companies exploit it shamelessly. One is urged to insure against all sorts of calamities. One is not told why the insurance company is so willing to give such insurance, and the question is not encouraged. The shareholders know the answer, because it appears regularly in the dividends. The majority of people who insure themselves do not need insurance. If they did, the insurance companies would be ruined.

It is the same in the realm of politics. Here too, it is a question of selling something by an appeal to appetite and emotion rather than intelligence. Words are used, thousands and thousands of suggestive words that tend to deaden the critical faculty. They are repeated again and again, on public platforms, in print and over the radio, and men come to accept them as true. It is done deliberately. It is difficult to think clearly and coherently under a barrage of propaganda, and politicians know this. It is *not* their business to encourage clear, coherent thought.

But, as individuals, it is our business to think thus. It is our duty, if we value our sanity. In all the thousands of words poured on us by the sellers of things, there is not one that brings peace of mind. They are words which tend to make us want things, to want the things that are for sale.

But peace of mind is not for sale. It is a gift which we give ourselves—if we are wise. It is a gift which the wise have given themselves, since the beginning of time. If we can shut out from our minds the clamour of those who are trying to sell us worthless things, we may hear one significant sentence that brings calm, a sentence such as the Buddha spoke when He said: "Whoso in the world controls this stupid, unruly craving, from him sorrows fall away, like waterdrops from a lotusleaf."

Ignorance—the Greatest Taint

Misconduct is a taint in a woman, niggardliness is a taint in a benefactor. All taints are evil indeed, in this world and the next. A worse taint than such as these is ignorance, the greatest taint. Abandoning this taint, be perfect, O bhikkhus.

Dhammapada

A Buddhist is sometimes asked why the Buddha did not tell people about certain things that are known today but were not known to his contemporaries. If he was omniscient, they argue, he must surely have known all about the solar system, the galaxy and so on. Then why did he not correct false notions about these and other matters?

The question is reasonable enough, provided the questioner is rather smug about what we know today, and chooses to ignore the whole purpose of the Buddha's life. To underline the smugness first, can we really presume to be dogmatic about our present views, or are they subject to revision in the light of further data? For all we know, we may be as far from the truth today as were the men of the Stone Age. A thousand years hence, if nuclear weapons have not made a dead planet of this earth, people may consider our present ideas as more or less on a level with pre-Copernican views of the geocentric structure of the universe. And, to a Buddha-mind, the ideas that will be in vogue a thousand years hence may be as fantastically and obviously untenable.

But, more important than this is the question of what the Buddha *wanted* to tell people, because it was vitally necessary for their deliverance. Once, in a forest, he compared a few leaves in His hand with the foliage around him, as illustrative of what He had taught, when compared with what he knew. And yet, what He taught was sufficient for man's deliverance from suffering. Nothing that needed to be said was left unsaid by that Supreme Teacher.

It would surely be naive to assume that such a being would bother to correct people's wrong ideas on such matters as the structure of the physical world. Just as a parent sees no harm in his child's happy belief in Santa Claus, so the Buddha saw no harm in existing ideas about the structure of the world. It did not matter to him whether people thought that the sun moved round the earth or the earth round the sun. Nor will it ever matter to anybody who values the world of mind rather than the material world as relevant to human progress. A man may be good and wise, though he believes that if one travels far enough one will come to the edge of the world. Many men, much better and wiser than we are, held that belief.

The Buddha was not concerned with knowledge as an end in itself. What then is that ignorance which he condemned as being the greatest taint? It is the ignorance that stands in the way of a being's progress to deliverance from suffering; the ignorance that feeds the fires of greed and hate; the ignorance that keeps us wandering, life after life, in saṃsāra.

We are all steeped in this ignorance, however smart and knowledgeable we may think we are. We have not realized that all phenomena are transient, not worth clinging to, ever passing to destruction, to be got rid of. So we cling and crave and hope and plan, sowing the seeds of further existence in this sorrow-laden world of fleeting shadows. Of what advantage, in this context, is the knowledge that the earth moves round the sun? All the discoveries of science have not helped humanity a hair's breadth forward on the road to happiness. Indeed, human folly is so great that the more we learn about the material world, the smaller and meaner we seem to become. Today humanity has become so mean that it finds difficulty in seeing any alternative to suicide, like a scorpion stinging itself to death with its own venom. If this is the result of knowledge, it is better to know less. Perhaps the Buddha foresaw this when he withheld from the world so much of what he knew. He came to teach Wisdom, not to impart useless and possibly dangerous knowledge.

The Power of Truth

In the world there surely is virtue, goodness, Truth, cleansing, improvement—
By this fact I make a supreme Act (assertion) of Truth.

Jātaka

The East has long believed that there is power in the assertion of truth. There are many instances in the Buddhist Scriptures of the use of this truth-power for various purposes, such as healing the sick. It is effective when the assertion is made by one in whom the truth relied on is manifest, as when a virtuous and good person says or thinks, "By the power of the truth that there is virtue and goodness in the world may so-and-so be cured of his illness." Such a person, quite understandably, would make the assertion with more confidence than would a person whose own virtue and goodness are questionable, and his mind therefore serves as a better conductor of the truth-power. There is no doubt that faith, or confidence, is necessary.

There was a time when it was considered fashionable and "modern" to scoff at anything so intangible as thought-force. But today even the materialistic West is awakening to the fact that the mind has certain capacities which defy all attempts at explanation on modern scientific lines. Matter-itself has ceased to be the dependable thing it was a few years ago, and has betrayed the materialist by turning out to be nothing more than a manifestation of energy. What is energy? Nobody knows. One can only call it by various other names and cite examples of its manifestation, such as electricity, magnetism, gravitation, heat, and light.

Is it not reasonable to suppose that thought also is a form of energy, and that such energy can and does affect the so-called material world?

Of course, it is not everybody who can split rocks by thinking, or, for that matter, generate enough thought force even to lift a feather off the ground. But then, how many people know how to generate enough electrical energy to split a rock or even lift a feather? In comparison with the world's population, very few. And yet, nobody will deny that electricity is a real and potent force.

The vital difference between electricity and thought-force is that whereas, in the modern world, the former has become the servant of any fool who knows how to pull a switch or press a button, the latter must still be generated and applied by each individual unaided by others, save for such advice as others may be able to give. Each individual must build his own mental dynamo and learn how to use it. Each must he a skilled technician and operator.

In the East there has been no lack of teachers, and today the methods taught by many of them are to be found in books. Supreme among such teachers was the Buddha. He understood the nature of thought-force as nobody else has understood it, and He knew that one way, a *relatively easy way,* in which such force may be generated and applied is by the Act (or assertion) of Truth (*saccakiriya*). It must be understood, though, that the sole purpose of His life was to teach people how to win freedom from the suffering inherent in all existence, and not merely to teach them how to develop thought-force. That was incidental, and He did not value power for its own sake.

But there is no denying that we worldlings sometimes need the power to help our fellow beings in various ways. The Act of Truth, properly used, does give us this power. But we must be qualified to use it. We must, in our own conduct, manifest the truth we seek to use. The laws of nature do not permit a libertine to exploit the truth of virtue, nor a miser the truth of generosity. If we are qualified to use it, the Act of Truth is an unfailing source of power. With it we can draw our fellows from sickness towards health, from madness towards sanity, from despair towards hope, from hate towards love.

Today, from the point of view of any kind person who does not wish to see this earth turned into shambles, such power is *urgently* needed. This essay is written in the hope that all such people, whatever their religion, will use it for the good of humanity.

The Happy Road

He who, discarding human bonds
And transcending celestial ties,
Is completely delivered of all bonds—
Him I call a Brāhmaṇa.

Dhammapada

The Buddha taught the way to absolute freedom from all bonds, human and celestial. To the worldling, enmeshed in human bonds such as the desire to win fame and wealth here in this life, it is hardly necessary to speak of celestial ties. Such a man does not begin to know the meaning of freedom before death overtakes him. He lives shackled to his worldly ambitions and dies with them. If those ambitions are still unfulfilled at the moment of death, as usually happens, because there is no such thing as "enough" for such a man, the chances of a happy rebirth are very slim.

But there are people who have the understanding to renounce worldly ambition in this gross sense for something higher. They know that death must come, and that it will mean leaving behind all such things as wealth and fame and worldly authority. So they live with one eye on the next life as it were, thinking of future rather than present success. Such people may get the reputation of being "unworldly," but really, they are more far-seeing than unworldly, just as a shrewd fellow who invests his money is more far-seeing than the man who spends it as soon as he gets it, but may be just as worldly.

Such foresight has its rewards, both in this life and the next, and we have the Buddha's word for it. Intelligence always pays, and the stupid have no cause to feel superior to the intelligent in that they have taken no thought for the morrow. And, when tomorrow comes, the stupid will have no justification to grumble at their bad luck, though they will certainly do so.

But, as we pointed out earlier, the intelligent person who invests in the next life is not really unworldly. He will reap the rewards of his foresight, but they will be worldly rewards, even if he is reborn in a celestial plane. He will still be in bondage for even celestial beings are mortal. In due course, after the lapse of a long, long time, such a person will die in that celestial plane and be reborn according to the balance of his kamma at that death moment. He may be reborn as a human once again, or as a being in some lower plane. And so the story of life goes on. It is never done until one attains Nibbāna. All living is in the world, and all desire for happy and safe living is worldly, if it goes no further.

The great danger is that mind is unstable. The man who lives wisely and well, storing up good kamma, may not live so wisely and well when, as a result of that very good kamma, he is reborn in a celestial plane. The steady, plodding human caterpillar of this life may turn into the light-headed celestial butterfly of the next. And, if such a man is reborn as a human, with no memory of the past, he will not even know why he is wealthy and fortunate. He may become a playboy and libertine.

So, the Buddha advised us to get rid of *all* bonds, human and celestial, and win final deliverance. Investment in future lives is good, but it is not enough. Such investment must be made only with a view to progress on the road to *Nibbāna.* Future happiness and security must be the means to an end, the end being freedom.

Aloofness

Seek no intimacy with the beloved, and never with the unbeloved.
Not seeing the beloved, and the sight of the unbeloved are both painful.

Dhammapada

Thoughts of "me" and "mine" are at the root of all our loves and hates. We may think highly of one person for his good qualities, and think poorly of another for his bad qualities, but we cannot love the one or hate the other unless there has been some personal contact. When parted from those whom we love, we feel a sense of personal loss. When forced to associate with those whom we hate, we feel a personal irritation. Both feelings are painful.

The Buddha saw that these feelings spring from the delusion of self, and are stimulated by personal contacts. The notion of self is a constant factor, and will remain so until we see things as they really are. It would be useless to pretend that we have eliminated it at the very beginning of our search for Enlightenment. So we are obliged to tackle the problem on the level of personal contacts, by making such contacts as light as possible.

Intimate association with the beloved and the un-beloved are both potentially painful. Aloofness, on the other hand, tends to lessen the intensity of such emotions and the pain they can engender. Such is the teaching of the Buddha, clear and uncompromising. Each of us is free to choose his own way of life. There may be those who will call this teaching cold and inhuman. They may say, "It is better to have loved and lost than never to have loved at all."

They are at liberty to love and lose as many times as they please, in this life and in future lives, until they realise that they are making fools of themselves. There may be others who pride themselves on being good haters. They too are free to go their own road until repeated suffering teaches them that the hater harms himself far more than he harms the object of his hate.

There are a few people, extremely few, to whom the teaching of aloofness has a strong appeal. They are the mature ones, the old campaigners of saṃsāra, who have had their fill of loving and hating. They are beginning to feel instinctively that freedom lies in letting go. It is to such people really that the Buddha spoke. The rest merely happened to be present, and to hear with their ears but not with their hearts.

Can such a teaching be called selfish? Surely not, when it leads to the elimination of the concept of self. Intimate association with people is *not* unselfish behaviour. It as the manure upon which the tree of Self grows and thrives, bearing in abundance its fruit of suffering. Aloofness is just the opposite of such behaviour. It is the nature upon which the tree of Wisdom grows and thrives, bearing at last the fruit of Insight.

Let us not delude ourselves. The world we live in is built upon the very notion of self which the Buddha sought to eradicate. All its activities, all its vested interests, are bound up with this basic idea. Any departure from the accepted standards of conduct will inevitably be branded as antisocial. Aloofness is such a departure, and is bound to be resented by those who love the world and its ways. Need that deter the wise?

Stillness

As in ocean mid-deeps
No wave arises, but all is still—
So be still, unmoved;
Pride let the bhikkhu nowhere entertain.

Tuvaṭaka Sutta, Suttanipāta

Deep down in the sea, where the sea is really deep, half a mile, a mile, two miles below the surface, all is still. Here there are no tempests, no storms. There is none of the fuss and bother that beset surface waters and shallows.

So it is with people who have attained Ultimate Deliverance. So it was with the Buddha and the Arahants. They had reached the Final Peace. Never again, for them, the flurry and turmoil, the longing and anxiety, the feverish, meaningless activity of the worldling.

The Buddha, in the stanza quoted above, advised *all* bhikkhus to be like that. The advice holds good for lay folk as well. Although the worldling has not attained that Final Peace, he can, by sedulous cultivation of calm, experience as it were a shadow of that stillness.

Why should he cultivate calm? The answer is simple. When one is in motion, it is difficult to judge motion in one's environment. Travelling in a moving vehicle, another vehicle, moving at the same speed in the same direction, seems to be still. An object that is actually still, like a tree, seems to be moving. One's impressions of one's environment are conditioned by one's own movement. It is so with the mind. When the mind is restless and flurried, it is difficult to realize the deep eternal Truths. Things that are actually changing are accepted as constant. Things that are actually constant, such as the Truth of *anicca*, *dukkha*, and *anattā* (impermanence, suffering and soullessness) are not perceived at all. The mind keeps rushing with changing phenomena, so busy and occupied that it is unable to see clearly or deeply or truly.

So the Buddha advised stillness. The whole system of *samatha-bhāvanā* (meditation for calm), as taught by the Buddha, has this one object in view. The mind, when purified of all sensual thoughts and concentrated on a *kammaṭṭhāna* (subject of concentration) becomes utterly still. It also grows very powerful, so powerful that such feats as levitation, clairvoyance, clairaudience, thought-reading, remembrance of past lives, and so on, become possible. But these are merely by-products of *samatha-bhāvanā*. The one and only object of such meditation is stillness—stillness which leads to clear, deep, true vision.

Lay people, in their daily lives, are badly handicapped when it comes to meditation. It is not so much the actual duties of the layman that interfere, though these do take up a large proportion of the layman's life. But the worst handicap is worry. We tend to worry about what we have done, are doing, and intend to do; about what has happened, is happening, and is likely to happen. This worry, says the Buddha, is useless and foolish. How can one stop it? Illustrations help. In times of worry and flurry one can think of the Buddha's own illustration—the mid-deeps of the ocean, where all is still. So thinking, one can become less excited about the fussy little things that cause worry.

Zeal

Look now, O bhikkhus, I urge you:
Transient innately are all compounds,
With zeal work out your aim.

Mahā Parinibbāna Sutta

These were the last words of the dying Buddha. They were plain, simple, direct words, going straight to the heart of things. For countless aeons he had perfected himself in order that he might teach living beings the way to end suffering, once and for all. In his final existence, as a Buddha, He bent all his tremendous power to that one end, never sparing Himself, never postponing for tomorrow that which could be done today. And at last, when that glorious life was at its end, these were the words he spoke. They crystalize the very essence, of His teaching, and may well serve as a motto for all Buddhists,

We Buddhists of today are feeble specimens indeed, in comparison with the Buddha and the mighty Arahants. We, most of us, regard life as desirable on the whole. We mouth the Buddha's words and profess to follow his teaching, but our actions are sadly lacking in that zeal, that wholehearted endeavour that is necessary for success. We are like people who have queued up and are patiently waiting at a motor bus halting-place. The Gotama Buddha bus has not yet arrived. So we are waiting, kicking our heels and whiling away the time in silly gossip about motor buses and the service they do for the public. We are waiting to pay our few miserable cents for a ticket to Nibbāna and to be carried there in comfort by Metteyya Buddha, without the slightest exertion on our part. Nothing on earth will induce us to walk.

But, alas, the dispensation of a Buddha is not a motor bus or any other kind of conveyance in which people are carried to Nibbāna. Buddhas are only teachers, though in the highest sense of the word, they teach the Way of Deliverance. Gotama Buddha's teaching still exists in the world, and if we are unable to profit from it and begin to work for Deliverance now, it is futile to expect that we will achieve that end when we hear the identical teaching from Metteyya Buddha. The teaching is clear enough and cannot possibly be made clearer. If anything is lacking, it is lacking in ourselves.

What then should we do? First of all we must get rid of the halting-place mentality. We must realise that Nibbāna is to be attained by our own personal endeavour and that it is not a paradise to which we can be carried by a Buddha. Buddhas are powerful, more powerful by far than any other living beings. But this is something that even Buddhas cannot do. All beings must work out their own salvation.

Having once realized this, we must get going here and now, following the Buddha's teaching and making a sincere effort to live the sort of life that leads to Nibbāna. "With zeal work out your aim," said the Buddha. Let us take that to heart. With zeal let us observe the precepts of virtue. With zeal let us practise the perfections. With zeal let us endeavour to purify and calm our minds, following the methods that he taught. Let us use the opportunities we have here and now.

ABOUT PARIYATTI

Pariyatti is dedicated to providing affordable access to authentic teachings of the Buddha about the Dhamma theory (*pariyatti*) and practice (*paṭipatti*) of Vipassana meditation. A 501(c)(3) nonprofit charitable organization since 2002, Pariyatti is sustained by contributions from individuals who appreciate and want to share the incalculable value of the Dhamma teachings. We invite you to visit www.pariyatti.org to learn about our programs, services, and ways to support publishing and other undertakings.

Pariyatti Publishing Imprints

Vipassana Research Publications (focus on Vipassana as taught by S.N. Goenka in the tradition of Sayagyi U Ba Khin)

BPS Pariyatti Editions (selected titles from the Buddhist Publication Society, copublished by Pariyatti)

MPA Pariyatti Editions (selected titles from the Myanmar Pitaka Association, copublished by Pariyatti)

Pariyatti Digital Editions (audio and video titles, including discourses)

Pariyatti Press (classic titles returned to print and inspirational writing by contemporary authors)

Pariyatti enriches the world by

- disseminating the words of the Buddha,
- providing sustenance for the seeker's journey,
- illuminating the meditator's path.

www.ingramcontent.com/pod-product-compliance
Lightning Source LLC
Chambersburg PA
CBHW020346170426
43200CB00005B/65
9781681721323